Communion of the Saints
Foundation, Nature, and Structure of the Church

Miguel M. Garijo-Guembe

Patrick Madigan, S.J.
Translator

A Michael Glazier Book
THE LITURGICAL PRESS
Collegeville, Minnesota

A Michael Glazier Book published by Liturgical Press

Cover design by Fred Petters. *Cover art:* Collection of the J. Paul Getty Museum, Malibu, California, artist unknown, "Psalter," ca. 1240-1250, tempera, 8 7/8 x 6 3/16 inches.

This book was originally published in German by Patmos Verlag GmbH under the title *Gemeinschaft der Heiligen: Grund, Wesen und Structur der Kirche,* © 1988 Patmos Verlag.

ISBN 13: 978-0-8146-5496-5
ISBN 10: 0-8146-5496-7

| 2 | 3 | 4 | 5 | 6 | 7 | 8 | 9 |

Library of Congress Cataloging-in-Publication Data

Garijo-Guembe, Miguel María, 1935-
    [Gemeinschaft der Heiligen. English]
    Communion of the saints : foundation, nature, and structure of the church / Miguel M. Garijo-Guembe.
        p. cm.
    Translation of: Gemeinschaft der Heiligen.
    "A Michael Glazier book."
    Includes bibliographical references and indexes.
    ISBN 0-8146-5496-7
    1. Church 2. Catholic Church—Doctrines. I. Title.
BX1746.G35713   1994
262'.02—dc20
                             94-7523
                               CIP

Contents

Foreword

There are two aspects under which the nature of the Church may be observed: pneumatological and Christological. The pneumatological aspect must be seen together with the fact that the Church, in its confession of faith, is said to be connected with the Holy Spirit. As the apostles were baptized in the Holy Spirit at Pentecost, in the same way the communion of the faithful is made fruitful today through the gifts of the Spirit. The Christological aspect, on the other hand, emphasizes the institutional character of the Church. Hence Christology and pneumatology must be understood as mutually complementary aspects of any satisfactory ecclesiology.

While Roman Catholic ecclesiology has traditionally first emphasized the significance of the Church as an institution, and thus the significance of its offices (thereby giving primacy to the Christological aspect), Protestant theology has stressed the pneumatological dimension. Confronted with this situation, Orthodox commentators have always striven after a synthesis of the two.

In order to arrive at a genuinely catholic vision of the Church, both aspects must be grasped together. This is also the position of the Second Vatican Council in its Constitution on the Church, *Lumen gentium*. This document has developed the tradition of the Church in a creative continuity; earlier documents and their pronouncements are reworked in a wider and unprecedented context. The teaching of *Lumen gentium* is central to this book; as with all official documents, it must be understood as a whole together with its complementary expressions.

Ecclesiology today can no longer be regarded as a purely Roman Catholic matter. The Orthodox and the Protestant (Lutheran) Churches have raised inquiries and demands which the Catholic Church must take seriously if she is to fulfill her call and effectively carry out her mission. I have attempted to integrate ecumenically these inquiries from the other Churches into this presentation of ecclesiology.

In the attempt to present what the Church is, different methodological requirements must be recognized.

Scripture is the *norma normans* of every theological reflection. For that reason the first part of the book is devoted to a purely exegetical study. We must ask ourselves: What ecclesiological perspectives may we tease out from the New Testament? How should we conceive the connection between Jesus Christ and his Church? What conclusions should we draw from the fact that the Scriptures offer us not one, but several distinct ecclesiastical models?

The *nature* of the Church must be described theologically. To what extent in this regard may we characterize the Church as a sacrament? How should we grasp the connection between Eucharist and Church? What is the relation between the Catholic Church, together with the other Churches, to the Church of Christ?

The Church is a *structured* community; she has offices and a hierarchy. The orientation of the offices toward the community and the episcopal structure of the Church must be analyzed in such a way that the *koinonia,* the community, is held up as the fundamental principle. In this connection the office of the papacy poses a particular ecumenical problem.

The Church has a *mission* and a task. Correctly discerning their true nature will affect her attitude toward society. The reciprocal movement between the Church's mission and society will be taken up in the final section.

The last three clusters of questions—corresponding to the second, third, and fourth parts of the book—are concerned with dogma, and are treated with attention to the ecclesial tradition.

It should now be apparent that the structure of this book is determined by these methodological considerations. If we attempt an adequate description of the Church, these elements must all be kept simultaneously in view; I hope I have succeeded in providing such a description.

In closing, may I thank my colleagues Barbara Boecker, Thomas Bremer, Mechtild Koslowski, Birgit Soisch, and Irmgard Wiegert for their support and patience.

Münster, 1987   Miguel Maria Garijo-Guembe

I.
Introduction: *"Credo Ecclesiam"*

1. The Position of the Church in the Creed

The Church is named in the creeds (for example, in that of Constantinople and in that of the Western Apostles) in the clause after the Holy Spirit: The Creed of Constantinople: "We believe in one God, the Father . . . and in Jesus Christ . . . and in the Holy Spirit . . . and in one, holy, catholic, and apostolic Church. We recognize one baptism for the forgiveness of sins. We await the resurrection of the dead and life eternal . . ."[1] The Apostles' Creed: "I believe in the Holy Spirit, the holy catholic Church, the communion of saints (that is, partnership in the saints), the forgiveness of sins . . ."[2]

This sequence of clauses can also be observed in other primitive creeds.[3] The reason the clause concerning the Holy Spirit is set before the others can be understood in light of the basic conviction of the primitive Church about the Spirit: (1) it was the Spirit who was active in the ancient prophets and who had prophesied the coming and experiences of the Savior; (2) the Spirit enlightens the Church and leads her into the truth; it fills her with its gifts (charisms), and it is effective in the sacraments (cf. the function of the *epiclesis*); (3) the Spirit guarantees the faithful a share in eternal life, that is, victory over death.

This ecclesial conviction about the nature of the Church was expressed by Irenaeus in the second half of the second century in the following terms:

---

1. DS 150 = NR 250.

2. DS 30. See DS 10 = 29.

3. For example, the *Epistola Apostolorum,* about 160–170 (DS 1), or the papyrus from Dèr-Balyzeh (DS 2). According to the *Traditio apostolica* of Hippolytus, the third baptismal question runs: "Do you believe in the Holy Spirit in the Church?" (B. Botte, *La Tradition apostolique de S. Hippolyte* [Münster, 1963] 50–61 and note 1).

God's gifts are given to the Church, just as God breathed life into those he had fashioned out of earth, so that in this way all the members receive life. And in this gift is the gift of Christ, that is, the Holy Spirit, contained—the earnest of eternal life, the confirmation of our faith, and the way to God. God placed apostles, prophets, and teachers in the Church (1 Cor 12:28) as well as the general working of the Spirit. Those who depart from the Church lose their participation in this working of the Spirit. . . . For where the Church is, there is also the Spirit of God. And where the Spirit of God is, there is also the Church and all grace; for the Spirit is the Truth.[4]

From the Creed itself it should be clear that ecclesiology can only be understood in connection with and as a consequence of pneumatology. The Church cannot be grasped apart from the Holy Spirit, and can only be grasped as the work of the Holy Spirit. Only after Pentecost, that is, after the sending of the Spirit through the Risen One—here we should keep in mind John 7:39: "for the Spirit was not yet there, because Jesus had not yet been exalted"—may we speak about a "Church"; the Church came to be at Pentecost. For that reason we must concur with Yves Congar when he calls the Holy Spirit the cofounder of the Church.[5]

The position of the Church in the Creed implies an essential perspective for ecclesiology that must be respected by every theology: the pneumatological perspective.

Although this methodological perspective is common to all Churches and their theologians, it does not imply ready agreement, since pneumatology is understood and emphasized differently by the different Churches. However, pneumatology cannot be separated from Christology; every pneumatological observation includes a Christological perspective, and vice versa.

Christology or Pneumatology as the Point of Departure for Ecclesiology?

Catholic theology has traditionally understood the Church on the basis of Christology. As a consequence, the institutional aspect of the Church

4. "Hoc enim Ecclesiae creditum est Dei munus, quemadmodum ad inspirationem plasmationi, ad hoc ut omnia membra percipientia vivificentur; et in eo deposita est communicatio Christi, id est Spiritus sanctus, arrha incorruptelae et confirmatio fidei nostrae et scala ascensionis ad Deum. In Ecclesia enim, inquit, posuit Deus apostolos, prophetas, doctores [1 Cor 12:28] et universam reliquam operationem Spiritus, cujus non sunt participes omnes qui non currunt ad Ecclesiam sed semetipsos fraudant a vita per sententiam malam et operationem pessimam. Ubi enim Ecclesia, ibi et Spiritus Dei; et ubi Spiritus Dei, ille Ecclesia et omnis gratia: Spiritus autem Veritas" (Adv. Haer. 3.24.1; PG 7:966).

5. Y. M. Congar, *Der heilige Geist* (Freiburg, 1982) 160 = *Je crois en l'Esprit Saint,* vol. 2 (Paris, 1980) 16.

is emphasized; correlatively, various offices are held up as the essential element of the institution. The Church is grasped on analogy with the mystery of the incarnation. In this context the Church is to be understood as a sacramental institution—occasionally, as the continuation of the incarnation. The office is accentuated as the instrumental cause which generates and fashions the Church.[6]

At the ecumenical convention in Amsterdam in 1948 a distinction was drawn between the "catholic" (not in the sense of "Roman Catholic") and the "evangelical" (Lutheran) concept of the Church. J. L. Leuba posed the contrast this way:

> The "catholic" conviction sees the continuity of the Church in its institutional character and the various properties that flow from this: a sacramental understanding of the offices, a reverence for tradition, and an emphasis on the apostolic succession (incidentally, in different forms). On the other hand the "protestant" conviction emphasizes the freedom of the Holy Spirit who engages us continually in new ways; through which God, in meditation on his Word, guides, nourishes, supports, quickens, and consoles his Church; the priesthood of all believers; and the charismatic character of every office."[7]

As an example of how Catholic authors regard the Protestant position—it remains open whether they are right or not—we cite here the opinion of Yves Congar:

> Protestants see the transcendent act of God (the Holy Spirit) as the only true foundation for the faith of believers. . . . We can diagram their understanding in the following flow-chart: God in his (heavenly) transcendence → Belief → Church, the totality of all believers.[8]
>
> In place of the sequence: *the Word made man* → *Church-as-Institution* → *christian life and Church as community* we have the sequence: *the heavenly Christ* → *christian living and Church as community;* one should better say simply Church, since no other meaning is attached to the word 'Church' than community of believers.[9]
>
> The Church is not only a holy community, but also "the totality of the means of sanctification": "a healing place," that is, "the sacrament of this reality."[10]

6. See Y. M. Congar, "Ministères et structuration de l'Église," in Congar, *Ministères et communion ecclésiale* (Paris, 1971) 34f. (the essay appeared originally in *La maison Dieu,* 102 [1970] 7–20).

7. J. L. Leuba, *Institution und Ereignis* (Göttingen, 1957) 7 (French, 1950).

8. Y. M. Congar, *Der Laie,* (Stuttgart, 1957; French 1952) 55.

9. Y. M. Congar, *Vraie et fausse réforme dans l'Église* (Paris, 1950) 442.

10. Congar, *Der Laie,* 58.

As concerns the offices, the Catholic understanding emphasizes the following: the historical Christ → the hierarchy of offices, which stem from Christ through the office of the apostles → Church or community of believers. Within the ecumenical movement one can discern the following schema: the Holy Spirit → the Church as altogether responsible for mission and for the office → offices. A different and, for Congar,[11] a better diagram that is also used in ecumenical circles is this one:

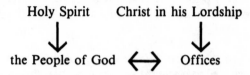

In Orthodox theology one hears about both Christological and pneumatological aspects of the Church. On the one hand the Church is understood in analogy with the mystery of the incarnation; on the other hand she is described as the continuing extension of Pentecost. The two aspects cannot be separated. G. Florovsky, whose opinion other authors endorse, writes: "The sacramental life of the Church is the continuation of Pentecost, and yet much more: the life of the Church has its foundation in two mutually complementary mysteries: the mystery of the Last Supper and the mystery of Pentecost. One will always discover this duality within the concrete existence of the Church."[12] The Christological aspect throws into high relief the Church as an institution and the function of its offices, while the pneumatological aspect surfaces more in its prophetic activity.

N. Nissiotis has criticized the Catholic position for being a "Christomonism." In his opinion, this is of a piece with the problem of the *filioque,* whose consequences for ecclesiology he describes in the following manner: Christ-based sacramentalism begins to dominate over spirit-founded prophecy; the hierarchy begins to dominate over the freedom of the faithful; the Petrine aspect overwhelms the Pauline, clericalism develops, and the Pope becomes the representative of Christ.[13] However, the fact that the Reformation introduced an (to the Orthodox) exaggerated pneumatological perspective into ecclesiology, though together with the entire Western tradition they retained the *filioque,* shows clearly that one cannot conclude to a causal connection between the presence of the

11. Congar, "Ministères," 38.
12. G. Florovsky, "Le corps du Christ vivant. Une interprétation de l'Église," in *La sainte Église universelle* (Neuchâtel-Paris, 1948) 19.
13. N. Nissiotis, "The main ecclesiological Problem of the Second Vatican Council," *JES* 2 (1965) 31–62 (esp. 48ff.); N. Nissiotis, "La pneumatologie ecclésiologique au service de l'unité de l'Église," *Istina* 12 (1967) 325; N. Nissiotis, *Die Theologie der Ostkirche im ökumenischen Dialog* (Stuttgart, 1968) 64ff.

filioque on the one hand, and a "Christomonism" or the failure to generate a sweeping pneumatology on the other.

The problems we are touching on here will be further developed in the appropriate chapters.

2. The Positive Meaning of *"Credo Ecclesiam"*

Already in the late patristic period authors such as Faustus of Riez (died before 500) concluded that the last clauses in the Creed were connected with the Holy Spirit. Faustus interpreted the text of the Creed in the following fashion: "Whatever in the Creed follows the words 'the Holy Ghost' should be understood without reference to the preposition 'in,' so that our belief about the Holy Church, the communion of saints, etc., is said as part of our appeal to God. This means we believe that these things have been ordered by God and derive their existence from him."[14]

Besides representatives from the late patristic period, Alcuin of York and figures from high Scholasticism, such as Alexander of Hales, Albert the Great, and Thomas Aquinas, also share this interpretation. The Roman Catechism expresses itself as a faithful witness to this long tradition with all desired clarity:

> Therefore one must believe that there is one Church that is one, holy, and catholic. In what concerns the three persons of the Trinity, the Father, the Son, and the Holy Ghost, we believe *in* them in the sense that we actually place our belief upon them. However, we then change our expression and say that we *believe the holy Church,* that is, not *in* the holy Church. Through these different ways of speaking, therefore, God, the source of all things, is distinguished from the rest of his creation, and we, as we receive them, also recognize all the precious gifts he has bestowed upon his Church as coming from this divine source.[15]

The intent of the Creed is clear: we believe in the Holy Spirit who sanctifies the Church and guides her into the Truth. Any divinization of the Church itself or its institutional features is therefore impossible. The Church may still, however, be regarded as a sacramental institution and therefore as a reference point for our belief in the three-personed God and his work of salvation. The constitution *Lumen gentium* compares the Church with the mystery of the Word-made-man (no. 8, 1). The Church and its function is not an end in itself, but rather an instrument for the Spirit of Christ, which utilizes even the social structure of the Church as its instrument. Its task is to be such an instrument—if always a human,

---

14. Faustus of Riez, *De Spiritu Sancto* 1.2; CSEL 21:103f.
15. Pars Prima, ch. X (de nomo articulo).

and therefore a sin-burdened instrument—for the "Word of God" and the Spirit of God. As the constitution *Dei Verbum* (no. 10, 2) states, the Church stands always under the Word of God.

We must not forget the social and ecclesial dimension of belief. "One believes in and with the Church."[16] Or as Karl Barth puts it: "The Church is first, and then through her and in her are the faithful."[17] Our common belief in Jesus as the Christ comes down to us as part of a tradition passed on by earlier ecclesial communities and finally by the apostolic witness concerning Jesus Christ. That is the reason we have to say that first comes the Church. Our own belief is essentially tied to tradition coming down through the Church. Over the centuries the various councils have done nothing more than try to render the Church's faith as clear as possible, as the formula "Haec est catholicae Ecclesiae fides"[18] ("This is the faith of the Catholic Church") attests.

16. H. de Lubac, *Credo,* (Einsiedeln, 1975) 143.
17. K. Barth, *Kirchliche Dogmatik* 1/2:230f.; 4/1:839.
18. A formula of the fourth synod of Toledo (635) quoted by de Lubac, *Credo,* 145 n. 16 (=DS 485).

First Part:

Fundamental Ecclesial
Directions in the New Testament

The New Testament is the *norma normans* for the Church. All Churches and all theologians base themselves upon its teaching to validate their own understandings.

Catholic theology is well aware of the fact that the elements of Catholic ecclesiology cannot all be directly and expressly found in the New Testament. For example, there is no indication of an office of bishop distinct from the office of presbyter.

These facts warrant a presentation, in our first part, of the ecclesiological directions to be found in the New Testament. Once this basis is established, these principles will be more closely examined in the later sections of the book.

This methodological decision will make clear the exact problems with which theological reflection must come to grips. The problematic of the apostolic succession of offices shows clearly that a principle like *sola scriptura* simply is not sufficient. It thus seems questionable, from a methodological point of view, to accept the New Testament as a canonical text, and at the same time to dispense with Church structures that the historical Church, which passes on to us certain books as canonical, takes to be essential. "Holy Tradition and Holy Scripture are tightly bound together." (*DV* 9)

The interpretation of the Scriptures in the Church does not exclude their analysis according to modern methods of exegesis.

II.
Fundamental Concepts of the
Church's Self-Understanding

Before the problematic of the connection of the Church with the historical Jesus can be treated, the self-understanding of the band of disciples of Jesus after the events of Easter/Pentecost should be presented. After Easter/Pentecost they understood themselves as the new people of God, as the Church of God. Only after this may we raise the question of how far the "founding" of a Church can be recognized in the announcement of the kingdom of God by the historical Jesus. Methodologically it is the same problem we have in Christology, that is, the problem of the relation between the Christ of faith and the historical Jesus; for the first community described the life of the historical Jesus in the light of their experience at Easter.

In both cases—Christology and ecclesiology—the early community saw their interpretation of Jesus as the Christ and themselves as the new people of God as being in continuity with Jesus' proclamation. For example, Matthew 16:18 has Jesus quite deliberately expressing his intention to found a Church. According to results of contemporary studies, we may confidently affirm that this text does transmit a statement of the pre-Easter Jesus; however, the significance of the text consists in the fact that Matthew presents the development of the Church as a logical consequence of both the words and deeds of Jesus, and as such as part of Jesus' direct intention ("on these stones I will build my Church").

1. *Ekklesia*—the Church of God

The *ekklesia* of God is the usual designation for the New Testament community or communities. The word is used as a term already stamped with a Christian reference.

9

In common Greek it stands for the assembly of a people, that is, a gathering of a people in their entirety (*in actu*). The Septuagint uses this as the primary term to translate *qahal Jahwe*.

The frequency of its usage in the New Testament is very uneven. Among the evangelists the word is used only by Matthew (16:18 and 18:17). The majority of its citations come in Paul and the communities that follow him: forty-six occurrences in the authentic Pauline letters and sixteen in those only attributed to him. In the Acts of the Apostles the word is invoked as the established term for the new communities of those who believe in Jesus: twenty-three times. It appears elsewhere in the New Testament: twice in Hebrews, three times in John's third letter, once in James and nineteen times in the Book of Revelation (in formal applications in connection with the seven letters: Rev 1–3).

Although Acts speaks only of the "Church"—20:28 is an exception: there it is a reference to the "Church of God" in the sense of the "Church of the Lord (Jesus)"—with Paul the usual expression is "Church of God" (*ekklesia tou theou*): 1 Corinthians 1:2; 10:32; 11:16, 22; 15:9, etc. He describes the persecution against those who believe in Jesus as a persecution of the Church of God (Gal 1:13; 1 Cor 15:9). Only in Romans 16:16 does he speak of the Church of Christ. The expression "Church of God in Christ" (1 Thess 2:14; Gal 1:22) emphasizes that the source of God's community consists in what took place with Christ. The designation of the Church as the *ekklesia Jesu* in Matthew 16:18 "most likely does not correspond to earlier speech habits."[1]

The disciples of Jesus understood themselves as the new people of God, which came into existence through the redemptive activity of Jesus. Most probably the Christian term arose under the influence of the Septuagint translation of *qahal Jahwe* by *ekklesia tou theou*.

This term encompasses three aspects:

(1) The assembly of the faithful, and especially as the gathering for worship. Paul speaks of the coming-together as a community with reference to the worship assembly (1 Cor 11:18; cf. also 1 Cor 14:34).

Christians understand themselves as Church when they are actually gathered together. "Even if the community is referred to as Church, '*ekklesia*,' apart from the cultic service, it still appears that the worshipful service is the authentic appearance of the essence of the community, and that the entire life of the community is dominated by it."[2]

Just as Israel experienced itself as the people of God in the Passover feast, so also the Christian community understands itself as rescued by

1. J. Roloff, *Ékklesia*, 1010.

2. R. Bultmann, "Kirche und Lehre im Neuen Testament," in Bultmann, *Glauben und Verstehen*, vol. 2 (1954) 165.

Jesus Christ to become the new people of God in the celebration of the Lord's Supper.

(2) The concrete community of that locale. In the Acts of the Apostles *ekklesia* designates the concrete community of that place, whether it be in Jerusalem (5:11; 8:1, 3; 15:4, 22), in Antioch (11:26; 13:1; 14:27; 15:3), or places of the Pauline mission (20:17: Ephesus). Paul speaks of the Church of God, for example, *in* Corinth (1 Cor 1:2). The Church of God comes into appearance in the community of that place. The term is also used for household communities (Rom 16:5; 1 Cor 16:19; Col 4:15), most probably because the Lord's Supper was celebrated in those houses, as Acts also shows.

Because the term *ekklesia* designates the individual community of a locale, one speaks of "churches" in the plural when one wants to refer to several local communities (Rom 16:4; 1 Cor 11:16; 14:33f.; 16:1, 19, etc.). The different churches subsist in relation to one another.

(3) The entirety of the Church. Paul speaks of the Church altogether: he had persecuted the Church of God; in the Church of God, God has called up apostles, prophets, etc. (1 Cor 12:28). According to Acts 20:28, it is the task of the bishops to care for the Church of God. Matthew employs the term in the same sense.

The expression "the Church of God *in* . . ." highlights the fact that the Church of God makes its appearance in the various local communities, so that in this way a general conception of the entire Church is implicitly operative.

In the deutero-Pauline letters the Church is understood as the intermediary for the cosmic role of Christ.

2. The Church as the Body of Christ

To describe the Church and its essence, Paul coined the specific phrase "the body of Christ," which was then incorporated into an altered framework in the deutero-Pauline letters.

a. The Phrase "Body of Christ" in Paul

Through baptism—so Paul says in Galatians 3:27f.—Christians have "put on Christ," so that they are altogether "one in Christ." The unity of Christians has as a consequence the overcoming of differences: "There are no more Jew and Greek, no more slave and free, no more male and female" (v. 28).

The same thought can be found in 1 Corinthians 12:13, where Paul speaks not of being "one in Christ," but rather of being "one body." "Through the one spirit we are all baptized into one body, whether we are Jew or Greek, slave or free." In this text (the internal development of 1 Cor 12:12-31 should be noticed), as well as in Romans 12:4-8, Paul uses a term that was already current in the Hellenistic world to designate a social unity, "one body": among the members of Christian communities, harmony and cooperation should prevail.

It is important for Paul that the source of this unity of Christians is Christ himself; for that reason he says that Christians make up one body in Christ. In this connection baptism and the Lord's Supper are given a high profile: through baptism Christians join the one body (1 Cor 12:13); through the sharing in the bread of the Lord's Supper, this unity is actualized and rendered concrete (1 Cor 10:17). Here the Hellenistic comparison is mystically deepened.

In both cases (1 Cor 12:12-31; Rom 12:4-8), Paul's discussion has the same goal, namely, to assert the complementarity of the different gifts of the Holy Spirit (charisms) for the Church. The phrase "body of Christ" shows that Paul places the emphasis on the Church as a community of *persons*.[3]

b. The Phrase "Body of Christ" in the Letters to the Colossians and Ephesians

Both these letters are concerned with the relation of Christ to the cosmos. According to Colossians 1:15-20, Christ can be the savior of the world because he took part in its creation. On this basis Christ is said to be before all creation and he is the firstborn from the dead (vv. 17, 18). In this context the Church is described as the body, and Christ as the head of the body: "He is the head of the body, that is, the Church" (v. 18).

The Church is also presented as the body of Christ in Ephesians (1:22, 23). Here also the context is cosmological. The Church is appreciated as the *pleroma* of Christ: she is understood as "the place of the 'fullness' of Christ, in which his power to sanctify becomes effective and powerful, that space where 'the fullness of Christ has come down and is present.' "[4]

In Ephesians 4:15f. and 5:23 the connection between Christ and the Church is also described as that between the head and its body. In the second text this description is complemented by a portrait of the Church as the bride of Christ, a picture which Paul used in 2 Corinthians 11:2, picking up a theme from the Old Testament (see, for example, Hos 2:4). In the analogy of Christ as the bridegroom and the Church as the bride, the accent falls on the dimensions of love and mutual devotion, while the

---

3. Against the position of H. Küng, *Die Kirche* (München, 1977) 145; see R. Schnackenburg and J. Dupont, "Die Kirche als Volk Gottes," *Conc* 1 (1965) 47-51.

4. R. Schnackenburg, *Der Brief an die Epheser* (Zürich-Köln-Neukirchen-Vluyn, 1982) 81.

metaphor of Christ as the head and the Church as his body stresses the superiority of Christ and the subordination of the Church.

We note here that Catholic theologians like Yves Congar and Heribert Mühlen base themselves on the expression "the Church as the pleroma of Christ" to justify their appreciation of the Church as a sacrament.

3. The Church as the Temple of God or the Temple of the Holy Spirit

Paul several times reminds the Corinthians that they are the temple of God and that the Holy Spirit lives in them (1 Cor 3:16; 6:19; 2 Cor 6:16).

In Ephesians 2:20-22 the Church is described as a holy temple and the house of God. It is qualified as a temple "in the Lord" (v. 21) or a house of God "in the Spirit" (v. 22). This deutero-Pauline letter employs two typically Pauline expressions: "in the Lord" and "in the Spirit." In this way the fact is emphasized that the Spirit of Christ lives in the Church.

The same idea appears also in 1 Peter 2:5, where the Church is spoken of as a spiritual home. "Temple of the Spirit" and "spiritual home" were common expressions for the Church in its early days.

BIBLIOGRAPHY

Cerfaux, L. *La Théologie de L'Église suivant Saint Paul*. Paris, 1965, 163–77, 223–40.
Roloff, J. *"Ekklesia."* In EWNT 1:998–1011 (with bibliography).
Scheikle, K. H. *Theologie des Neuen Testamentes* 4/2. Düsseldorf, 1976, 35–43.
Schlier, H. *Ekklesiologie des Neuen Testaments*. In MySal 4/2. Einsiedeln 1972, 152–63.
Schweizer, E. *"Soma."* In ThWNT 7:1024–1091.
_____. *"Soma."* In EWNT 3:770–779 (with bibliography).

III.

Jesus and the Church: Jesus' Proclamation of the Kingdom of God and the Church that Arose after the Events of Easter/Pentecost

1. Sketch of the Problematic

For traditional Scholastic Catholic theology it was assumed that Jesus—the historical Jesus—had founded the Church. The anti-modernist oath of Pius X (Sept. 1, 1910), which was obligatory before the installation in every office of the Church at least until the end of the Second Vatican Council, states: "I firmly believe that the Church, the protector and teacher of the revealed Word, was personally and directly set up by the true and historical Christ himself during his life among us, and that it was built upon Peter, the head of the apostles, and upon his continuous successors."[1] This theology emphasized that the kingdom of God proclaimed by Jesus Christ was "not only eschatological, spiritual, and interior, but also exists on the earth, is external and visible."[2] The founding of the apostolic college supposedly indicates "the form toward which Christ had begun to orient the external kingdom he was announcing":[3] Christ passed on to the apostles complete authority, so that he may be viewed as "the founder of a hierarchical society, which he called the Church."[4] The choosing of the Twelve together with the authority Jesus bestowed upon them, and Matthew 16:18 (the statement to Peter), was foundational for this theology. In this way Catholic theology reacted

---

1. DS 3540 = NR 63.

2. J. Salaverri, "De Ecclesia Christi," in Salaverri, *Sacrae theologiae summa,* vol. 1 (Madrid, 1952) thesis 1, 509. Salaverri is quoted as a representative example, in that his handbook was widely read.

3. Salaverri, Explanation of the second thesis, 524.

4. Salaverri, thesis 3, 532.

against the representatives of a merely eschatological interpretation of Jesus' proclamation, as well as against modernism.

From the modernist Alfred Loisy came the famous sentence: "Jesus proclaimed the kingdom of God, and what appeared was the Church."[5] This sentence poses the problem clearly: Although the kingdom of God (*basileia tou theou*) is the characteristic expression of Jesus' announcement—the three Synoptics are one in interpreting Jesus' mission through this phrase (Mark 1:15; Matt 4:17, 23; Luke 4:43; 8:1)—after Jesus' resurrection (after Easter/Pentecost) the language among his followers shifts to that of the Church. From that fact arises the question of the exact relation—if there is one at all—between the "kingdom of God" and the "Church." Does the intention to set up a Church fit with Jesus' proclamation? Also one should not forget that Matthew 16:18 speaks of building a church *in the future.* There can be no doubt that the Church "arose for the first time after Easter,"[6] so that we can speak of a Church in a true sense "only after Jesus' ascension and the sending of the Spirit."[7]

On the other hand, the fact that the post-Easter Church placed in Jesus' mouth such words as Matthew 16:18—which the majority of even Catholic scholars consider a post-Easter composition—shows that there must be at least a minimal continuity between Jesus' proclamation of the kingdom of God and the appearance of the Church after the events of Easter/Pentecost: "The post-Easter Church understood itself to be a community founded by Jesus."[8] *TRUE*

These reflections arise a posteriori, that is, from the perspective of the already founded Church after Easter/Pentecost. However, once the issue of the historical Jesus and his announcement is thoroughly analyzed, the problem immediately presents itself whether the Church is compatible with Jesus' proclamation of the kingdom of God. For example, Hans Conzelmann is convinced that they are incompatible: With Jesus' "eschatological preaching the setting up of an organized eschatological society simply does not fit";[9] Jesus' "eschatological consciousness excludes any thought of an actualized Church."[10] The problem becomes greater when the texts

5. A. Loisy, *L'évangile et L'Église* (Paris, 1902). On the meaning of this sentence in Loisy: Heinz, *Kirchenenstehung,* 122ff. It is his opinion that this sentence is frequently misunderstood.

6. A. Vögtle, "Jesus und die Kirche," in *Begegnung der Christen* (FS O. Karrer), (Frankfurt a. M., 1959) 54–81 (here 58).

7. R. Schnackenburg, "Kirche," in LThK 6:167.

8. K. H. Schelke, *Theologie des neuen Testaments* 4/2 (Düsseldorf, 1976) 33. K. Kertelge, *Gemeinde und Amt im neuen Testament* (München, 1972) speaks of a "manner that was legitimate for its time of invoking the original intention of Jesus" (54).

9. Hans Conzelmann, "Eschatologie II," in RGG 2:668.

10. Hans Conzelmann, *Grundriss der Theologie des neuen Testamentes* (München, 1968) 50.

in which Jesus speaks of the nearness of the kingdom are scrutinized: "If Jesus truly expected and proclaimed the imminent outbreak of God's dominion, there would seem to be no place for a Church oriented toward the 'world' and equipping itself for a long duration; at most one could see in her only a transitional solution and an ephemeral institution erected for a short interval."[11]

2. Overview of the Different Positions of Researchers

a. The "New Consensus" and Its Decline

In 1942 the Catholic theologian F. M. Braun spoke about a "new consensus" concerning the foundation of the Church by Jesus among Lutheran theologians, as a parallel to the so-called "consensus of eighty years of the nineteenth century";[12] his position may be summarized as follows:[13]

(a) Establishing a Church is part of the essential work of the Messiah; the Messiah's work is not private, but rather a community is attracted to him. F. Kattenbusch, who was the first to think along these lines, appealed almost exclusively to Daniel 7:13-14: the Son of Man is in Daniel a single person who at the same time must be seen as the representative of the people of the Most Holy. Correspondingly, Jesus interpreted his own person and his mission as that of the representative of the people of the Holy One.[14] Thus "the question whether the Church was established by Jesus is the same as the question whether he was the Messiah."[15]

(b) Jesus undoubtedly was conscious of being the Messiah, and he had begun to fulfill this obligation already during his earthly life. The figure of twelve apostles called by Jesus has here a special importance, for the number twelve is a goal of the messianic program: to refound Israel (the

11. W. Trilling, "Implizite Ekklesiologie," in Trilling, *Die Botschaft Jesu* (Freiburg, 1978) 57–72 (here 60).

12. O. Linton, *Das Problem der Urkirche in der neuen Forschung. Eine kritische Darstellung* (Uppsala, 1932) 3–30.

13. F. M. Braun, *Aspects nouveaux du Problème de L'Église,* 1942; there is a German translation of an expanded and reworked version in *Neues Licht auf die Kirchen. Die Protestantische Kirchendogmatik in ihrer neuesten Entfaltung* (Einsiedeln-Köln, 1946) 93ff. Heinz, *Kirchenenstehung,* 213ff., presents an expanded list of authors who have opted for this orientation.

14. "Der Quellort der Kirchenidee," in *Festgabe für A. v. Harnack* (Tübingen, 1921) 160. K. L. Schmidt, in his article "Ékklesia," in ThWNT 3:525, agrees with this understanding: "The 'son of man' of Daniel is indeed not simply an individual, but the representative of the 'People' of the 'Most High,' who has given himself the task of presenting this People of God, that is, the *ekklesia.*"

15. Schmidt, "Ékklesia," 3:525.

twelve tribes). For that reason the Church should understand itself as the new people of God. According to F. Kattenbusch, a special meaning should be attached to the final meal celebrated by Jesus with his disciples: "The Last Supper is the act through which Jesus founded his *ekklesia,* which had been his community as such." Because Jesus interpreted the Last Supper as the precursor of the messianic banquet, he "established his discipleship by means of a cultic act."[16]

(c) A common opinion was that the intention of founding a Church lay at the basis of Jesus' entire preaching, so that "it is not right to look for isolated moments for this event."[17] The members of the "New Consensus" emphasized that the actual construction of the Church succeeded through the salvation events of the death and resurrection of Jesus.

"The 'victory march' of the 'New Consensus' was decisively stopped by an article by R. Bultmann in 1941 entitled 'Question concerning the genuineness of Mt 16, 17-19.'[18] Bultmann found support for his criticism of the 'New Consensus' especially with W. G. Kümmel."[19]

For Kümmel the eschatological proclamation of Jesus is the central point, and not an a priori demand, in the sense that "Jesus *had* to gather a new community, if he was truly to make a claim about being the Messiah."[20] For the fact of the matter is that up to the end Jesus was oriented toward the entire *old* people of God. "There is nowhere any indication that Jesus seized upon the prophetic notion of the 'Remnant,' nor that during his life he culled out a Holy Remnant as the foundation for an eschatological people of God. . . . Certainly Jesus intended to found a 'Church,' but certainly not *his* Church, that would necessarily have to be separated from the *one* people of God." The group of twelve disciples clearly shows that Jesus oriented himself toward the whole of Israel. Kümmel concedes that Jesus gave the Twelve "the task of collaborating in his eschatological effectiveness" and that "thus within the circle of Jesus' disciples the coming Lordship of God is already effective." However, he still rejects the notion that the Church was founded by the twelve

16. "Der Quellort," 169. K. L. Schmidt writes: "From this point forward [from Daniel's understanding of the 'son of man'], the so-called establishment of the Last Supper can be interpreted as an act of founding a Church" (Ékklesia, 525).

17. H. D. Wendland, *Eschatologie des Reiches Gottes bei Jesus* Gütersloh, 1931) 184f.

18. *Exegetica. Aufsätze zur Erforschung des Neuen Testaments,* ed., pub., and with an introduction by E. Dinkler (Tübingen, 1967).

19. Heinz, *Kirchenenstehung,* 218. "A Presentation of Kümmel's Reflection": ibid., 230ff.

20. W. G. Kümmel, "Jesus und die Anfänge der Kirche," in Kümmel, *Heilsgeschehen und Geschichte. Gesammelte Aufsätze* 1933–1964 (Marburg, 1965) 289–309 (here 295). The work was first published in *Studia theologica* 7 (1053) 1–27.

apostles: "Since there is no talk of a *new* people of God in the circle of these disciples or those they influenced, one cannot say that the group of the Twelve is the germ of the new people of God."[21] Further, Matthew 16:17-19 cannot be used as an argument, for the text envisages no "organized" community.[22] Also the final meal lends no support to this hypothesis.[23] "Jesus gave absolutely no thought" to the time between his resurrection and his parousia.[24]

In spite of that, Kümmel adds, it would be incorrect to draw the conclusion that the appearance of the Church has absolutely no direct connection with the activity of Jesus. For the disciples came together on the basis of their experience of the resurrection. "These events are not based upon the sayings and wisdom of the earthly Jesus, but on God's activity in raising up the crucified one and in the gift of the Spirit that is to characterize the last age of the world. . . . The Church has its origins in the whole effectiveness of God in Jesus Christ, from his birth, his ministry and calling of the disciples, down to the gift of the Spirit upon the witnesses to the resurrection."[25]

b. Positions within Catholic Theology

Catholic theology seemed to see in the "New Consensus" a validation of its own position. The most important points to mention are Jesus' consciousness of being the Messiah—whether or not it can be demonstrated according to critical literary methods that Jesus understood himself as the "Son of Man" in the sense of the Book of Daniel—and the fact that Jesus had celebrated the final meal with his disciples in the fashion that his disciples should follow after his death in his memory. The institution of the Eucharist should be appreciated as a kind of "covenant that leads to the setting up of a new religious society, a new people of God." "In other words here we find one of the most compelling reasons to assert that Jesus effectively founded his Church in his final meal and, indeed, primarily as a cultic gathering, as a 'worshipping community,' " as J. Coppens puts it.[26] In a similar vein R. Schnackenburg writes:

21. Ibid., 294.

22. Ibid., 307.

23. Ibid., 309. In his work "Kirchenbegriff und Geschichtsbewusstsein in der Urgemeinde und bei Jesus" (Uppsala, 1943), Kümmel concedes that "the Last Supper clearly presumes the existence of a community of disciples after Jesus' death and thereby a point of departure and an anticipation for the development of an eschatological community."

24. "Jesus," 300.

25. Ibid., 309.

26. J. Coppens, "L'eucharistie. Sacrement et sacrifice de la nouvelle alliance. Fonde-

If Jesus instituted the holy Eucharist with the intention described earlier, then we can no longer say that he took no thought about the time after his death; rather, he had the most important thing already set in place: that his community should retain, and even increase, the powers and gifts of God's dominion that had broken out in his own ministry, and even more: that those things which had been won through the outpouring of his blood, the atonement power of his death, and the definitive forgiveness and reconciliation, would be bestowed upon her in their fullness.[27]

A. Vögtle expresses himself in a similar fashion: "With this fact a completely new situation appeared in the economy of salvation with the fact that Jesus understood his imminently expected violent death as an atonement sacrifice approved by God for 'the many' (that is, for the numberless people from all lands) that had the power to found a new covenant. The evidence for this consciousness of Jesus of his own death is the truly decisive point on the question of the institution of the Church."[28]

It should be noted that R. Schnackenburg and A. Vögtle speak of the Church as arising only after Easter and Pentecost. Schnackenburg writes: "Only after the ascension of Christ and the sending of the Spirit can we begin to speak of the Church in an authentic sense."[29] According to Vögtle, "the Church appears unambiguously only after Easter."[30] However, for both authors it is crucially important to connect the appearance of the Church after Easter/Pentecost with the words and deeds of the historical Jesus, in whatever way they conceive this connection concretely;

How church Founded

---

ment de l'Église," in J. Giblet et al., *Aux origines de l'Église,* Recherches Bibliques 7 (Bruge, 1965).

27. R. Schnackenburg, *Gottes Herrschaft und Reich* (Freiburg, 1963) 178. "If we look at the group of the saints after Jesus' departure who celebrated their Lord's farewell meal, it looks a bit different from a band of disciples abandoned by their leader, or a group of eschatologically enflamed fanatics awaiting the parousia and the final coming of God's kingdom. Rather, it is more the people of God gathered around Jesus, and gathering more progressively the new people of God, to the extent that—after the rejection by the old 'people of God'—it is built upon a new foundation" (177). See also 134 and 156. Schnackenburg writes in his article "Kirche 1. Die Kirche im NT," in LThK 6 (1961) 169: "The Last Supper opens up a new order of salvation to view, it makes manifest . . . that the group of disciples should continue, and promises to the community celebrating his memory an eschatological fulfillment in God's kingdom."

28. A. Vögtle, "Der Einzelne und die Gemeinschaft in der Stufenfolge der Christusoffenbarung," in *Sentire Ecclesiam* (FS H. Rahner) (Freiburg, 1961) 50–91 (here 90). See Vögtle, "Jesus und die Kirche," 76 note 48.

29. Schnackenburg, "Kirche," 167.

30. Vögtle, "Jesus und die Kirche," 58.

Schnackenburg speaks of "Jesus' acts of instituting the Church,"[31] H. Schlier of a "pre-formation of the Church," insofar as Matthew, for example, "stresses the empirical continuity of this community with the discipleship of the earthly Jesus."[32]

H. Küng summarizes this position as follows:

> a) *Before Easter* and during his earthly life, Jesus *did not found a Church;* b) *Before Easter,* however, through his preaching and deeds Jesus had *laid the foundations* for the appearance of the Church after Easter; c) The Church exists from the moment there is faith in the resurrection; d) Thus the Church derives its origin not exclusively from the intention and deeds of Jesus before Easter, but rather *from the complex of events that concern Jesus:* that is, in all that God achieved through Jesus the Christ, from his birth, through his calling of the disciples, his ministry, down to his death and resurrection and even down to the sending of the Spirit upon the witnesses to the resurrection. Not just the preaching and instructions of the pre-Easter Jesus, but also the will of God in raising up the crucified one and later sending the Spirit brought it about that from this group who together believed in the risen Jesus there developed a community of those who claimed, in contrast to the old, unbelieving people of God, to be the new and eschatological people of God.[33]

Küng attempts to show that among exegetes on this admittedly difficult question there is a fundamental agreement.[34] Some, however, would hold that he does not pay enough attention to the elements present at the farewell meal.[35] Küng's thesis was later taken up and extended by L. Boff in a work with the suggestive title, "Did the Historical Jesus Intend Only the Institutional Form of the Church?"[36] His position runs as follows: in its essential elements (proclamation, the twelve apostles, baptism, Eucharist), the Church was "pre-formed" by the historical Jesus; in its concrete, historical shape, however, it goes back only to the decisions of the apostles who were being led by the Holy Spirit (cf. Acts 15:28).[37] And that means that "the power to make decisions with regard to the commu-

31. "Kirche," 168.

32. H. Schlier, "Ekklesiologie des Neuen Testaments," in MySal 4/1, 111f.: "Thus the band of disciples together with Simon Peter is for Matthew *a preformation* of the future Church. . . . The evangelist is certainly conscious of the factual continuity of the community with the discipleship of the earthly Jesus." See also 209.

33. H. Küng, *Die Kirche,* 90–95.

34. "In their main features the numerous exegetes represented by Kümmel and Vögtle are in basic agreement" (ibid., 95).

35. He is there referring to page 96.

36. L. Boff, *Die Neuentdeckung der Kirche* (Mainz, 1980) 79–100.

37. No. 42, p. 95.

nity on discipline and dogma belongs essentially to the Church,"[38] that is, these functions should not be exercised "as dominion *over* the community," but rather they should arise "from *within* the communities."[39] In my opinion this theme is not necessarily best treated in this context. It will be the subject of the following chapters, in which the relation between the apostles and the community will be analyzed. ⟶named by vatican

Recently the International Commission of Theologians has taken up the theme of the institution of the Church. Their conclusion states: "Numerous marks of the Church, although they only appear in their fullest expression after Easter, are already apparent in the earthly life of Jesus and have there their foundation."[40] On that basis we may speak of "stages in the progress of the institution of the Church." For the commission it is important and undeniable that "in this process simultaneously the foundational, enduring, and final structure of the Church is being formed."[41]

It is H. Fries' opinion that "there is no single, specific act in the life of Jesus whereby he founded the Church, something like the proclamation of such an institution; on the other hand, there is an entire series of events, interactions, and exchanges which together indicate that Jesus had thought in terms of and planned a Church, in the sense of a fellowship united with himself."[42]

The historical difficulties have led W. Trilling, and with him H. Frankenmölle, to speak of an implicit ecclesiology, analogous to the way one may speak of an implicit Christology: "God leads into the present

38. No. 42, p. 96.

39. No. 49, p. 98 (my own translation from the corrected original).

40. Commissio theologica internationalis, *Themata selecta de ecclesiologia* (Vatican, 1985) 1.3, p. 11 and 1.4 = Internationale Theologenkommission, *Mysterium des Gottesvolkes* (Einsiedeln, 1986) 18. The concretization is very similar to Schnackenburg's description in "Kirche," 168f. See also Commissio theologica internationalis, "La conscience que Jésus avait de lui-même et de sa mission," in *Gregorianum* 67 (1986) 413–28, third thesis: "To accomplish his mission of salvation, Jesus wished to gather mankind with a view toward God's kingdom and to call them together around himself. With reference to this plan he carried out specific deeds whose only possible meaning, if one regards them in their entirety, is that of the preparation of the Church, which was definitively established in the events occurring from Easter to Pentecost. For that reason we must say that Jesus wished to found a Church" (422).

41. *Themata selecta* 1.4, p. 12 = *Mysterium*, 20.

42. H. Fries, *Fundamentaltheologie* (Graz-Wien-Köln, 1985) 376f. In nos. 47–49 Fries discusses the traditional themes: the calling of the disciples, the selection of the Twelve, the call of Simon Peter, and the Last Supper. For G. Lohfink, "Jesus and the Church," in *Handbuch der Fundamentaltheologie*, vol. 1, third tractate, "The Church" (Freiburg, 1988) 92, "formulations of this type are at the very least misleading as long as it is not also said that such acts 'relevant to the Church' have to do with a Church which, as concerns its identity, is in no way separate from Israel."

the construction of his *basilica,* which was begun in the Old Testament, refounded in a definitive way by Jesus, and awaits the future to be fully realized."[43]

In an article entitled "The Extraction of the Church in Salvation-History from Jesus' Death and Resurrection,"[44] K. Rahner speaks rather of a "derivation of the Church from Jesus, from the crucified and risen One," instead of a founding: if Jesus' resurrection is "God's enduring expression of himself toward the world," "God's irreversible statement to himself," then "naturally there must always have been a community of believers." "Such a community of believers is constitutive, and therefore necessary, for the realization of Jesus (as God's 'self-expression,' and not simply as a 'preacher of moral reform' or revivalist)." It is noteworthy that Rahner uses a theocentric point of departure, and to that extent depends upon Jesus' announcement of the kingdom of God.

3. Analysis and Reflection

a. *Jesus' Proclamation of the Kingdom of God*[45]

The Gospel of Mark joins his proclamation of Jesus at the beginning of his public ministry together with a typically Markan sentence: "The time is fulfilled, the kingdom of God is near. Repent and believe in the Gospel" (Mark 1:15; the same phrasing can be found in Matt 4:17). Matthew 4:23; 9:35, and Luke 4:43; 8:1 all maintain that Jesus preached a gospel of the kingdom of God. The phrase "basileia tou theou" doubtless expresses the kernel of Jesus' preaching. When Jesus sent out his disciples, they received from him the commission to say to the people: "The kingdom of God is near" (Luke 10:9; cf. Matt 10:7). They proclaimed what Jesus himself proclaimed. Jesus also taught his disciples to pray in a way that reflects this preaching: "Thy kingdom come!" (Luke 11:2; Mark 6:10).

43. H. Frankenmölle, "Kirche, Ekklesiologie," in NHthG 2:302. Trilling, "Implizite Ekklesiologie," 71: "God leads the development of his *Basileia* which has begun with Jesus, for this *Basileia* was not fully achieved in Jesus the Christ. . . . God remains true to this beginning when, after Easter, he entrusts it to a Church and simultaneously binds the Church to this beginning."
44. In *Schriften* 14:73–91 (here 79–86).
45. Selected bibliography: R. Schnackenburg, *Gottes Herrschaft;* Schnackenburg, *Die sittliche Botschaft des Neuen Testaments,* vol. 1 (Freiburg, 1986) 31ff.; H. Schürmann, *Jesu ureigener Tod* (Freiburg, 1974); Schürmann, *Gottes Reich und Jesu Geschick* (Freiburg, 1983). H. Merklein, *Jesu Botschaft von der Gottesherrschaft. Eine Skizze* (Stuttgart, 1983); L. Goppelt, *Theologie des Neuen Testaments* (Göttingen, 1981) nos. 7 and 8; E. Schillebeeckx, *Jesus* (Freiburg, 1975) 102ff.; U. Luz, *"Basileia"* in EWNT 1 (1979) 481–91.

When Jesus announced the coming of the kingdom, he did not add any new notion to this, but merely brought forward the expressions that had become common since deutero-Isaiah. The call "Your God is King" (Isa 52:7) expressed the hope for a final sovereignty by God, and this hope remained a frequent theme in post-Exilic prophecy (cf. Mic 2:12f.; 4:6-8; Zeph 3:14f.; Zech 14:6-11, 16f.). "As a matter of substance, above everything else the insistence on *the uniqueness of the name of Jahweh* is tied to the notion of God's dominion." This connection is clearest in Zechariah 14:9: "Then Jahweh will be King over the whole earth. On that day Jahweh will be the only one, and his name the only one." The same connection is present with Jesus, as the Our Father shows, so that "the hallowing of God's name and the advent of his Lordship" should be understood "as two sides of one and the same reality."[46]

Following R. Bultmann, the eschatological notion of the "kingdom of God" can be described in the following way: "It indicates the forces of God that put an end to the world's course up till now, that destroy everything ungodly, satanic, under which the world now groans, and therewith, by overcoming all need and suffering, inaugurate a condition of sanctification for God's people, which was waiting for the fulfillment of the prophetic promises."[47]

Because of its character as an eschatological event, Jesus' announcement that God's kingdom has "come near"[48] should be regarded as an eschatological pronouncement. "Jesus proclaimed the eschatological reign of God as near and breaking in, as effective and perceptible, bound together as one with his own person and ministry, and calling the hearer to an ineradicable decision. In this sense it is already present in him, in his words and deeds."[49] Jesus first raises the claim that the reign of God is present in connection with the miracles he performs: "But if I drive out demons through the finger of God [Mark: Spirit of God], then is the reign of God come among you" (Luke 11:20; Matt 12:28). The answer he gives to John's disciples, "The blind see, the lame walk, lepers are cleansed, the deaf hear, the dead rise, and the poor have the good news preached to them" (Matt 11:5; Luke 7:22) retrieves Old Testament signs for the time of salvation (Isa 29:18f.; 35:5f.; 61:1f.). What now takes place through Jesus should be reported with the words from these prophecies, in such a way that Jesus is seen in connection with the Lordship of God. "God's sovereignty and Jesus' person are joined intimately and indissolubly. Jesus not only announces, he is also the manifestation of God's Lordship." "This manifestation and execution of God's sovereignty are

46. Merklein, *Jesu Botschaft,* 40.
47. R. Bultmann, *Theologie des Neuen Testaments* (Tübingen, 1961) 3.
48. Schnackenburg, *Gottes Herrschaft,* 53.
49. Ibid., 109.

one and the same, to the extent that without the person of Jesus there would be neither manifestation nor execution."[50] For that reason the acceptance or the rejection of his person is determinative for the eschatological judgment of God (Mark 8:38; Matt 19:28).

Still the future retains its interest, and Jesus' attention stays fixed upon the kingdom to come. This is the fundamental meaning of the petition in the Our Father: "Thy kingdom come!" (Matt 6:10 = Luke 11:2). The language of entering the kingdom of God is often employed (Matt 5:20; 7:21; 18:3; 19:23; 21:31; 22:23; 23:13; 25:10, 21, 23; Mark 9:47). In this regard one should also mention the images for the coming reign of God, among which the grand banquet God invites us to is certainly primary (Matt 8:11f. = Luke 13:28; Matt 22:1-10, 11-13; 25:1-12, 21, 23). Jesus avails himself of this image during the Last Supper: "I will no longer drink from the fruit of the vine until the day on which I drink it anew [+ Matt: with you] in the kingdom of God [Matt: of my Father]" (Mark 14:25 = Matt 26:29; cf. Luke 22:15, 18: until the reign of God has come).

Was Jesus expecting the inbreaking of a completed kingdom of God in a fairly short time interval? This question is one of the most difficult exegetical problems of the New Testament. Three texts are relevant: Mark 9:1; 13:30; Matthew 10:23. These texts appear to indicate a limit of the expectations to the end of the present generation. The fact that the first community was indeed expecting the imminent arrival of the Lord would be an indication that such texts repeat actual sayings of Jesus. However, according to other texts like Luke 17:20 and Mark 13:32 among others, Jesus spoke indeed of the imminent arrival of the kingdom of God, but without giving a more precise time indication.[51]

Therewith the problem of an error by Jesus is excluded.[52] The problem is all the more important in that not only does the possibility of the projection of the Church by Jesus depend upon it, but also the question whether he could have seen his death as a death-bringing-salvation, and as such, in a logical connection with preaching of the kingdom.[53]

---

50. Merklein, *Jesu Botschaft,* 152f.

51. Thus Schnackenburg, *Gottes Herrschaft,* no. 16: "Die Frage der Naherwartung." See also Schillebeeckx, *Jesus,* 134f. The positions of the exegetes show no agreement.

52. For example, Grässer, *Die Naherwartung Jesu* (Stuttgart, 1973) 123-26, maintains that Jesus made a mistake.

53. On the problem with a bibliography: Schürmann, *Tod,* 41ff.; Trilling, "Implizite Ekklesiologie," 60ff.; R. Pesch, *Das Abendmahl und Jesu Todesverständnis* (Freiburg, 1978) 107ff.; Merklein, *Jesu Botschaft,* 137ff. Merklein tries to find a fundamental model according to which the problem Jesus had to wrestle with of the possible unity between his own death, which he had to reckon with, and the legitimacy of his mission, could be resolved.

Fundamentally it may be stated: "Jesus' proclamation of the king- *← Guembes* dom, with its undeniable dimension of an 'imminent expectation' . . . *A to* is contextualized by the <u>radical reference to God characterizing his entire</u> *Ron 24* <u>ministry</u>, which finally includes a forfeiture of his own ambitions and will, in which, however, this activity is maintained as completely transparent, open, and at disposal."[54] "Jesus had to carry out the specific task God had assigned him, to announce the kingdom, but equally to hold himself ready for the other possibility God might have in mind, specifically the effectuality of God's grace through his own failure, or even through his self-offering for death."[55]

b. Jesus' Farewell Meal

There is no difficulty with the notion that, shortly before his death, as the end he could foresee approached, Jesus would have given his disciples at an evening meal a concrete indication about the mystery of his persona and an insight into his own understanding of his approaching death. At the same, the descriptions we have of the farewell meal Jesus celebrated with his disciples are all colored and shaped by the post-Easter insights and reflections of his disciples; as a consequence, we cannot definitively prove that the words of institution carry precisely the meaning Jesus saw in his death—as an atoning death for many or for you, and a new covenant.

talking about future

On the other hand, the eschatological language is accepted by almost all exegetes as authentically from Jesus,[56] since it expressly corresponds to Jesus' proclamation of the kingdom of God: "I will no more drink of the fruit of the vine until the day when I drink it new in the kingdom of God" (Mark 14:25; Matt 26:29). In Luke 22:18 it runs "until the kingdom of God comes."

This eschatological language expresses Jesus' conviction that his farewell meal with his disciples, summing up their table fellowship on earth, is oriented toward completion in the kingdom of God. Jesus had frequently represented the kingdom through the metaphor of a meal (Matt 8:11; Luke 13:28f.; 14:15-24, etc.). For that reason "it is difficult to separate the thought of the Last Supper and that of the eschatological banquet."[57] In that the exchange of bread, and still more of wine, in Jewish thought had

54. Trilling, "Implizite Ekklesiologie," 63.
55. Schürmann, *Tod*, 45.
56. X. Léon-Dufour, *Abendmahl und Abschiedsrede im Neuen Testament* (Stuttgart, 1983) 118, with reference to H. Merklein, "Erwägungen zur Überlieferungsgeschichte der neutestamentlichen Abendmahlstradition," *BZ* 21 (1977) 236.
57. Schürmann, *Tod*, 83.

an eschatological connotation,[58] the offering of bread and the cup must be seen as signs of an eschatological salvation, that is now promised. This is the way the words over the cup should be understood in Luke and Paul (Luke 22:20; 1 Cor 11:25), that is, as participation in the promised eschatological salvation. However, it cannot be demonstrated that the expression about a "new covenant," echoing Jeremiah 31:31, goes back to the pre-Easter Jesus. Luke 22:30, "You shall eat and drink with me in my kingdom," passes on the essential message of the historical words of Jesus, in that they express Jesus' conviction about the connection between his own person and the eschatological kingdom of God.

Jesus appreciated "his own death as somehow drawn into the salvation-coming-down-from-God."[59] On the other hand, the eschatological language of Jesus validates the acceptance of a "between-time" between Jesus' death and his parousia. These two elements express the fundamental assumptions needed to clarify why the disciples, after their experience that Jesus would be raised up by God, could understand themselves as *ekklesia,* as the new *qahal Jahwe.* Jesus' farewell meal with his disciples, with the pre-Easterly group of the Twelve, "looks forward to and presages the completion of the eschatological salvation company after Jesus."[60] The fact that this meal could and should be repeated by the disciples as a memorial of Jesus (1 Cor 11:24, 25; Luke 22:19) became apparent when Jesus appeared to the disciples as the Risen One. From this moment on it was clear to the disciples that Jesus' death had a soteriological significance for "the many," that is, for all of humanity, and that Jesus' death was the foundation of a "new covenant" (from the words over the cup in Luke and Paul). If we could trace back the thoughts of the words of institution to the historical Jesus, then it would be very clear that it was the explicit and historically demonstrable intention of Jesus—at least after the representatives of Israel had rejected his message—to found a new community.

Easter clarifies and presents how the entire life of Jesus was drawn into God's plan of salvation. The soteriological interpretation of Jesus' death is the correlate of what is expressed in the term *ekklesia.* In as much as Jesus' farewell meal expresses Jesus' own consciousness in which he had associated his own death with the divine plan of salvation, it may be interpreted as a "symbol" of the new community of God founded on Jesus' death.

---

58. J. Jeremias, *Die Abendmahlsworte Jesu* (Göttingen, 1966) 225–28.

59. Schillebeeckx, *Jesus,* 275.

60. L. Goppelt, *Die Apostolische und Nachapostolische Zeit,* Die Kirche in ihrer Geschichte 1, A (Göttingen, 1966) 9 note 21.

c. Additional Observations *Attempts to [handwritten] between his [handwritten]*

It is my experience that every attempt to e[
the Church without a direct connection to the
cessful. The term *implicit ecclesiology* is helpf
implicit Christology, it attempts to do justice t
in the New Testament between the situation a[
cal Jesus.

It has correctly been emphasized that all the way through
end of his career, even with his lack of success, Jesus was oriented exclusively toward all of Israel. The pre-Easter group of the Twelve is evidence
for this: the number twelve relates to the twelve tribes of Israel, for although at that time the system of twelve tribes no longer existed, the hope
still persisted for an eschatological period of salvation when the twelve
tribes of the people would be reestablished.[61] Mark 7:24 and Matthew 8:5-
13 should be regarded as exceptions to Jesus' usual sphere of operation.
Further, Jesus had given his disciples instructions not to go outside the
borders of Israel (Matt 10:5, 23). Since Jesus hoped to win over the entirety of Israel for his eschatological salvation community, it is understandable that he would not tend to the constitution of a special group.

In that the group of the Twelve prefigured the final people of God,
we are justified in regarding Jesus' circle of disciples as "the seed of the
eschatological salvation community."[62] *[handwritten: Why?]*

It is our interpretation that Jesus' farewell meal was of crucial significance for establishing a connection between the historical Jesus and the
post-Easter reality of the Church. The Church must be understood as a
community set up for worship. In the celebration of the Last Supper the
new community discovers its identity as the new people of God founded
in the death and resurrection of Jesus (Jesus Christ as the new Passover),
just as Israel discovered its identity as the people of God in the celebration of Passover. Otherwise expressed, it is here that the power for salvation of the reign of God proclaimed by Jesus, and the salvation offered
to all humankind by God through the death and resurrection of Jesus,
becomes efficacious. For that reason, if we want to know what the Church
is, we must look to the Lord's Supper. The kingdom of God announced
by Jesus has a concrete people for its correlate, the new people of God.[63]

61. See J. Jeremias, *Neutestamentliche Theologie* (Gütersloh, 1971) 225; T. Holz,
"Dodeka," in EWNT 1:876.

62. Lohfink, *Jesus,* 85 note 140. He qualifies these statements with "only to the
extent." Schnackenburg, *Gottes Herrschaft,* calls the band of Jesus' disciples the "seed
of the salvation community in the future kingdom of God" (151). Vögtle, *Der Einzelne,* 82, accepts this terminology, all the while remarking that such terminology is
"misleading." Schlier, *Ekklesiologie,* speaks of a "preformation of the Church."

63. Lohfink, *Jesus,* 93.

BIBLIOGRAPHY

nz, G. *Das Problem der Kirchenentstehung in der deutschen protestantischen Theologie des 20. Jahrhunderts.* Mainz, 1974. (This work offers a complete presentation of the various opinions. Several Catholic authors are also discussed.)

Articles in Lexicons:

Frankenmölle, H. "Kirche/Ekklesiologie, A. Biblisch." In NHthG 2:294–309.

Schnackenburg, R. "Kirche, I. Die Kirche im NT." In LThK 6:167–72.

Exegetical Contributions:

Descamps, A. L. "L'origine de l'institution ecclésiale selon le Nouveau Testament." In J. L. Monneron et al., *L'Église: institution et foi.* Brussels, 1979, 91ff.

Dias, P. V. "Kirche in der Schrift und im 2. Jahrhundert." In HDG 3:3a. Freiburg, 1974, 14–33.

Goppelt, L. *Theologie des Neuen Testaments.* Göttingen, 1981, nos. 6, 7, 20, 21.

Lohfink, G. "Jesus und die Kirche." In *Handbuch der Fundamentaltheologie,* Bd. 3: Traktat Kirche. Freiburg, 1986, 49–96.

Schelkle, K. H. *Theologie des Neuen Testaments,* 4/2. Düsseldorf, 1976, 30ff.

Systematic Discussions:

Boff, L. "Die Neuentdeckung der Kirche." Mainz, 1983, 79–99 ("Did the historical Jesus intend only an institutional form for the Church?" as a Quaestio Disputata).

Küng, H. *Die Kirche.* München, 1977, 88–98.

IV.
The Church,
"Built on the Foundation of the Apostles"

1. The Term "Apostle"; The "Twelve Apostles"

Among researchers there is agreement that "in the New Testament we do not have a single notion of what it is to be an apostle, but rather different suggestions, between which there is a certain amount of tension. The clearest conceptions seem to arise with Paul and Luke."[1]

For Luke the "Twelve" are identical with the "apostles." The notion of apostle is reduced and limited to the circle of the Twelve. The Twelve were named apostles immediately after they were called: "Jesus called them apostles" (Luke 6:13). According to Luke 22:14, Jesus celebrated his farewell meal with his apostles, where Matthew 26:20 and Mark 14:17 speak only of the Twelve. Because after Judas' betrayal the circle of apostles was no longer complete, Matthias was added. According to Luke, two conditions had to be fulfilled for someone to be admitted to the circle of the twelve apostles: the candidate must not only have been a witness to the resurrection, but also must have accompanied Jesus during his earthly ministry (Acts 1:22). As a consequence of this second condition, in the Acts of the Apostles Luke cannot view Paul as an apostle, a position he maintains consistently. There is a palpable tension between the condition of having been a witness to the earthly life of Jesus and Paul's conception of an apostle.

The importance of the Twelve as the source of the Church is testified to by various traditions which the Gospels, the Acts of the Apostles, and 1 Corinthians 15:5 pass on. This importance is understandable only if this circle had a pre-Easter existence, that is, if it goes back to the historical

1. Schnackenburg, *Apostolizität,* 53.

Jesus. The report that Judas forfeited his position as an apostle (Acts 1:25) is a clear argument for this; it can scarcely be imagined that Jesus' disciples would have invented this after their experiences with the Risen One.

When Paul speaks of himself as an apostle, he mentions two elements to justify this designation: he has seen the Lord (1 Cor 9:1; 15:7), and he was both called and missioned by the risen Lord ("an apostle not by men or through a man, but through Jesus Christ and God the Father": Gal 1:1).

Compared with the apostolate of the Twelve, Paul's notion of apostolate has a special character. Here lies the tension between the Pauline and the Lukan notion of apostle, which can be expressed as follows: if the group of the Twelve is regarded as an "institutionalized" circle, then by contrast Paul's notion of apostle may be described as "charismatic." The use of such terminology should make us conscious of the fact that Paul presents himself as an apostle before a previously closed circle (the Twelve of 1 Cor 15:5 or all the apostles of 1 Cor 15:8),[2] that is, before those who were apostles before him (Gal 1:17-19).

This tension between the Pauline and Lukan conceptions of apostle is further reflected in the presentation of Church structures within the New Testament and their further development. For Paul it was necessary to remain in *koinonia* with the other apostles: he wanted to be sure that he "was not running or had not run" in vain (Gal 2:2); James, Cephas, and John, who were esteemed as the "pillars," recognized the grace that Paul had received (v. 9). The apostles maintained their unity. The same is shown by Luke in the Acts of the Apostles: the apostles are responsible for the preaching, so that every preaching of the gospel must be kept in contact with them. The departure of the apostles for Samaria also demonstrates this, for the purpose of this trip was to pass on the "gift of the Spirit" after receiving the news that "Samaria had accepted the Word of God" (Acts 8:14).

The apostles are witnesses to Jesus' resurrection. It is their task to preach God's gospel concerning Jesus the Christ. They were commissioned to this task by the Risen One himself.

The term *apostle* is also used in a wider sense. Paul differentiates his commission as apostle from a notion of apostlehood that comes "from men" or was set up "by a man" (Gal 1:1).[3] He is thus not a member of

2. See Roloff, *Apostel*, 434: "The addition of v. 8f. to v. 7 makes clear that Paul, by presenting himself as having received an Easter appearance, is drawing over himself the criterion required and accepted in Jerusalem for being an apostle; the supposed closed company of 'all the apostles' is thereby again exploded."

3. According to Hahn, *Apostolat*, 59, "*oudi di' anthropou* . . . shows that his apostolate was not passed on through a man, that is, that it is not a matter of task announced by a prophet through the Spirit." According to this interpretation there

the community of apostles. He talks about this community in 2 Corinthians 8:23. However, according to Acts 13:3f., Paul and Barnabas are regarded as members of the band of apostles. Andronikus and Junia are called apostles by Paul (Rom 16:7). It cannot be absolutely determined from the text whether the term "apostle" should be understood here in the narrower or wider sense.[4]

2. The Missionary Commissioning of the Apostles by the Risen One

The conception of apostle in the New Testament assumes that the apostle has received a missionary commission from the Lord. All four Gospels testify to this: Matthew 28:19; Mark 16:16; Luke 24:47; John 20:23.[5] The apostles were sent by the Risen One to preach the gospel (Mark) in his name (Luke). They are to make all people into disciples of Jesus (Matt). Luke's wording corresponds to the wording of the message of Jesus: "They [all peoples] should repent, so that their sins may be forgiven." Matthew, Mark, and John all speak specifically about baptism. This also corresponds to Peter's answer to the question from his audience after his sermon, as Acts 2:38 shows. The proclamation is a call to repentance, the request to let oneself be baptized in the name of Jesus Christ (Acts 2:23).

The comparison of Mark and John is particularly instructive:

Mark: "Whoever believes and is baptized will be saved; however, he who does not believe, will be damned."

John: "Whose sins you shall forgive, they are forgiven them; whose sins you shall retain, they are retained."

Both texts contain an antithesis: "saved or damned" (Mark); "forgiveness or retention of sins" (John). The comparison makes clear that John's text may also be understood in connection with baptism.[6]

---

would be three types of apostleship: (1) an apostle through empowerment by the Risen One, (2) an apostle through empowerment by the community, and (3) an apostle through empowerment by the Spirit. Other authors do not distinguish between these last two types.

4. According to Roloff, *Apostel,* 434, "in all probability Andronicus and Junias also (were members of) the Jerusalem apostles," for "that they were already 'in Christ' before him . . . corresponds" to the argument in 1 Cor 15:9ff.

5. Bibliography for John's Gospel: R. Schnackenburg, *Das Johannesevangelium,* vol. 3 (Freiburg, 1976) 386–90; R. E. Brown, *The Gospel according to John* (13–21) (New York, 1978).

6. During the first three centuries the texts were interpreted primarily in terms of baptism. Thus, for example, Cyprian concludes that "only the presiders of the Church are authorized to baptize and to forgive sins" (*Ep.* 73.7; CSEL 3:783. The Reforma-

In the opinions of various authors,[7] the logion in John should be regarded as a variation of the logion in Matthew 18:18.[8] Both texts have a Semitic foundation: while John uses a passive formula, Matthew speaks of a binding and losing in heaven. Both expressions refer to God's activity, so that the apostles' judgment, that is, the Church's, may be viewed as ratified by God himself.

Matthew's terms "binding" and "losing" reflect rabbinic terminology. These terms "normally mean 'forbidden' or 'allowed,' separated or 'imposed' with regard to a 'lifting of the ban,' and indeed both with the claim of authorization from God or his high court."[9]

Here and only here John employs a terminology that is common in the Synoptics. The meaning of the text becomes clear when we see the connection between verse 23 and verses 21 and 22; the disciples can forgive or retain sins, because they have been sent by Jesus (v. 21). And this means that the relaxation or the retention of sins by the disciples should be understood in the light of Jesus' behavior with regard to sin (John 3:17-21; 9:39-41; 17:18). "[We] must understand the forgiveness of sins by the disciples as the application of the salvation which Jesus has fashioned. . . . The authoritative command of the Risen One, which precedes the evangelist, is for him the foundational promise that the forgiveness of sins indeed occurs, and will occur further, within the community."[10] As for what concerns the commissioning of the apostles by the Risen One, it is exegetically indisputable that after his resurrection Jesus extended partnership to his disciples in his authority, although one must concede that we cannot exclude a shaping of this authority by the Church. This participation in Jesus' authority should be seen in connection with Jesus' bestowing of the Spirit upon the apostles: "Receive the Holy Spirit!" (John 20:22).

With regard to Matthew 18:18, we must inquire whether the text refers to the narrower circle of disciples or to the whole community. In the opin-

---

tion's thesis that this text should be interpreted as referring only to baptism was rejected by the Council of Trent (DS 1703 = NR 662). The council invoked this text to justify the establishment of the sacrament of penance.

7. See Schnackenburg, *Johannesevangelium*, 388 note 87; C. H. Dodd, *Historical Tradition in the Fourth Gospel* (Cambridge, 1963) 347–49.

8. On Matt 18:18, see B. Rigaux, " 'Lier et délier.' Le ministère de reconciliation dans l'Église des temps apostoliques," *La maison Dieu* 117 (1974) 86–135 (Rigaux also analyzes Matt 16:18 and John 20:23). A fuller bibliography and a complete exegetical presentation is given by H. Vorgrimler, "Busse und Krankensalbung," HDG 4/3 (Freiburg, 1978) 10ff.

9. A. Vögtle, "Binden und Lösen," in LThK 2:481. See also J. Jeremias in ThWNT 3:750f.; Rigaux, "Lier et délier," 87ff.

10. Schnackenburg, *Johannesevangelium,* 389.

ion of R. Schnackenburg, "the present placement and connection of the logion does not permit a final decision."[11] The word is here transmitted in a Matthean composition which presents a kind of community pattern (cf. vv. 15-17). Because of this it is pointed out that the "you" of verse 18 should be placed in connection with the Church of verse 17 and the previous "you" of the group (vv. 2, 10, 12, 13). Thus the "you" of verse 18 refers to the community. This is the preferred interpretation among gospel exegetes. However, it is the opinion of most Catholic and also several Lutheran exegetes that this text refers to the twelve apostles, on the basis that "Matthew 18:12ff. gives Jesus' counsel for the '*mathetai*' in their uniqueness as shepherds of Jesus' flock, and that vv. 15-18 appear to be thought of as a direct continuation of this."[12]

It is my experience that such an interpretation must explain two points: on the one hand the text contains a claim to full authority, which parallels the commissioning of the apostles by the Risen One; it thus becomes difficult to defend an interpretation which applies this claim to the entire community. On the other hand, however, this text is transmitted as part of a deliberate composition whose intention is to show a type of "community pattern," so that the relationship between the apostles and their communities is important in order to make clear the New Testament understanding of the matter.

With reference to John 20:23 Schnackenburg poses the following question: "Is this a special authority bestowed on the disciples as officeholders, that would be transmitted to their successors, or is it rather an empowering of the whole community?"[13] His answer runs: "This is a false dilemma, for we must keep the unfolding of the historical development of offices within the community in view. . . . The authoritative word of the Risen One, which precedes the evangelist, is for him the foundational promise that the forgiveness of sins occurs within the community, and will occur further. *A concentration on the present disciples, which means on the later holders of their offices, is not part of the evangelists' intention.*"[14]

---

11. Schnackenburg, *Apostolizität,* 60. He defends the same position in "Die Mitwirkung der Gemeinde durch Konsens und Wahl im Neuen Testament," *Conc* 8 (1972) 484-89 (here 487).

12. J. Jeremias, "Kleis," in ThWNT 3:751. This is also the opinion of H. Schlier, *Ekklesiologie des Neuen Testaments,* in MySal 4/1, 11. Rigaux, in "Lier et délier," puts forward as arguments: (1) the change in number: singular in vv. 15-17 and plural in v. 18, as well as (2) the literary genre: casuistry is replaced by the statement of a sacred law (118). Besides that there is, according to him, no doubt that the text refers to the office of governing "if we understand the word in its sense in the Church milieu of the years 80-85" (117).

13. Schnackenburg, *Johannesevangelium,* 388.

14. Ibid., 388f. (my emphasis).

3. Clarification of the Missionary Commissioning through the Apostles' Practice[15]

Since the words of the Risen One have been transmitted to us in and through a reflection by the community, we should attempt to understand the commissioning of the apostles through their practice, that is, through their relationships to the communities. For this purpose the New Testament offers the descriptions in the Acts of the Apostles, as well as the relations of Paul to his communities.

a. Paul and His Communities

Paul is anxious lest the communities he has founded accept some other gospel than the one he has preached (Gal 1:9). He reminds the faithful in Thessalonica about the command that he gave them through the Lord Jesus Christ (1 Thess 4:2). Through different images Paul emphasizes the importance of his person as an apostle for their community existence: he sees himself as the master builder who through his preaching of the gospel has laid the foundation, which is Christ himself (1 Cor 3:9-17); he is the father who through the transmission of the gospel has engendered his communities (1 Cor 4:12f.; Gal 4:12-20).

Paul asks the communities sarcastically whether he should come to them carrying a stick or with love and a gentle spirit (1 Cor 4:21). We find an idiom of command in 2 Thessalonians 3:6: "We order you . . . in the name of our Lord Jesus Christ, that you should pull back from any brother who lives a disorderly life and not according to what you have received from us." As 2 Corinthians 13:10 puts it, "For this reason I write thus while still so far away, so that when I am present, I will not have to use strong means with the full authority [*exousia*] that the Lord has given me, to build up, not to tear down" (cf. also 2 Cor 10:8). We may thus say that the apostle is fully conscious of the authority he has with regard to the community. The incident of indecent behavior presents a particular example of this. In light of the fact that the community has not expelled this person, Paul writes that he has already decided the case, as if he were already among them ("as if I were with you": v. 3). He adds: "When you are gathered together in the name of our Lord Jesus Christ and my spirit together with the power of our Lord Jesus is with you, this man should be given over to Satan" (v. 4f.). Schnackenburg comments: "In no way does Paul wish to act independently of the community; on the contrary, his intention is that the community should concur with his decision—even more, they should themselves reach this decision and carry it out. This shows that Paul sought an authentic consensus between him-

---

15. Schnackenburg's "Mitwirkung" is an important contribution to this topic.

self and the community, a consensus behind which stood the power of Christ."[16]

b. Apostle and Community in the Acts of the Apostles

Without doubt Luke presents a theologized depiction of the beginnings of the Church.

He describes the office of apostle as though founded by the risen Jesus, received through the gift of the living Spirit. All preaching about Jesus the Christ must take place in connection with the apostles (this is particularly clear in the preaching done by Philip in Samaria, after which "the apostles in Jerusalem heard that Samaria had accepted the Word of God" [Acts 8:14]). The apostles appear as the guarantee of unity. In the contentious discussions over whether pagan converts must be circumcized as well as baptized, the community decides to consult the apostles and the elders in Jerusalem (15:2).

In its own way the entire community takes part in the decisions. To replace Judas in the group of twelve, Peter convenes not only the other members of the group, but all the brothers (1:15-26). Equally when it came to choosing the seven deacons, the Twelve called in the entire community (6:2ff.). Paul won the approval, not only of the other apostles, but also of the entire community, for his decision to baptize non-Jews (11:1, 2, 18).

The already mentioned Council of Jerusalem (Acts 15), in which the early community confronted perhaps the most difficult question of this period, shows how the relation between the apostles and the community should be understood. Even though at 15:3 and 6 there is talk of a gathering only of the apostles and the elders, and even though the decision is spoken of as a decision by the apostles and the elders (15:25), it is conceded that "the apostles and the elders reached their decision together with the entire community" (15:22). One can therefore understand why Schnackenburg writes: "In the important question the community exercised its right to express itself."[17]

16. Ibid., 486. H. von Campenhausen, *Kirchliches Amt und geistliche Vollmacht in den ersten drei Jahrhunderten* (Tübingen, 1963) 51, writes: the apostle "can not simply give commands, he does not by himself create a norm which afterwards must be obeyed; rather the community of those who possess the Spirit should follow him freely, and this is what the norm appeals to." In my opinion both elements, the norms of the apostle and that the community should follow the apostle in freedom, are present in Paul.

17. R. Schnackenburg, "Lukas als Zeuge verschiedener Gemeindestrukturen," in *Bibel und Leben* 12 (1971) 232–47 (here 238). George, in Delorme, *Ministère,* 212, writes: "Luke several times shows that the apostles exercised a *rather discrete* leadership role in the Church of Jerusalem," with a reference to Schnackenburg. In Gal 2:1-10 Paul emphasizes that the "esteemed" recognized his apostleship. This is the main point of

4. Conclusion

The apostles are witnesses to Jesus' resurrection. It is their task to preach the good news of God's activity in Jesus Christ. They were commissioned by the Risen One himself. Their duties are to be appreciated in analogy with the duty of Jesus, who had enlisted them. In them the commissioning One is present: they receive from him *exousia*, "authority." We cannot exclude the possibility that the account of this commissioning has been passed on to us in a form edited by the community.

The tension between the Lukan and the Pauline conceptions of "apostle" takes form in the fact that Paul was received by the other apostles as an outsider. Paul distinguishes his office as apostle from that of Peter paradigmatically by saying that his activity is to be among the Gentiles, while Peter's is to be carried out among the Jews (Gal 2:8).

In what concerns the relation of the apostle to the community, it is to be noticed that the apostles included the communities in their decision-making processes, so that a cooperation by the community in the execution of their commission can be detected, in spite of the fact that—as is clear in the case of Paul—they were conscious of their authority in relation to the community.

BIBLIOGRAPHY

Bühner, J. "Apostolos." In EWNT 1:342–51.
Delorme, J. (publisher). *Le ministère et les ministères selon le Nouveau Testament.* Paris, 1974. (The themes of apostle and the Twelve is treated by different authors: J. Delorme, for Mark, 164–81; A. George, for Luke and Acts, 209–14; J. Delorme, 288ff., systematically).
George, A. "Des douze aux apôtres et à leurs successeurs." In *Le ministère sacerdotal; un dossier théologique.* Lyon: R. Didier, 1970, 23–53.
Hahn, F. "Der Apostolat im Urchristentum. Seine Eigenart und seine Voraussetzungen." *KuD* 20 (1974) 54–77.
Holz, T. "Dodeka." In EWNT 1:874–79.
Rengstorf, K. H. "Apostéllo, apóstolos." In ThWNT 1:406–46.
_____. "Dodeka." In ThWNT 2:321–28.
Rigaux, B. "Die Zwölf Apostel." *Concilium* 4 (1968) 238–42.
Roloff, J. "Apostel/Apostolat/Apostolizität." In TRE 3:430–45.
Schnackenburg, R. "Apostles before and during Paul's Time." In *Apostolic History and the Gospel.* Grand Rapids: F. F. Bruce, 1970, 287–303 = *Schriften zum Neuen Testament.* München, 1971, 338–58.
_____. "Apostolizität: Stand der Forschung." In *Katholizität und Apostolizität* (KuD. Beihefte 2). Göttingen, 1971, 51–73.

Paul's position. According to Schnackenburg, "Mitwirkung," 485, in spite of all the remaining unclarity, Paul's looking backward on the proceedings in Jerusalem gives no justification for excluding consensus by the community.

V.

The Organization of the Church
in Its Successive Developmental Stages;
Community Structures in the New Testament

0. Preliminary Remark on the Problematic

An analysis of community structures in the New Testament assumes *on Exam* a clarification of certain methodological problems, which here at the beginning must at least be mentioned. The fact that the later Church looked back to New Testament times as characterized by unity does not overshadow the fact that one may, and in fact must, speak of a multiplicity of voices in the New Testament. The Lima document endorses this point of view with regard to offices: "The New Testament does not present a unified hierarchy of offices that should serve as the model or enduring norm for every future office in the Church. Rather in the New Testament we find a variety of forms which developed in different places and at different times."[1] *[end] for today — NT does not present unified hierarchy of offices*

The greatest attention must be paid to difference in time and place for the development of the New Testament texts. It appears that "we must distinguish two distinct periods: the first in which the return of the Lord was believed to be so near that there was little concern for the future of the Churches and their organization, and a second in which the apostles, knowing that they would soon die and that already the danger of false teaching and division was threatening, set up offices that were intended to insure the continuation of their work after them."[2] This statement of Congar can be substantiated through an examination of the development

---

1. No. 19 in DwÜ, 574.
2. Y. M. Congar, "Die Wesenseigenschaften der Kirche," in MySal 4/1 (Einsiedeln, 1972) 550.

within the Pauline communities after the death of the apostle (the Pastoral Epistles). The fact that this development was executed through pseudepigraphical letters testifies clearly to such an evolution. At the same time this also shows that such development was in itself not self-evident, at least for various communities or persons. If we compare the Churches as Luke describes them in Acts—even if we concede here a certain theologizing in his description—with the picture of the Church given in 1 Corinthians, perhaps we should conclude that the Jerusalem community was from the very beginning more strongly structured than the Pauline communities.

Both aspects raise the important question of the significance of the fact that a certain structure in the Church—office as the guarantee of the continuity of the apostolic tradition—should appear everywhere. Because of this development, had an older pattern of the Church within the New Testament, for example, that of the Church at Corinth, lost its meaning for the life of the Church in the course of its history? The Church's situation in this second phase is commonly designated as "early Catholicism."[3] Must we view this development as a betrayal of an earlier understanding the Church had of itself, as some do? Even if we answer this question no, we must still take up the matter of the difference between a "primitive" testimony on the one hand and a "cultivated" testimony on the other.[4] Even if we view only the Scriptures themselves as the *norma normans,* we must still not attempt to drag New Testament sources out of the New Testament period, for the context helps to bring out explicitly what in the text remains only implicit.

3. On "Early Catholicism" (*"Frühkatholizismus"*): E. Käsemann, ed., *Das Neue Testament als Kanon. Dokumentation und kritische Analyse zur gegenwärtigen Diskussion* (Göttingen, 1970) (with essays by various authors); Käsemann, "Begründet der neutestamentliche Kanon die Einheit der Kirche?" idem, 124-33 = "Exegetische Versuche und Besinnungen I" (Göttingen, 1960) 214-23; H. Küng, *Strukturen der Kirche* (Freiburg, 1962) 142ff.; Küng, "Der Frühkatholizismus im Neuen Testament als kontroverstheologisches Problem," idem, 175-204 = *Kirche im Konzil* (Herder-Bücherei 140) 125-55 = *ThQ* 142 (1962) 385-424; Küng, *Die Kirche* (statement of the problem, 31; application, 217); F. Hahn, "Das problem des Frühkatholizismus," *EvTh* 38 (1978) 340-57; U. Luz, "Erwägungen zur Entstehung des Frühkatholizismus," *ZNW* 65 (1974) 88-111; J. Rogge and G. Schultze, eds., *Frühkatholizismus im ökumenischen Gespräch* (Berlin, 1984) esp. H. Schürmann, "Auf der Suche nach dem 'Evangelisch-katholischen' zum Thema Frühkatholizismus," 71-107, and J. Rogge, "Die Diskussion um den Frühkatholizismus im Neuen Testament," 27-51 (with a presentation of various positions).

4. See H. Küng, *Die Kirche,* 202 and 217.

1. The Pauline Communities during Paul's Lifetime

a. The Charisms in the Community

In his authentic letters Paul speaks twice about charisms in the community: in 1 Corinthians 12, where he answers a question posed by some Corinthian Christians about the gifts of the Spirit ("the hymn concerning love [1 Cor 13] and the extended discussion concerning speaking in tongues and prophecy in chapter 14 are both essential elements in Paul's understanding of the charisms"[5]) and in Romans 12:3-13. In both cases the teaching on charisms is developed in connection with the understanding of the Church "as the body of Christ" (1 Cor 12:12-27; Rom 12:4f.). Paul emphasizes that all the members belong to one another. He specifies the authentic goal of the differentiated spiritual gifts ("from the grace that has been bestowed upon us": Rom 12:6) to be the building up of the community (1 Cor 14:12, 26, where prophecy is expressly discussed; 12:7). "Paul at no time assumes that such charisms would be only an ephemeral development within the Church."[6]

In 1 Corinthians 12 Paul twice specifies the charisms. He uses "four traditional specific terms (gifts of the Spirit = *pneumatika*, effective powers = *energemata*, servers = *diakoniai*, gifts of grace = *charismata*) in connection with a variety of developments within the life of the community."[7] A first description of the charisms (gifts as talents) is given in verses 8-11. After the description of the Church as a body there follows a second list of charisms. In this list persons endowed with a grace come first: apostles, prophets, teachers (vv. 28a and 29) with the rank designations "first," "second," "third"; then other, mostly extraordinary gifts are named. The Greek construction suggests that "Paul is here taking over a list that is not original with him":[8] apostles, prophets, teachers. It is noteworthy that the *kybernesis* (the role of leader) appears in the second group!

The list of charisms in Romans 12:6 does not mention apostles. There prophecy stands first together with teaching. After these two comes *diakonia*, which should be regarded as a general category. Here also the later leadership charisms (specifically, of "one who stands before," *ho proistamenos:* v. 8) are placed in second place.

In contrast to these two descriptions stands that of Ephesians 4:11, although according to most exegetes we are here dealing with a deutero-

5. J. H. Schütz, "Charisma IV," in TRE 7:690.

6. H. Schlier, *Ekklesiologie,* 171.

7. H. Schürmann, *Gnadengaben,* 499.

8. R. Schnackenburg, "Apostel vor und nach Paulus," in Schnackenburg, *Schriften zum Neuen Testament* (München, 1971) 354; H. Merklein, *Das kirchliche Amt nach dem Epheserbrief* (München, 1973); Cothenet, *Prophétisme,* 1293.

Pauline epistle. The sequence runs: apostles, prophets, evangelists, pastors, and teachers. (Apparently the last two terms refer to the same group.)[9]

A comparison of the texts reveals a triad: apostles, prophets, teachers. The question of why Paul does not name apostles in the list of charisms of Romans 12 is answered in different ways by researchers. While some regard the "apostles" of 1 Corinthians 12:28 as meant in the narrow sense, others see this term used here in a wider sense, that is, for wandering missionaries who were officially sent out by the communities, without, however, excluding the possibility that they could be apostles in the narrower sense. In Romans 12, A. Lemaire believes, Paul is thinking of the life of a local community. Hence it is easy to understand why he does not mention this office.[10] In the later text of Ephesians 4:11, he is doubtless using the term "apostle" in the narrower sense.

To understand more precisely what is meant by the terms *prophets* and *teachers,* we should refer to Paul's remarks about prophecy and the other New Testament sources which discuss prophets and teachers. Acts 12:1 speaks about prophets and teachers in the community. According to the same source Paul and Barnabas belonged to this circle, and they were sent out by the community (Acts 13:3). The *Didaché* also speaks of prophets and teachers in the primitive Church in the sense of wandering missionaries.[11] The meaning of the term *prophets* becomes clear in Ephesians 2:20: the Church is "built on the foundation of the apostles and the prophets."[12] In the last texts which complete the New Testament, the

9. See, for example, J. Jeremias, *"poimain,"* in ThWNT 6:497; K. H. Rengstorf, *"didáskalos,"* ThWNT 2:161. According to H. Schlier (*Der Brief an die Epheser* [Düsseldorf, 1963]) "the identity [cannot] be proved." Nevertheless, they "belong with one another. In practice . . . their functions were probably often joined together" (196f.).

10. A. Lemaire, "Les épitres de Paul: La diversité des ministères," in Delorme, *Ministère,* 61. See also 60 and the note.

11. In 11.3-5 the topic is (wandering) apostles and prophets; they are the same people. Prophets and teachers are mentioned in ch. 13. The transition to bishops and deacons as permanent structural elements in the community seems to have provoked controversy. For that reason it is emphasized that the bishops and deacons also carry out the service of prophets and teachers, that is, a service that is naturally accepted by the community (ch. 15).

12. It is disputed whether the prophets should be understood as a separate group, or whether "prophets" should be seen as a more precise description of "apostles," in the sense of "the apostles who are prophets." ("Thus the foundation of the Church as a heavenly construction are the two of them: those who are authorities through the principle of having been commissioned directly for mission, and those who are charismatic authorities:" R. Schnackenburg, *Der Brief an die Epheser* [Freiburg-Zürich-Neukirchen, 1982] 184.) For the second interpretation see, for example, Cothenet, *Prophétisme,* 1308f.

Pastoral Letters and the Catholic Letters, the fight against false prophets appears prominently. All this demonstrates that in the primitive Church prophets played an important role.

Paul never refers to himself as a prophet, but only as an apostle: "The title of 'apostle' was enough for him, since it also contained that of 'prophet.' "[13] Also for Paul prophecy is nothing extraordinary; thus he can urge the Corinthians to acquire the gift of prophecy (1 Cor 14:1). The purpose of prophecy is the building up of the community (vv. 3, 4, 26). The role of an apostle (v. 6) should be seen in a closer connection with what prophecy is also bringing about. Like other charismatic gifts, prophecy is dependent upon a fundamental apostolic witness (cf. Rom 12:6; 1 Thess 5:21). According to Paul prophecy is a normal gift of the Spirit and appearance in a community; this inspiration may unexpectedly fall upon anyone (1 Cor 14:30). For that reason the apostle counsels not to stifle the Spirit (1 Thess 5:19f.). "The only restriction he places is that those gifted by the Spirit should retain their faith and that during the worship service, for the sake of the members of the community and the dignity of the proceedings, everything should take place in order."[14] Prophecy is subjected to the community's judgment (1 Cor 14:29).

In the description of the charisms a picture of the life of the community is given that differs sharply from the picture of the community given in the Pastoral Letters, where the role of the offices is much more strongly emphasized. "When Paul expresses concern over the unity and the building up of the community, his emphasis is not on setting up a board of directors, but rather on the 'Spirit,' which is working in the community and that speaks primarily through the prophets (cf. 1 Cor 14:30-33)."[15] Spontaneity and freedom characterize the life of the community. However, this does not mean that we may not speak of a principle of order; next to the apostolic leadership there is a self-regulation of the charismatic order out of love.[16] Beyond that it should not be forgotten that already in 1 Corinthians Paul speaks about a mutual deference among those who work with the community and exert themselves on its behalf (16:16).

However, one should not so emphasize these facts as to give the impression that Paul's description of the community and the charisms was typical of all community structures in the New Testament.

b. The Role of Those Who Minister to the Community

On various occasions Paul speaks of his coworkers, whom he sends to the communities. Among them Timothy stands in the first place: "When

13. L. Cerfaux, *La théologie de L'Église suivant S. Paul* (Paris, 1965) 365.
14. H. Schlier, *Ekklesiologie,* 171.
15. Kertelge, *Gemeinde,* 124.
16. Thus Schürmann, *Gnadengaben,* 515.

Timothy arrives, conduct yourselves in such a way that he will have nothing to fear; for he is as busy about the Lord's work as I am. Let no one despise him!" (1 Cor 16:10, 11). Other coworkers with Paul are Titus (Gal 2:3; 2 Cor 2:13; 7:6-14; 8:6-23; 12:18), Epaphras (Col 4:12f.), Epaphroditus (Phil 2:25), Tychikus (Col 4:7), and Onesimus (Col 4:9). These collaborators work in dependency on the apostle. Especially important for an understanding of the local Pauline communities are the apostle's remarks on the respect which the faithful in the communities owe toward those who are expending themselves on the community's behalf. Because of the service which the family of Stephanas did for the community, the faithful should submit to him (1 Cor 16:15). The meaning of this subjection becomes clear when we notice that the term *hypotassomai* used here by Paul he employs elsewhere to designate religiously grounded subordination to the civil authority (Rom 13:1, 5) or to declare that all is subject to Christ (1 Cor 15:27). In this context 1 Thessalonians 5:12 is an especially important text: "Respect those who work among you [*kopiontes*] and who lead you [*proistamenoi*] in the Lord." We should presume a link between the two terms, in the sense that those who particularly exert themselves on the community's behalf occupy a preeminent place in it.

About various women Paul says that they "have toiled for the Lord" (Rom 16:6, 12); in this way their particular mission work is emphasized.[17] Phoebe is described as a *diakonos* of the community at Kenchre, the port of Corinth (Rom 16:1). Although we know nothing more precise about her work, it must have been important, since Paul refers to her so highly.

Philippians 1:1 is the only place in the authentic Pauline letters where *episkopos* and *diakonos* can be found as descriptions of activities, and which later became fixed as titles for offices. While normally the greeting in Paul's letters is directed only to the community, here after the community the *episkopoi* and *diakonoi* are named. Were these added on, as the letter was compiled out of two or three different letters?[18] This is a possibility. In any case, however, this text is the only example in the authentic Pauline writings that testifies to the existence of these structures in the Pauline communities. In Acts 14:22-24 and 20:17-38 it is said that Paul set up *episkopoi*, specifically *presbyteroi* and *diakonoi,* in his communities. This is doubtless a theological, and not a historical, presentation,

17. For these women special Pauline technical terms ("exert oneself," "labor") were used for missionary activity. See W. H. Ollrog, *Paulus und seine Mitarbeiter* (Neukirchen-Vluyn, 1979) 75.

On the role of women in the early Church, see A. Weiser, "Die Rolle der Frau in der urchristlichen Mission," in *Die Frau im Urchristentum,* eds. G. Dautzenberg, H. Merklein, and K. Müller (Freiburg, 1983) 158–81; G. Dautzenberg, "Zur Stellung der Frauen in den paulinischen Gemeinden," ibid., 182–224; G. Lohfink, "Weibliche Diakone im Neuen Testament," ibid., 320–28.

since the establishment of such offices is nowhere mentioned in the authentic Pauline letters. No doubt the communities Paul founded developed later such structures; the question is whether this transition occurred during the lifetime of the apostle. This appears doubtful to me. Paul's letters consistently present a perspective in which all the members are answerable to the community and "that leadership tasks grew organically out of the community's life."[19] The leadership assignments should be understood in a "charismatic" perspective, in such a way that the community in Corinth is a model of the typical Pauline community.[20]

2. Community Structures in the Acts of the Apostles[21]

Although Acts of the Apostles was probably composed around A.D. 80, it contains important historical data from the earlier period. On the negative side, it presents a theologized portrait of these facts, as a comparison of their description of Paul with Paul's own letters makes clear.

I wish to draw out three topics within Acts: (a) the Jerusalem community, (b) the Antioch community, and (c) the situation of the community at the time the text was composed.

a. The Jerusalem Community

The Apostles. Acts clearly maintains that the apostles were the leaders of the Jerusalem community. Luke emphasizes that everything in the community indeed took place, and had to take place, in connection with the apostles: the later choice of a twelfth apostle (1:15-26), the choice of the Seven (6:1-6), the evangelizing of Samaria (8:14ff.). A leading role is ascribed to Peter; after Easter he speaks as the representative of the apos-

18. Thus Lemaire, *Les Ministères*, 97.

19. J. Gnilka, *Der Philipperbrief* (Freiburg, 1968) 33.

20. In my opinion, an exaggerated description of the Corinthian community can be found in H. Küng, *Die Kirche*, 475f. Küng's entire presentation of charisms and authority is interesting. On the reaction of Catholic exegetes to the book, see P. Grelot, "La structure ministérielle de l'Église d'après S. Paul," *Istina* 15 (1970) 389–94 (a shorter presentation can be found in H. Häring and J. Nolte, eds., *Diskussion um Hans Küng "Die Kirche"* [Freiburg, 1971] 114–27); Grelot, "Sur l'origine des ministères dans les églises pauliniennes," *Istina* 16 (1971) 452–69; M. M. Bourke, "Reflections on Church Order in the New Testament," *CBQ* 30 (1968) 495–511 (a shorter version in Häring and Nolte, *Diskussion,* 127–33); O. Pesch, "Amtsstrukturen im Neuen Testament," in Häring and Nolte, *Diskussion,* 133–54.

21. From the bibliography given above the following items are especially recommended: Schnackenburg, *Lukas;* Lemaire, *Les ministères,* 45–71; A. George, in Delorme, *Ministere,* 207ff. Besides these, S. Docks, "L'ordination de Barnabé et de Saul d'après Actes 13, 1-3," *NRTh* 98 (1976) 238–50.

tles (2:14ff.); he plays an important role in decisive situations, either alone, as in the question about baptizing Gentiles (chap. 11), or together with John (3:1; 4:1; 8:14ff.), or together with James in the decision from Jerusalem (chap 15).

James. After Peter's departure, James, the "brother of the Lord," moves almost imperceptibly into prominence. Even before his departure Peter says: "Say this to James and to the brothers" (12:17). Also according to 21:18, as Paul comes for the third time to Jerusalem, James occupies the leadership role in the community.

Through Paul also we discover that James was an important personality in Jerusalem. During his first trip there Paul had come to know Peter, but no other apostle except James, the brother of the Lord (Gal 1:18-20). At the Council of Jerusalem, James, Cephas, and John, who were regarded as the "pillars" of the community, recognized the grace that the Lord had given to Paul (Gal 2:9). We must add to this that the appearance of the Lord to James in the earliest Christian kerygma is particularly mentioned among the appearances of the Risen One (1 Cor 15:7).

There is no basis for equating this James and the apostle James.

The theory that after his departure from Jerusalem Peter left jurisdiction in the hands of James, as O. Cullmann suggests, cannot be demonstrated.[22] Already during Peter's presence James was a powerful figure in the Jerusalem community, as the description of the Jerusalem Council shows (15:13ff.). Until the destruction of the Temple, Jerusalem was the central reference point for all the Christian communities.

The Seven. The election of the Seven indicates a decisive stage in the development of the Jerusalem community. The question about the function of the Seven raises a problem: according to the description in the Acts of the Apostles, their function was to take care of table service, leaving the apostles free to attend to the Word of God (6:2). However, Luke describes the activity of Stephen and Philip (for Stephen: 6:8-10; 8:26-40; for Philip: 8:4-13; 21:3 describes Philip as an evangelist) as the task of preaching the Word of God, that is, they carry out the same task for which the Twelve, according to 6:2, wanted to be freed from "table service."[23] This raises the suspicion that the Seven received a commission to direct themselves toward the Hellenistic-Jewish community. It is noteworthy in this connection that the names of all seven are Greek.

The fact that "according to the Law, the governing body of the Jewish community consists in seven men"[24] partially explains the number seven. Besides that, seven has a symbolic character and stands for completion or perfection.

22. O. Cullmann, *Petrus. Jünger-Apostel-Màrtyrer* (Zürich-Stuttgart, 1960) 47f.
23. Schnackenburg, *Lukas,* 236.
24. K. H. Rengstorf, "hepta," in ThWNT 2:630.

The investiture took place through the laying on of hands (6:7), probably by the apostles, since the initiative came from the apostles, although the text does not give us more information. This first community took over a ritual that was common and traditional for the installation of a rabbi.[25]

The Elders. Nothing is reported about their installation; they are suddenly presented in 11:30. They appear together with the apostles at the Council of Jerusalem (15:2, 6, 23; 16:4) and later in connection with James (21:28). "This term is common in the Jewish world with reference to a circle of counselors for the community."[26] It is thus an advisory and consultative board.

b. The Community in Antioch

Acts 13:1-3 gives us a brief description of the community in Antioch: "However, there were in Antioch in the community prophets and teachers, namely. . . . Because they fasted and served the Lord, the Holy Spirit spoke: 'Set aside Barnabas and Saul for the work to which I have called them.' Then they fasted and prayed and laid hands on them and allowed them to depart."

"This report surprises us, for otherwise Barnabas and Paul are nowhere called prophets or teachers."[27] We are already informed in 11:22-26 about the activity of Barnabas and Paul in Antioch: Barnabas went to Antioch as the emissary of the community in Jerusalem, and brought Paul there. Verse 27 says that prophets came into the community from outside.

Barnabas and Paul were sent by the community. The laying on of hands was employed as a ritual to indicate this. On the basis of this mission Luke regards both of them as apostles (14:4, 14). After their mission they shared with the community what God had done through them (14:27).

Luke nowhere describes the investiture of these prophets by any authority figure. This corresponds to the biblical tradition, according to which prophecy is simply understood as a charismatic gift. Prophets had always

25. See E. Lohse, "Cheir," in ThWNT 9:420-23. E. Maurer, "epitíthemi," in ThWNT 8:161-62; E. Lohse, *Die Ordination im Spätjudentum und im Neuen Testament* (Göttingen, 1951); A. Ehrhardt, "Jewish and Christian Ordination," *JEH* 5 (1954) 125-28; K. Hruby, "La notion d'ordination dans la religion juive," *La Maison-Dieu* 102 (1970) 52-72.

26. A. George, in Delorme, *Ministère,* 218. See also G. Bornkamm, "presbys" in ThWNT 6:659-61.

27. Schnackenburg, *Lukas,* 240. Because of the expression in 4:36, "son of consolation," which could be understood as "son of prophecy," several authors are of the opinion that Barnabas was a prophet in Jerusalem. Other authors reject this interpretation.

been called through the unforced election of the Spirit. Luke gives no indication how the prophets were recognized as such, while Paul names a criterion: the judgment of the community (1 Thess 5:19-20) or perhaps of other prophets (1 Cor 14:29); but fundamentally he holds that recognition by the apostles is needed (1 Cor 14:37).

There are other sources that tell us about the role of the prophet in the early Church: Paul's description of the charisms (1 Cor 12:28; Rom 12:6); the Didache and Matthew 10:41[28] (a logion found only in Matthew).

Most probably the expression "prophets and teachers" has already become "a fixed designation for officeholders who work charismatically."[29] In all the communities teachers were necessary (cf. also Acts 11:26). Their activity may be observed in the conservation, spread, and fruitfulness of the tradition.[30]

The distinctive aspect of the Antioch community is described by R. Schnackenburg in the following terms: "The charismatic element has a higher profile in this community than in the Jerusalem community, since this community structure more closely resembles that of the community in Corinth, which is blessed with many charismatic gifts. However, the leadership was more tightly controlled by these prophets and teachers, while the community in Corinth had a greater variety of charismatic individuals, and owed their direction to their founder Paul."[31]

c. Community Structures at the Time of the Composition of the Acts of the Apostles

It appears that the author of the Acts of the Apostles has woven several glimpses of contemporary community structures into his presentation. There is one unmistakable indication of this: he names presbyters as community leaders in Pauline foundations (14:22-24 and 20:17-38), although Paul himself never mentions presbyters.

Without verse 23 the thrust of 14:22-24 would be clearer. Luke has interjected a theological goal into this verse, to link the installation of presbyters with the founders of the community. In 20:28 the image of shepherding, which can also be found in 1 Peter 2:25 and 5:2, is employed: the presbyters are responsible for the community. For that reason they must "shepherd God's people" and "give their attention" to the community.

---

28. Matt 7:15, 22f. differs from Luke 13:25ff. and Mark 13:22 by the warning against false prophets. This fact shows that there were Christian prophets in the area of Syrian-Palestine.

29. Schnackenburg, *Lukas,* 241, poses this as a question.

30. Thus Schnackenburg, *Lukas,* 241, with a reference to H. Greven, "Propheten, Lehrer, Vorsteher bei Paulus," *ZNW* 44 (1952/53) 1–43, here 4ff. See also G. Friedrich, "prophétes," in ThWNT 6:849ff.; F. Schnider, "prophétes," in EWNT 3:442–48.

31. Schnackenburg, *Lukas,* 242.

The situation is close to that in the Pastoral Letters; it is a period in which false teachers are confusing the faithful (v. 30). "Just as in the Pastoral Letters the office of Church leadership, which has as its responsibility to conserve the apostolic teaching and tradition and to protect the faithful, takes on greater importance. Faced with these new situations and dangers, the community structures change."[32]

3. Community Organization in the Post-Apostolic New Testament Period

In the Acts of the Apostles Luke describes the community structures of his own time, and in their light he gives us a theological presentation of the first community. Luke's description corresponds fundamentally with the picture that other writings which come from the same period offer us.

A preliminary remark concerning pseudo-epigraphic literature is necessary. Pseudo-epigraphic writings invoke the unquestionable authority of a person for situations or decisions which in themselves, at least for certain persons or groups, are exceedingly questionable. Evidently *Didaché* 15 evidences a suspicion by various communities, when it says: "Choose for yourselves bishops and deacons . . . for these will carry out for you the offices of prophets and doctors [teachers]. Do not despise them, for they should be honored in the same way as prophets and doctors." The pseudo-epigraphic writers are convinced that the new form of Church offices should be understood as a necessary transformation in view of a new situation; this terminology should be accepted as a consequence of the direction of the apostles to their followers and as corresponding therefore to the spirit and intention of the apostles.[33]

a. In the Sphere of the Pauline Communities

Ephesians 4:11-13 contains a list of the charisms and services. A comparison with 1 Corinthians 12:28-31 and Romans 12:6-8 shows that here new names, specifically evangelists and teachers, have been added. The Greek construction (*men . . . de . . . de . . .*) allows us to distinguish four groups: apostles, prophets, evangelists, and shepherds and teachers.

In Ephesians 2:20 and 3:5 apostles and prophets were mentioned: "The Church is built on the foundation of the apostles and prophets" (2:20); "In former times the children of man did not know about what has now been revealed to the holy apostles and prophets through the Spirit" (3:5).

The first two groups do not pose any particular problem, in that both are mentioned by Paul himself. We can find the term *evangelist* in the

32. Ibid., 245.
33. This perspective is emphasized by H. Schlier, *Ekklesiologie*, 479, for the Pastoral Letters.

New Testament: in Ephesians 4:11; in Acts 21:8 for Philip, "one of the Seven"; and in 2 Timothy 4:5 for Timothy. These records "make it possible to discern men therein who take up the 'apostolic' proclamation and carry it forward."[34] The expression *pastor*—here together with *doctor,* which is a new term—is used in 1 Peter 2:25 for Christ. The image of pastors is employed in Acts 20:28 and in 1 Peter 5:2 for community leaders (see also John 21:15-17). In Ephesians 4:12 the reason is "so that the saints may be properly outfitted for the work of service." The author casts a glimpse at the contemporary situation of the community: "The 'basic' meaning of apostle and prophet is equally carried out in the different activities of the evangelist, the pastor, and the teacher."[35]

The theme of the Pastoral Letters is the conservation of the tradition, of the *paratheke* of the apostles: "O Timothy! Preserve what has been entrusted to you" (1 Tim 6:20; cf. also 2 Tim 1:10-14). It is a question here of an undefiled teaching that must be retained (1 Tim 1:10; 2 Tim 4:3). It is also Titus' obligation to preach what corresponds to this undefiled teaching (Titus 2:1; see also 1:9).

The task is similar in these letters for persons designated as bishops, presbyters, or deacons: the bishop must hold himself to the authentic word of the teaching (Titus 1:9); he must care for God's Church (1 Tim 3:5). The deacons should preserve the mystery of faith with a pure conscience (1 Tim 3:9).

At the center stands the unabridged transmission of the apostolic good news: "What you in the presence of many witnesses have heard from me, entrust to reliable persons who are capable of teaching others" (2 Tim 2:2). Office in the Church is appreciated in these letters as a means by which to maintain the authentic gospel. The emphasis in the Pastoral Letters on the offices in the Church has as a consequence that the community's charisms, of which Paul speaks, retreat into the background. It is different in 1 Peter (see below, section 3b).

The officers are introduced with the titles *bishop, presbyter,* and *deacon*. What a bishop is supposed to do is made clear by a comparison between the Church and the bishop's household (1 Tim 3:4; Titus 1:7), so that one may conclude therefrom that the bishop should play the same role in the community as a father plays in his family. Since it was Titus' task to install presbyters in every city (Titus 1:5), we may conclude that the bishop of Titus 1:7 may not be distinct from the presbyter. The same thing follows from 1 Timothy 5:17. Thus, at this time, there is as yet no difference between a bishop and a presbyter. If one insists on distinguishing between them, then the bishop must be viewed as something like the

34. R. Schnackenburg, *Der Brief an die Epheser* (Zürich-Neukirchen, 1982) 184.
35. Ibid., 183.

leader of a "team of presbyters."[36] It is interesting that there is nowhere any mention of the liturgical functions of these officers.

With reference to the deacons it should be mentioned that 1 Timothy 3:8-12 provides grounds for speaking about women in the service functions. After the qualities that a bishop ought to have have been described, there follows the text: "In the same way [*hosautos*] should the deacons . . ." (v. 8); "in the same way [*hosautos*] should the women . . ." (v. 9); "the deacons should . . ." (v. 12). The repetition of "in the same way" indicates that women also perform a service.[37]

To the question how a person is installed in office, the answer is given in 1 Timothy 4:14 and 2 Timothy 1:6: through the laying on of hands. It is a matter of a gift of God, of a *charisma,* that is received through the laying on of hands. The two texts do not completely agree on *who* lays on hands; the first text speaks of presbyters, the second of Paul. The comment "on the basis of prophetic words" reminds us of Acts 13:1-4: it is a matter of an inspired choice. "The transmission of office is as much concrete and ecclesial as it is a spiritual and sacramental act."[38]

b. In the "Petrine" Sphere (1 Peter)

"Outside the Pauline sphere, but not completely unaffected by Pauline perspectives, stands the letter 1 Peter."[39]

Although the author has introduced himself with the title "apostle" (1:1) he describes himself as a "co-elder" (*sympresbyteros:* 5:1). This gives prominence to the respect that has come to surround the title *presbyter.* "In 5:1-4 we have something like an early Christian job description of the *presbyteroi.* They should 'pastor God's flock,' that is, provide the local Church with leadership, nourishment, and protection."[40] The role of the presbyters is here emphasized so that the apostle Peter as the founder of the community may, with a becoming modesty, place himself on the same level as the presbyters.

In 1 Peter 4:10f. we have a short text that treats the charisms: "Serve one another, each with the gift that he has received from God, as a good steward of the many-sided grace of God." Only the kerygmatic ("if someone speaks")[41] and the diaconal ("if someone serves": *diakonei*) gifts

---

36. E. Schillebeeckx, *Das kirchliche Amt* (Düsseldorf, 1981) 30, poses the question: "Is the *episkopos* a *presbyteros,* perhaps the leader of the presbyteral team?" See also G. Bornkamm, *"présbys,"* in ThWNT 6:663-72 ("Die Presbyter in den urchristlichen Gemeinden").

37. See Lohfink, *Weibliche Diakone,* 332ff.

38. Campenhausen, *Kirchliches Amt,* 126.

39. Hahn, *Charisma und Amt,* 225.

40. Schlier, *Ekklesiologie,* 198.

41. *Der Luthertext* (1984 revision) translates this: "if someone preaches."

are named. The fact that next to the office of presbyter the charisms are also named shows that the emphasis on the role of office does not exclude the tasks of the other Christians in the community, and vice versa.[42] It is again noteworthy that also in 1 Peter there is no word about the liturgical function of these offices.

The Church is presented as "the holy People," as "God's own people": "You are a chosen race, a royal priesthood" (2:9).[43] It is the task of the holy priesthood to bring forth "spiritual [*pneumatikai*] sacrifices through Jesus Christ that are pleasing to God" (2:5). A similar thought is found in Romans 12:1: "I exhort you to present yourselves as a living and holy offering." Through their baptism the entire community is priestly. One can place the text about the charisms in connection with the text concerning the royal priesthood, since the latter gives the presupposition for that specific gift.[44] The function of presbyter is also a gift; however, we may exclude the possibility that the function of presbyter may be extracted from that specific gift. There is no basis in the text for such a deduction.

c. In the Johannine Sphere

There are sharply divergent opinions among exegetes about life in the Johannine communities and their corresponding Church structures. E. Schillebeeckx puts the problem this way:

> Do the Johannine writings say anything concrete about the structure of offices in the ecclesial community? Exegetes come to different opinions. According to E. Schweizer (Gemeinde, 105–124), there were no structured offices in the Johannine communities, and as little were specific charisms given to a few of the faithful. If we restrict our attention to the Fourth Gospel, we must come to the conclusion that this gospel neither denies nor confirms the existence of offices; we simply have nothing on which to base such a judgment. However, the Johannine letters from the same circles testify throughout to the office of presbyter (2 John 1:1; 3 John 3). Closer study has in the meantime brought to light that the Johannine communities indeed

42. Schlier, *Ekklesiologie,* 198: "Next to these 'bureaucratic' offices there are also others of a purely charismatic nature."

43. Bibliography: L. Cerfaux, "Regale sacerdotium," in *Recueil L. Cerfaux,* vol. 2 (Gembloux, 1954) 283–315; E. Cothenet, "Le sacerdoce des fidèles d'après la 1ª Petrie," *Esprit et vie* 79 (1969) 169–73; this is a review of the book by J. H. Elliot, *The Elect and the Holy* (NT. S 12) (Leiden, 1966) (especially the "Conclusion" 13, p. 225).

44. Hahn (*Charisma und Amt,* 225f.) writes thus: "The demand to serve one another as good managers of 'God's multiform grace' is expressly grounded with reference to that charism in which all have a share which corresponds, in the viewpoint represented in chap. 2, to the priesthood of all believers."

had structures of offices, but without, however, any automatic claim to authority, to such an extent that the Johannine tendency from the start fought against any institutional authority for teaching or comportment, in contrast to other Christian communities.[45]

The First Letter of John tries to lead the community into authentic ecclesial, that is, Johannine traditions: "What you have heard from the beginning" (1 John 2:24). Christians must remain in the truth that they have received. They should not "follow every spirit," but rather "test the spirits to see if they are from God, for many false prophets have gone out into the world" (1 John 4:1). The author confronts the community directly (1 John 1:3), and the goal of the letter is that the community will accept this clarification of the author (1 John 1:3: "so that you also may have communion with us").

In reaction against the false prophets who "are leading you into error," the author puts forward the following principle: "The anointing that you received from him remains in you, and you do not need to be advised by anyone. His anointing has instructed you about all things, and it is the truth and is no lie; and as he instructed you, so you must remain in him" (1 John 2:27). In this way the activity of the Spirit is emphasized. Since the author makes belief dependent upon the acceptance of what they have received (1 John 1:2, 3, 5; 2:7, 24; 3:11), "[it is completely unthinkable] that he intended to assure them that they should not submit to any authority in doctrine."[46] On the other hand, the text says that the anointing of the Spirit is enough for Christians. Evidently the text may be so interpreted; it concerns the Word of God which Christians receive through preaching and which has intensified in the lives of Christians.[47] On the basis of these texts Schillebeeckx presents the following opinion: "[The presbyter] wishes to convince his opponents that they have deviated from what they have received. He can do no more, for he can only persuade, and not speak with authority."[48] Without question the author is trying to impress his point of view through persuasion. There is no other possibility within the Johannine Church. That he distinguishes himself from the community and challenges the community also implies that he speaks with authority: "John appears in the writing of his letter to be carrying out a service function in the authentic sense."[49] The author calls himself

---

45. Schillebeeckx, *Christliche Identität*, 116f. He wrote the same thing in his book, *Das Kirchliche Amt.*

46. R. Schnackenburg, *Die Johannesbriefe* (Freiburg, 1963) 161.

47. Thus I. de la Potterie, "L'onction du chrétien par la foi," in I. de la Potterie and S. Lyonnet, *La vie selon L'Esprit* (Paris, 1965) chap. 7.

48. Schillebeeckx, *Christliche Identität*, 119.

49. X. Léon-Dufour in Delorme, *Ministère*, 252.

a presbyter in 2 John 1 and 3 John 1. Doubtless this is an honorific title,[50] perhaps in the manner "of a prophet or a teacher in the old style."[51] In 3 John the author challenges a certain Diotrephes; the function he exercised can only be indirectly surmised from the reproaches made against him: "he would be first among them" (v. 9); "he himself does not receive the brothers [apparently wandering missionaries] and hinders all that they wish to do, and excludes them from the community" (v. 10). Two points are clear: on the one hand he does not recognize the authority of the presbyter; on the other hand the impression is created that he alone leads the community. Since the presbyter turns not to the council of presbyters, but to Gaius as his beloved disciple, some exegetes have surmised that Diotrephes was a "monarchical" bishop.[52]

4. Conclusions and Remaining Problems

a. Conclusions

The communities were led from the very beginning by the apostles. The leadership role appears most clearly in the Jerusalem community. The author of Acts has a special interest in emphasizing that everything—evangelization, the decision about Gentile baptism, etc.—took place and had to take place in connection and solidarity with the apostles.

Leadership by the apostles does not exclude a certain coresponsibility of the community, but rather includes it. The Jerusalem Council, as well as the way in which Paul relates to his communities (1 Cor 5:1-5) are clear examples of this.

During the lifetime of the apostles there were two basic types of communities. One is typified by the Jerusalem community: the other is represented by the Corinthian community. Compared with the second, the first type may be regarded as an institutionalized model. There the Seven and the Elders were installed as helpers for the apostles through the latter's decision and with the laying on of hands. In the Corinthian community the (spontaneous) charisms were cast into such prominence that the leadership roles which eventually had to be set up could not be regarded as primary or special charisms.

The little data that Luke passes on about the Antioch community indicates that this community had prophets and teachers and was "led" by

50. Schlier, *Ekklesiologie*, 147, is of this opinion.

51. Campenhausen, *Kirchliches Amt*, 132. See also Schnackenburg, *Johannesbriefe*, 305f.

52. Schnackenburg, *Johannesbriefe*, 329, writes: "We find ourselves in a time of transition in which the monarchical episcopacy is becoming solidified, as we recognize from the letters of Ignatius."

these. The existence of prophets and teachers—the prophets by themselves open up the problem of the free gifts of the Spirit—are testified to by various sources, for example by the two Pauline lists of charisms. What they indicate about development within the New Testament may be summarized as follows:

First, the institutionalization within the Church with a growing emphasis on offices, which the pseudo-epigraphic Pastoral Letters show, could only take place through the invocation of the authority of the apostles.

Second, the oldest tradition of the Church is located in Ephesians 2:20, in that there prophets are ranked next to the apostles. Through Paul we know of the existence of various members of the faithful—both men and women—who participated especially in the evangelization efforts of the earliest Church. Their particular *diakonia* is emphasized by the apostle. Not a word is said about how these persons came to have their *diakonia*. The individual initiative of these people, as well as recognition by the apostle or by the community, doubtless played the most important role. If we compare the facts contained in the authentic Pauline letters with the description of the installation of the presbyters in their communities, as the author of the Acts of the Apostles fashions this (Acts 14:22; 20:17, 28), it then becomes clear that Luke is passing on a heavily theologized story.

It is certain that in the Pauline communities, after the death of the apostle, an institutionalization took place that emphasized the role of offices. The development of "Early Catholicism" (*Frühkatholizismus*) cannot be put into doubt.[53] However, we should reject the view which sees this development as a deviation or decline; the New Testament as a whole must be taken seriously. This does not mean that we are not obligated to distinguish between derivative or misleading witnesses in the New Testament, and those on which the later writings depend.[54]

Still this development of the function of office is defended either by invoking the intention of the apostle (the Pastoral Letters) or Paul's deeds (the Acts of the Apostles). The fact that the invented Peter introduces

53. Consult the bibliography given in note 3. There is here a difference not only between Catholic and Lutheran exegetes, but also within Lutheran theology. Schürmann, "Auf der Suche," 71, notes that *frühkatholisch* refers to distinctive features of preaching and teaching that must be held to be distortions: "The postulation of a 'break' or a 'fall,' is from the very beginning a more or less automatic reflex simply from the way the question is posed." It is not surprising that Catholic theologians say that the recognition of *Frühkatholizismus* inside the New Testament is evidence for the correctness of the Catholic position. In this connection Küng's comparison of Schlier and Käsemann in his two works (see note 3) is worth noticing.

54. See Küng, *Frühkatholizismus*, 196f.

himself as a *sympresbyteros* further supports this development. This is an instance of a theological justification for offices. In this context Luke's conception in Acts is noteworthy, since there the theological interpretation is sharpened.[55] The function of office is emphasized in connection with the conservation of the apostolic inheritance and teaching. "Office as service is subordinated to the preservation of the apostolic deposit; precisely to preserve the *continuity* of this tradition, there must be offices within the Church."[56] "Office . . . is the visible testimony of the continuity of the gospel; through its interrelated structure and verifiable continuity, the community is assured of the constancy of what is passed on."[57] To that extent and in a certain way it is a guarantee of the preservation of the apostolic tradition.[58]

The difference between the community in Corinth and the picture of community that comes out of the Pastoral Letters because of the emphasis on the role of office is very clear. It is perhaps a bit surprising that such a development could take place. The pseudo-epigraphic literature shows that there were difficulties in this transition.

This difference corresponds somewhat to that between the Pastoral Letters and 1 Peter. While the former do not speak about the charisms of the members of the community—we should say that the charisms recede into the background—the latter has no hesitation in speaking of charisms, although it places first that of shepherd of the flock. The Johannine Letters with their teaching of the anointing through the Spirit should be mentioned in this context.

Any view of the developing situation which only takes into account the Pastoral Letters would lead to a false conclusion. To complement this one-sided presentation, two points must be held in view: the role of office in the preservation of the apostolic deposit, and the *diakonia* of all the members of the community (1 Pet 4:10). The fact of having offices does not diminish the service of the community members, but rather increases it.

It is expressly maintained by the Pastoral Letters that office itself must

55. Several authors refer to this fact and on the basis of it discover *frühkatholizismus*. For his part Schlier (*Ekklesiologie,* 134) writes: "There is already stirring in the *Ekklesia* that Luke describes the elements of the tradition and succession and of the teaching office and leadership, thus, in short, of authority." A. George is of a similar opinion in "Les douze aux apôtres et à leurs successeurs," in *Le ministère Sacerdotal,* ed. R. Didier (Lyons, 1970) 21.

56. Schillebeeckx, *Amt,* 29.

57. Roloff, *Amt,* 527.

58. Against this, Roloff writes (ibid.): "Authority has no power over the gospel; it neither produces it nor guarantees it (against this, Schlier, *Zeit der Kirche,* 144; Kertelge, *Gemeinde,* 144), but rather it is its more visible expression."

be regarded as one of the charisms. For that reason we must distinguish between office-as-charism and those charisms that do not involve any office. The laying on of hands is specified for the installation in office, a fact that must be appreciated in the context of the laying on of hands by the apostles on the Seven (Acts 6:6), as well as the laying on of hands given to Paul and Barnabas.

It is nowhere expressly stated in the various New Testament writings that only the person who occupies an office should be the presider at the Eucharistic celebration. Following Jewish categories we must conclude that the apostles occupied this role. The fact that the celebration of the Lord's Supper took place in house churches, as well as the existence of charisms, makes it appear probable that this central celebration was not always led by ordained officeholders.

b. Remaining Problems

We must attend to the problems that remain concerning the apostolic succession. That the bishops are the successors of the apostles—as the central thesis of the Catholic position maintains—in the sense that they were installed by the apostles, as the latter were by Christ (and so the linear succession runs: Christ → apostles → bishops), does not allow of historical proof. It is the answer of the Church in its polemic against Gnosticism since the second half of the second century (see the Excursus). Clement of Rome gives essentially the same answer (around A.D. 90) in his letter to the Corinthian community, when he speaks of the installation of the bishops or presbyters directly through the apostles or of the installation of their successors through the bishops or presbyters.[59] Clement makes explicit what appears only implicit in the contemporary New Testament sources such as the Pastoral Letters and the Acts of the Apostles. It cannot be proved historically that an assertion of linear succession is valid for all the communities. On the basis of the pseudo-epigraphic literature we may say that this development and reflection could only be

---

59. "Also our apostles learned through our Lord Jesus Christ that there would be disputes about the office of bishop. For this reason, since they had been forewarned, they now set the above named persons in place and let it be known that, when they died, other seasoned persons should take over this ministry. Thus these, and later other respected individuals, with the consensus of the community, were set in office . . ." (44.1-3; translation by J. Fischer, *Die apostolischen Väter* [München, 1981] 81). See J. Martin, *Die Genese des Amtspriestertums in frühen Kirche (Der Priesterliche Dienst 3, QD 48)* (Freiburg, 1972) 67ff.; A. M Javierre, *El tema literario de la sucesión. Prolegómenos para el estudio de la sucesión apostolica* (Zürich, 1963); Javierre, "Das Thema von der Nachfolge der Apostel in der christlichen Literatur der Urkirche," in Y. M. Congar, ed., *Das Bishofsamt und die Weltkirche* (Stuttgart, 1964) 185–239.

carried through with difficulty. For that reason we may say that "within the context of its essential apostolicity the Church has given itself (or received) the offices that it needed."[60]

On the other hand the distinction between *episkopos* and *presbyteros* is the result of a development that comes to an end only in the post-New Testament period. With Clement of Rome and surprisingly with Polycarp the two terms are still interchangeable. The difference is clear in Ignatius of Antioch (d. around 110). This is unmistakably a post-New Testament development.

The entire problem of the "apostolic succession" is a complex and, from the point of view of method, important problem. Catholic authors like Congar point out that here one may not simply apply the principle of *sola scriptura*.[61]

It is worth noticing how several contemporary Catholic exegetes approach this problem. Schnackenburg is one example we may cite:

> Is this ordination through the laying on of hands [about which the Pastoral Letters speak], through which a charism, a grace of office is bestowed, the essence of apostolic succession? Is apostolic succession even presented as the most important element if the "apostolicity" of the Church is to be preserved? The New Testament does not offer a firm answer to this question. The Pastoral Letters were written for a specific situation and concern, and show only what was being carried out in a few communities. By themselves they do not suffice to demonstrate this to be *the* principle of apostolicity, nor to show the relationship of apostolic succession to this principle.[62]

Another problem is the significance of the Corinthian community for the later Church. This problem has been discussed by H. Küng and E. Schillebeeckx. The latter writes: "Because she included the Pauline writings in the canon, the Church has also recognized the possibility, for its contemporary life, of a charismatic basis for Church offices."[63] It is his

60. Y. M. Congar, *Ministères et communion ecclésiale* (Paris, 1971) 49; a revised presentation of an article from *La Maison Dieu* 102 (1970) 20.

61. Y. M. Congar, "Die Wesenseigenschaften der Kirche," in MySal 4/1, 550: "A rigid application of the principle *sola scriptura* would here lead necessarily to disappointing results, from the very nature of the things which are being questioned."

62. Schnackenburg, *Apostolizität*, 65. See also Vögtle, *Exegetische Reflexionen, seine Zusammenfassung*, 577ff. (excellent work). Of a similar opinion are P. Dornier in Delorme, *Ministère*, 98; B. SesboÜé, idem., 409; A. Sand, in Hainz, *Kirche*, 235f.

63. Thus E. Schillebeeckx, *La mission de L'Église* (Brüssel, 1969) 363; see also 354 = *TTh* 8 (1968) 420 = *TS* 30 (1969) 575f.; see Küng, *Die Kirche*, 475ff., 357; Schillebeeckx, *Amt*, 31: the concretization of authority "is thus evidently a *pastoral* question that the Church must ever regard anew." In this direction see also L. Boff, *Kirche:*

opinion that, dogmatically speaking, the episcopal and presbyteral leadership structure of the Church is not unchangeable. The only thing that is necessary is a collegial unity among the leaders of the Church. Clearly such a theory would offer an important solution to the ecumenical problem. On the other side, the Lima document on Church office emphasizes that "the New Testament does not present a unified pattern of offices which could serve as a model or enduring norm for all future offices in the Church."[64]

In my opinion the Catholic side may respond by asking whether in this situation the principle *sola scriptura* suffices. On the other hand one can wonder whether a post-New Testament development like the monarchical model of the bishop's office belongs to the essential structure of the Church.

BIBLIOGRAPHY

Campenhausen, H. von. *Kirchliches Amt und geistliche Vollmacht in den ersten drei Jahrhunderten.* Tübingen, 1953 (chs. 3-5).

Cerfaux, L. *La theologie de l'église suivant S. Paul.* Paris, 1965, 351-400.

Cothenet, E. "Le Prophètisme dans le Nouveau Testament." In DBS 7 (1971) 1222-337.

Delorme, J., ed. *Le ministère et les ministères selon le Nouveau Testament.* Paris, 1974.

Hahn, F. "Charisma und Amt. Die Diskussion über das kirchliche Amt im Lichte der neutestamentlichen Charismenlehre." *ZThK* 76 (1979) 419-49—*Exegetische Beitrage zum okumenischen Gesprach.* Göttingen, 1986.

Hainz, J. *Ekklesia. Strukturen paulinischer Gemeinde—Theologie und Gemeinde im Neuen Testament.* München, 1972.

_____, ed. *Kirche im Werden. Studien zum Thema Amt und Gemeinde im Neuen Testament.* München, 1976.

Käsemann, E. "Amt und Gemeinde." In *Exegetische Versuche und Besinnungen I,* Göttingen, 1960, 109-34.

Ketelge, K. *Gemeinde und Amt im Neuen Testament.* München, 1972.

_____, ed. *Das Kirchliche Amt im Neuen Testament.* Darmstadt, 1977. (A collection of important contributions from Harnack, Sohm, Lietzmann, etc. which have played an important role in contemporary research.)

Küng, H. *Die Kirche.* Freiburg, 1967. (Esp. C II 3; E II 1.2. For the reaction of Catholic exegetes to this book, cf. note to this chapter 20).

Lemaire, A. *Les ministeres aux origines de l'église.* Paris, 1968.

Roloff, J. "Amt/Ämter/Amtsverständnis IV. NT." In TRE 2:509-33.

Charisma und Macht (Düsseldorf, 1985) 119-22; Boff, *Die Neuentdeckung der Kirche* (Mainz, 1983) 95 and 97.

64. No. 19 in DwÜ 574. See also no. 22, ibid., 575.

_____. "Apostel/Apostolat/Apostolizität I. NT." In TRE 3:430-45.

Schelkle, K. H. "Dienste und Diener in den Kirchen der neutestamentlichen Zeit." *Conc* 5 (1969) 158-64.

Schillebeeckx, E. *Das kirchliche Amt.* Düsseldorf, 1981, 13-67.

_____. *Christliche Identität und kirchliches Amt.* Düsseldorf, 1985, 55-148.

Schlier, H. "Ekklesiologie des Neuen Testaments." In MySal 4/1, 101-221.

Schnackenburg, R. "Apostolizität, Stand der Forschung." In *Katholizität and Apostolizität* (OR. B 2), Göttingen, 1971, 51-73.

_____. "Lukas als Zeuge verschiedener Gemeindestrukturen." *BiLe* 12 (1971) 232-47.

_____. "Die Mitwirkung der Gemeinde durch Konsens und Wahl." *Conc* 8 (1972) 484-91.

_____. "Ursprung und Sinn des kirchlichen Amtes." In *Masstab des Glaubens,* Freiburg, 1978, 119-54.

Schürmann, H. "Die geistlichen Gnadengaben." In *Baraúna* 1:494-519.

Schweizer, E. *Gemeinde und Gemeindeordnung im Neuen Testament.* Zürich, 1959.

Vögtle, A. "Exegetische Reflexionen zur Apostolizität des Amtes und zur Amtssukzession." In *Die Kirche des Anfangs* (FS H. Schürmann), Freiburg, 1978, 529-82.

Excursus: The Apostolic Succession

In this excursus we shall show how the monarchical conception of the bishop's office established itself and how the primitive Church understood apostolic succession. The theme of "apostolic succession and the apostolic tradition" was already the central point in the great struggle between the Church and the Gnostics. This quarrel can even be detected in the later writings of the New Testament.

1. The Transition to the Monarchical Bishop

Ignatius of Antioch (ca. 110) is the first historical witness to the monarchical episcopacy: "Bishops have been installed even to the ends of the earth."[1] The bishop appears as the guarantee of unity, of liturgy, and of doctrine in the Church: "All who are with God and Jesus Christ are with the bishop."[2] "Only those Eucharistic celebrations may be considered valid [bebaia] which take place under the bishop or his appointed delegate. . . . Without the bishop one should neither baptize or celebrate the Love Meal."[3] The offices in a community consist of a bishop, a college of presbyters for counsel, and deacons.[4]

Ignatius views Polycarp as a bishop.[5] Polycarp speaks of himself together with his presbyters ("Polycarp and the presbyters with him").[6] The community of Philippi, to whom Polycarp's letter is addressed, is still led

1. Eph. 3.2. In J. A. Fischer, *Die apostolischen Väter* (München, 1981) 145.
2. *Philad.* 3.2; Fischer, 197.
3. *Smyrn.* 8.1, 2; Fischer, 211.
4. *Magn.* 6.1; Fischer, 165.
5. *Ad Polyc.*, Greeting; Fischer, 217.
6. *2 Phil.*, Greeting; Fischer, 249. Fischer translates: "The presbyters with him (syn autô)."

by a college of presbyters.[7] The First Letter of Clement of Rome to the Corinthians (ca. 90) equally testifies that the two terms *bishop* and *presbyter* are interchangeable. The leaders of the Corinthian community were called *hegoumenoi* or *proegoumenoi* or *presbyteroi*.[8] In the famous text that treats of the apostolic succession in the office and the bishops, these persons are also characterized as presbyters:

"So they preached in the street and in the country and installed their first followers, after a thorough examination in the Spirit, as bishops and deacons for the believers who were coming in."[9]

"Our apostles also knew through our Lord Jesus Christ that there would be arguments about the bishop's office. For this reason they installed those named above, since they had exact information beforehand, and gave instructions that, when these died, other tested individuals should take over their service. . . . For it would be no small sin for us to remove from the bishop's office [*tes episkopes*] blameless and pious men who made the offering. The presbyters who have preceded us have all been holy . . ."[10]

The function of the presbyter is the *episkope*. In Clement there is no foundation for a monarchical bishop's office. The Shepherd of Hermas (written before 150), a Roman document of apocalyptic character, speaks about prominent members of the Church,[11] about presbyters who administer the Church,[12] as well as about *episkopen* and *diakonen*.[13] "All three groups could, as in Clement's letter, represent the same office."[14] With Hermas the terms *episkopoi* and *presbyteroi* have the same meaning.[15] In what concerns the transition to the monarchical office of the bishop, O. Linton has put forward the hypothesis that the monarchical system resulted from the Eucharistic celebration, in view of the fact that the role of presider would normally fall to the most respected participant.[16]

---

7. Ibid., 5.3: "For that reason it is necessary to hold oneself aloof from such people and to follow the presbyters and deacons as God and Christ" (Fischer, 255–57).

8. *1 Clem.; hegouménoi/proegouménoi:* 1.3; 21.6; *presbýteroi:* 21.6; 44.5; 47.6; 54.2; 57.1.

9. 42.4; Fischer, 79.

10. 44.1, 2, 4, 5; Fischer, 81.

11. *Vis.* 2.2.6; 3.9.7.

12. *Vis.* 2.4.3; see 3.1.8.

13. *Vis.* 3.5.1; *Sim.* 9.26.2; 9.27.2.

14. Martin, *Genese*, 78. He adds, without, however, giving any reason: "It cannot be ruled out that the *episkopoi* of Hermas were already monarchical bishops."

15. See Lemaire, 164; G. Bornkamm, *"présbys,"* in ThWNT 6:673f.

16. O. Linton, *Das Problem der Urkirche in der neueren Forschung. Eine kritische Darstellung* (Uppsala, 1932) 200ff. In agreement with him is Colson, *Ministre de Jésus-Christ ou le sacerdoce de L'Évangile* (Paris, 1966) 277f.

The principal conclusion is that the monarchical office of the bishop which Ignatius mentions had not at his time established itself everywhere. Besides, Ignatius does not indicate how we should understand the difference between the bishop and the presbyters.

2. Apostolic Tradition—Apostolic Succession

The terms *apostolic tradition* and *apostolic succession* appear very clearly in the letter from the Gnostic Ptolemy to Flora (ca. 165): "You will receive later a more specific explanation, when you are worthy of the apostolic tradition [*paradosis*], which we also have received through succession [*diadoché*]."[17]

It is disputed whether these concepts first appeared among the Gnostics and were then applied by Church authors, as Campenhausen believes,[18] or the Gnostics picked up terms that were already in use within the Church.[19]

The Church polemic against Gnosticism is all the more important in that for both sides it was a question of a concretization of the apostolic inheritance. The Gnostics invoked the oral transmission of a supposedly secret doctrine: there are certain teachings that Christ either did not share with the apostles, or which the apostles passed on esoterically, that is, not to the entire Church, but only to the pneumatics. Against this position, the authors of the "Great Church" maintained that there was no esoteric apostolic tradition, but rather that the apostles had passed on to the Church and its leaders the entire teaching of Christ. As a consequence, a teaching can only be rendered legitimate in the Church if the Church that stands behind this position can look back over a legitimate and unbroken chain of succession in such a way that the bishop of this Church may trace back his office either to an apostle or to a bishop installed by an apostle.

This style of argument used by Irenaeus in his work *Adversus haereses* (ca. 180–85), by Tertullian in *De Praescriptione Haereticorum* (ca. 200), and by Origen in *De Principiis* (finished between 220 and 230).

Irenaeus holds that the tradition (*paradosis*) originates with the apos-

---

17. 7.9 in Epiphanius of Salamis, *Panarion* 33.7, ed. K. Holl, GCS Epiphan, 1:457.

18. Campenhausen, *Kirchliches Amt,* 174: "It can come as no surprise that the thought of clearly indicated tradition assured by definite, named witnesses did not first arise where a 'catholic' feeling existed, but rather in opposing quarters."

19. Against Campenhausen, L. Cerfaux has emphasized the inconspicuous *kai* ("and") in the relative clause of the quotation from Ptolemaus. In his opinion this word indicates that "a counter-offensive by the Gnostics was only possible through the reference to a hidden succession unknown to the Christians" (*RHE* 50 [1955] 570).

tles (*ab apostolis*)[20] and comes to expression in the Church.[21] With reference to the presbyters who have become heretics, he says that they have separated themselves from the succession.[22] Irenaeus regards the episcopal succession as a sign that what is taught today in the Church stands in continuity with the apostolic instruction. The central point is the identity of this teaching with the tradition coming down from the apostles. The (legitimate) succession of bishops is a sign of this. This argument presumes that the bishops, as teachers of the Church, are a sign of the identity of the Church with the apostolic tradition: "qui cum episcopatus successione charisma veritatis acceperunt."[23]

On the other hand, Irenaeus attributes a special role to the Churches of Rome, Smyrna, and Ephesus, who, because of their apostolic foundation, are the most reliable witnesses of authentic Church doctrine.[24] Tertullian also uses this argument.[25] Not only the presider in a Church, but the Church as such is important here. A split between the presider and the community is for this patristic conception impossible, for any candidate must demonstrate before his consecration that his confession of faith agrees in all aspects with that of the Church.[26] Summing up, one may say

20. "Cum autem ad eam traditionem quae est ab apostolis, quae per successiones presbyterorum in Ecclesia custoditur . . ." (3.22.2, eds. A. Rousseau and L. Doutreleau, *Sources Chrétiennes* 210:26).

21. "Traditionem itaque apostolorum in toto mundo manifestatam in omni Ecclesia adest perspicere omnibus qui vera velint videre, et habemus adnumerare eos qui ab apostolis instituti sunt episcopi et successores eorum usque ad nos, qui nihil tale docuerunt neque cognoverunt quale ab his deliratur" (3.3.1, ibid., 30). See also 3.3.3, ibid., 38.

22. "Quapropter eis qui in Ecclesia sunt presbyteris obaudire oportet, his qui successionem habent ab Apostolis, sicut ostendimus, qui cum episcopatus successione charisma veritatis certum . . . acceperunt; reliquos vero qui absistunt a principali successione et quocumque loco colligunt suspectos habere" (4.26.2, ed. A. Rousseau, *Sources Chrétiennes* 100:718). Similar formulations in 4.26.4, 5, ibid., 722, 728.

23. 4.26.2, ibid., 718.

24. 3.3.2-4: Rome was founded by Peter and Paul; in Smyrna Polycarp was installed as bishop by the apostles; the Church of Ephesus was founded by Paul, and John lived there.

25. Tertullian emphasizes the apostolic origins of Corinth, Philippi, Thessalonica, Ephesus, and Rome: *De praescriptione haereticorum* 36, in PL 2:49.

26. According to the *Traditio Apostolica* of Hippolytus, it was presumed that a bishop was ordained to minister to a Church that stood in the apostolic tradition: "ut ii qui bene docti sunt id quod fuit usque nunc traditum custodientes" (1 prologue, B. Botte, *La tradition apostolique de S. Hippolyte* [Münster, 1963] 2f.). Other later texts: *Const. Apost.* 8.4.2.6; *Cyprian, Epis.* 38.1; *Statuta ecclesiae antiquae,* ed. Ch. Munier (Paris, 1960) 75f. See H. Legrand, "Die Ordinationspraxis der Alten Kirche," in *Gemeinsame Römisch-Katholische/Evangelische Kommission, Einheit vor uns* (Paderborn-Frankfurt, 1985).

that "For Irenaeus the apostolic succession of the episcopacy represents first of all the identity of that Church in time and space with the Church of God . . . and this identity is evidenced through the succession of bishops."[27]

Origen says the same thing: he regards the tradition as apostolic and ecclesial. This teaching of the Church has its source in the principle of succession.[28]

What we find in Irenaeus, Tertullian, and Origen is in its essentials also testified to in the report transmitted by Eusebius about Hegesippus. Under Anicet (ca. 154–66), he passed through Corinth on the way to Rome.

"The Corinthian community remained with the correct doctrine down to its bishop Primus. . . . After my arrival in Rome I made a *Diadoché* to Anicet, whose deacon was Eleutheros. Soter took over from Anicet, and Eleutheros from him. In each succession [*diadoché*] and in each city it was so maintained as the law, the prophets, and the Lord prescribed."[29]

"*Diadoché* . . . here takes on the later common meaning of 'list of bishops.' "[30]

The *Traditio Apostolica* of Hippolytus (ca. 215) reports the first prayer known to us for a bishop's consecration. The congregation asks for an outpouring of the Spirit that Christ gave the apostles on this candidate: "Nunc effunde eam virtutem, quae a te est, principalis spiritus, quem

---

27. A. Schmemann, "La notion der primauté dans l'ecclésiologie orthodoxe," in N. Afanassieff et al., *La primauté de Pierre dans L'Église orthodoxe*, (Neuchâtel, 1960) 134.

28. "Servetur vero ecclesiastica praedicatio per successionis ordinem ab apostolis tradita et usque ad praesens in ecclesia permanens; illa sola credenda est veritas, quae nullo ab ecclesiastica et apostolica traditione discordat" (*De principiis*, Praef. 2, ed. P. Koetschau [GCS Grig. 5] 8). "Accepting the canon of the heavenly Church of Christ according to the succession [*diadoché*] of the apostles" (ibid., 4.2.2 [9] 308). See also *In Math. comm. ser.*, no. 46 in PG 13:1667D. With Clement of Alexandria and Origen we find the traditional terminology: that of a tradition coming down from the apostles; without referring specifically to the *episcopal* succession, they speak only generally of succession. In his homily *In Isaias*, Origen speaks of the successors to the apostles ("eorum successores": *In Is* 7; PG 13:243B), but without saying whom he means. Usually he speaks of doctors in the Church (*Hom. in Jos.* 20.5, ed. A. Jaubert, *Sources Chrétiennes* 71:422; *Hom. in Lev.* 6.6; PG 12:473B), who may not necessarily be set at the same level as bishops. Even as a lay person Origen was very influential in dogmatic questions, as his work "Disputation with Heraclides" shows.

29. In Eusebius, *Church History* 4.22.2-3. Translation from Martin, *Genese*, 96.

30. Campenhausen, *Kirchliches Amt*, 183. Of the same opinion is Martin, *Genese*, 96; E. Molland, "Le développement de l'idée de succession apostolique," *RHPhR* 34 (1954) 1-29 (here 20). Of a different opinion is G. G. Blum, *Tradition und Sukzession* (Berlin-Hamburg, 1963) 87. On the list of bishops, see L. Koep, "Bishofslisten," *RAC* 2:410-15.

dedisti delecto filio tuo Jesu Christo, quod donavit sanctis apostolis, qui constituerunt ecclesiam per singula loca."[31]

Hippolytus concludes his description of the heretics with the following words: "This heretical teaching will be refuted by none other than the Holy Spirit who has been sent into the Church, whom the apostles first received and then led orthodox people to. We are their successors and have a share in the same gift of the high priesthood (*archierateia*) and the teaching; we are numbered among the protectors of the Church. For that reason we cannot close our eyes nor keep silent with regard to the true doctrine."[32] The policy concerning the bishops receives with Hippolytus its fullest expression: the bishops are the successors to the apostles; the Spirit received in the bishop's consecration is compared to the Spirit received by the apostles.

One historical fact must be mentioned in order to clarify the role of the bishops: already by the end of the second century Church problems that concerned different communities were being handled by synods of bishops. The local Churches were represented by their bishops. The bishops as a corporate group made decisions that affected the life of the communities.

3. Conclusion

That the bishops should be seen as successors to the apostles was established as a fundamental theological statement in the polemic against Gnosticism, although the sequence Christ → apostles → bishops appears not to admit of historical demonstration. For many communities the bishop was probably simply the first in the college of presbyters.[33]

In what concerns the office of bishop, we are doubtless dealing with something that developed over time. Should we not put this development into connection with that of the canon, that is, with the self-developing consciousness of the Church with reference to the canon? In that case we may say that the Church, which accepted certain books as its canon, came to the conviction that an office of bishop in the above sense belonged to its structure.

---

31. Botte, 8. The spirit bestowed in the priestly ordination is called the "spiritus gratiae et consilii" (7; Botte, 22). With reference to the ordination of deacons, it states that these do not receive the same spirit as the presbyters: "non accipiens communem presbyterii spiritum" (8; Botte, 24).

32. *Elenchus* 8.18.2, ed. P. Wendland, GCS Hippol. 3:238. Translation by Campenhausen, *Kirchliches Amt,* 192.

33. Thus P. Fransen, "Weihen, Heilige," in HTTL 8:99, with a reference to Alexandria and—with reservation—to Lyons.

BIBLIOGRAPHY

Benoit, A. "L'apostolicité au second siècle." *Verbum Caro* 15 (1961) 173-84.

Blum, G. G. "Apostel/Apostolat/Apostolizität II. Alte Kirche." In TRE 3:445-66.

Campenhausen, H. von. *Kirchliches Amt und geistliche Vollmacht in den ersten drei Jahrhunderten.* Tübingen, 1963, 91ff., 163-94.

Dix, G. "The Ministry in the early Church. A.D. 90-140." In *The Apostolic Ministry,* London: K. E. Kirk, 1946, 183-203.

Garijo-Guembe, M. M. "La 'sucesión apostolica' in los tres primeros signlos de la Iglesia." *Dialogo ecumenico* 2 (1976) 179-231.

Kötting, B. "Zur Frage der 'successio apostolica' in frühkirchlicher Sicht." *Catholica* 27 (1973) 234-47.

Lemaire, A. *Les ministeres aux origines de l'eglise.* Paris, 1971.

Martin, J. "Die Genese des Amtspriestertums in der frühen Kirche." *Der priesterliche Dienst* 3 QD 48, Freiburg, 1972.

Schillebeeckx, E. *Christliche Identität und kirchliches Amt.* Düsseldorf, 1985, 149-68.

VI.
Peter in the New Testament

The Protestant and Catholic authors who collaborated on a book entitled *Peter in the Bible* reached a consensus on the following points: "Whatever one thinks of the justification that the New Testament provides for the establishment of the papacy, in its developed form the papacy cannot be projected back into the New Testament; and it helps neither the defenders nor the opponents of the papacy in their discussions over the role of Peter to have this model of the later papacy cloud their vision."[1]

When one compares the results of Catholic exegetes with those of their Protestant colleagues, it becomes clear that their scholarship shows signs of their confessional identity. Some Catholic exegetes come close to the position of the Protestant exegetes. In this case there is the danger that the Catholic position may appear no longer justified. Without question, method here is of major importance; is it sufficient to proceed in this matter with the principle of *sola scriptura* alone?

1. The Common Tradition Concerning Peter

Statistically speaking, Peter is the apostle most often named in the Gospels: 114 times, while John, who comes in second, is mentioned only 38 times.

In the post-Easter period Simon Peter took on a leadership role in the circle of disciples. This can be discerned from the fact that to him was granted the first appearance of the resurrected Christ (cf. 1 Cor 15:5; Luke 24:34; Mark 16:7, and also John 21:15ff.). On this point there is complete agreement among scholars. The role of Peter after Easter is made clear in the first part of the Acts of the Apostles; there Peter appears al-

1. *Der Petrus der Bible,* 18.

66

ways in first place, and notably at the most important moments in the development of the Church: during the election of Matthias he leads the discussion (1:15f.); at Pentecost he speaks in the name of all the apostles (2:14ff.); he is sent together with John to Samaria after it is reported that, through the preaching of Philip, Samaria has accepted the Word of God (8:14); on the important question of whether Gentiles may be baptized, he plays the decisive role (10:34-48). Acts 12:17 states that Peter went off to another place; after that, there is no more mention of Peter, apart from the Council of Jerusalem (Acts 15:5ff.), during which Peter spoke after James. In my opinion there can be no doubt that, according to Acts, at the Jerusalem Council James, and not Peter, was the most important personality. After Peter leaves Jerusalem, James appears to be the leader of the Jerusalem community. On the other hand, the suggestion of O. Cullmann that during this second period Peter was dependent upon James is not convincing. At least this position has not established itself among researchers.

A second ancient source on the role of Peter in the primitive community is Galatians 1:12-2:14: Paul went up to Jerusalem "to meet Cephas" (1:18). On this occasion Paul also saw James, the brother of the Lord (1:19). Fourteen years later Paul went up again to Jerusalem, as a question had been raised whether he was preaching the correct gospel (2:2). It is noteworthy that this is the same problem that, according to Acts 15:5, was discussed in Paul's presence at the Council of Jerusalem. Paul reports that the gospel he preaches was accepted by the pillars James, Peter, and John—the order is important. Paul's concern is to place himself on the same level as Peter: "The gospel has been entrusted to me to preach to the uncircumcised, while it has been given to Peter to preach to the circumcised" (2:8). Paul's opponents in Galatia are people in contact with James (Gal 2:12). Evidently to quiet his critics, Paul here places James first. However, one may not conclude from this fact that Paul ranks James first, as the entire context makes clear that the comparison of himself with Peter is Paul's main concern.

Peter's preeminence after Easter most probably extends and corresponds to a leadership role he exercised among the Twelve already during the earthly ministry of Jesus. Otherwise we could not explain why, in every description in the Gospels about the establishment of the circle of twelve, Peter always occupies the first place. Just as we can only understand the significance of the circle of twelve after Easter if there was indeed a group before Easter, in the same way the preeminent role of Peter in the group after Easter presupposes that Peter also exercised a leadership role before Easter within the circle as spokesperson for the disciples. The expression "Peter and his companions" (Mark 1:36; Luke 9:32) indicates the important position of Peter among the disciples.

In the catalogue of apostles (Mark 3:16-19; Matt 10:2-4; Luke 6:14-16), he is mentioned as Simon Peter: according to Mark and Luke Jesus gave Simon the name Peter when he founded the circle; Matthew says simply: "in the first place Simon, called Peter" (10:2). According to John 1:42 Simon received the name Peter from Jesus at their first meeting. "You are Simon, son of John; you shall be called Kephas."

After Easter the name "Peter" gradually pushed his original name "Simon" into the background in the early Church. Paul refers to him using the Aramaic form Cephas in 1 Corinthians 15:5 and with the more felicitous form Peter in Galatians 2:7f. He nowhere uses the original name Simon. In Acts only the name Peter is used.

It is very probable, if not absolutely certain, that Simon actually did receive the name Peter from the earthly Jesus.

2. Special Status in the Tradition of Matthew's Gospel (Matt 16:18-20)

It is interesting to compare Matthew 16:18-20 with the parallel passages at Mark 8:27-30 and Luke 9:18-21. All three gospels transmit a question by Jesus together with Peter's answer (Matt 16:13-16; Mark 8:27-29; Luke 9:18-20), but only Matthew's version contains additional words that Jesus says to Peter (vv. 17-19). In all three Synoptics the conclusion of the pericope is again similar (Matt 16:20; Mark 8:30; Luke 9:21).

As a result of this comparison the question arises whether Matthew has added these words to the original story, or whether Mark and Luke have simply left them out. Since we know of no reason why Mark and Luke should have left such verses out, had they been present in their sources, the first hypothesis seems the more probable. In that Matthew has set up the section encompassing chapters 14–18 as a book about the Church, it is easier to understand why he would add such ecclesially relevant words to his account.

The Semitic character of the text is undisputed and comes to the fore in such terms as "Simon Barjona," "flesh and blood," "revealed," "my Father in heaven," "Peter Cephas," "the gates (powers) of the underworld or of Hades," "the key to the kingdom of heaven," and "bind and loose." In its original form this text arose out of an Aramaic-speaking community, for "only there would its wordplay with the 'kepha' used twice have its full effect":[2] "You are the rock, and on this rock I will . . . ."

The text contains a clue that it may be a matter of a post-Easter reflection or at least a post-Easter reformulation. It speaks about "my *ekklesia*," while generally Jesus only referred to the eschatological kingdom

---

2. Hahn, *Verheissung*, 188.

of God. Although the normal term of the (post-Easter) primitive Church is "community of God" (*ekklesia tou theou*) (cf. 1 Cor 1:2; 10:32; 15:9), the expression *ekklesia tou Christou* may also be found in Paul (Rom 16:16). On that basis one can understand the placing of the term "my Church" in Jesus' mouth. "The primitive Church firmly and with unanimous consistency held onto the conviction of an original causality by Jesus in all Church business, especially in everything that had to do with preaching and cult. Thus this is nothing other than the conviction of the enduring presence of Christ, as it also comes to expression in the final chapter of Matthew's Gospel (Matt 28:20). So there is no obstacle, theologically speaking, to seeing this as a post-Easter expression."[3]

a. Peter as the Rock on Which Christ Will Build His Church

In the Old Testament a rock is a place of protection for the persecuted. This theme is present in several psalms (18:3ff.; 31:3ff.; 71:3ff.): God is the rock from whom the persecuted seek protection. The midrash *Yelamdenu* comments about Numbers 23:9: "When God looked upon Abraham, he said: See, I have found a rock upon which I can found and build the world. For that reason he called him Abraham."[4] Abraham and the patriarchs generally constitute the foundation for the construction of the chosen people.[5] The comparison of Matthew 16:18-20 with the images of building a house on rock or on sand (Matt 7:24-27) yields interesting results: "Whoever hears my words and acts upon them is like a clever man who builds his house on rock" (v. 24). On that basis the text of the renaming of Peter may be interpreted in the following way: "Jesus' *ekklesia* is a house that will be built upon rock and that cannot be destroyed; and she is this finally because she is founded on a word and a teaching for which Peter is here presented as the most important witness."[6]

As for what concerns the content of the text, it is worthwhile to compare this with Ephesians 2:20, for there the apostle is described as the foundation of the Church: "You have been built on the foundation [*themelion*] of the apostles and the prophets; the ground stone [*akrogoniaios*] is Jesus Christ himself" (cf. also Rev 21:14, where twelve ground stones, the twelve apostles, are referred to). In 1 Corinthians Christ is described as the foundation (*themelion:* 3:11) and as the rock (*petra:* 10:4).

The Reformers interpreted the word "Rock" as referring not to the person of Peter, but to his faith. Several gospel exegetes have distanced

---

3. Blank, *Petrus,* 82.

4. Strack and Billerbeck, *Kommentar zum Neuen Testament aus Talmud und Midrasch,* 1:733.

5. See Rigaux, *Der Apostel Petrus,* 595, with the reference in note 86.

6. Blank, *Petrus,* 81.

themselves from this interpretation and now accept that it refers indeed to the person of Peter, but only insofar as he confesses Christ. This emphasis can already be found in Origen, and the text was so appreciated by various Eastern bishops at Chalcedon and other ecumenical councils: any person who confesses the orthodox faith may be regarded as Peter.[7]

b. The Construction of the Church and Its Endurance

The statement "the powers of the underworld will not overcome it" (v. 18b) is a negative expression for what Jesus expresses positively by saying that he will build his Church upon the rock that is Peter. The depiction of a conflict between God's enemies and the community of the people of God is a common topos of apocalyptic. With J. Jeremias we may appreciate the gates of Hades as a symbol for the hellish powers, as a symbol for Satan and the evil spirits who set themselves to attack the Church.[8]

This idea can also be found in Luke 22:31f.: Satan seeks to try the disciples; it is Peter's task after his conversion to strengthen his brothers.

c. The Giving of the Keys and the Power to Bind and to Loose

The picture of the keys is employed as the opposite to the gates of Hades; just as Hades is the kingdom of death, so the kingdom of heaven is that of life.

The power of the keys is "a divine authorization to allow mankind to participate in the eschatological kingdom (the kingdom of heaven), that is, to open up access to salvation (the power over the keys that the steward of the house possesses)."[9] The image of keys is used in Revelation 1:18 and 3:7, in dependency upon Isaiah 22:22: Christ possesses the key to the kingdom of heaven. Just as God places the key to David's house on the shoulders of Eliakim, so Christ gives Peter the key to the kingdom of heaven. This implies that Peter is installed as the steward controlling access to the kingdom of heaven.

This role is explained through the images of binding and loosing (about these powers, cf. above IV 2). It is very important to notice that Matthew 16:19 speaks only of Peter, while according to Matthew 18:18 as well as John 21:23 this power was extended to all the apostles.

basis for collegiality

---

7. Origen, *In Mt* 12.10; PG 997: "Every student of Christ is a rock"; 1004: "All who follow after Christ bear the name of rock." For the history of the understanding of this word, see J. Ludwig, *Die Primatworte Mt 16, 18.19 in der altkirchlichen Exegese* (Münster, 1952), as well as Cullmann, *Petrus,* 183ff.

8. J. Jeremias, "Hades," in ThWNT 1:146–50.

9. Schnackenburg, "Die Stellung des Petrus 27," with reference to Jeremias, in ThWNT 3:749–51.

3. Complementary Texts:
Luke 22:31f.; John 21:15-19, and the Petrine Letters

Luke 22:31f. contains the prediction of Peter's denial and reversal. Besides that, the text also clarifies the new name: in verse 31 Jesus speaks of Simon, and in verse 34 of Peter. The injunction to "strengthen your brothers" of verse 32 is said in reference to their faith. This text is concerned with a function that Peter should play in the circle of disciples: as the first witness to the Risen Christ, Peter should play a special role in the conversion of the other apostles to faith in this event.

John 21:15-19, a passage that is contained in the supplementary chapter to the Gospel, is the most important text in the Johannine tradition dealing with Peter. The commission arises during an appearance of the Risen One. To the answer Peter makes three times to Jesus' question (whether Peter loves him) follows immediately three times Jesus' instruction: "Feed my lambs." This expression "feed" or "pasture" is best explained as coming from the Johannine shepherd analogy (John 10:14-16): Jesus Christ is the shepherd of the community, he is the chief shepherd (*archipoimen*), as 1 Peter 5:4 puts it. As 1 Peter 5:1-4 shows, the understanding of office as that of a shepherd was already widespread in the early Church.

This Johannine text may be put into a fruitful comparison with Matthew 16:17-19: for in Matthew the horizon of the text is that of the universal Church.

Some Catholic exegetes, such as R. Schnackenburg or R. E. Brown, dispute whether this Johannine text provides any basis for the interpretation that Peter has authority over the other apostles, an interpretation that has at least been commonly made in Catholic systematic theology.[10]

The two pseudo-epigraphical Petrine Letters allow us to recognize the significance of Peter, that is, his authority for the Church. Otherwise such pseudo-epigraphical letters would never have been written. In 1 Peter, Peter imposes himself with full authority on all the Churches in Asia Minor (1:1). The letter comes from "Babylon" (5:13), which means very probably or almost certainly from Rome, where Peter had been martyred. Peter, an apostle of Jesus Christ (1:1) is described as a "co-elder" (*sympresbyteros*). He admonishes the other presbyters. In this way Peter's authority over the authority of the other shepherds who pasture the community is graphically presented. The second Petrine Letter is directed toward Christians

---

10. See R. Schnackenburg, *Das Johannesevangelium*, vol. 3 (Freiburg, 1975) 436; R. Brown, *The Gospel according to John* 13-21 (New York, 1970) 1116. Brown points out that the meaning of the Johannine text was not defined by Vatican I (DS 3053-55). He criticizes U. Betti, *La costituzione dommatica 'Pastor Aeternus' del Concilio Vaticano I* (Rome, 1961) 592.

who know of Paul's Letters (3:15). Perhaps here Peter's authority is invoked against the use which the Gnostics were making of Paul. At the same time Peter's authority does not exclude that of Paul; rather, the letters of both apostles are authoritative statements of doctrine for the post-apostolic generation.

The importance which the two apostles have here in 2 Peter is further reflected in the earliest patristic sources; according to Irenaeus both apostles are the founders of the Roman Church,[11] even though Paul's Letter to the Romans shows that even before his arrival a Christian community already existed in Rome. The same holds true for Peter. Ignatius expresses himself laconically: "I do not command you like Peter and Paul. Those two are apostles; I am one condemned."[12] Respect for the community in the chief city of the Empire is bound up with belief in the presence there of both Peter and Paul.

4. Concluding Reflection

The special significance of Peter in the Church is attested by writings from distinct traditions in the New Testament. It cannot be doubted that Peter had a special authority among the apostles and in the primitive community. Also, long after his death his special role in the Church was the object of theological reflection. Since a change in name in the Bible always occurs in connection with a commission, it is not surprising that the first community pondered over this. To that extent Matthew's and John's post-Easter ruminations may be explained. There we find a theological reflection over what Paul and the Acts of the Apostles present as a historical reality, that is, the leading role which Peter exercised in the earliest community. Matthew and John speak from a universal Church perspective; that is, they have the entire Church before their eyes. For this Church the two of them present Peter's task as intended by Jesus Christ.

It is worth noting that Peter's task is described by images which are also valid for the other shepherds, or that to Peter is ascribed what also corresponds to the other apostles. The comparison between Matthew 16:19 and 18:18 is very important here. Whichever the first, redactionally speaking, may be, in any case "16:19 and 18:18 (for the evangelist) cannot contradict one another."[13]

It would surely run contrary to the spirit of the New Testament to so emphasize this parallel that finally there would be nothing specific left

---

11. *Adv. Haer.* 3.3.2: "a gloriosissimis duobus apostolis Petro et Paulo Romae fundatae et constitutae ecclesiae."

12. Rom. 4.2, in J. A. Fischer, *Die apostolischen Väter* (München, 1981) 187.

13. Schnackenburg, *Stellung des Petrus,* 29.

to Peter's function. However, one should not forget what kind of leadership role results for Peter from the descriptions given by Paul and the Acts of the Apostles (even if Acts gives a "theologized" presentation). On the one hand, the *koinonia* emphasis becomes clear; on the other hand, Paul attempts in some ways to place himself on the same level as Peter ("to me the ministry to the uncircumcised is entrusted, just as to Peter is the ministry to the circumcised": Gal 2:7), although he also concedes that it is essential that his ministry be confirmed by Peter, as one of the pillars (Gal 2:9).

The interest of the New Testament in Peter lies in the fact that he was seen as a witness to the appearances of the Risen Jesus. "This appreciation . . . was early joined to the opinion that Peter was entrused by Jesus with a special leadership role, one invested with his full authority."[14] Perhaps one could also say that "in Peter was seen the special guarantee of the genuine tradition about Jesus, in as much as he had been an authentic eyewitness to the public ministry of Jesus."[15]

That there could be successors to this task of Peter in the history of the Church is denied by Protestant exegetes.[16] Catholic exegetes at first, understandably, strongly supported the notion.[17] Today, however, even Catholic exegetes express themselves more cautiously, when they do not simply deny the proposal.[18]

---

14. F. Mussner, "Petrusgestalt und Petrusdienst in der Sicht der späteren Kirche," in J. Ratzinger, ed., *Dienst an der Einheit* (Düsseldorf, 1978) 27–45 (here 42).

15. Ibid., 43; Blank, *Petrus,* 89, writes: "As our interpretation has shown, the promise to Peter in Matt 16:17-19 validates Peter first of all as *a witness to the revelation of Christ and as a guarantor and teacher of the authentic tradition concerning Jesus.*"

16. See Cullmann, *Petrus,* 237ff., 244ff.; Hahn, *Verheissung,* 195f., among others.

17. Vögtle, *Petrus,* 338f., recognizes the difficulty. Nevertheless, he writes: "From a purely exegetical point of view, there thus (in view of the *ekklesia* as a community of mortal individuals) remains the possibility and the necessity of a second and third bearer of Peter's function, as a consequence of the images of a foundation that ensures continuity (in the Old Testament, recognized as the highest office) of the one who holds the keys as well as that of the shepherd for the sheep" (339).

18. For example, O. Kuss ("Jesus und die Kirche" [1955], in Kuss, *Auslegung und Verkündigung* 1 [München, 1963] 25-77) writes: "Doubtless it cannot be denied that in Matt 16:17-19, the reference is only to Peter; there is absolutely no word about any successor, nor an entire line of successors" (43f.). Nevertheless, Kuss maintains that the primacy of Rome is here intended. Rigaux, *Der Apostel Petrus,* 597, ends his article with a quotation from F. Refoulé, with whose position he apparently associates himself: "The gospel texts neither expressly mention the possibility of such an extension, nor do they expressly exclude it" (F. Refoulé, "Primauté de Pierre dans les Évangiles," *RSR* 38 [1964] 39). Blank, *Petrus,* 89: "Matthew's understanding of the role as foundation is hardly transferable; this evangelist would not understand the notion of a 'successor to Peter.' " G. Schneider (" 'Strengthen your Brother!' [Luke

Exegesis on this point should not leave out of consideration the consciousness of the Church in the second and third centuries (cf. below chap. 13, section 3).

BIBLIOGRAPHY

Blank, J. "Petrus und Petrus-Amt im Neuen Testament." In *Papsttum als ökumenische Frage,* Die Arbeitsgemeinschaft ökumenischer Universitätsinstitute, München and Mainz, 1979, 59–103.

Brown, R. E., K. P. Donfried, and J. Reumann, eds. *Peter in the New Testament. A Collaborative Assessment by Protestant and Roman Catholic Scholars.* Minneapolis and New York, 1973.

Cullmann, O. *Petrus. Jünger-Apostel-Martyr.* Zürich and Stuttgart, 1952, 1960.

_____. "Petrus, Cephas." In ThWNT 6:99–112 (Cullmann's book and article have played an important role in research).

Grässer, E. "Neutestamentliche Grundlagen des Papsttums." Ibid., 33–58.

Hahn, F. "Die Petrusverheissung Mt 16, 18f." In *Exegetische Beitrage zum ökumenischen Gesprach,* Göttingen, 1986, 185–200.

Hoffmann, P. "Die Bedeutung des Petrus für die Kirche des Matthäus." In J. Ratzinger, ed., *Dienst an der Einheit,* Düsseldorf, 1978, 9–26.

Mussner, F. *Petrus und Paulus—Pole der Einheit.* Freiburg, 1976.

Pesch, R. "Die Stellung und Bedeutung Petri in der Urkirche des Neuen Testamentes. Zur Situation der Forschung." *Conc* 7 (1971) 240–45.

Rigaux, B. "Der Apostel Petrus in der heutigen Exegese. Ein Forschungsbericht." *Conc* 3 (1967) 585–600 (excellent presentation with a thorough bibliography).

Schelkle, K. H. *Theologie des Neuen Testaments* 4/2. Düsseldorf, 1976, 90–103.

Schnackenburg, R. "Die Stellung des Petrus zu den anderen Aposteln." In A. Brandenburg and J. J. Urban, eds., *Petrus und Papst,* Vol. 1, Münster, 1977, 20–35.

Thiede, C. P., ed. *Das Petrusbild in der neueren Forschung.* Wuppertal, 1987.

Vögtle, A. "Petrus, Apostel." In LThK 8:334–40.

22, 32]. Die Aufgabe des Petrus nach Lukas," in *Petrus und Papst,* eds. A. Brandenburg und H. J. Urban [Münster, 1977] 36–42) writes: "The author of Matthew's gospel (imagines) the continuation of Peter's task in the Church in a similar way, if more strongly concentrated in the power to bind and to loose. Peter is conceived as the one and only 'foundation' of the Church (Matt 16:18). His power to bind and to loose lives on as such in the community (16:19; 18:18)" (42).

Second Part:
The Nature of the Church and Its Essential Characteristics

The nature of the Church—the title of the first chapter of the constitution *Lumen gentium* is "The Mystery of the Church"—must always be described from the perspective of its being *in Christ:* "The Church is indeed *in Christ* like a sacrament" (*LG* 1).

The Church must be understood in the light of the Trinitarian history of salvation (nos. 2-4). "The entire Church appears as 'the people (*plebs*) come together through the unity of the Father and of the Son and of the Holy Spirit,'" says the constitution (no. 4, 2), making use of a formula going back to the Church Fathers Cyprian, Augustine, and John Damascene.

The Church comes out of God's *convocatio*. This means that the Church is to be understood as the assembly of those who have accepted the message of Jesus Christ in faith, that is, as a *congregatio fidelium*. Word and sacrament are the two elements through which the community of believers comes to be and lives.

VII.
Essential Elements in a Theological Description of the Church

[handwritten: 2 DIFFERENT DIMENSIONS]

[handwritten: TOO MUCH CHRISTOLOGICAL]

The history of ecclesiology shows that in different epochs certain aspects were so emphasized that others were neglected or almost lost. An example of this is the First Vatican Council. *[handwritten: → christological pneomatological]*

> As the bishops assembled together in council heard the definition of the Church as the Mystical Body of Christ, a substantial part of them—and not the worst—reacted negatively and critically to what they heard. Some found this notion obscure or too abstract, or metaphorical. Many feared that it would prompt an understanding of the Church as an invisible affair made up only of the righteous. Some recalled that the Jansenists had used this very expression, and saw in this one fact a sufficient ground for rejecting the formula. The entire assembly asked for a definition with a more "Bellarminish" stamp, "from the outside" (Mgr. Dupanloup), that would express the visible features of the Church. They wanted the Church to be defined as a *society,* and not merely as a *Communio,* or a *Collegium,* or as a *Coetus . . .*[1]

[handwritten: VATICAN I]

These words from Y. M. Congar, one of the most insightful commentators on ecclesiological history, show how terms must be appreciated contextually; this is the only way we can grasp how such a biblical term as the "mystical body of Christ," which had become widespread in the tradition, could be held suspect by some.

[handwritten: THEOLOGY OF ROBERT B. EXTERNAL DEALING WITH THE PYRAMID]

1. Congar, *Heilige Kirche,* 36f.

77

No

cannot prove God exists → mystery)

Is there an essential definition of the Church? Various theologians before the Second Vatican Council had answered this question by saying that "the Church can only be *defined* in a descriptive way."[2] The facts are that, in the New Testament and in the tradition of the Church, there are various notions, and more importantly *images,* that complement one another. This is also the path which the constitution *Lumen gentium* took: "The Council describes the Church in various ways as the people of God, the body of Christ, the bride of Christ, the temple of the Holy Spirit, and the family of God. These various descriptions of the Church complement one another and must be appreciated in light of the mystery of Christ or of the Church in Christ."[3]

Here we must illustrate the notions of "people of God," "body of Christ," "community" (*koinonia*), "society" (*societas*), and "sacrament" in their historical significance as well as in their utilization in *Lumen gentium.*

1. The Church as the Fruit of Salvation and the Means to Salvation

The ecumenical task force of Protestant and Catholic theologians founded by Archbishop L. Jaeger and Bishop W. Stählin views the Church as "both the means to salvation (institution) and the fruit of salvation (the community in the Holy Spirit)."[4] Congar writes: "As the actualization of salvation (community of those being saved), the Church is the community of believers. At the same time she is the totality of the means of calling people to salvation. One could say that she is, if we understand the word in the widest sense, the sacrament of this actualization (the institution of salvation)."[5]

2. Ibid., 16; evidence for this in note 1. There is a presentation of the positions of various Catholic theologians in U. Valeske, *Votum Ecclesiae* (München, 1962) 26ff. For Orthodox theology, see P. Trembelas, *Dogmatique de L'Église orthodoxe catholique* (Chevetogne, 1967; Greek original, 1959) vol. 2, 366f., with references to Androutsos and K. Mouratidou.

3. Synod of Bishops 1985, Final Document 2.3, in *Zukunft aus der Kraft des Konzils. Die ausserordentliche Bishofssynode '85. Die Dokumente mit einem Kommentar von W. Kasper* (Freiburg, 1986) 26.

4. *Evangelium-Sakramente-Amt und die Einheit der Kirche. Die ökumenische Tragweite der Confessio Augustana,* eds. K. Lehmann and E. Schlink (Freiburg-Göttingen, 1982) 185 (a general explanation of the signs of unity in the Church following the CA 1.5).

5. Y. M. Congar, *Der Laie* (Stuttgart, 1957; French original, 1953) 58. The expressions *Heilsgemeinschaft* and *Heilsanstalt* are also in the French text left in the original German.

It goes without saying that the Church is the community of believers. The Augsburg Confession calls the Church *congregatio sanctorum* or "assembly of believers."[6] As Melanchthon makes clear in the apology, it is a matter of replacing *communio sanctorum* with *congregatio sanctorum*,[7] which in relation to the Middle Ages should not be viewed as a major or suspicious innovation, in that there we repeatedly find the Church described as the *congregatio fidelium*.[8]

The Augsburg Confession offers a powerful description of the Church: "Est autem ecclesia congregatio sanctorum, in qua evangelium pure docetur et recte administrantur sacramenta."

The Church is "the assembly of all believers, in whose presence the gospel is preached in its authenticity and the holy sacraments are publically administered according to the gospel."[9]

The Church is understood as the community of believers in which the true gospel is preached and the sacraments of this proclamation are appropriately dispensed. This extremely simple formula puts into high profile what makes the Church a Church. The essential elements are word and sacrament. Here there should be no argument between the confessions. The well-known words of Luther in his letter to Ambrosius Catharinus (1521): "Tota vita et substantia Ecclesiae est in verbo dei,"[10] or his description of the Church as "creatura verbi"[11] should not be so understood as to oppose sacrament and Word of God, as appears to be the case when we characterize the Protestant Church as the Church of the Word and the Catholic Church as the Church of the sacrament.[12]

The wording of the Confessio Augustana has a formal Protestant stamp, in that this "clear emphasis on the proclamation of the gospel as

---

6. CA 7, in BSLK 61.

7. *Apologie* 7.4, in BSLK 235.

8. H. Meyer and H. Schütte, "Die Auffassung von Kirche im Augsburgischen Bekenntnis," in *Confessio Augustana. Bekenntnis des einen Glaubens* (Frankfurt-Paderborn, 1980) 169–97 (here 179). See, for example, Thomas Aquinas, *Summa theologiae* 3.8.4. obj. 2 and ad 2; 1.117.2, obj. 1. Further evidence in Congar in MySal 4/1, 375, note 29.

9. CA 7, in BSLK 61.

10. WA 7:721.

11. "Cum ecclesia verbo Dei nascatur, alatur servetur et roboretur" (WA 12:191, 18); "tota vita et substantia Ecclesiae est in verbo Dei" (WA 7:720, 321). See P. Althaus, *Die Theologie M. Luthers* (Gütersloh, 1963) 249f.

12. See E. Kinder, *Der evangelische Glaube und die Kirche* (Berlin, 1960) 85ff.; P. Althaus, *Die Christliche Wahrheit* (Gütersloh, 1966) 536ff. Althaus says that the sacrament "safeguards the 'objectivity' of the Word" (539); W. Pannenberg, "Sakramente und kirchliches Amt," in H. Fries, ed., *Das Ringen um die Einheit der Christen* (Düsseldorf, 1983) 791.

central both in preaching and in the administration of the sacraments was intended to defend *the sovereignty of the gospel over the Church.*[13] The fact that Church offices are not expressly mentioned is not at all accidental, although they are certainly presumed.[14] In contrast, Bellarmine's equally well-known definition of the Church adds to this confession of the true faith and celebration of the same sacraments, the shepherd's function, and especially that of the pope.[15] That is the way the Catholic side formulated the conditions which had to be observed to achieve *koinonia* within the Church and between the various local Churches. It is worthy of note that Melanchthon complains of "a new Roman definition of the Church"[16] "that concentrates primarily on Church office [expressly on the *'monarchia externa'* of the papacy]."[17]

This theme will be thoroughly discussed in connection with the Church as *koinonia* and as *communio sanctorum.*

Besides characterizing it as a community in the Holy Spirit (the fruit of salvation), both Roman Catholic and Orthodox theology speak of the Church as a *sacramental institution.* In the text quoted above, Congar speaks of the Church as a sacrament in the widest sense. For that reason, before we try to apply the notion of *sacrament* to the Church, we should first ask the question whether there may here lie an ecumenical problem.

2. Fundamental Conceptions of the Nature of the Church

The texts of the curial canonists concerning the papal *potestas,* the documents from the fifteenth century concerning the Hussites and conciliarism (especially that of Turrecremata, *Summa de Ecclesia*), and finally and especially the anti-Protestant controversy (Bellarmine, Peter Canisius, etc.) are factors that have left a deep stamp on Roman Catholic ecclesiology. As a consequence of these controversies the role of authority (the teaching office) and especially (when not exclusively) the understanding of the Church as a hierarchy have been so emphasized as the norm of faith that ecclesiology has been reduced to a justification for this hierarchy. "In such an ecclesiology the aspect of community plays, in effect,

13. H. Meyer, "Amt und Ordination," in Fries, ed., *Das Ringen,* 96.

14. CA 5 shows this: "To secure this faith God instituted the office of preaching and bestowed the gospel and the sacraments"; "ut hanc fidem consequamur, institutum est ministerium docendi evangelii et porrigendi sacramenta" (BSLK 58).

15. "(Ecclesiam esse) coetum hominum ejusdem christianae fidei professione colligatum, et eorundem Sacramentorum communione collegatum, sub regimine legitimorum pastorum, ac praecipue unius Christi in terris Vicarii Romani Pontificis" (*Controversiae 4 [De Conciliis],* Book 3, chap. 2: "De Ecclesia").

16. *Apologie* 7.23, in BSLK 239.

17. Meyer, *Amt,* 96. The words in parentheses come from the Apology.

almost no role. It is characterized by institution, impersonality, and the exclusion of all human reality, by the themes of the spiritual combat and the new man, which also characterize the ecclesiology of the Fathers and of the High Middle Ages."[18]

We shall treat these notions in the sequence which corresponds to the role they have played in modern ecclesiology since the Reformation.

a. The Church as a Society (Societas)

The understanding of the Church as a society was emphasized by Bellarmine[19] in order to stress the visibility of the Church against the errors of (1) Wyclif and Hus, (2) the Pelagians, (3) the Novatians, and (4) the teaching of the *Confessio Augustana*. Bellarmine represents the reaction against the one-sided understanding of Augustine through Hus and Wyclif, a reaction that turned against the notion of a completely invisible and spiritual Church.

Bellarmine also makes us aware of the fact that, according to the Reformation, there are indeed two Churches: the true Church is only the assembly of *authentic* believers, and this is only visible to the eyes of faith. The external Church is the assembly of people who meet in the liturgy and for the reception of the sacraments. In the external Church there are both the righteous and sinners. For that reason the external Church is no real Church; she does not deserve the name "Church."

Bellarmine believes that the Church is an assembly of people that is as visible (*visibilis et palpabilis*) as France or the Venetian republic.

This emphasis on visibility does not imply an insensitivity to the "pneumatic" or the "interior" dimension in the Church. Bellarmine's conception of membership in the Church makes this clear. Like Augustine, he distinguishes between the body and the soul of the Church. The "soul" is the gifts of the Holy Spirit, faith, hope, and love (*fides, spes, caritas*). By "body" he intends the external confession of faith and the external participation in the sacraments. From this he divides the members of the Church into three categories: (1) Those who belong both to the body and the soul of the Church. These are complete members of the Church; they belong *perfectissime* to the Church, in that they are its living members. (2) Those who only belong to the body of the Church, fulfill only the minimum that membership in the Church demands. These are sinners. (3) The catechumens and those who have been excommunicated, who still belong to the soul of the Church if they have faith and love.[20]

18. Congar, *Heilige Kirche*, 31.
19. Text in note 15.
20. *Controversiae 4 (De Conciliis)*, Book 3, chap. 2: "De Ecclesia."

Bellarmine's assertion that the perfect members belong to both the body and soul of the Church shows that he recognizes in principle the pneumatic nature of the Church.[21] However, he does not express it clearly enough. The problem consists in the fact that "what is not expressly spelled out easily runs the danger of being thought not to be present."[22] That happened in the explanatory letter: the "connection [of the Church] with the Pneuma . . . its spiritually active nature as 'Unity of the Holy Spirit' and as the 'communion of saints' withdrew into the background. . . . Of Christ's activity on and in the Church there remained nothing but his founding and establishment of a hierarchy. . . . The Church is nothing more than a species of human sociability, that lives and operates according to the same scientific principles of social grouping which hold everywhere."[23]

The term *society* threatened to push discussion about the Church in the direction of an emphasis on authority in the Church. "The study of the Church is thereby reduced to the study of its constitution," often without "making clear the specifically Christian character of this authority" or "the connections between a society and its superior."[24] Society expresses neither directly nor formally what is distinctive to the Church, that Christ through his Spirit is the principle of the Church's life. The notion of a supernatural society serves as a corrective to this. In the Second Vatican Council's constitution *Lumen gentium,* the idea of the Church as a society is not especially emphasized. This does not mean that the positive content of the notion is denied; it is rather integrated within the notion of sacrament, in the sense that the latter unites the visible and *societal* element with the invisible and spiritual (no. 8, 1).

b. The Church as the Body of Christ

This expression which comes from Paul, was often used by the Fathers to describe what is distinctive about the Church. Over the course of history it received various nuances. J. Ratzinger distinguishes "three historical modifications."

> 1. The biblical-patristic notion: Church as the people of God, that comes together in the Eucharist as the body of Christ. One could speak of a *sacramental-ecclesiological understanding* of the Church; a valid comparison would be: *ecclesia = communio = corpus Christi.*

21. Thus Mühlen, *Una mystica persona,* 1.09, against F. X. Arnold, *Grundsätzliches und geschichtliches zur Theologie der Seelsorge, das Prinzip des Gottmenschlichen* (Freiburg, 1949) 80.

22. Fries, *Wandel,* 259.

23. Arnold, *Grundsätzliches,* 83.

24. Congar, Heilige Kirche, 31, 33.

2. Next to that stands the understanding of the Middle Ages: the talk turns to the "mystical body of the Church"; the Church appears as the corporation of those in Christ. One could speak here of a *juridical-corporate* conception of the "body of Christ."

3. The modern period introduces a romantic notion: *corpus Christi mysticum*—the obscure, mysterious, living body of Christ; the word "mystical" derives from "mystic." We have here an understanding of the Church as a mystical organism.[25]

The Church Fathers emphasized that the incarnation touched the humanity of *all* human beings.[26] Through it the objective inclusion of all human beings into Christ has occurred. This takes place through baptism or more concretely on the basis of the new status of being a child of God received through baptism. The binding of each individual with Christ leads to the unity of all believers with one another. On the basis of their life in Christ, all Christians constitute one body, and the Church is described as the body of Christ. Participation in the Eucharist, or Holy Communion, should be placed in this context: the celebration of the Eucharist is the founding moment of the Church as the body of Christ. Theodore of Mopsuestia (here typical of many) writes: "Through the new birth and through the Holy Spirit we have become the one body of Christ. Through the food of the holy mysteries . . . we attain communion with Christ our Lord. . . . As we all partake of the body of our Lord . . . we all become the one body of Christ. So, through this means we are all in connection and communion with our head."[27]

Augustine coined the formula "totus Christus, caput et corpus." The sentence "Verbum caro factum est" is explicated by him as follows: "The Church is attached to or fused with this [incarnated] flesh, and so the entire Christ arises, head and body."[28] The formula "Christ is the head of the Church" is so clear and basic that the Byzantine bishops and patriarchs rejected the claim of the bishop of Rome to be the head of the Church.[29]

During the Western Middle Ages there was a shift in terminology. Following the patristic tradition the Church was described as the true body

25. J. Ratzinger, *Das neue Volk Gottes* (Düsseldorf, 1969) 99.

26. Here the works of E. Mersch, L. Bouyer, S. Tromp, and others are important. An overview can be found in J. N. D. Kelly, *Early Christian Doctrines* (London, 1960) 401–21.

27. Homily 16.24, in R. Tonneau and R. Devresse, *Les homélies catéchétiques de Théodore de Mopsueste,* Studi e Testi 145 (Rome, 1949) 571. In Cyril of Alexandria we find the following text: "The Church is named the Body of Christ and we are members . . . because we are all united in Christ through his holy body" (*In Joh.* 11.11; PG 74:560).

28. *Tract. in ep. Io.* 1.2e: PL 35:1779.

(*corpus verum*), while the Eucharist received the title *corpus mysticum,* that is, "sacramental body." In the thirteenth century the Church itself, and no longer the Eucharist, was described as the mystical body of Christ.[30] This change in terminology did not, however, indicate a change in the fundamental axiom that Eucharist and Church must be seen together, since the Church realizes itself fully when it comes together to celebrate the Eucharist. The Eucharist is described as the sacrament of the unity of the Church (see below, chap. 8). It is interesting and noteworthy that Thomas Aquinas treats the theme "the Church as the body of Christ" in a section concerning the grace of the headship of Christ.[31] The Church may thus be characterized as the body of Christ only in the sense that it depends upon Christ.

"*Corpus Christi mysticum* was soon perceived as a loaded Protestant term."[32] Luther had compared the mystical body with the soul, or with an invisible society.[33] It is supposedly the achievement of the so-called Roman School (Perrone, Passaglia, Schrader, Franzelin) to have emphasized the meaning of the term "body of Christ." The schema of Vatican Council I begins with the question on the nature of the Church and describes the Church as the mystical body of Christ. Only in a second moment is the Church described as a visible society. This decision was taken on the following grounds: the body of Christ is the most common image for the Church in the New Testament; only through this image may the nature of the Church be adequately described. Besides that, due attention to the Church's external side (as a society) requires attention also to its internal dimension.[34] In the discussion, however, this schema provoked such a negative reaction that a new schema was prepared in which the term "society" was moved to first place.

In the encyclical *Satis cognitum* (29 June 1896), Pope Leo XIII used the term "Corpus Christi" to refute the erroneous assertion that the Church is a merely human institution: "The Church is . . . the body of Christ endowed with a supernatural life." It is also noteworthy that the

29. This is what Patriarch Ignatius said in his letter to the pope about Christ being the head of the Church, when the pope said that Rome was the head of the Church. See D. Stiernon, *Konstantinopel 4* (Mainz, 1975) Mansi 16:47D.

30. See de Lubac, *Corpus mysticum,* 89–135.

31. *Summa theologiae* 3.8: "De gratia Christi secundum quod est caput Ecclesiae."

32. Ratzinger, *Leib Christi,* 911. Nevertheless the term was also used in Catholic theology. See Jáki, "Tendances," with reference to J. Willen, in *Catholica* 4 (1935) 75–86.

33. See W. Wagner, "Die Kirche als Corpus Christi Mysticum beim jungen Luther," in *ZKTh* 61 (1937) 29–98.

34. F. van der Horst, *Das Schema über die Kirche auf dem Ersten Vatikanischen Konzil* (Paderborn, 1964).

Church is compared with the mystery of the incarnation.[35] Between the two world wars this term was the subject of more intensive study. The encyclical *Mystici corporis* (29 June 1943)[36] by Pope Pius XII sought to make more precise the doctrine of the Church as the mystical body of Christ. It responded to two opposed points of view: against naturalism, which saw the Church as a purely human organization, excluding the transmission of supernatural life through the visible Church (62), the encyclical stresses the significance of the external and visible dimension of the Church as a means of grace. The encyclical also rejects the opposed error which would so emphasize the interior dimension of the Church (its connection with Christ, love, or *caritas*) as to make the Church a purely spiritual entity (14), and which suggests that there is a contradiction between the juridical Church on the one hand and the Church which subsists in Love (the spiritual Church) on the other (63). This position is called ecclesiological mysticism (79, 85).

The central purpose of the encyclical is to emphasize that the structure of the Church is both human and divine: the visible dimensions of the Church are appreciated as the instrument for the invisible, that is, for the activity of Christ as head of the Church and for his Spirit as its soul. The Church is expressly characterized as the fullness and completion of the Redeemer ("plenitudo ac complementum redemptoris": 78). (Several of these aspects will later be taken up in *Lumen gentium* under the rubric "Sacrament.") *Mystici corporis* understands the Church as "the mystical body of Christ" in the following sense:

Body designates the social and institutional character of the Church; thereby the external side of the Church and its visible structure is emphasized.

The phrase "of Christ" stresses the absolute dependency of the Church upon Christ. The Church is appreciated as a kind of extension of Jesus Christ's incarnation.

Lumen gentium uses the term "body of Christ" early (no. 3) in a eucharistic context. The Church is expressly treated as the body of Christ in no. 7. Its main assertion runs: "By sharing his Spirit, . . . he [Jesus Christ] virtually transformed his brothers and sisters in a mysterious way into his body." No. 7, 2-3 reflects the way this term is used in 1 Corinthians and Romans, while no. 7, 4-8 reflects the theology of Colossians and Ephesians.[37]

---

35. DS 3301.

36. The numbers correspond to the edition of S. Tromp (Rome, 1958).

37. See L. Cerfaux, "Die Bilder für die Kirche im Neuen Testament," in *Baraúna* 1:220–35 (especially 230ff. and note 11).

c. The Church as Sacrament

Lumen gentium begins its description of the Church with the terms *mystery* and *sacrament:* "The Church is truly in Christ as a sacrament, that is, as a sign and instrument for achieving the most intimate union with God and also towards the union of all humanity" (no. 1). Other passages in the same constitution employ the term *sacrament* to refer to the Church.

God has "called together and established his Church so that she might be for one and all the visible sacrament of this saving unity" (no. 9, 3). In no. 9, 2 the Church is characterized as the tool (*instrumentum*) of salvation.

"Risen from the dead, he shared his life-giving Spirit with his disciples and through them he made his body, the Church, into an all-embracing sacrament of salvation" (no. 48, 2; cf. also no. 59).

The term *sacrament* also appears in the constitution on the divine liturgy, *Sacrosanctum Concilium,* which was issued as the first document of the council: "Out of the side of Christ dying on the Cross the wonderful mystery of the entire Church came forth" (no. 5, 2); "The liturgical exercises are not of their nature private, but rather public celebrations of and by the Church, which is the 'sacrament of unity'" (no. 26).[38]

For the elucidation of the term *sacrament,* the following is to be found in the documents: "Normally the term 'sacrament' in the wide sense, or 'mystery,' or sign of 'salvation,' is used for Jesus Christ. . . . With the Church Fathers this term often refers to the whole economy of salvation, which includes the various liturgical exercises of the Church. For that reason the same Church is called 'sacrament' or 'mystery.' . . . In the narrow sense the term can only be applied to the seven sacraments which Jesus instituted."[39]

The text makes clear in what sense the Church may be regarded as a sacrament, namely, only as coming from Christ and thus only in dependency upon him. For that reason in no. 1 the term *veluti* (like) is used. The Church does not constitute a sacrament *along side of* the other seven sacraments; rather, it is the fundamental sacramental reality which actualizes its own sacramental nature through the seven specific sacraments.[40]

---

38. Attention should also be paid to no. 6 of the same constitution.

39. *Schema constitutionis dogmaticae de Ecclesia* (Vatican, 1963) Pars 1, p. 15, "5" = *Acta synodalia* 2/1, 233, note 5. According to Congar and Beinert, Thomassin was the first theologian to use the term *sacrament* for the Church, based on the Church Fathers. On Thomassin, see P. Nordhues, "Der Kirchenbegriff des Louis de Thomassin in seinen dogmatischen Zusammenhängen und in seiner lebensmässigen Bedeutung," EThSt 4 (Leibzig, 1958) especially 163–73.

40. This perspective was developed especially by E. Schillebeeckx, *Christus, Sakra-*

K. Rahner has made this especially clear: "Christ is the historical witness to the mercy of God which [with him] has become eschatologically victorious." The Church is only "the continuation, the extension into the present of this eschatological witness to the victorious and final grace-filled will of God in Christ, now established in the world. The Church is the remaining-present of that fundamental sacramental Word of final and definitive Grace, that Christ is in the world. . . . *Already as coming from Christ* has the Church within her a sacramental structure. . . . He never abandons the Church, and can never give her up, if he intends to remain humanly available for eternity. *Seen as coming from Christ,* the Church is the enduring promulgation of his own graced presence in the world; *seen from the seven sacraments,* she is the Ur-sacrament."[41]

According to Rahner the seven concrete sacraments should be seen as the "self-realization" of the Church or as the "stages of highest realization of the essence of the Church."[42] Among them the Eucharist properly occupies a special place;[43] it should be appreciated as the source of the other sacraments, for there the sacrifice that founds the New Covenant becomes *sacramentally* present.[44]

In a second movement, the term *Ur-sacrament* is reserved for Christ himself; both Semmelroth and Rahner refer to the Church rather as the fundamental sacrament.[45] Thereby any "ecclesiological triumphalism" is avoided.

This employment of the term *sacrament* for the Church resembles and calls to mind the analogy between the incarnation and the Church presented in *Lumen gentium:*

> The society fitted out with a hierarchical structure and the mysterious body of Christ, the visible assembly and the spiritual community, the earthly Church and the Church endowed with heavenly gifts, should not be regarded as two different entities, but rather build to-

---

ment der Gottbegegnung (Mainz, 1959; Dutch original 1957); Schillebeeckx, "Sakramente als Organe der Gottbegegnung," in *Fragen der Theologie Heute,* eds. J. Feiner, J. Trütsch, and F. Böckle (Einsiedeln, 1957) 379–401; O. Semmelroth, *Die Kirche als Ursakrament* (Frankfurt, 1953); K. Rahner, *Kirche und Sakramente,* QD 10 (Freiburg, 1960).

41. Rahner, *Kirche,* 13, 17f. My emphasis.

42. Ibid., 68 and 22.

43. Ibid., 73: "These should not simply be arranged all at the same level under the other sacraments."

44. An expression from M. de la Taille, *Mysterium fedei* (Paris, 1931), which Rahner quotes.

45. For Rahner: *Grundkurs des Glaubens* (Freiburg, 1982) 396. One also encounters the expressions "Root sacrament, complete sacrament, sacrament of the salvation of the world." Evidence in Bernards, *Zur Lehre,* 361.

gether a single complex reality, that grows together out of divine and human elements. For that reason she is similar through a significant analogy to the Word-Become-Man. Specifically, just as the assumed human nature serves the divine Word as a living, indissolubly fused tool for salvation, in the same way the societal frame of the Church serves the Spirit of Christ who enlivens it toward the growth of his body (no. 8, 1)."[46]

Again we should pay attention to the term *analogy*. Through it an attempt will be made to nuance the comparison between the Church and the incarnation that J. A. Möhler and the Roman School initiated.[47]

This analogy presumes that the Church should be understood as a sacrament. It is very typical of theologians who operate in the Catholic style to state that the social framework of the Church serves the Holy Spirit. But is that true *only* for theologians who operate in that style?

THE ECUMENICAL PROBLEM

The Sacramental Ecclesiology of the Eastern Church. In the Orthodox world these remarks caused great satisfaction. According to the Rumanian Orthodox theologian A. Scrima, the Church is the place of the *phanie* of God's transcendence. Its nature is "theandric."[48] One finds such statements in Orthodox theologians of all persuasions. P. Evdokimov sees in theandrism what is specific and distinctive of the Church: the Church is "the *theandrical organism, God's life among men*. This directly determines its structure: *a sacramental community*. . . . The sacraments bring forward and disclose the essence of the Church." "The Church has its historical origin in the *acta et passa Christi in carne,* in the Last Supper, and came to reality in the gift of the Holy Spirit at Pentecost." For that reason we must speak of a "Eucharistic ecclesiology." "The Eucharist is the *sacrament of sacraments . . .* and it is simultaneously the presenta-

---

46. There are two footnotes in the text: the first (10) refers to the encyclicals *Mystici corporis* and *Humani generis* of Pius XII, the second (11) to the encyclical *Satis cognitum* of Leo XIII.

47. J. A. Möhler speaks of the Church as the "enduring incarnation": *Symbolik* no. 36, ed. J. A. Geiselmann (Darmstadt, 1958) vol. 1, 389. For an interpretation see W. Kasper, *Die Lehre von der Tradition in der Römischen Schule* (Freiburg, 1962) 103. Evidence concerning the Roman school in Congar, *Die Lehre von der Kirche,* 92ff. This analogy is also discussed by M. Scheeben, *Die Mysterien des Christentums,* no. 81.

48. A. Scrima, "Gedanken eines Orthodoxen zur Konstitution," in Barauna 2:514f. See D. Staniloae, *Theologia dogmatica orthodoxa,* vol. 2 (Bucharest, 1978) 208ff. (on the theandrical structure of the Church).

tion of the Church. The Church is an ongoing Eucharistic *koinonia.*"[49]
Evdokimov borrows his phraseology from S. Boulgakov,[50] G. Florovsky,[51]
N. Afanassieff ("Eucharistic ecclesiology"),[52] and others. For the Greek
Orthodox tradition, one is referred to the following authors: J. N. Karmiris describes the Church as the center of salvation and the instrument
of the Holy Spirit. . . . She is the *worksite* and vessel of healing, the steward and distributor of the justifying and sanctifying grace of God."[53] The
Church has "a theandric nature."[54] P. Trembelas takes it for granted that
the Church is an institution of salvation.[55] Earlier C. Androutsos had bor-
rowed the term from J. A. Möhler.[56]

The Lutheran Position. Möhler's description of the Church as the "on-
going incarnation" was sharply criticized by Lutheran theologians because
such a Church could easily usurp the divine prerogative—infallibility—
for itself. Moreover, the complaint was lodged that this formulation does
not preserve the difference between God and the Church, nor does it reflect the dependence of the Church upon God.[57] This last criticism is often

49. P. Evdokimov, *L'orthodoxie* (Neuchâtel, 1959) 126ff.
50. S. Boulgakov, *L'orthodoxie* (Lausanne, 1980) 125: "The nature of the sacraments (or of the mysteries) is a connection of the visible and the invisible, of an exterior form and an interior content. The essence of the Church is here mirrored again,
in that she presents the invisible in the visible and the visible in the invisible." He
describes the Church as the "Complete Mystery" (presented by R. Hotz, *Sakramente
im Wechselspiel zwischen Ost und West* [Zürich-Köln, 1979] 190.)
51. G. Florovsky, "Le Corps du Christ vivant," in *La sainte Église universelle*
(Neuchâtel-Paris, 1948) 9–57 (29, 36f.). Florovsky sees no problem in the statement
that "the incarnation is extended and completed in the Church" (21). "The sacramental
life of the Church is the extension of Pentecost, or better the life of the Church is
grounded upon two related mysteries: the mystery of the Last Supper and the mystery
of Pentecost" (19).
52. The notion developed by Afanassieff and his students of a "Eucharistic ecclesiology" is discussed in chapter 8.
53. J. N. Karmiris, "Abriss der dogmatischen Lehre der orthodoxen katholischen
Kirche," in P. Bratisiotis, ed., *Die Orthodoxe Kirche in Griechischer Sicht,* 1 Teil (Stuttgart, 1959) 91.
54. J. N. Kasmiris, *Orthodoxos ekklesiologia (Dogmatikes tmema E)* (Athens, 1973)
103 (the title of the second chapter: "He theanthropopiné phúsis tes Ekklesías," 179f.,
with discussion of Florovsky).
55. Trembelas, *Dogmatique,* 366ff.
56. Chr. Androutsos, *Symboliké* (Athens, 1930) 70.
57. H. Küng has especially occupied himself with this problem: *Strukturen der Kirche*
(Freiburg, 1962) 323ff.; *Die Kirche,* 286. With this sentence Möhler wished to make
clear the continued activity of Christ in the sphere of the Church; thus W. Kasper,
Die Lehre von der Tradition in der Römischen Schule (Freiburg, 1962) 103.

raised by some Lutheran theologians against the phrase "Church as sacrament," although other Lutheran theologians have no difficulty with it.[58]

For the next position we have at our disposal the publications of several official commissions. In the *Reformed* (Calvinist) tradition, "many theologians see in the application of the analogy of the incarnation to ecclesiology an under-appreciation of the work of the Spirit and of Christ's lordship over the Church. Others believe that the analogy of the incarnation may be applied to the Church if this occurs in a Trinitarian context, which makes clear and does justice to the dynamic of Christ's activity through the Holy Spirit." Thus reads the document "The Presence of Christ in the Church and in the World."[59] The document "Unity Before Us" puts it this way: "This expression [the Church as sacrament] is viewed skeptically in the Lutheran tradition and is even often criticized. However, its intention should meet with approval from Lutherans: as the body of Christ and the '*koinonia*' of the Holy Spirit, the Church is both the sign and instrument of God's grace."[60] The document "Church Community in Word and Sacrament" maintains that "this expression proves helpful also for understanding Church community as a sacramental community, whether the statements of Vatican II about the Church as a sacrament are accepted or criticized."[61] U. Kühn sums up the negative reaction from the Lutheran side as follows:

> Does not this formulation [the thesis of the sacraments as the self-realization of the Church] destroy the difference between Christ as the redeemer and the Church? Does it not basically maintain that the Church "can develop the sacraments on its own design and principally out of itself, to any number and with any significance," and so

---

58. There is a presentation of the various positions in Beinert, *Die Sakramentalität*, 44–49, and in Döring, *Grundriss*, 160; see also A. Birmelé, "La sacramentalité de l'Église et la tradition luthérienne," *Irenikon* (1986) 482–507. W. Pannenberg has modified his opinion; see *Thesen zur Theologie der Kirche, these* 98 (München, 1970): ". . . nevertheless it is advisable to completely abandon this rich and many-sided term"; in the second edition, 1974: "One could consider . . . abandoning this many-sided term. Then still a renewed term may refer correspondingly to the sacramental dimension present in the transactions of God and in the connection with Christ in the founding depths of the Church, since the Church itself is a sign of the divine will for the salvation of the world." In both editions the Church is described as the "visible sign of divine grace."

59. No. 104, in DwÜ, 513.

60. Gemeinsame römisch-katholische/evangelisch-lutherische Kommission, *Einheit vor uns* (Paderborn-Frankfurt, 1985) no. 85.

61. The document was published by the bilateral committee of the German Bishops' Conference and the Church Leadership of the VELKD (Paderborn-Frankfurt, 1984) no. 43.

"manipulate" them as its own instruments of salvation (Dantine[62])? Does not such an expression disturb the *extra nos* that is an essential element of salvation? Do we not have here before us *in nuce* the same "expanding ecclesiology," (Maron),[63] against which we must protest in the name of justification?[64]

E. Jüngel emphasizes that:

> in the attitude of the listening Church and in the posture of the assembly of the faithful receiving God's grace, there takes place in its most fundamental way the *repraesentatio Christi.* The Church presents Christ in so far as she declines to present herself. . . . In that the Church nourishes itself from Jesus Christ as the one and authentically only sacrament, she celebrates the sacramentality *of his* nature. And only to the extent that she celebrates his sacramentality, together with the story of Jesus Christ showing forth and sharing the gracious presence of God may we call the Church, not directly a *(foundational) sacrament,* but indeed the great *sacramental sign* showing forth Jesus Christ. She is like an *analogatum,* that directs us to Jesus Christ as the *analogans.* As the analogatum she allows us to recognize that it is Jesus Christ who energizes and transforms individuals into an answering Church.[65]

62. W. Dantine, "Kirche und Sakrament," *MdKI* 18 (1967) 44. See also 46f. (note by Kühn).

63. G. Maron, *Kirche und Rechtfertigung* (Göttingen, 1969) 261. See also G. Ebeling, *Wort Gottes und Tradition* (Göttingen, 1964) 197–218 (here 216) (note by Kühn).

64. U. Kühn, *Sakramente* (Gütersloh, 1985) 211.

65. E. Jüngel, "Die Kirche als Sakrament," *ZThK* 80 (1933) 432–57 (here 449f.; see also 436 and 442). See Jüngel, "Das Sakrament - Was ist das?" in E. Jüngel and K. Rahner, *Was ist ein Sakrament?* (Freiburg, 1971). Jüngel refers to the remarks of Luther and Melanchthon. In "De captivitate Babylonica," Luther emphasizes that there is only one sacrament, Christ, and three sacramental transactions: "quamquam si usu scripturae loqui velim, non nisi unum sacramentum habeam, et tria signa sacramentalia" (WA 6:501 = Ausgabe Clemens 1:304). In the "Disputatio de fide infusa et adquisita," theses 17 and 18 maintain "17. Nullum sacramentorum septem in sacris litteris nomine sacramenti censetur. 18. Unum solum habent sacrae litterae sacramentum, quod est ipse Christus" (WA 6:86, 5ff.). Melanchthon says the same: "Quae alii sacramenta, nos signa appellamus aut, si ita libet, signa sacramentalis. Nam sacramentum ipsum Christum Paulus vocat" (Loci Communes . . . 1521, Studienausgabe 2/1, 143, 29f.). It is worthy of note that both Luther and Melanchthon ally themselves with the Augustinian expression "Non est aliud dei mysterium nisi Christus" (*Epistola* 187; CSEL 57:113).

A comparison with Thomas Aquinas is enlightening. In *Contra gentes* 4.41, Thomas characterizes the sacraments as separated instruments (*instrumenta separata*), while the humanity of Jesus Christ is regarded as the tool of God's activity (*instrumentum coniunctum*). In *Summa theologiae* 3.65.1 Thomas discusses the problem that there

Correctly understood, the Catholic formula intends to say no more than what E. Jüngel here maintains. Both sides seek to express that the Church is the visible sign of God's grace.

The danger that the idea of its sacramentality may lead to a certain divinization of the Church must also be recognized by Catholic theology. At the same time other things must here be kept in mind, specifically how the transcendence of God's word is to be understood and lived, and how the function of office should be exercised within the *koinonia* that is the Church.

d. The Church as the Communion of the Faithful

KOINONIA AND THE PEOPLE OF GOD

The Church as Communio. Lumen gentium characterizes the Church as a "community of faith, hope, and love" (no. 8, 1), that is, as a community of persons who live from faith (or from the virtues). Here we have to do primarily with a "communio ecclesiology," in which it is taken for granted that there is "a variety of members and tasks [*officiorum*]" (no. 7, 3). The Decree on the Apostolate of the Laity puts these perspectives together: "There exists in the Church a variety of servants [*ministerii*], but a unity of mission [*missionis*]" (no. 2). The word *ministerium* is here used in a broad sense and means that "the laity also carry out their own share in the mission of the entire people of God" (ibid.).

The term *communio* is set out in a systematic way in no. 4 of the constitution: "[The Spirit] leads the Church into all Truth, unites her in fellowship [*communione*] and mutual service [*ministratione*], prepares and guides her by way of the different hierarchical and charismatic gifts."

We should notice that community is mentioned first, and only then mutual service. The Church is thus first characterized as a community of persons—*congregatio fidelium,* in the terminology of medieval theology—and only then is there mention of service, in that the office or offices are set up to serve the community. As G. Philips says, "it corresponds to the priority of *communio* that the offices were set up for its service."[66] The topic of the charisms, which will be further discussed in no. 12, 2, first appears here in connection with the hierarchical gifts.

---

can only be *one* sacrament, since there is a *single* divine power and only a *single* passion of Christ. Thus, Christ would be the authentic sacrament (obj. 1). Thomas accepts this principle and adds that Christ works in us through various sacraments as through different instruments (ad 1). This means that both Catholic theology and Lutheran theology speak of a single sacrament in Jesus Christ and of three, or seven, sacramental signs.

66. G. Philips, *L'Église et son mystère au IIe Vatican* (Paris, 1967) ad locum.

Some have claimed that in the council documents we can find two ecclesiologies "that are not reconciled with one another."[67] Without denying that in some texts the role of all believers, while in others more the role of the hierarchy, is emphasized, we should recognize that the term *communio* is integrated within a conception of the Church in which the hierarchy has an important role to play.

The Church as the People of God. The concrete significance of *communio* becomes clear if we attend to the content of chapter 2 of the constitution, "The People of God." Placing the chapter on the people of God before the chapter on the hierarchy emphasizes that all believers represent a common reality, before one begins to speak about the different functions in the Church: "By the term 'people of God' is not meant only the faithful, insofar as they are distinguished from the hierarchy, but rather the community of all who belong to the Church—shepherds and faithful."[68]

The thrust of the chapter clearly shows what "people of God" means concretely in the constitution: *first* the Church is spoken of as the new people of God (no. 9). Here the notion of the new covenant and election by God (1 Peter 2:9-10) plays a special role. *Then* the talk turns to the priestly status of the entire people—the universal priesthood of all believers (no. 10)—and of their prophetic function (no. 12)—the sense of the faith of the entire people of God.

Without doubt this notion correctly emphasizes the pilgrim nature of the Church as well as its historical character. *Communio* and "people of God" both correctly emphasize the role of all believers in the Church. Already in 1952 Y. Congar, in my opinion, had properly stated that "the 'classical' theology must be complemented and completed by a theology of fellowship (*communio*). We urgently need to integrate the axioms of our classical 'hierarchology' again within the still more classical '*ecclesiology*' of the tradition of the Fathers and the Middle Ages."[69]

Congar puts forward this statement in his reflection on the ecclesiology of *Sobornost* by A. Chomjakov, which may be described as a synodality of the entire community. Those who exercise the greatest powers

67. Thus H. J. Pottmeyer, "Die zwiespältige Ekklesiologie des Zweiten Vaticanums - Ursache nachkonziliarer Konflikte," *TThZ* 92 (1983) 272-83 (here 276). A. Acerbi is of the same opinion in *Due ecclesiologie. Ecclesiologia giuridica ed ecclesiologia di communione nella Lumen gentium* (Bologna, 1975). See also Acerbi, "Die ekklesiologische Grundlage der nachkonziliaren Institutionen," in *Kirche im Wandel*, eds. G. Alberigo, Y. M. Congar, and H. J. Pottmeyer (Düsseldorf, 1982) 208-40.

68. *Schema constitutionis de Ecclesia* (Vatican, 1964) 56 = Acta Synodalia 3/1, 209.

69. Y. M. Congar, *Der Laie,* 450.

in the hierarchy must never be "isolated from the body of the Church, but always regarded in connection with it."[70]

The two terms raise a variety of significant ecclesiological problems: the Church as the community of believers, the relation between community and office, the entire Church as a *koinonia* of the various local Churches, etc. These problems will be taken up in the third part of this book.

If we compare "people of God" with "body of Christ," can we maintain, as H. Küng does,[71] that the fundamental multilayered structure of the Church must be understood on the basis of the people of God? Without question, "body of Christ" is used in *Mystici corporis* in such a way that the hierarchical appears first, although the charisms of the people of God are also discussed. From this perspective Küng's reaction appears to me understandable. Still we must not forget that Paul tied the charisms together with the expression "body of Christ." On the other hand, and speaking purely exegetically, "people of God" does not play any special role in Paul's writings, in as much as the apostle quickly moves from the people of God to the body of Christ.

BIBLIOGRAPHY

Congar, Y. M. *Heilige Kirche*. Stuttgart, 1966 (orig. French, 1961) (especially: Can the Church be Defined? 16–41; Christological Dogma and Ecclesiology; The Validity and Limits of this Parallel, 65–104).

—————. "Die Lehre von der Kirche. Vom Abendländischen Schisma bis zur Gegenwart." In HDG 3:3d. Freiburg, 1971.

Fries, H. "Wandel des Kirchenbildes und dogmengeschichtliche Entfaltung." In MySal 4:223–85.

Holböck, F. "Das Mysterium der Kirche in dogmatischer Sicht." In F. Holböck and Th. Sartory, eds., *Mysterium Kirche*, Salzburg, 1962, vol. 1, 201–346.

Jáki, St. *Les tendances nouvelles de l'ecclesiologie*. Rome, 1957. (Excellent work. It contains a presentation of the sources of modern ecclesiological orientations: ch. 1; "Non-Catholic Ecclesiologies": ch. 2; "The Return to the

70. Ibid.

71. H. Küng, *Die Kirche*, 145. What the "people of God" means for Küng is clearly shown by his theses: "a) *All* the faithful are the people of God; a clericalization of the Church is thus out of the question. . . . b) All are the people of God *through God's own call;* a *privatization* of the Church is thereby excluded. . . . c) All are God's people through their *personal decision;* thus a *hypostatization of the Church* is impossible. . . . d) The people of God of all believers is an *historical* people: no *idealization* of the Church can thus take place" (151–58).

Sources [Bible, Church Fathers, Scholastic Thinkers]": ch. 3; also a systematic approach: ch. 4.)

Mühlen, H. *Una mystica persona*. München and Paderborn, 1968, nos. 1, 3 (Mystici Corporis), 7 (The Difference and Connection between Incarnation and Church), 10 and 11 (Vatican II).

On The Church as the Body of Christ:

Lubac, H. de. *Corpus mysticum. L'eucharistie et l'église au moyen age*. Paris, 1949.

Ratzinger, J. "Leib Christi, II. Dogmatisch." In LThK 6:910-2 (with a bibliography).

On the Church as a Sacrament:

Alfaro, J. "Cristo sacramento de Dios Padre. La Iglesia sacramento de Cristo glorificado." *Gregorianum* 58 (1967) 5-28.

Beinert, W. *Die Sakramentalitat der Kirche und Sakrament*. Zürich, Einsiedeln, and Köln, 1980, 13-66 (excellent presentation of different positions).

Bernards, M. "Zur Lehre von der Kirche als Sakrament. Betrachtungen aus der Theologie des 19 und 20 Jhs." *MThZ* 20 (1969) 29-54.

Boff, L. *Die Kirche als Sakrament im Horizont der Welterfahrung*. Paderborn, 1972.

Congar, Y. M. *Un peuple Messianique*. Paris, 1975 (first part: "The Church, Sacrament of Salvation").

Döring, H. *Grundriss der Ecclesiologie*. Darmstadt, 1986, 100-67 (the sacramental structure of the Church).

Kasper, W. "Die Kirche als universales Sakrament des Heils." In *Glaube im Prozess,* eds. E. Klinger and K. Wittstadt, Freiburg, 1982, 221-39.

Ratzinger, J. "Kirche als Heilssakrament." In J. Reikerstorfer, ed., *Zeit des Geistes,* Vienna, 1977, 59-70.

Semmelroth, O. "Die Kirche als Ursakrament." In MySal 4/1, 309-56.

Smulders, P. "Die Kirche als Sakrament des Heils." In *Barauna* 1:289-312 (excellent work).

Vorgrimler, H. *Sakramententheologie*. Düsseldorf, 1987, 44-57.

On the Church as Koinonia and the People of God:

Congar, Y. M. "Die Kirche als Volk Gottes." *Conc* 1 (1965) 5-16.

Küng, H. *Die Kirche*. Freiburg, 1968, 131ff.

Schnackenburg, R. and J. Dupont. "Die Kirche als Volk Gottes." *Conc* 1 (1965) 47-51.

VIII.
Church and Eucharist

1. The Church Realizes Itself in the Celebration of the Eucharist

A variety of documents from Vatican II establish the connection between the Eucharist and the Church.

The Constitution on the Sacred Liturgy characterizes the liturgy—the celebration of the Eucharist is preeminently the liturgy—as "the highpoint, towards which all that the Church does is striving." Around that all apostolic labor is oriented (no. 10, 1; cf. also no. 41, 2). Also the Decree on the Priesthood returns to the theme of the Eucharist as the highpoint of apostolic labor (nos. 52, 2 and 6, 5).

Lumen gentium discusses the connection between the Eucharistic celebration and the Church three times. No. 3: "Through the sacrament of the Eucharistic bread the unity of the faithful is made manifest [*repraesentatur*] and realized [*efficitur*]"; no. 11, 1: "Strengthened through the body of Christ in the holy celebration of the Eucharist, they then manifest the unity of the people of God, which through this sublime sacrament is powerfully represented [*significatur*] and wonderfully realized [*efficitur*] in a visible way"; no. 26, 1 takes up the sacerdotal role of the bishop.

In the Decree on Ecumenism (no. 2, 1) this same terminology is once again repeated (through the Eucharist "unitas Ecclesiae et significatur et efficitur").

It is worth noting that the same terminology is employed with regard to the Orthodox Churches, but not, unfortunately, for the Churches of the Reformation: "In the same way the Church of God is built up and grows through the celebration of the Eucharist of the Lord in these separated members" (no. 15, 1).

In the celebration of the Eucharist—through participation (=communion) in the celebration of the Eucharist—the nature of the Church

96

is presented on the symbolic and sacramental plane, so that one could say that the Church realizes or fulfills itself in the celebration of the Eucharist. In this way the deeper implications of using the term *sacrament* for the Church become clear.

Through this formulation the Second Vatican Council assimilates a long-standing principle in the tradition that is also prominent in the consciousness of modern Orthodox, especially Russian, theology.[1] The so-called Eucharistic ecclesiology that has been developed by the Orthodox theologian N. Afanassieff is based on this connection between Eucharist and Church.[2] The connection between Eucharist and Church is treated expressly as a fundamental axiom by the official commission between Orthodox and Catholics,[3] as well as by that between Orthodox and Anglicans.[4]

1. Among many authors we here quote G. Florovsky, "Le Corps du Christ vivant," in *La sainte Église universelle* (Neuchâtel, 1948) 9–57: "One could say that the Church is transcribed through the sacraments. . . . The Church of Christ is not constituted only through the Word of God or through its authentic proclamation. It is rather constituted through the presence of the Lord, a presence which must be characterized as sacramental but true. And his presence in the Eucharistic mysteries especially safeguards the catholic unity or identity of the body. . . . In an exalted sense each and every Eucharistic occasion is a sublime revelation of the entire Christ" (28f.). "The Eucharist is the mystical center and the spiritual source of the Church and of its catholic unity" (36).

2. A bibliography for "Eucharistic ecclesiology": N. Afanassieff, "L'apôtre Pierre et l'Éveque de Rome," *Theol* (A) (1955) 465–75, 620–42; Afanassieff, "La doctrine de la Primauté à la lumière de l'ecclésiologie orthodoxe," *Istina* 4 (1957) 401–20; Afanassieff, "Das Hirtenamt der Kirche: In der Liebe der Gemeinde vorstehen," in *Der Primat des Petrus in der Orthodoxen Kirche* (Zürich, 1961; French original, 1960) 7–65; J. Meyendorff, *Orthodoxie et catholicité* (Paris, 1965) 7–20 ("Sacrements et Hiérarchie dans l'Église); A. Schmemann, "Der Begriff des Primates in der orthodoxen Kirche," in *Der Primat des Petrus,* 119–51. Reactions: (a) from the Orthodox side: P. Trembelas, "Theoriai aparadektoi peri ten Unam Sanctam," *Ekkl* (A) 41 (1964) nos. 7–13; J. D. Zizioulas, *Being as Communion* (New York, 1985) 24f.; Zizioulas, *He henotes tes ekklesias en te theia eucharistía kai to episkópo katá tous treis protous aionas* (Athens, 1965); (b) from the Catholic side: B. Schultze, "Eucharistie und Kirche in der russischen Theologie der Gegenwart," *ZKTh* 77 (1955) 257–300; P. Plank, *Die Eucharistieversammlung als Kirche. Zur Entstehung und Entfaltung der Eucharistischen Ekklesiologie N. Afanas'vs* (Würzburg, 1980). Eucharistic ecclesiology was developed in opposition to the Primacy (universal ecclesiology).

3. The document in *Una sancta* 37 (1982) 334–40.

4. *Anglican-Orthodox Dialogue. The Dublin Agreed Statement 1984* (London, 1985) no. 13 (p. 12f.), with reference to the *Moscow Agreed Statement 6. The Church as the Eucharistic Community,* idem, 55f. (esp. no. 24: "The Eucharist actualizes the Church. The Christian community has a fundamental sacramental character. . . . The Church celebrates the Eucharist as the central act of its existence"). See also the re-

The principle that the Church fulfills or realizes itself in the celebration of the Eucharist is prominent in the writings of both the Eastern and Western Church Fathers; this link is forged as part of the discussion of the Church as the body of Christ.[5] This teaching continues through the entire post-patristic period down to High Scholasticism.[6] Thomas Aquinas (to name one Scholastic figure) describes the Eucharist as the sacrament of Church unity.[7] The Council of Trent for its part puts it this way: "Our Savior left behind in his Church the Eucharist as a sign of its unity and love, in which he wished to be assured that all Christians would be united and bound to one another."[8]

With regard to the New Testament roots of this principle, which has never been contested in the course of the Church's history, we must first attend to the notion of *ekklesia:* in 1 Corinthians 11:18, *ekklesia* refers to the community when it comes together, that is, for the weekly worship service. The context clearly shows that an assembly for the celebration of the Lord's Supper is referred to. Moreover, it must be emphasized that the Lord's Supper was set up as a celebration which those who believed in Jesus were supposed to celebrate regularly ("Do this in memory of me"). The command "do this in memory of me" may at the very least be regarded as a reflection by the post-Easter community. Here lies the foundation for what the tradition of the Church has formulated.

Since "the Church in its deepest nature is the historical remaining-present in the world of the incarnate Word of God, it arises most accessibly and intensively there where the 'new and eternal covenant' which he [Christ] has established takes on its most accessible and actual presence in the holy *anamnesis* of its establishment. The Eucharistic celebration is thus the most intensive rising up of the Church."[9] This reflection by K. Rahner should not be misunderstood. Every word in the Church (proclamation of God's word, the Church's missionary activity) must be

---

marks of K. Ware in *Anglican-Orthodox Dialogue. The Moscow Agreed Statement* (London, 1977) 68ff.

5. See in chapter 7, note 27 the example of Theodore of Mopsuestia and Cyril of Alexandria. In Augustine there is the following text: "If you are the body of Christ and members of Christ, then 'signs' of you (that is, the Eucharistic elements) are placed on the Lord's table, and you receive yourself [*mysterium vestrum in mensa Dominica positum est et mysterium vestrum accipitis*]" (*Homily* 272: PL 38:1246). Leo I writes: "Participation in the Body and Blood of Christ brings it about that we are transformed into that which we receive" (*Homily* 63.7: PL 54:357C).

6. See H. de Lubac, *Corpus Mysticum* (Paris, 1949).

7. *Summa theologiae* 3.82.2 ad 3: "Eucharistia est sacramentum unitatis ecclesiasticae"; 3.73.3: "Res sacramenti est unitas corporis mystici."

8. DS 1635 = NR 567.

9. Rahner, *Episkopat*, 26.

understood in connection with the anamnetic word of the Eucharistic celebration (the Eucharistic celebration *is* proclamation). This is the source for the saying that the celebration of the Lord's Supper as such is a proclamation of the saving Word of the Lord, as Paul says expressly in 1 Corinthians 11:26.

The Lima document on the Eucharist says the following: "The *anamnesis* is the effective proclamation of the Church about what God has promised and done" (no. 7). "In that the '*anamnesis*' of Christ constitutes the central content of both the word that is preached and the Eucharistic meal, the one strengthens the other. It is an essential part of the Eucharistic celebration that it includes a proclamation of the word" (no. 12). "The celebration of the Eucharist in itself is an example of the participation of the Church in God's mission to the world" (no. 25).

When this text's point of view is taken into account, it follows that "its celebration [that of the Eucharist] remains the central act of the Church's worship" (no. 11).[10] This sentence must be understood in light of the connection between word and sacrament (no. 12).

A comparison with the Lutheran tradition is useful here. As an example we may quote P. Althaus, who writes concerning word and sacrament:

> The Word of the gospel calls mankind into the community of Christ. . . . The Word stands in the Church, the Word attaches us to the body of Christ. As Luther acknowledges in the Great Catechism: I am led through the Holy Spirit to the holy community or Christianity through the fact that I have heard the Word of God and continue to hear it. The meaning of the Word becomes explicit in the sacraments and becomes event or happening. . . . In this way the sacraments "build up" (Eph 2:20; 1 Pet 2:5) the Church in the biblical sense of the word and set the borders of the Church against the world. . . . In this sense the sacraments are "powers that construct the Church" (G. Thomasius).[11]

---

10. In DwÜ 559, 560, 564, 558. See also "The Lord's Supper" from the Gemeinsam römisch-katholischen/evangelisch-lutherischen Kommission, no. 17, ibid., 277.

11. P. Althaus, *Die Christliche Wahrheit* (Gütersloh, 1966) 540f. Althaus refers to the strong emphasis of the meaning of the sacraments for the upbuilding of the Church by Melanchthon in his later writings. See also Althaus, *Die Theologie Martin Luthers* (Gütersloh, 1963) 297ff. ("Sacrament and Gospel"); E. Kinder, *Der evangelische Glaube und die Kirche* (Berlin, 1960) 85ff. (" 'Word and Sacrament' as the instruments of the Church"). The United Roman Catholic/Evangelical Lutheran Commission described the Eucharist as the "source and high point of Church life": "The Lord's Supper," no. 26 (see also no. 25), in DwÜ, 279. The Reformed/Roman Catholic Commission called the Church the "Eucharistic community": *Die Gegenwart Christi in Kirche und Welt*, no. 88, in DwÜ, 508.

Word and sacrament together build a unity. One can describe a sacrament, as Augustine does, as a "visibile verbum."[12] This text stands in the foreground of the Reformation's reflection.

The sacraments should be viewed as "Church-building powers" (P. Althaus). Baptism is the entrance into the Church, and eucharist is the source of Church life. There we Christians come into contact with our Christian identity.

Nevertheless, a difference in accent does exist between the Churches formed by the Reformation on the one hand, and Churches of a more "Catholic" style on the other, in that the former emphasize especially the role of the Word. With regard to the Catholic position it is worthy of note that the Constitution on the Liturgy recognizes that "cult (that is, sacrament) and Word are most intimately bound together."[13]

From the fact that the Church realizes itself in the celebration of the eucharist results the following for the understanding of the Church on both the local and universal planes, and for the problem of community through the tools of salvation (a sacramental community).

2. The Universal Church as the *Koinonia* of Local Churches

We must here distinguish two orientations. One can speak of "the Church" in the singular, that is, of the universal Church, in such a way that the local Churches are regarded as only a part of this universal Church. The other alternative would be to speak of "the Churches" in the plural; in this perspective the "universal Church" should only be understood as following from the life of various local Churches in *koinonia*. This latter understanding "arose first in the primitive Church, and has remained the dominant conception in Eastern ecclesiology"; in contrast to that is the other conception, which may be regarded as the conception of a unified organization—"the one that the papacy very early sought after and which Latin Catholic ecclesiology in general has raised to a theory down to the present."[14] As an example, Thomas Aquinas' understanding is "una Ec-

---

12. *Tract. in Io.* 80.3: PL 35:1840.

13. No. 35. In this way Catholic theology confronts the demands of the Reformation. See H. Meyer, "Exkurs: Eucharistie-Wort-Verkündigung," in Gemeinsame römisch-katholischen/evangelisch-lutherischen Kommission, *The Lord's Supper* (Paderborn-Frankfurt, 1978) 90–92. No. 7 discusses the different ways the Lord is present: in the Eucharist, in the sacraments, in his Word, and in the prayer of the Church. If the connection between Word and sacrament is better observed, then one must first speak of the presence of the Lord in his Word, and only then in the sacraments.

14. Congar, *Wesenseigenschaften*, 399.

clesia = unus populus christianus''; the necessary conclusion from such an understanding is a head for the entire Church, the pope.[15]

Historically, *communio* ecclesiology[16] was the first ecclesiology in the Church. *Communio* is the bond of unity between believers, that is, between bishops and the faithful on the one hand, and also between the local Churches who are represented through their bishops. The union is actualized and at the same time rendered manifest through Eucharistic communion. *Whoever sets up a distinct communion, sets up a distinct Church.* Since the Church community comes to expression through the Eucharistic community, when the Churches began to split apart, the fundamental axiom held true that each person belongs where he or she receives communion.

It was common for the Churches to exchange communion letters. This seemed to be the normal way to assure unity. The participants in the synod at which Paul of Samosata was excommunicated in 268 wrote to the bishops of Rome and Alexandria, asking these to write to the new bishop and receive communion letters (*koinonika grammata*) from him.[17] Another example of this early *communio* mentality is presented by the reply of Bishop Firmilian of Caesarea to Pope Stephan (in the middle of the third century): "You have committed a very great sin in separating yourself from so many communities. For you have cut yourself off. Do not deceive yourself: the true schismatic is the one who makes himself disloyal to the *communio* of Church unity."[18]

In this conception any bishop can excommunicate any other. If it comes to appear that the other bishops, that is, the other Churches, do not agree with him, then the excommunication rebounds upon himself: the opposite of remaining "in communion" is ex-communication. The unity of the Church was hidden behind the community of bishops. Questions of doctrine, as well as any important problem that occupied the

15. *Contra gentes* 4.76. Further evidence in Congar, *Wesenseigenschaften,* 399 note 89.

16. Bibliography: L. Hertling, "Communio und Primat," in *Una sancta* 17 (1962) 91–125 (the work first appeared in *Miscellanea historiae pontificiae 7* [Rome, 1943] 1–48; a second, improved version: *Communio. Chiesa et papato nell'antichita Cristiana* [Rome, 1961]; the text in *Una sancta* follows the second edition); W. Elert, *Abendmahl und Kirchengemeinschaft in der Alten Kirche, hauptsächlich des Ostens* (Berlin, 1954); Elert, "Abendmahl und Kirchengemeinschaft in der Alten Kirche," in *Koinonia. Arbeiten des ökumenischen Ausschusses der vereinigten evangelisch-lutherischen Kirche Deutschlands* (Berlin, 1957) 57–78; Y. M. Congar, "Von der Gemeinschaft der Kirchen zur Ekklesiologie der Weltkirche," in Congar, ed., *Das Bischofsamt und die Weltkirche* (Stuttgart, 1964; French original, 1962) 245–82 (here 249ff.).

17. Eusebius, *Church History* 7.30.17.

18. In Cyprian, *Ep.* 75.24.

different local Churches, were resolved through synods in which the bishops from the local Churches took part.

In the ecumenical dialogue the question must be posed to what extent the Roman Catholic conception of primacy, as it was formulated in the second millenium, is compatible with a full-blown or developed ecclesiology of the local Churches, and why Vatican II did not develop any adequate theology of the local Church. These problems will be treated in the third part of this book in connection with the collegiality of bishops and the primacy.

3. The Problem of Communion in the Means of Salvation (*communicatio in sacris*)

In the ecumenical movement the question of intercommunion arises. Two orientations are clear. While some believe that communion at the Lord's table presupposes community among the Churches, so that intercommunion must in principle be rejected, others see intercommunion as a means by which to overcome the split between the Churches.[19] The Decree on Ecumenism rejects this second opinion: "Nevertheless, we may not regard community at the Lord's table [*communicatio in sacris*] without distinction as a valid general means for restoring the lost unity among Christians" (no. 8, 4). According to the same document, on which all later documents of the Catholic Church base themselves, "two principles are here determinative: the generation of unity within the Church, and the participation in the means of grace. The generation of unity forbids in most cases a common worship service, while the concern for grace in many cases recommends it. The way one should act in a particular case should, with a consideration for all the circumstances . . . be decided by the authority of the local bishop"[20] (no. 8, 4).

The first principle corresponds to the statement the council has made several times that the Eucharist makes manifest and actualizes the Church.

19. See, for example, the Report on the Section on Unity, no. 20ff. of World Conference of Churches in New Delhi, 1961, in *New Delhi. Dokumente,* ed. F. Lüpsen (Witten, 1962) 73f.

20. "Spätere Dokumente: Ökumenisches Direktorium," in *AAS* 59 (1967) 574–92 = NED 7 (Latin and German edition Trier, 1967); "Instructio de peculiaribus casibus admittendi alios christianos ad communionem eucharisticam in Ecclesia catholica," in *AAS* 64 (1972) 518–25 (= Instructio) = NKD 41 (Trier, 1975) 18–41; "Communicatio quoad interpretationem Instructionis . . ." in *AAS* (1973) 616–19 = ibid. 50–59. "Una dichiarazione del Secretariato per L'Unione dei cristiani. La posizione della Chiesa catolica in materia di Eucaristia comune tra cristiani di diverse confessioni," in *AAS* 62 (1970) 184–88 = *L'Osservatore Romano,* 12–13 January 1970; can. 844 CIC 1983.

This principle was emphasized by the Old Catholics,[21] and the Orthodox Churches also take it as a fundamental axiom.[22] "Also in the thought of the Reformers, from the outset the correlation remains valid between the community at the Lord's Supper and the community of the Church."[23]

The second principle recognizes exceptions, but always under the assumption that the first principle is being retained. The second principle is fundamentally the expression of the pastoral concern of the Church for the faithful. The Orthodox refer to this principle as the economy. From the Catholic side, Orthodox believers are handled differently than Christians of the Church communities of the Reformation. Here we find again the distinction made in the Decree on Ecumenism between the Orthodox *Churches* and the Reformation Church *communities*. The same distinction holds true for the participation of Catholics at the Eucharist of the Orthodox Churches or of Church communities: "A Catholic should request the sacrament only from a minister who has received a valid priestly consecration."[24]

---

21. See Elert, *Abendmahl* (1954), 143: "The modern theory that a person in a Church of a different creed would be admitted as a guest to communion, or that one could mutually communicate as guests in each other's Churches, if there was not full communion between the Churches, cannot be found in the ancient Churches; indeed, it is unthinkable."

22. Bibliography: R. Erni and D. Papandreou, *Eucharistiegemeinschaft. Der Standpunkt der Orthodoxie* (Freiburg, 1964) (Erni, 31ff., gives complete information on the positions of various Orthodox theologians: J. Meyendorff, B. Bobrinskoy, E. Simonod, E. Timiadis, among others). For that as well: I. Bria, "Intercommunion et unité," *Istina* 14 (1969) 220–37; G. A. Galitis, "Le problème de l'intercommunion sacramentelle avec les non-Orthodoxes d'un point de vue orthodoxe," *Istina* 14 (1969) 197–219; J. Klinger, "Le problème de l'intercommunion: point de vue d'un orthodoxe," in *Vers l'intercommunion, Église en dialogue* 13 (Tours, 1970) 69–118; K. T. Ware, "Intercommunion: the Decisions of Vatican II and the orthodox Standpoint," *Sobornost* 5 (1965–68), 258–72; Chr. Konstantinidis, "Interkommunion aus der Sicht der Orthodoxie," in *Eucharistie—Zeichen der Einheit* (Regensburg, 1970) 86–98.

23. H. Meyer and H. Schütte, "Abendmahl," in *Ökumene Lexikon* (Frankfurt, 1983) 6. See also V. Vajta, *Intercommunion avec Rome?* (Paris, 1970) 35f.

24. *Direktorium*, nos. 55, 79. For a concrete example, see *Direktorium*, nos. 42, 50, 55, 69, 73, 77, 79. For what concerns the concrete application of this model within the Catholic Church, we should consult the decision of the bishop of Strassburg with regard to mixed celebrations, since he raised this particular problem of the Western Church to public attention and made possible a more open approach: "L'Hospitalité eucharistique pour les foyers mixtes. Directives de Mgr. Eichinger aux fidèles du diocèse de Strasbourg," in *La documentation catholique*, no. 1629 (1973) 161–69. See the critical reaction from L. Scheffczyk, "Eucharistische Gastfreundschaft?" *MThZ* 24 (1973) 263–68.

To the decision by the patriarch of Moscow that in certain circumstances Catholics may participate in Eucharistic communion, most Orthodox Churches reacted in a critical fashion.[25] Later the patriarch retracted this permission.

The decision of the Lutheran Churches in West Germany is based on the principle that it is the Lord who invites his faithful. On this basis Christians of other Churches who happen to be present are invited to take part in the Lord's Supper.

BIBLIOGRAPHY

Allmen, J. J. von. "L'Eucharistie, l'Église et le monde." *L'eucharistie* (Églises en dialogue 12). Paris, 1970, 137–83.

Bouyer, L. *Die Kirche Gottes.* Einsiedeln, 1977 (French orig., 1970), vol. 2.

Rahner, K. *Kirche und Sakrament.* Freiburg, 1960, 15–18, 73ff.

_____. "Episkopat und Primat." In K. Rahner and J. Ratzinger, *Episkopat und Primat,* Freiburg, 1961, 21ff.

Tillard, J. M. R. "Eucharistie et Église selon le Vatican II." *Parole et pain* no. 21, 285–309.

_____. "Eucharistie et Église." *L'eucharistie* (Églises en dialogue 12). Paris, 1970, 75–135.

_____. "Les sacrements de l'Église." *Initiation à la pratique de la théologie* 3, (Dogmatique 2). Paris, 1983, 458–63.

Zizioulas, J. "Abendmahlsgemeinschaft und Katholizität in der Kirche." *Katholizität und Apostolizität* (KuD. B 2). Göttingen, 1971, 31–50.

25. There is a presentation in *Proche orient chrétien* 20 (1970) 185–88. The position of the Greek Orthodox Church is especially critical. The decision of the Moscow Patriarch followed the mentioned principle of "Economy"; the opposed principle, on which the other Orthodox Churches based their rejection, is called "Acriby."

IX.
The One Church and the Many Churches

In the Creed the Church is referred to as *one*. As a matter of fact, however, the Churches are divided; that is, they do not live in *koinonia*.

0. Different Models of Unity

The conceptions the various Churches have of unity are different:

The *Roman Catholic* Church emphasizes three elements with regard to the unity of the Church: unity of belief, unity in worship (sacraments), and community in the life of the Church under the leadership of legitimate pastors. These three mutually interrelated aspects, which go back to Bellarmine's famous definition of the Church,[1] also appear in Vatican II's Decree on Ecumenism: Christ "called his community toward unity: in the confession of one faith, in a common celebration of worship, and in the fraternal harmony of God's family" (no. 2, 4) under the leadership of the bishops together with the successor of Peter as head (ibid.).

These same three elements are emphasized by the *Orthodox* Churches. For example, J. N. Karmiris writes: "It [unity] is strengthened through the grace of the Holy Spirit and by the mutual living love of members united and bound together with the one body of Christ, that is of individual Christians. However, this interior unity of the Church comes also to expression exteriorly, namely as a unity in faith, in administration, and in worship."[2] The difference between the two Churches lies in the fact that the Orthodox Churches defend the principle of a *communio* ecclesiology, that is, of a community of Churches and consequently of a collegiality of bishops, while the Catholic Church presents itself, on the basis of

1. See chapter 7, note 15.
2. "Summary of the Dogmatic Teaching of the Orthodox Catholic Church," in P. Bratsiotis, ed., *Die orthodoxe Kirche in griechischer Sicht*, 1. Teil (Stuttgart, 1959) 94.

its claims to the primacy, as "the basis for organizational unity, that is, of a Church that constitutes a single people with even the visible structure as such a single people."

The conceptions of the Anglican communion as well as that of the Old Catholic Church are similar to the Orthodox.

Those Churches which come out of the *Reformation* locate unity immediately in the community of the local Church. The Reformation understanding and its spirit becomes clear in article 7 of the Augsburg Confession: the Church "is the assembly of all believers, by whom the gospel is proclaimed in its purity and the holy sacraments are administered according to the Gospels. For this is enough to preserve the unity of the Christian Churches, that there according to a pure understanding the gospel is proclaimed harmoniously and the sacraments are administered according to God's Word. Further, it is not necessary for the unity of the Christian Churches that similar ceremonies, which after all are human creations, be carried out everywhere, as Paul says to the Ephesians at 4:4f."[3] "In the '*satis est*' . . . doubtless is contained a '*necesse est*':[4] what is required is a community which confesses the same faith, the criterion of which is the true gospel; in the view of the Reformation, therein lies the unity of the Church "deriving from the Word and sacrament and always dependent upon them."[5] "This understanding led to the model for unity of the 'Church community,' as it was unfolded and realized in the so-called Leuenberger Concord (1973)."[6]

Life in unity is destroyed through heresy. The ancient Church reacted against heretics by employing the anathema. In this the ancient Church

---

3. The Latin text runs: "Et ad veram unitatem ecclesiae satis est consentire de doctrina evangelii et de administratione sacramentorum. Nec necesse est ubique similes esse traditiones humanas seu ritus ac cerimonias ab hominibus instituta; sicut inquit Paulus . . ." (BSLK 61).

4. E. Kinder, *Der evangelische Glaube und die Kirche* (Berlin, 1960) 206 note 3; see also the entire chapter 199–209: The unity of the Church—a) The Reformation View, with bibliography, p. 199 note 1. "Sometimes Luther lists a *whole series* of factors by which the Church of Christ in the empirical sense can be identified." It is "not that these others are added to the two essential *notae* of proclaiming the gospel and administering the sacraments, but rather . . . these others all stand in a functional relationship to Word and Sacrament. Such things as the Church offices or the creed or the cult or proper behavior or suffering are not of themselves autonomous indications or *per se* valid *notae verae ecclesiae,* but they are signs through which the Church in this world gives evidence of itself and preserves itself; *they depend upon Word and Sacrament and refer always to them*" (107 and 109). For the Reformed understanding, see J. Rohls, *Theologie der reformierten Bekenntnisschriften* (Göttingen, 1985) 205ff.

5. Kinder, *Glaube.*

6. U. Kühn, *Kirche* (Gütersloh, 1980) 203.

may serve as a model, because through it the understanding of the undivided Church of the ecumenical councils becomes visible. Those who do not accept the defined doctrine of the Church—*de-finition* means marking the boundary of true teaching—were excluded from life in the Church (*ex-communication* means exclusion from the *communio*). The contemporary separation of the Churches thus means that the Churches mutually excommunicate one another, if we understand this term in its original meaning.

This is the way the problem of what the "other Churches" are from the point of view of the Catholic Church presents itself: may one say that the Church of Christ is realized not only in the Catholic Church, but also in the other Churches? Does the conviction that the Catholic Church alone is the true Church lead us necessarily to say that the other Churches cannot be called Churches?

1. The Relation of the Catholic Church to the Church of Christ

The encyclical *Mystici corporis* says that the Catholic Church is (*est*) the Church of Christ. This formulation was also planned in the proposal for the constitution *Lumen gentium*. However, the final draft states rather that the Church of Christ is realized (*subsistit*) in the Catholic Church. To avoid a misinterpretation we must pay attention to the entire context:

> "Christ, the unique intermediary, has established here on earth his holy Church, the community of faith, of hope, and of love, as a visible structure, and continues unceasingly to sustain her as such" (no. 8, 1).
> "This is the only Church of Christ, which we confess in faith to be one, holy, catholic, and apostolic. . . . This Church, established and structured in this world as a community, is realized (*subsistit*) in the Catholic Church, which is led by the successor of Peter and by the bishops in community with him. This does not mean that outside its structure numerous examples of holiness and of truth are not to be found, which as the distinctive gifts of the Church of Christ impel us towards a catholic unity" (no. 8, 2).[7]

The context shows clearly that the unique and true Church of Christ exists as a concrete historical reality, so that the Catholic Church may

---

7. On the interpretation of the text: H. Mühlen, *Una mystica persona* (München, 1968) 399–406; A. Grillmeier, "Kommentar zum I. Kapitel der konstitution über die Kirche," in LThK. El here 174ff. Both authors give a more precise commentary. Further: Ricken, *Ecclesia,* 367ff.; F. A. Sullivan, " '*Subsistit in.* ' The Significance of Vatican II's Decision to say of the Church of Christ not that it 'is' but that it 'subsists in' the Roman Catholic Church," *OIC* 22 (1986) 115–23.

be characterized as the concrete form of existence of the Church of Christ. The documents validate this interpretation, which is made certain by the context:

> The *purpose* [of no. 8] is to show that the Church [of Christ] . . . can be found on earth concretely [*concrete*] in the Catholic Church. This empirical Church reveals the mystery, but not in sweeping away all darkness. . . . For that reason we propose a clearer distinction, in which next to each other one may find the following:
>   a) The mystery of the Church is present and reveals itself *in the concrete community*. . . .
>   b) The Church is *one, unique (unica)*, and present (*adest*) here on earth in the Catholic Church, although elements of the Church may be found outside her. Instead of *"est,"* *"subsistit in"* is used, so as to better correspond with what is said elsewhere about the elements of the Church to be found outside the Catholic Church.[8]

The expression *subsistere* is to be found also in the Decree on Ecumenism, a text which, according to the express word of Pope Paul VI, should be seen as complementing the teaching of *Lumen gentium:*[9] The obstacles which "stand in the way to full Church community" must be overcome, so that "all Christians may unite around the same celebration of the Eucharist, in the unity of the one and only Church. . . . a unity which according to our belief perdures [*subsistere*] immemorially in the Catholic Church" (no. 4).

These statements correspond to nos. 2 and 3 of the same decree, where the unity of the Church is expressed in the clearest language.

Quite consciously the council rejected the identity put forward in *Mystici corporis* between the Church of Christ and the Catholic Church, so as to acknowledge the elements of the Church present in the other Churches. The communities of non-Catholic Christians are thus recognized as Church communities in the most positive sense. Through this terminology the communities *as such,* and not merely isolated individuals, are taken into account.[10]

---

8. *Schema constitutionis de Ecclesia* (Vatican, 1964) 23f. = Acta Synodalia 3/1, 176.

9. *AAS* 56 (1964) 1012f.

10. See below note 11: This terminology is common in the ecumenical movement. It has its origin in Calvin (*Institutio*). See the "Toronto Declaration" (1950) nos. 10 and 12, and the documents of the Ecumenical World Conference at Lund (1952) no. 44. For a presentation of the positions of various Catholic theologians: E. Lamirande, "La signification ecclésiologique des communautés dissidents et la doctrine des Vestigia Ecclesiae; panorama théologique des vingt-cinqt dernières années," *Istina* 10 (1964) 25–57; Dietzfelbinger, *Grenzen*, 135ff.; U. Valeske, "Vestigia Ecclesiae. Die nicht-

Since the Catholic Church understands herself as containing the fullness of the means to salvation,[11] one may say about the other Christian communities only that they contain *elements* of this fullness. The Catholic Church judges the degree of actualization of the Church in the other Churches according to her understanding of what belongs to the nature of the Church. This recognition of Church elements outside the Catholic Church is not incompatible with a simultaneous insistence that the Catholic Church is the concrete form of existence of the Church established by Christ. The other Church communities, whose Church elements the council emphasizes, are called either "Churches" (the separated Eastern Churches) or "Church communities" (the Protestant Churches),[12] according to whether or not they have maintained the apostolic succession of office according to the Catholic understanding.[13]

Although the Roman Catholic Church understands herself as the one true Church of Christ, she does not identify herself with the Church of Christ and recognizes Churches outside herself. Does that not imply that "the Church of Christ subsists also in other Christian Churches"?[14] In

---

römischen Kirchen in der Sicht der heutigen römisch-katholischen Theologie," in *Nachrichten der evang. luth. Kirche in Bayern* 15 (1960) no. 21.

11. "Only through the Catholic Church . . . does one have access to the fullness of the means of salvation" (Decree on Ecumenism no. 3, 5).

12. *Lumen gentium* no. 15 and the Decree on Ecumenism in the subtitle to the third chapter as well as no. 3, 4. As the Relatio to no. 15 says, it is about titles that can already be found in papal documents: *Schema constitutionis,* 51 = Acta Synod. 3/1, 204. "The elements detailed in no. 15 concern not only individuals, but also communities." On the use of official documents, see Y. M. Congar, "Note sur les Mots 'Confession,' 'Église,' et 'Communion,' " in *Chrétiens en dialogue* (Paris, 1964) 227ff. (originally in *Irénikon* 23 [1950] 3–36). As a justification for the term *Churches* for the separated Churches of the East, the Decree on Ecumenism no. 3, 4, note 4, refers to the Fourth Lateran Council, the Second Council of Lyons, and the Council of Florence.

13. "The term *ecclesia* clearly remains connected with acknowledgment of the apostolic succession" (J. Ratzinger, *RGG* 5 [1961] 665, in dependency upon Congar's analysis). The Decree on Ecumenism speaks of a "defectus ordinis" with regard to the ecclesial communities of the Reformation (no. 22, 3), while apostolic succession is recognized by the Churches of the East (no. 15, 3).

14. This is the way L. Boff, *Kirche: Charisma und Macht* (Düsseldorf, 1985) 140, formulates it. To this the Congregation of the Faith has reacted: "However, the council specifically chose the word 'subsistit' to make clear that there is only one 'subsistence' of the true Church [in Italian: "esiste una sola 'sussistenza' della vera Chiesa], while outside its visible structures there are merely 'elementa Ecclesiae' " (*AAS* 71 [1985] 758f.). The document also refers to the Decree on Ecumenism nos. 3–4 as well as to the document *Mysterium Ecclesiae* no. 1 (*AAS* 65 [1973] 396–98). Sullivan, *Subsistit in,* 121, is of the opinion that the document of the Congregation of the Faith presents the teaching of the council in a narrow sense.

my opinion, such a concession does not contradict the statement that the Church of Christ in all its fullness is to be found in the Roman Church and only there.[15] This statement also does not support the so-called branch theory (that the Church is only *de facto* and not *de jure* divided, and that only its external, visible unity has been broken; thus the Orthodox, Anglican, and Roman Catholic Churches could be regarded as equally legitimate limbs of the same paternal reality). The recognition of the Church character of the other Christian communities is a consequence of decisions coming down from the patristic era (the conflict over the validity of baptism administered by heretics; Augustine's arguments with the Donatists), according to which sacraments administered outside the Church must be viewed as valid if they were administered in accordance with the rubrics of the Church. This principle is also supported by various contemporary Orthodox theologians.[16] This is the basis for the special prob-

---

15. Here I am following the paraphrase of G. Philips, *L'Église et son mystère au IIe concile du Vatican* (Paris, 1967) ad locum.

16. G. Florovsky, "Les limites de l'Église," in *Messager de l'exarchat* no. 37 (1961) 28–40, maintains that the historical practice of the Churches of the East and West shows clearly that the sacraments may validly be administered outside the *canonical* boundaries of a specific church. For that reason the statement of Cyprian, that only within the Church do the sacraments have their effect, should be turned around: that "wherever the sacraments have their effect, there the Church is present." Florovsky criticizes Augustine's thesis (30). Orthodox theologian J. Klinger writes: "The Orthodox Church has to choose between the rejection of the validity of sacraments administered outside of the Orthodox Church, if she regards herself as the only true Church, or, if she will accept the validity of at least a few of the sacraments administered by other Christian communities, she must then acknowledge these communities as representations of the one true Church." ("Le problème de l'intercommunion: point de vue d'un orthodoxe," in *Vers l'intercommunion* [Paris-Tours, 1970] 71–118, here 88f.). This thesis by Florovsky is referred to by both J. Bria in *Istina* 14 (1969) 229ff., and N. Nissiotis, "Die Zugehörigkeit zur Kirche nach orthodoxen Verständnis," in P. Meinhold, ed., *Das Problem der Kirchengliedschaft Heute* (Darmstadt, 1979) 366–90, here 369f.

In general, Orthodox theology maintains that sacraments administered outside the Orthodox Church must be rejected according to the principle of acriby; however, under certain circumstances they can be recognized by the Church according to the principle of economy. D. Wendebourg has analyzed the historical problematic and has established by very good arguments that this practice at least as regards baptism does not correspond to the entire history of the Orthodox Church, but is rather a novel development of the eighteenth and nineteenth centuries: "Taufe und Oikonomia. Zur Frage der Wiedertaufe in der Orthodoxen Kirche," in *Kirchengemeinschaft—Anspruch und Wirklichkeit,* FS G. Kretschmar, eds. W. D. Hauschild, C. Nicolaísen, and D. Wendebourg (Stuttgart, 1986) 93–110 (an excellent presentation of the Orthodox position as well as of the most recent literature).

lem with the Reformation Churches, for according to both the Catholic and Orthodox understanding, this principle assumes an essential connection between Church and Eucharist (cf. above chap. 8), and a *valid* celebration of the Eucharist presupposes a validly ordained ministry.

2. The Significance of the Other Churches and Their Traditions for the Catholicity of the Church

The elements of the Church and the qualities out of which together it is built up and through which it carries out its life, and which also exist outside the visible borders of the Catholic Church, "belong by right to the unique Church of Christ" (Decree on Ecumenism, *Unitatis redintegratio* no. 3, 2), so that "as the distinctive gifts of the Church of Christ they push towards a catholic unity" (*Lumen gentium* no. 8, 2). These statements must be understood as coming from the Roman Catholic Church, which sees herself as the true Church. Since Christians of the other Churches believe the same thing about their own communities,[17] the dialogue between the Churches must be carried out on the basis of equality.

What the other Churches and their traditions mean for the Catholicity of the Roman Catholic Church is expressed by the Decree on Ecumenism in the following way: "However, the split between Christians is an obstacle for the Church in her attempt to bring about that fullness of catholicity which is proper to her in her children, who indeed belong to her by their baptism, but who are cut off from full community. Indeed, it thereby becomes more difficult for the Church to impress the fullness of her catholicity under that aspect upon the actuality of life" (no. 4, 10).

As regards the Eastern tradition, the Decree on Ecumenism clearly states that the apostolic inheritance in the Church was differentiated from the very outset (no. 14, 3). The difference of methods that correspond to a difference of mentality leads to the statement "that sometimes certain aspects of the revealed mysteries are better understood and more clearly brought to light by one side, sometimes by the other, and indeed in such a way that, in the various theological expressions, one should better speak of a mutual complementarity and completion than an opposition or contradiction" (no. 17). These basic principles may also be applied, *mutatis mutandis,* to the Churches of the Reformation.

17. J. Karmiris, "Zur dogmatischen Konstitution über die Kirche," in D. Papandreou, ed., *Stimmen der Orthodoxie, zu Grundfragen des II. Vatikanums* (Freiburg-Basel-Wien, 1969) 55–91, writes correctly about the Orthodox understanding: the Orthodox catholic Church "does not at all believe that it possesses merely *elements* (*elementa* or *vestigia Ecclesiae*), but rather the *fullness* of the sanctifying and saving divine grace and of the revealed truth."

The ecumenical perspective means for Catholic ecclesiology that the Roman Catholic Church may complement or be complemented by the other Churches, in case the aspects developed by the other Churches are only present in it *in potentia*, but not *in actu*. As an example of Catholic theological reflection over the meaning of ecumenism before the Second Vatican Council, K. Rahner has correctly written that the history of the separated Christian communities "is not *only* a history of error and of the continuing substantial deprivation of Christian reality. It is at the same time . . . the history of an unfolding of authentic Christian possibilities which in fact, in their disposition and root, are available to the one true Church and may there be cultivated, but whose development may not always and everywhere reach as far in the Church in actuality, as they are currently cultivated in the separated Churches."[18]

It must be the attempt of every theology that describes itself as ecumenical to strive after catholicity. The principle of catholicity is also of central importance for a theology of mission; thus it is able to integrate the apostolic inheritance into the variety of cultures. Only in this way may the Church and its theology follow the model of the New Testament, where we witness the translation of a Semitically grounded proclamation into Hellenistic categories.

On the Expression "Catholic"[19]

The expression *catholic* appears for the first time in Ignatius of Antioch: against the heretics Ignatius emphasizes that the community is present where the bishop is present, just as the Catholic Church is present where Christ is present.[20] Here *Catholic* means no more than the Church in its fullness.

The term is used by Clement of Alexandria and Tertullian to distinguish the true Church from the heretical sects.[21] In 251 Cyprian produced a work called *De catholicae ecclesiae unitate*. From the third century on the epithet *Catholic* established itself with the meaning of "the true, world-spanning Church" or "a local Church in connection with this Church."[22]

The excommunication formula of the Council of Nicaea runs: "The Catholic Church bans . . . those who say . . ." (DS 126). The documents

18. K. Rahner, *Schriften*, 2:32.

19. Bibliography: Congar, *Wesenseigenschaften*, 478–502, 597 (bibliography); W. Beinert, *Um das dritte Kirchenattribut* (Essen, 1964); J. Salaverri, "Katholizität der Kirche," in LThK 6:90–92; G. W. H. Lampe, *A Patristic Greek Lexicon* (Oxford, 1965) 690 ("Katholikós"); V. Lossky, *A l'image et à la ressemblance de Dieu* (Paris, 1967) 167–79 ("Du troisième attribut de l'Église").

20. Smyrn. 8.2, ed. Bihlmeyer, 108.

21. Clement: PG 9:547, 551; Tertullian, *De praescriptione* 26.9; 30.2; PL 2:45B, 48B.

22. Congar, *Wesenseigenschaften*, 480.

speak of "bishops of the Catholic [that is, the true] Church"; specifically in Nicaea, canon 19 (DS 128). Gregory of Nazianzus calls himself "bishop of the Catholic Church in Constantinople."[23] Pope Paul VI witnessed the documents of the Second Vatican Council with the title "Ego Paulus Catholicae Ecclesiae Episcopus."

With Cyril of Jerusalem the term has the twofold meaning of a geographical universality as well as the fullness of truth.[24] The dispute between the Donatists and Augustine had particular significance for this term. Against the Donatists Augustine emphasizes the geographical interpretation of universality. He refers to the universal scope of the proverbs in Holy Scripture. To be Catholic for Augustine means to stand in communion with all the Churches (*in communione omnium gentium*). Against the particularism and exclusivism of the heretical groups Augustine emphasizes that the Church is called this everywhere in the world.[25] Against the geographical interpretation of Catholicity the Donatists posed a qualitative understanding: *Catholic* is any Church that has preserved the purity of its sources and celebrates the true sacraments.[26]

For High Scholasticism, *Catholic* indicates fullness: "not primarily a quantitative or numerical worth, but the fullness of the bread of life that Christ is and which the Church carries forth in faith and in the sacraments of the faith."[27]

The controversy between the Donatists and Augustine is reflected in the apologetic disputes between the Churches. Catholic apologetics has concentrated upon the universalist or geographic interpretation of *Catholic*, while the Orthodox and Protestant Churches have focused more strongly upon the qualitative meaning.

3. Church Membership or To Be in Communion with the Church

Together with the themes of the relation of the Catholic Church to the Church of Christ and the ecclesial character of the other Churches, the theme of Church membership was discussed at the Second Vatican Council and taken up in a new perspective.

23. See H. Marot, "Note sur l'expression 'Episcopus Ecclesiae, Catholicae,' " *Irénikon* 37 (1964) 221-26.

24. *Cat.* 18.23; PG 33:1044.

25. "Katholiké graece appelatur quod per totum orbem terrarum diffunditur" (*Ep.* 52; PL 33:194; see also *Ep.* 93.7; PL 33:333 and PL 34:128). See Augustine, *Traités antidonatistes*, vol. 1 (Paris, 1963) with the introduction by Y. M. Congar 77-80 and 83ff.

26. At the assembly of 411, Gaudantius said: "Cum hoc sit catholicum nomen quod sacramentis plenum est, perfectum, quod immaculatum, non ad gentes" (*Coll. Carthag.* 3.102: PL 2:1381).

27. Congar, *Wesenseigenschaften*, 484.

A comparison of the final form of sections 14 and 8 of *Lumen gentium* with the approach in 1963 (nos. 15 and 8) shows the following:[28]

First, both texts emphasize the necessity of the Church for salvation, "into which humans enter through baptism as through a door" (no. 14, 1).

Then the members of the Roman Catholic Church are mentioned: the final text talks about those who "have been fully [*plene*] incorporated into the community of the Church" (no. 14, 2), while the schema of 1963 reads: "actually and simply [*reapse et simpliciter loquendo*] . . . integrated." In order for a person to be fully incorporated into the community of the Church, both texts insist that the bonds of a confession of faith, the sacraments, and Church leadership and community are required (no. 8, 2).

As a third step the schema of 1963 speaks of a vote for the Church by catechumens, by all non-Catholics, and by non-Christians. The final text, however, mentions only catechumens (no. 14, 3). In this way it is made clear that non-Catholic Christians, since they have been baptized, are not to be placed on the same level as those who have not been baptized.

a. The Problem of Church Membership before Vatican II

Bellarmine approached the theme of Church membership with the help of Augustine's distinction between the body and the soul of the Church: *some* belong to the body and the soul of the Church, since they are bound together with Christ, the head of the Church, interiorly (through the life of grace) as well as exteriorly (through a connection with the true Church as an institution, through the confession of the true faith, and through participation in the same sacraments); these belong *perfectissime* to the Church. They are like living members of the body. *Others* belong either only to the body or only to the soul of the Church. To the body alone belong those who do not live in grace, that is, sinners; however, they still fulfill the minimum that is required for membership in the Church. Catechumens and those who have been excommunicated, if they retain faith and love, belong only to the soul of the Church. Heretics and schismatics also belong to this group.[29]

Bellarmine's position is based solidly on the doctrine of Augustine, according to which the spirit is only to be found "in corpore Christi," that is, in that Church which has excluded heretics. Augustine had also recognized the problem of the status of sinners, and concluded that they retain only an exterior membership. The fundamental plank of Augustine's position may be expressed as follows: "The true and holy Church, in which

---

28. *Schema Constitutionis* 35f. (Text) 49f. (Relatio) = Acta Synod. 3/1 188f.; 201ff.

29. Bellarmine, *De Conciliis* 3 (= "De ecclesia militante"), ch. 2. See J. Beumer, "Die kirchliche Gliedschaft in der Lehre des hl. Robert Bellarmin," *ThGI* 37–38 (1947/48) 243–57.

alone man may be saved, is hidden like an invisible core within the visible Church."[30]

Under the influence of Augustine's teaching, Thomas Aquinas appreciates the Church primarily in its interior dimension. Christ is the head of the mystical body. As concerns one's relation with Christ, Thomas distinguishes between those who are actually (*actu*) and those who are only potentially (*potentia*) connected with Christ. Besides the saints in heaven, those who are *actu* bound with Christ are those who live without sin, that is, *in caritate*. Sinners are in actuality not members of Christ, only *in potentia,* insofar as they have faith (*per fidem informem*). Unbelievers also are members *in potentia,* for the redemption to be found in Christ is sufficient for the salvation of all humanity.[31] Is it true that in Thomas the visible side of the Church disappears behind the invisible side, as A. Grillmeier, for example, maintains?[32] No, for Thomas Christ is the head of the Church to the extent that he gives it his grace. The role of the Church is to be an intermediary. For that reason Thomas can say of those outside the faith that they do not belong *actu* to the Church (*etsi actu non sint de Ecclesia*), and of sinners that, *in actuality,* they are not members of Christ.[33] For that reason I reject Grillmeier's opinion; Thomas quite clearly maintains that to be a member of the Church is not the same thing as to be a member of Christ. He bases himself on the empirical fact of baptism, which integrates us into Christ. Those who, after baptism, live in grace are members of Christ and of the Church. The two aspects (membership in Christ and membership in the Church) are bound together, since the Church has this intermediary role.

Bellarmine's position established itself within theology. Before *Mystici corporis,* the general theological opinion could be expressed as follows:[34]

Membership in the Church consists in the baptized, and only the baptized, in that baptism should be regarded as the door through which one enters the Church.

It was generally assumed by theologians that heretics and schismatics were no longer members of the Church in spite of their baptism. Those who had *formally* committed heresy or schism were regarded as heretics

30. Ricken, *Ecclesia,* 355. Text of Augustine: *Tract. in Io.* 26.13; 27.6; 32.8 (PL 35:1612, 1618, 1645); *Ep.* 185.11.42 (PL 33:811).

31. Thomas Aquinas, *Summa theologiae* 3.8.3 and ad 1 and 2. See also 3 Sent. d. 13, q. 2, a. 2, sol. 2.

32. A. Grillmeier, "Kommentar zum II. Kapitel der Konstitution Lumen gentium," in LThK. E I, 196.

33. *Summa theologiae* 3.8.3. ad 1 and 2.

34. Here I follow J. Salaverri in *Sacrae theologiae summa,* vol. 1 (Madrid, 1952) nos. 1026–32, p. 838ff.

and schismatics, since heresy and correspondingly schism presupposes *pertinacia,* or obduracy.

Still, a majority of theologians applied this principle also for *material* heretics and schismatics, even if authors like Franzelin or d'Herbigny took these to be members of the Church. Several theologians emphasized that the expression "material heretic" can only be understood analogically. The term *heresy* characterized a doctrine, not, however, the persons who represented this teaching in good faith and with the best of intentions. If this perspective is appropriated, then one must say that those who have been baptized into heresy or a schism have become *de se* by their baptism members of the Church; however, with them the connection with the Church, that is, with the Roman Catholic Church, is shattered through the position they have personally adopted (at least through having grown up within a separated community).

It is generally agreed that those who have been formally excommunicated by the Church with a complete excommunication (*excommunicatio perfecta*) are not members of the Church.

Mystici corporis states: "Only those should be counted as real [*reapse*] members of the Church who have received the bath of rebirth, confess the true faith, and who have not by their opposition been separated from connection with the body, nor been excluded through the regular course of Church authority because of serious errors. For these reasons those who are separated from one another in faith or in leadership [*qui fide vel regimine invicem dividuntur*] may not live in this one body and from its one divine spirit" (DS 3802 = NR 402).

The encyclical reinforces the traditional opinion: to be *reapse,* really or in reality, a member of the Church, not only is baptism required, but also the reality bound up with it of unity in the faith as well as in government. This statement must be understood in connection with the identification the encyclical makes between the Roman Catholic Church and the Church of Christ or the body of Christ. This identification was repeated by the encyclical *Humani generis* (1950) (DS 2319). Catholic theologians had availed themselves of the distinction between the mystical body of Christ and the Roman Catholic Church in order to clarify the situation of non-Catholic Christians. Both encyclicals attack these opinions. In addition *Mystici corporis* insists on the necessity of the Roman Catholic Church for salvation. For that reason it is maintained that non-Catholic Christians "do not live in this body and from its one divine spirit." The connection of non-Catholic Christians to the Church is described through the term *votum:* "With loving hearts we invite each and every one of them freely and joyfully to cooperate with the inner impulses of divine grace, and to free themselves from a situation in which they cannot be certain about their own eternal salvation. For even though they may well already through an unconscious yearning and desire stand in connection with the mystical body of the Savior [*etiamsi inscio quodam desiderio ac voto ad mysticum Redemptoris Corpus ordinentur*], still they are doing without the many efficacious divine graces and helps which are only available within the Catholic Church" (DS 3821).

The encyclical's solution consisted in a distinction between a membership in the Church that was *reapse* (in reality) or *votum* (by desire). This solution places non-Catholic Christians *de facto* on the same level as heathens, for the desire to belong to the Church may also be ascribed to the latter.[35]

b. The Emphasis on Baptism by Vatican II

Vatican II's approach emphasizes the significance of baptism and with it the different situations of non-Catholic Christians and of heathens. Baptism is entrance into the Church. For that reason all baptized persons constitute "a certain, if also not complete community [*in quadam communione etsi non perfecta*] with the Catholic Church" (Decree on Ecumenism no. 3). The incorporation of Catholics into the Church is described as full (*plena*) (*Lumen gentium* no. 14). Full incorporation demands the three elements already mentioned by Bellarmine (ibid.).

These three elements should be understood as a consequence of baptism. Through baptism every Christian is connected with the Church. Baptism is administered in connection with the Church's confession of faith and in the *koinonia* of the Church, or Churches, in the event a baptism administered outside one particular Church is recognized by other Churches. Seen denominationally, baptism joins one to the Roman Catholic Church. However, this fundamental incorporation into the Catholic Church is partially diminished if the individual grows up in a separated Church: the connection with the Catholic Church given in baptism is interrupted.

---

35. There were two directions in Catholic theology, represented by the names Mörsdorf and Rahner. There was also a third, which spoke of Church membership in stages. See H. Schauf, "Zur Frage der kirchengliedschaft," *ThRv* 58 (1962) 217–24. While Rahner emphasizes the three conditions named in the Church's doctrinal statements for Church membership in reality (*reapse*), Mörsdorf distinguishes between a constitutional Church membership on the basis of baptism and a factual Church membership. The former holds for non-Catholic Christians; at the same time, they do not possess the second. Mörsdorf's position criticizes Rahner for not taking baptism seriously enough, with the consequence that heathens and non-Catholics are placed on the same level. This also appears to be the case in the schema of the constitution *Lumen gentium* of 1963. See C. Vaggagini, "L'unione alla chiesa e la salvezza. Per un chiarimento della terminologia," *L'osservatore romano*, 14–15 May 1962, 5.

4. The Necessity of the Church for Salvation

Lumen gentium treats the topic of Church membership in connection with the necessity of the Church for salvation (no. 14), a connection which historically was expressed through the sentence *extra ecclesiam nulla salus.*

a. The Historical Meaning of the Sentence
Extra ecclesiam nulla salus[36]

The pre-Nicene Fathers clearly maintain that outside of membership in the institution of salvation of the Church there is neither eternal life nor salvation. For them membership means baptism. Irenaeus says, "Where the Church is, there is the spirit of God, and where the spirit of God is, there is the Church and all grace."[37] Cyprian argues in the following way against the baptism by heretics: God offers salvation to humanity through Christ, and Christ extends this salvation through the Church, so that the Church must be described as the instrument of salvation. Outside the Church there is only space for the antichrist. "Habere non potest Deum patrem, qui ecclesiam non habet matrem."[38]

Origen writes at the same period: "Whoever will be rescued from these [Jewish] people, let him come into this house to obtain salvation. He then comes into that house in which Christ's blood stands as a sign of redemption. . . . Let no one delude himself, let no one deceive himself. Outside this one house, that is, outside the Church, no one will be rescued. If anyone nevertheless should depart from this house, he alone is responsible for his own death."[39]

Similar statements are to be found by various later Church Fathers and Church writers. For example, Lactantius and Jerome make statements to this effect.[40] Augustine produced the following noteworthy text: "Outside the Catholic Church one can find everything except salvation. One can take the sacraments, one can sing Alleluias, one can have faith and preach in the name of the Father and of the Son and of the Holy Spirit. But nowhere else except in the Catholic Church can one find salvation."[41]

The following remarks should be made apropos of that passage. Augustine concedes that there are people who will be saved outside express membership in the Church in its canonical visibility; there is an *ecclesia*

---

36. Here I follow the work of Congar, *Ausser der Kirche kein Heil* (Essen, 1961).
37. *Adv. haer.* 3.24.1; PG 7:966.
38. *De cath. ecclesiae unitate* 6; PL 4:502. See also *Ep.* 55.24; 73.21.
39. *In Jesu Nave* 3.5; PG 12:841.
40. Lactantius, *Divinae institutiones* 4.30.11; CSEL 19:396; Jerome, *Ep. ad Damasum;* CSEL 54:63.
41. *Sermo ad Caes. Eccl. pleb.* 6; PL 43:695. See also *De baptismo* 1.12.18; 3.13.13; PL 43:119, 146.

ab Abel, that is, the Church already existed beginning with the first humans. Nevertheless, he frequently states that the Jews after Christ, the pagans, and the heretics will all be damned. Even though he recognizes that there are sacraments outside the Church, he maintains that the heretic draws no nourishment from his sacraments, insofar as he has embraced the ruination of heresy.[42]

It was a student of Augustine's, Fulgentius of Ruspe (468–533), who first coined a phrase that later impressed itself upon the Western Christian consciousness. This formula runs: "Believe firmly and doubt not that, not only all pagans, but also all Jews, heretics, and schismatics who end their lives outside the Catholic Church are given over to the everlasting fire that has been prepared for the devil and his angels."[43]

The influence of this text can be clearly discerned in the doctrinal decisions of the Council of Florence concerning the Jacobites: The holy Church "firmly believes, confesses, and proclaims that no one outside the Catholic Church—neither pagan nor Jew, heretic nor schismatic—will have a part in eternal life, but will rather fall into the everlasting fire that has been prepared for the devil and his angels, if before death they do not enter her [the Church]" (DS 1351 = NR 381).

Before this council the teaching office of the Church had maintained against the Waldensians (DS 792) and the Albigensians (DS 802 = NR 920) that "there only exists one universal Church of believers" and that "outside of her, no one will be saved."

Neo-Augustinianism is represented in the two following formulae that were condemned by the Church's teaching office:

The statement from Jansenius (condemned 1653): "It is semi-Pelagian to say that Christ died for all people" (DS 2005 = NR 875).

The statement from Quesnel (condemned 1713): "Outside the Church there is no grace" (DS 2429).

The condemnation of both these statements by the teaching office makes clear the boundaries within which the axiom *extra ecclesiam nulla salus* must be understood: "The sentence 'there is no salvation outside the Church' from that point on could only and today can only be stated as one part of a dialectical unity together with a rejection of the statement 'outside the Church there is no grace.' *From this point on only the self-conscious acceptance of this dialectic corresponds to the Church's teaching.*"[44]

---

42. *De bapt.* 4.17.24; PL 43:170. See F. Hofmann, *Der Kirchenbegriff des hl. Augustinus in seinen Grundlagen und in seiner Entwicklung* (München, 1933) 212–43; J. Ratzinger, *Volk und Haus Gottes in Augustins Lehre von der Kirche* (München, 1954) 136–58.

43. *De fide ad Petrum* 38.79; PL 65:704.

44. Ratzinger, *Volk Gottes,* 348. My emphasis.

How the axiom is to be interpreted is made clear in the letter of the Holy Office of 8 August 1949 with regard to the case of L. Feeney (DS 3866–73). The Church and baptism are necessary not only *necessitate praecepti,* but also *necessitate medii.* However, just as the necessity of baptism can according to the patristic tradition be replaced by a desire (*voto*), in the same way the necessity of the Church can be replaced: "For someone to reach eternal salvation it is not always necessary that they in actuality [*reapse*] be incorporated as a member of the Church. However, it is at least necessary that the person attach himself to her by desire [*voto et desiderio*]" (DS 3870). It is sufficient that there be an implicit desire (*implicitum votum*), that may be simply part and parcel of a "correct disposition of the soul, by the power of which a person intends his will to be in accord with the will of God" (ibid.). As the specific content of a will so disposed are mentioned love ("such a desire should be formed by complete love") and supernatural faith.

Vatican II extended this orientation in the direction of heathens: "A person who, through no fault of his own, does not know the gospel of Christ and his Church, but who seeks God with a sincere heart, and who tries in his actions to follow his will as he recognizes it under the influence of his grace, may obtain eternal salvation. Divine providence does not refuse the means necessary for salvation to those who, through no fault of their own, have not yet arrived at an express recognition of God, but still exert themselves, not without God's grace, to lead an upright life" (*Lumen gentium* no. 16).

b. Theological Reflection

The necessity of the Church for salvation means nothing else but that the Church itself is the general sacrament of salvation. *Lumen gentium* points out the necessity of faith and of baptism (cf. Mark 16:16; John 3:5), to ground the need for the Church (no. 14). Positively expressed, this means that every divine grace has an ecclesial character. In accord with this, modern Catholic sacramental theology (E. Schillebeeckx, K. Rahner, O. Semmelroth) has stressed the ecclesial character of the sacraments.

The axiom *extra ecclesiam nulla salus* was deployed against the heretical sects because God's spirit is only to be found within the Church, according to the overwhelming conviction of the Church Fathers. The most graphic example of this would be Cyprian, who simply does not recognize the validity of a baptism performed outside the Church. If the validity of sacraments administered outside the Church were to be recognized, as Augustine does in his controversy with the Donatists, it is then very difficult to understand that the axiom may also be employed with regard to schismatics, as at the Council of Florence. In other words, if the Orthodox and Eastern Churches are recognized as Churches, and the communities coming out of the Reformation are recognized as ecclesial communities, then this axiom could no longer be used, at least in the sense intended by the Council of Florence, but one would rather have to say with the Decree on Ecumenism that "the separated Churches and communities [*are*] not without significance and importance within the mystery of salvation. For the Spirit of Christ has seen fit to use them as means of salvation" (no. 3, 4). In this way the axiom is viewed from another perspective than in the patristic Church, though on the basis of the Fathers' own reflection, which recognized the validity of sacraments administered outside the Church.

There still remains concealed within this axiom a problem regarding non-Christians. On the one hand we must here emphasize the necessity of faith and of baptism, and therefore of the Church, for salvation; but on the other hand we must not forget that God's desire for salvation embraces all of humanity (cf. 1 Tim 2:4) in its particular concrete situations.

We should here notice that the New Testament supplies two mutually complementary responses to the question of what is necessary from the human side for salvation to be attained: on the one hand faith in Jesus Christ (and baptism) is emphasized; on the other hand it is said that whoever has love, has everything. This comes clearly to the surface in the discussion between Jesus and the teacher of the Law (Matt 22:35-40), as well as in Paul, who describes love as the completion of the Law (Rom 13:9f.), and especially in the daring depiction of the last judgment (Matt 25:31-46).

With the help of this second perspective, K. Rahner[45] has developed his conception of the "anonymous Christian," a conception which must be grasped as the union of love of neighbor and love of God. The principle evidenced by the New Testament, that God's will for salvation includes all of humanity in its concrete situations, can only be clarified if through their worldly affairs every human being stands before the gracious offer of God, even though, as non-Christians, they are completely unaware of the fact that there is a gracious offer by God and, as unbelievers, they do not indeed recognize God.

One may pose the following question: if one may obtain divine grace outside the sacramental medium of the visible Church, then what in fact remains of the necessary intermediary role of the visible Church?

Following K. Rahner, this question may be answered in the following way: just like the Greek Fathers, we may speak of an objective salvation; that is, humanity "has ontologically already in advance become the con-

45. K. Rahner, "Über die Einheit von Nächsten- und Gottesliebe," in *Schriften* 6:277-98; *Grundkurs des Glaubens* (Freiburg, 1976) 301f.

crete gracious salvation of individual persons into the community of God's children. To the extent that humanity 'consecrated' in this way is already a real unity, there already exists—in advance of any social or legal organization of humanity as a supernatural unity in the Church—a 'people of God' which is as wide as all humanity."[46] Otherwise expressed: one can distinquish between the "Church as an 'established formally correct organization,' and the Church as 'a humanity consecrated through the incarnation.'"[47] The first expression presumes the second, and the second has the first as its goal according to Christ's will. Since the simply "natural" no longer exists, "ultimately every personal act in man's concrete nature . . . also has a historical aspect (a constituting sign) that it is a *votum Ecclesiae.*"[48]

BIBLIOGRAPHY

General:

Baum, G. "Die ekklesiale Wirklichkeit der anderen Kirchen." *Conc* 1 (1965) 291–303.

Bläser, P. "Die Kirche und die Kirchen." *Cath* 18 (1964) 89–107.

Congar, Y. M. "Die Wesenseigenschaften der Kirche." In MySal 4/1, 372f. (The Types of Unity), 411f. (The Divisions within the Unity), 500f. (Ecumenism and Catholicity).

Küng, H. *Die Kirche.* Freiburg, 1967, 313ff.

Mühlen, H. "Der eine Geist und die vielen Kirchen nach den Aussagen des Vaticanum II." *ThGl* 55 (1965) 329–66.

Ökumene, Konzil, Unfehlbarkeit (Pro Oriente 4). Innsbruck, 1979. Contents: "The one Church and the many Churches (from an Old Eastern perspective): M. K. Krikorian, 164ff.; from an Orthodox perspective: St. C. Alexe, 169ff.; from a Roman Catholic perspective: H. Mühlen, 175ff.; from a Lutheran perspective: K. Lüthi, 181ff.

On Church Membership and the Necessity of the Church for Salvation:

Congar, Y. M. *Heilige Kirche.* Stuttgart, 1965 (orig. French 1963), 434ff. (No Salvation Outside the Church)

Jáki, St. *Les tendances nouvelles de l'ecclésiologie.* Rome, 1957, ch. 4.

Mörsdorf, K. "Kirchengliedschaft, I. Fundamentaltheologisch und kirchenrechtlich." In LThK 6:221-23.

Rahner, K. "Die Gliedschaft in der Kirche nach der Lehre der Enzyklika Pius' XII '*Mystici Corporis.*'" In *Schriften zur Theologie* 2:7–94.

_____. "Kirchengliedschaft. II Dogmatisch." In LThK 6:223-25.

46. Rahner, *Gliedschaft,* 89.
47. Ibid., 93.
48. Ibid., 94.

_____. "Kirchengliedschaft (Kirchenzugehörigkeit)." In SM 2:1209-15 = HTTL 4:159-64.

Ratzinger, J. *Das neue Volk Gottes.* Düsseldorf, 1969, 101ff., 339ff.

Ricken, F. " 'Ecclesia . . . universale salutis sacramentum.' Theologische Erwägungen zur Lehre der Dogmatischen Konstitution 'De Ecclesia' über die Kirchenzugehörigkeit." *Schol* 40 (1965) 352-88.

Thils, G. "Die das Evangelium nicht empfangen haben." In Baraúna 1:602ff.

Willems, B. "Die Heilsnotwendigkeit der Kirche." *Conc* 1 (1965) 52-59 (with bibliography).

Presentations of Catholic Theology by Protestant Theologians:

Dietzfelbinger, W. *Die Grenzen der Kirche nach römisch-katholischer Lehre.* Göttingen, 1962.

Valeske, U. *Votum Ecclesiae.* München, 1962.

X.
A Pilgrim Church

In the Church there are always two aspects to distinguish. On the one hand the Church is the community of the saints, that is, of believers, in the sense that it consists of those persons who believe in Jesus. On the other hand, it is a sacramental institution, a means or agency of salvation.

In the Creed the Church is confessed to be *holy*. Thus she is seen first and foremost in Christ and in his Spirit. Just as the people of Israel are holy (Exod 19:6), the Church is also holy, because through baptism Christ has purified her (Eph 5:25-27). In the New Testament believers are called holy on the basis of their call from God and their salvation in Christ. The Church is also holy for this reason. The holiness of the Church consists in the fact that Christ and his Spirit are bound to the Church by an unbreakable connection, and that the Holy Spirit works in it and through it, as *Lumen gentium* says expressly (nos. 4 and 39). The holiness of the Church emphasizes this aspect of the Church as the *communio sanctorum,* in the sense of having "a participation in holy things" (*sancta*), most especially in the Lord's Supper.[1] In *Lumen gentium* (no. 8) the Church

1. Most probably the formula comes from the East, where *tá hágia* designated the consecrated elements. Evidence for this is in W. Elert, *Abendmahl und Kirchengemeinschaft in der Alten Kirche, hauptsächlich des Ostens* (Berlin, 1954) 5-17 and 170ff.; Elert, "Der Herkunft der Formel 'Sanctorum communio,' " *ThLZ* 74 (1949) 577-86. See also J. N. D. Kelly, *Altchristliche Glaubensbekenntnisse* (Göttingen, 1962) 381-90, J. Mühlsteiger, "Communio sanctorum," *ZKTh* 93 (1970) 113-72.

The formula was used by Nicetas of Remesiana (Serb, d. after 414) and by Faustus of Riez (consecrated bishop ca. 452) in the sense of the assembly of the saints of all ages. See the texts in Kelly, 384.

In the Middle Ages *sanctorum* was commonly interpreted as the masculine genitive. For example, Abelard (d. 1142) understands the formula as "that community through which the saints are strengthened toward holiness and in their holiness through participation in the divine sacrament." He nevertheless adds that *sanctorum* may also

is presented in analogy with the mystery of the incarnation; in this way a species of ecclesiological "Nestorianism" is avoided, according to which there is no substantial relation between the divine and human element. The opposite of an ecclesiological "Nestorianism" would be an ecclesiological "Monophysitism,"[2] according to which everything in the Church is so "divine" that the historicity of the Church, and with it the limitations, impoverishments, and faults of this sacramental organization, are not recognized. When the pilgrim character of the Church is kept in mind, certain ecclesiological problems and aspects come forward. Here we will take up two aspects of major significance: first, the sinfulness of the Church, and second, the relation of the Church to its eschatological fulfillment.

1. *Ecclesia Semper Reformanda*

Lumen gentium says of the Church that she "embraces sinners in her own bosom" and that she is "simultaneously holy and always in need of purification; she must perpetually tread the path of penance and of renewal" (no. 8, 3). Corresponding to this, the Decree on Ecumenism speaks of the *necessary* reform and renewal of the Church: "The Church in the midst of its pilgrimage is called by Christ to this continuing reform, of which she is perpetually in need, to the extent that she is a human and earthly institution" (*UR* 6).

In the patristic tradition, the Church is deliberately named the *casta meretrix,* the "chaste whore." The Church Fathers[3] emphasize that Christ found the Church sinful and has cleansed her. They see the Church symbolized in the sinful women of whom Holy Scripture speaks. "The Church is holy only because she has been snatched away from sin. Of herself, on the basis of her *causa materialis,* or human nature, she is a sinner."[4] The

---

be interpreted as the neuter, that is, as referring to the consecrated elements (PL 178:629f.). Thomas Aquinas comments on the formula as follows: "Because all the faithful constitute one body, the good deeds that belong to one are shared with the others. In the Church there is thus a participation in good deeds (*communio bonorum*), and they are meant when we say 'sanctorum communio.' " (*Expositio super symbolorum apostolorum ad fin.,* vol. 3 of the Parisian edition of 1634, 133).

2. These expressions were used by the International Commission of Theologians, *Mysterium des Volkes* (Einsiedeln, 1987) 54 (6, 1) = Commissio theologica internationalis, *Themata selecta de Ecclesiologia* (Vatican, 1985) 36.

3. See Balthasar, *Casta meretrix;* S. Tromp, *Corpus Christi quod est Ecclesia,* vol. 1 (Rome, 1946) 128–41 (excellent summary); H. Riedinger, *Die Makellosigkeit der Kirche in den lateinischen Hoheliedkommentaren des Mittelalters* (Münster, 1958).

4. Congar, *Wesenseigenschaften,* 470. Unfortunately these images associate sin with the feminine. The identification goes: Church = human nature. For that reason

claim that the Church is without blemish (*non habentem maculam aut regam*) Augustine explains by reference to the eschaton. The Church on pilgrimage, because of the sins of its members, who even though sinners still remain members, must pray each day: Forgive us our fault.[5] At the same time, this admission in no way hinders Augustine from speaking of the holiness of the Church. In his opinion the Church is holy on the basis of the means to salvation which Christ has entrusted to it (that is, the sacraments), and on the basis of the holiness of its members, if the majority live according to the principles of the Church (*caritas*).

a. A Sinful Church?

Quite understandably the Lutheran tradition applies the anthropological principle *simul justus et peccator* to the Church itself; the Church must be viewed as simultaneously holy and sinful. In the ecumenical assembly at Evanston (1954), this statement was emphasized in connection with the pilgrim status of the Church: "The Church takes its point of departure from the received unity, and travels towards the unity of complete revelation (Eph 4:3, 13). In this sense may we say of the Church as a whole what is said of each individual Christian: it is holy and sinful at the same time (*simul justus et peccator*). . . . The Church is already one in Christ . . . and she must become one in Christ, in order to reveal her authentic unity, for whatever she separates, she kills."[6] This comparison was rejected by the Orthodox representatives.[7]

On the side of Catholic theology, Chr. Journet refused to budge in defending the position that, while the Church always contains sinners, it itself is without sin. Sin touches only the members of the Church, and these only to the extent that they are untrue to their membership and have something in themselves that does not belong to the Church. From his point of view, one could only attribute something sinful to the Church if one regarded it *materialiter,* not *formaliter,* that is, in what pertains to its essence. The Church as such is without sin since it is the Church and as such consists in union with God and in the means to such a union.[8]

---

one should speak of the *sinful* people of God, so as to avoid misunderstandings such as Eve (without Adam) = the cause of sin.

5. *Retract.* 2.18; PL 32:637. (This is only one text among many others.)

6. *L'espérance chrétienne dans le monde d'aujourd'hui* (Evanston, 1954; Neuchâtel-Paris, 1955) 23.

7. See *The Orthodox Church in the Ecumenical Movement. Documents and Statements 1902-1975*, ed. C. G. Patelos (Geneva, 1978) 91ff. (especially nos. 2 and 5).

8. Following *Lumen gentium* Journet writes (in Baraúna 1:287): "All contradictions are removed once one understands that, to the extent that the members of the Church are sinful, the Church is betrayed. For the Church is indeed not without *sinners,* but she is without sin."

This understanding drew the criticism of working with a Platonic notion of the Church.[9]

K. Rahner presented a different point of view. He conceded that the constitution avoided using the expression "sinful Church." "However, the question is clearly broached whether the Church itself is affected by the sins of its members."[10] Rahner drew attention to the fact that the Church could not be "the *subject* of such a renewal and purification of its *self* [as the constitution asserts], if it has not previously been, and is now also, in some sense the subject of sin and guilt."[11]

b. Conclusions

In its concrete existence, the life of the Church and its historical dealings correspond only partially with the ideal that it should realize. For that reason it is of the greatest importance that the effectiveness of a sacrament does not depend upon the holiness of the person who administers the sacrament. The Church has received God's promise that as a whole it will never completely fall from grace and truth. Because of this promise it has the certainty that sin will never so dominate it that it could *definitively* be unfaithful to God's truth (the indefectibility of the Church). However, it does not possess God's promise that in its historical decisions it will always follow the Spirit or that in a concrete situation its decisions have been or will be the best possible.

The history of the Church demonstrates that it has experienced progress and decline; its life is changeable, and at times its steps backward have been larger than those forward.

The pilgrim status of the Church means that the entire history of the Church must be kept in mind should one attempt to speak of structures of divine activity. Only a theory that does justice to the facts of this history can support a teaching about such structures in the Church. This methodological principle will have to be carefully observed in the third part of this book.

Vatican I speaks about the Church directly as a sign of credibility for belief, so that "anyone who has once embraced the faith under the teaching authority of the Church, could never have a proper reason to change this belief or to cast it into doubt" (DS 3014 = NR 36 and 37). Even if on the purely objective level this statement is accurate, one should still not forget that individuals must decide according to their own conscience and following their own experience, so that one could defend the position that a given Catholic individual could *without guilt* decide otherwise.

9. Thus for example, Küng, *Kirche,* 382f.
10. Rahner, *Sündige Kirche,* 336.
11. Ibid.

Objectively seen, as a sign of credibility the Church should be compared with the person of Jesus. Even the sinless humanity of Jesus did not make it possible for his contemporaries, without further help, to recognize God's activity in him. No wonder, then, that the concrete Church can often be a hindrance to its own credibility. We must expect from the concrete Church that it renew itself, so as to become as little as possible an imperfect sign of salvation. However, it cannot be expected that it should ever become a perfect sign of salvation, precisely because of its human and sinful dimension. The Church has God's promise that the Spirit supports it and will help it further. Because of this divine promise, and in spite of the sin of the members who make up the Church, one may still speak of the indefectibility of the Church, that is, of its ultimately decisive faithfulness to the word of God. Error will not have the last word, although partial errors are always possible and cannot be excluded.

2. The Church Is Oriented toward the Eschatological Kingdom of God

The Church, that is, the community of believers, is on a pilgrimage toward the eschatological kingdom of God: "The essence of the Church is pilgrimage toward the still outstanding future."[12] This statement requires no particular justification, since the dialectic between the "already" and the "not yet" belongs to the essential character of Christian life. The baptized have already received the Spirit, but as *arrabon,* as a first share (2 Cor 1:22; Eph 1:14), and as *aparche,* as the first gift (Rom 8:23). Both terms emphasize that the reality received by Christians is oriented toward its eschatological completion. Paul, in Romans 8:13-30, relates this dialectic to the salvation of the world.

The Church must therefore be described as "the community of those hoping, of those waiting, of pilgrims, who are still seeking their authentic homeland, of those who understand and grasp their present in terms of their future."[13]

Lumen gentium establishes this eschatological character of the Church even when it speaks of the Church as the "people of God": "Its ultimate orientation is the kingdom of God, which was founded on earth by God himself, which must further expand, until at the end of time it will also be completed by him" (no. 9, 2; see also nos. 2 and 5). In chapter 7 of the same constitution, which speaks of the "final character of the pilgrim Church" (the chapter title), appears the following text: "Thus the resto-

---

12. Rahner, *Kirche und Parusie,* 351.

13. Ibid., 350. The image of Christians as pilgrims was strongly emphasized in the early Church.

ration which we have been promised and which we await has already begun in Christ, was continued in the sending of the Holy Spirit, and through him is extended in the Church [*pergit*]" (no. 48, 2). In the same section, immediately before this text, the Church is described as the all-embracing sacrament of salvation. One could conclude from this that the Church can be understood as the sacrament of the kingdom of God. Since the Church is the sacrament of salvation, one can also analogously call her the sacrament of the kingdom, to the extent that "the Church is not simply an empty sign [*sacramentum tantum*]; rather the reality referred to by the sign [*res et sacramentum*] is present as the kingdom of God."[14] An identification of the Church and the kingdom of God, which was the dominant position among Catholic theologians, cannot be exegetically defended.[15]

When the Church is regarded from the standpoint of "service to God's lordship,"[16] we may then say with K. Rahner: "The Church, properly understood, lives continually from the proclamation of her own preparatory status and her eventual historical replacement in the coming kingdom of God, toward which she is on pilgrimage."[17] This perspective is strongly underlined in Protestant theology.[18] On the other hand Catholic theology has typically hardly stressed the preparatory character of the Church. However, when this is taken as seriously as it should be, it means that it is not possible to absolutize or divinize either the Church or her structures.[19] The eschatological character of the Church is taken by various theologians as the programmatic principle for the *mission* of the Church (see the fourth part of this book). It may also however contain a programmatic meaning for the understanding of the *structural* elements of the Church: even if there are structures in the Church which should be regarded as *ius divinum,* as God's law, still the historical conditions with which these elements of *divine law* are stamped must not be forgotten; the same principle is valid for a definition of the Church that is formulated in a specific context. The effort to distinguish between the absolute tradition of the Church on the one hand, and the various customs that have developed into parts of that tradition on the other, must always be

14. International Commission of Theologians, *Mysterium,* 10, 3, S. 85/58.

15. See the remarks of R. Schnackenburg, *Gottes Herrschaft und Reich* (Freiburg, 1965) no. 23.

16. Küng, *Die Kirche,* 119.

17. Rahner, *Kirche und Parusie,* 351.

18. See: *Bedeutung der Reich-Gottes-Erwartung für das Zeugnis der christlichen Gemeinde. Votum des Theologischen Ausschusses der Evangelischen Kirche der Union* (Neukirchen-Vluyn, 1986).

19. Küng, *Kirche,* 114, points out this difficulty.

regarded as an urgent problem, when the preliminary character of the Church is taken duly into account.

BIBLIOGRAPHY

Balthasar, H. U. von. "Casta Meretrix." In *Sponsa verbi: Skizzen zur Theologie,* Einsiedeln, 1961, 203–305.
Congar, Y. M. *Heilige Kirche.* Stuttgart, 1966 (original French, 1963), 133–58 (How the Holy Church should endlessly renew itself).
_____. "Die Wesenseigenschaften der Kirche." In MySal 4/1, 458ff. (the Holy Church, with a bibliography).
Journet, Ch. *L'église du verbe incarné,* vol. 2. Paris, 1950, 904.
_____. *Theologie de l'église.* Paris, 1958, 236.
Küng, H. *Die Kirche.* Freiburg, 1967, 379ff.
Lubac, H. de. *Katholizismus als Gemeinschaft.* Einsiedeln and Köln, 1943, 61ff.
Rahner, K. "Kirche der Sünder." In *Schriften* 6:301–20.
_____. "Die Sünde in der Kirche." In Baraúna 1:346–62; reworked as "Sündige Kirche nach den Dekreten des Zweiten Vatikanischen Konzils," in *Schriften* 6:321–47 (with a bibliography, 346f.).
_____. "Kirche und Parusie Christi." Ibid., 348–67.

Third Part:
The Structures of the Church

It is the general conviction of all the Churches that authority belongs to the essential structure of the Church. However, there are different opinions about the specific relation between authority and community and about the specific function of authority. This is where the ecumenical problem lies.

It is the general conviction of both the Orthodox and the Catholic Churches that authority as such resides in the bishop's office, in such a way that the other offices of the community, such as presbyter and deacon, should be viewed as sharing in the bishop's authority. Here there is a difference with the Churches of the Reformation. The primacy of the bishop of Rome is a specific teaching of the Roman Catholic Church that is rejected by both the Orthodox Churches and the Churches of the Reformation. Chapters 12 and 13 are dedicated to the themes of the office of bishop and the primacy of the bishop of Rome, respectively.

An examination of the Church's structures must begin with the relation between the community and authority, since the function of authority must be viewed within the context of a community that is in its own way coresponsible. This also matches the structure of *Lumen gentium,* which first discusses what concerns the entire people of God, that is, all the members of the Church (chap. 2), and only then moves on to discuss the various offices, functions, and responsibilities of the different members.

XI.
Community and Office

1. The Teaching of *Lumen gentium*

In the second chapter of the Constitution on the Church two themes are discussed, namely, the priesthood of all believers and the sharing of all members of the Church in the prophetic office of Christ. This is the way the constitution describes the role of *the entire people* of God. The starting point for this presentation is the threefold office of Christ, in which all believers share through baptism and confirmation, and in which someone who holds office through ordination shares in a different way than the other believers.[1]

a. The Priesthood of All Believers[2] (LG 10)

Even though the New Testament speaks of the priestly character of the entire people of God and even though this theme is present in the Church Fathers and also in the theology of High Scholasticism,[3] it played

1. For the office of bishop: *LG* nos. 25, 26, 27; for the presbyterate: *PO* nos. 2, 3; for the laity: *LG* nos. 34, 35, 36; *AA* nos. 2, 2; for the entire people of God: *LG* nos. 10, 12. This terminology was first used by Protestant, especially Reformed theology, and then later by Catholic theology. See M. Schmaus, "Ämter Christi," in LThK 1:457–59. The encyclical *Mystici corporis* (1945) recognizes a threefold office only as regards the hierarchy. In his work *Der Laie* (1952), Y. M. Congar patterned his theology of the laity on the three offices or functions of Christ (chs. 4, 5, and 6).

2. This heading, as well as the next one, was given to the council fathers as an explanation of the text of the constitution. However, neither appears in the final draft.

3. Thomas Aquinas, for example, describes the character bestowed in baptism as a participation in the priestly office of Christ: *Summa theologiae* 3.63.3.

no role in Catholic ecclesiology after the Reformation. The term practically disappeared from the vocabulary of Catholic theology, since, according to the understanding of Catholic theology, it had been used by the Reformers in an anti-hierarchical sense. In this regard it was important that the Council of Trent rejected Luther's opinion that "all Christians are in the same way priests of the new covenant or that all are entrusted without differentiation with the same spiritual powers" (DS 1767 = NR 710). At the same time one must remember that the *Catechismus Romanus* speaks expressly of the priesthood of all believers.⁴

Through the influence of the liturgical movement this theme took on more importance again for Catholic theology.⁵ From the official side, the encyclical *Mediator Dei* (November 20, 1947) took up the theme of the universal priesthood of all believers, although with the caution that this must not be understood in an anti-hierarchical sense.⁶

Lumen gentium grounds the theme of general priesthood on Revelation 1:6 and 5:9-10. Also 1 Peter 3:4-10, on which Luther based himself in this connection, is quoted by the constitution.

Terminologically the constitution distinguishes "the priesthood of all believers" (*sacerdotium commune fidelium*) from "the priesthood of service or the hierarchical priesthood" (*sacerdotium ministeriale seu hierarchicum*). Each "participates in its distinctive way in the priesthood of Christ" and the two are "related to one another" (no. 10, 2). An important statement is added, which maintains that "the two differ in their essence, and not merely in their degree" (*essentia et non gradu*). The distinctive way each participates in the priesthood of Christ is described in the following terms:

> The priest by ordination [*sacerdos ministerialis*], through the holy power [*potestas*] which he possesses, builds up the priestly people and guides them; in the place of Christ [*in persona Christi*] he carries out the Eucharistic sacrifice and brings it forward in the name of the entire people; the believers on the other hand cooperate through the power of their royal priesthood in the Eucharistic offering, and exercise their priesthood through the reception of the sacraments, in prayer, in thanksgiving, in the witness of a holy life, in self-denial and in daily love. (Ibid.)

4. *Cat. Trid.* 2.7.284. The constitution bases itself upon the following New Testament texts: Rev 1:5; 1 Pet 2:5; Rom 12:1.

5. Here the following works should be cited: E. Mersch, *Morale et corps mystique* (Paris, 1941) 143-69; B. Botte and others, *Le sacerdoce des fidèles* (Louvain, 1946); P. Dabin, *Le sacerdoce royal des fideles*, vol. 1: *Daus les livres saints* (Paris, 1941); vol. 2: *Dans la tradition ancienne et moderne* (Paris, 1950); Congar, *Der Laie*, ch. 4, esp. 207ff.

6. DS 3849-53 = NR 721-23.

To the ordained priest a leadership role, as well as the function of presenting the sacrifice in the person of Christ, is attributed. The terms of the distinction *essentia et non gradu* derive from the address *Magnificate Dominum* by Pius XII (November 2, 1954). This address, as well as the encyclical *Mediator Dei*—both documents are quoted by the constitution—indicate what is meant by this expression.

The address counters attempts to characterize the person who occupies the office of priesthood as merely delegated by the people, or to speak of an undifferentiated "concelebration" of everyone taking part in the Eucharistic meal.[7] *Mediator Dei* has the same apologetic context; however, there the expression *essentia et non gradu* is not used.[8]

The substance of this address is that the person who occupies the office of priesthood through ordination has a particular power (*potestas*) which other baptized Christians do not have; for that reason one cannot simply refer to this person as the delegate of the people. Church authority is not derived from the community. At the same time, someone who holds office in the Church is not a Christian in some higher degree. This is the point of the passage from Augustine quoted by *Lumen gentium* (no. 32, 3): "For you I am a bishop; with you I am a Christian. The one has reference to position, the other to grace." In the words of Y. M. Congar: "The priesthood of ministry lies not at the level of the essential ontology of being a Christian, but at the level of *service*. It is a *functional* participation, which implicitly involves an ontological foundation, but at the level of a functional ontology."[9]

At the council there were various attempts to distinguish the universal priesthood of all believers from the ministerial priesthood; all were rejected by the commission in charge. It is the teaching of the council that

---

7. See *AAS* 46 (1954) 669.

8. The encyclical describes as errors the following opinions: (1) that the only priesthood present in the New Testament is that which extends to all the baptized; (2) that the people have true priestly power and that the priest carries on his office only "in persona ecclesiae" through the commission he has received from the community; (3) that it is better if the priests celebrate ("concelebrent") together with the people present, than if they confect the Eucharist privately ("privatim"), separated from the people (DS 3850 = NR 721). The theses of the encyclical: (a) "The priest officiates in the place of the people only because he represents the person of our Lord Jesus Christ" (DS 3850 = NR 721); "the unbloody sacrifice is the work of the priest alone, in the sense that he represents the person of Christ, not in the sense that he presents the persons of the faithful" (DS 3852 = NR 723). (b) "The rituals and prayers of the Eucharistic sacrifice express no less clearly that the confection of the Eucharist occurs through the priest together with the people" (DS 3851 = NR 722).

9. Y. M. Congar, "Quelques problèmes touchant les ministères," *NRTh* 93 (1971) 785-800 (here 790).

the universal priesthood is an authentic priesthood. Since both participate in different ways in the priesthood of Christ, one can speak of an analogy between the two.

The significance of this theme for a renewed ecclesiology as the council understands this becomes even clearer if we widen our perspective to include the discussion in section 12 of the constitution.

b. The Sense of the Faithful and the Charisms of the Christian People

Lumen gentium, no. 12, presents the participation of the entire people of God in the prophetic office of Christ:

> The totality of the faithful, who have received anointing from the Holy One (see 1 John 2:20), cannot err in the faith. And this particular characteristic reveals itself through the supernatural sense of the faith, when it expresses itself in a universal consensus in matters of faith and of customs 'from the bishops down to the last lay believer' [*Augustine*]. Specifically through this sense of the faithful, which is awakened and nourished by the Spirit of Truth, the people of God holds fast to the faith given at one time definitively to the saints (see Jude 3), under the leadership of the holy teaching office, in the true adherence to which it is no longer received as the word of men, but as truly the word of God (see 1 Thess 2:13).

By "sense of the faithful" a power (*facultas*) of the *entire* Church is understood, "through which it grasps in faith the transmitted revelation, so that it can distinguish between truth and error in matters of belief."[10] One of the most important discussions of the council, which absolutely must be kept in mind for a proper understanding of the ecclesiology of Vatican II, concentrates on this text.

The text takes it for granted that there is guidance by the teaching office: "under the guidance of the teaching office [*sub ductu Magisterii*]." The difference consists in the fact that first the entire people of God and their sense of the faith are emphasized: "The totality of the faithful cannot err in their faith."

Some of the Council Fathers criticized the text, saying it underappreciates the role of the hierarchy.

After the First Vatican Council the theology of the schools had normally placed first the *infallibilitas in docendo,* the infallibility in teaching, while the *infallibilitas in credendo,* the infallibility in belief, was usually presented as a simple deduction from the first.[11] Basing themselves on such

10. *Schema Constitutionis de Ecclesia* (Vatican, 1964) 46 = Acta Synod. 3/1, 199.

11. Congar, in *Der Laie,* 471 and note 168, has already pointed out the importance of this problem for all of ecclesiology. As authors who emphasize the infallibility *in*

an understanding, the conservative wing of Vatican II reacted against this text: the *sensus fidei* is exercised and realized by the teaching office, while the faithful believers should simply receive it passively. Only in this way, it was added, could one avoid the error of modernism[12] (according to which "the teaching Church had nothing more to do than to identify and sanction the consensus of opinions of the hearing Church" [DS 3406]).

Against this the commission pointed out that the best post-Tridentine theologians, in spite of the Reformation, saw no danger for the role of the hierarchy when one argued from the faithful toward the hierarchy, that is, from the infallibility *in credendo* toward the infallibility *in docendo*.[13]

In accord with this understanding the constitution *Dei verbum* speaks of the role of the community first and of the teaching office only second, not the other way around—as the conservative wing wished—when it treats of the development in our understanding of the apostolic deposit in the Church: "The understanding of revealed things and words grows through reflection and study by the faithful . . . through interior insight, which arises from spiritual experience, through the proclamation of those who, in solidarity with the successors to the bishop's office, have received the assured charism of the truth" (no. 8, 2).

In connection with the sense of the faithful of the entire people of God, the topic of charisms is taken up in no. 12, 2. By the word *charism* the council understands not only the free charisms which the Holy Spirit "imparts to individuals as he will" (1 Cor 12:11), but also the gifts which the people who hold an office in the Church receive through ordination: "In Paul, the term '*charisma*' has a wide meaning, which also, or rather principally includes the enduring offices [*officia*]."[14] The constitution insists

---

credendo, Congar quotes M. J. Scheeben, *Katholische Dogmatik,* vol. 1, *Erkenntnislehre* (Freiburg, 1948) nos. 11–14, esp. no. 102; J. V. Bainvel, *De magisterio et traditione* (Paris, 1905) no. 94. The main opposing opinion is represented by the following authors among others: L. Billot, *De ecclesia Christi* (Prato, 1903) 721; A. Tanquerez, *Sinopsis theol. dogm. fundamentalis* (Paris, 1925); L. Lercher, *Institutiones theologiae dogmaticae,* vol. 1 (Innsbruck, 1939) nos. 478 and 475.

12. "Infallibilitas passiva seu in credendo, ab activa tamquam effectus a causa oritur" (*Schema Constitutionis* 46 = Acta Synod. 3/1, 198). "Sensus fidei efficitur per Magisterium et passive accipitur a fidelibus. Ut praecaveatur 'instinctus' ad modum modernistarum, insistere oportet super munus Hierarchiae" (*Modi a Patribus conciliaribus propositi . . . II. De Populo Dei* [Vatican, 1964] 8 n. 30 = Acta Synod. 3/6, 971).

13. *Schema Constitutionis* 46 = Acta Synod. 3/1, 198. The work that stands in the background is G. Thils, *L'infaillibilité du peuple chrétien "in credendo." Notes de théologie posttridentine* (Paris-Louvain, 1963).

14. *Schema Constitutionis* 47 = Acta Synod. 3/1, 199.

that "the judgment about their [*the charisms*] authenticity and their proper use resides with those who have leadership in the Church." The same was also programmatically established in no. 7, 3: "Under these gifts the grace of the apostles streams out, whose authority in the Spirit also underlies the charismatics (see 1 Cor 14)."

In the chapter on the laity *Lumen gentium* establishes the principle that the laity, "participating in the priestly, prophetic, and royal offices of Christ in their own way, take part in the mission of the entire Christian people in the Church and in the world" (no. 31; the same in *AA* no. 2, 2). Here the council sets forth a principle that should be appreciated as calling for the coresponsibility of the entire people of God.

2. The Ecumenical Problem

In this context the Orthodox and Protestant positions should be sketched out, so that thereby the ecumenical problematic will become clearer.

a. The Orthodox Position[15]

Orthodox theologians of various orientations welcomed the development that took place within Catholic ecclesiology. *Lumen gentium,* no.

15. A selected Orthodox bibliography: N. Afanassieff, "The Ministry of the Laity in the Church," *ER* 10 (1957/58) 255–63; Afanassieff, *L'Église du Saint Esprit* (Paris, 1957); O. Clément, "Après Vatican II: Vers un dialogue théologique entre catholiques et orthodoxes," in *La pensée orthodoxe* (Paris) 2 (13) (1968) 39–52; P. Evdokimov, "Le sacerdoce royal, état charismatique du chrétien," in *Le mystère de l'Esprit Saint* (Tours, 1968) 111–40; A. Kallis, "Volk Gottes und Lehrautorität," *US* 32 (1977) 139–51; J. Karmiris, "Zur dogmatischen Konstitution über die Kirche," in D. Papandreou, ed., *Stimmen der Orthodoxie* (Vienna, 1969) 55ff.; H. Kotsonis, "Die Stellung der Laien innerhalb des kirchlichen Organismus," in P. Bratsiotis, ed., *Die orthodoxe Kirche in griechiscer sicht,* vol. 2 (Stuttgart, 1960) 92–116; G. Larenzakis, "Die dogmatische Begründung der Synodalität und der Gremialität," in *Konziliarität und Kollegialität,* Pro Oriente 4 (Innsbruck-Vienna, 1975) 64–69; J. Meyendorff, "Die Lehrautorität in der Tradition der orthodoxen Kirche," *Conc* 12 (1976) 426ff.; N. Nissiotis, "L'unité du laicat et du clergé dans la tradition orthodoxe," *VC* 18 (1964) 162–67; J. Zizioulas, "Priesteramt und Priesterweihe im Licht der östlichen orthodoxen Theologie," in H. Vorgrimler, ed., *Amt und Ordination in ökumenischer sicht,* Der priesterliche Dienst 5 (Freiburg, 1973) 72–113. Presentations of Orthodox positions: M. M.ª Garijo-Guembe, "La conciliaridad eclesial. Aspectos sobre el 'Pueblo de Dios' in la teologia ortodoxa actual," *Lumen* (Victoria) 19 (1970) 438–63; Garijo-Guembe, "La naturaleza del ministerio sacerdotal in la teologia ortodoxa moderna," in *Teologia del sacerdocio,* vol. 12 (Burgos, 1980) 207–36; H. Marot, "Erste Reaktionen auf die Dekrete des 2. Vatikanischen Konzils von orthodoxer Bedeutung," *Conc* 2 (1966) 298ff.; B. Schultze, "Die byzantinische-slawische Theologie über den Dienst der Laien und der Kirche," *OstKSt* 5 (1956) 243–84.

12, was especially appreciated. Several authors have compared this text with that of the Orthodox patriarchs who in 1848 responded to an encyclical of Pope Pius IX with the following words: "For us neither patriarchs nor synods can introduce anything new, for the defender of the confession of belief is the body of the Church, that is, the people themselves, who seek to maintain their belief forever unchanged and the same as that of their fathers."[16]

Orthodox theology, especially that of Russian stamp, speaks of conciliarity or *Sobornost:* there is an organic and ontological connection between the hierarchy and the people of God. This connection can be described in the following way: First, the hierarchy must be seen *within* the Church, and not *over* the Church.[17] Second, the hierarchy acts not only *in persona Christi,* but also *in persona ecclesiae.* The hierarchy must never operate *ex sese,* that is, by itself, but rather always *ex consensu ecclesiae,* that is, in organic relationship with the Church. This is the position of G. Florovsky, P. Evdokimov, and many others.[18] It is worthy of

16. Mansi 40:407C = J. Karmiris, *Dogmatica et symbolica monumenta orthodoxae ecclesiae* (Graz, 1968) 2:920 (1000).

17. Y. M. Congar, *Ministères et communion ecclésiale* (Paris, 1971) 198f. (the article was written in 1969 as a preparation for the synod of bishops) writes in my opinion correctly: "The urgent problem of ecumenical theology as well as of Catholic ecclesiology consists in thinking and showing that the 'above' does not destroy the 'in,' but rather includes it in itself. . . . In this way Catholic ecclesiology would respond to one of the deepest demands of the East, one that rests upon a Christian and critical ontology, and lies beneath the encumbrances of a Slavic tendency toward over-systematization." One of the best reflections on the position of A. Chomjakov is that of Congar, *Der Laie,* 447ff.

18. G. Florovsky, "Le Corps du Christ vivant," in *La sainte Église universelle* (Neuchâtel-Paris, 1948) 9–57 (here 38f., 50, and 52) writes: "Of course the authority of the Ordo belongs to the bishops, and the administration of the sacraments is restricted to ordained officials. And this authority and this power to administer does not arise from the people, but comes from above. . . . Thus officials exercise their office *in persona Christi* on the basis of a specific charism. However, this sacramental power is given to them for the Church, for the faithful, in the sense that they are part of the faithful, established as their shepherds. In this sense the officials also operate *in persona ecclesiae.* Truthfully, these two aspects, Christ and the Church, cannot be separated. . . . Authority and priesthood are in the Church, not above or outside the Church. . . . The truth is protected by the entire body (that is, by the community); the priesthood is only to give a reliable, authentic witness to this. The authenticity of its witness rests upon the charismatic continuity of the Church, which is directly assured through the hierarchical succession. The *potestas magisterii* is fundamentally nothing other than the power to give witness, and therefore it is limited by the nature and the content of the truth that is its reference. For that reason this ordinary teaching authority should be exercised never *ex sese,* but rather always *ex consensu ecclesiae.*" There are similar statements in P. Evdokimov, *L'orthodoxie* (Neuchâtel-Paris, 1959)

note that these Orthodox authors apply to the hierarchy the terminology used by the First Vatican Council for the definition of the pope, but in the opposite sense. Third, the Orthodox theologians quote as an axiom the words of Cyprian: *"episcopus in ecclesia"* and *"ecclesia in episcopo"* or *"nihil sine consilio vestro* [that is, of the presbyter] *et sine consensu plebis mea privatim sententia gerere."*

The rejection by the people of the union with Rome that was agreed to in Florence in 1439 by the Orthodox bishops is a difficult problem for Orthodox theology. A. Chomjakov developed the theory that reception by the people of God is necessary for the validity of the decisions of an ecumenical council; however, this theory has not established itself within Orthodox theology. Still, the problematic that Chomjakov sketches plays an important role even with those authors who distance themselves from his position. For example, the Greek theologian P. N. Trembelas writes: since "the history of the Church shows that not every synod of bishops ('even when they are canonically convened') has the assurance of the truth and is not free from error," and since "the tradition of the Church is the active possession of the Church as a whole," the endorsement by the people of God is "an essential, most official, and indefeasible witness of its [the synod's] sacred character," that is, that we are dealing with an authentic synod. Against the propositions of A. Chomjakov, Trembelas adds: "Their recognition . . . through the ecclesial *'pleroma'* does not refer to a recognition of the conciliar decisions, such that without this they would not be valid."[19]

b. The Position of the Reformation[20]

In a polemic against the understanding developed during the Middle Ages of priestly office, Luther and with him the other Reformers stressed

---

160, 163f.; N. Afanassieff, "L'Infallibilité de l'Église du point de vue d'un théologien orthodoxe," in *L'infallibilité de L'Église* (Chevetogne, 1963) 199. For his part, J. Zizioulas writes: "No authority may place itself outside the community or over it, as if it were an individual or ontological property" ("L'Eucharistie," in *L'Eucharistie* [Tours, 1970] 48).

19. P. Trembelas, *Dogmatique de L'Église Orthodoxe Catholique,* vol. 2 (Chevetogne, 1967) 434. Similar positions were defended already by Chr. Androutsos, *Dogmatiké tes Orthodoxou Anatolikes Ekklesias* (Athens, 1956; first ed. 1907) 280. See G. Larentzakis, "Die dogmatische Begründung," 67, which St. Harkianakis, *Perí ta altheton tes Ekklesias en te orthodoxo theologia* (Athens, 1965) 148f. quotes (in Greek) to make clear that the majority of (Greek!) Orthodox theologians reject the theory of *Sobernost.*

20. Bibliography: P. Althaus, *Die theologie M. Luthers* (Gütersloh, 1963) 279ff.; E. Kinder, *Der evangelische Glaube und die Kirche* (Berlin, 1960) 146–64; H. Schütte,

the universal priesthood of all baptized Christians. All believers are *con-sacerdotes* with Christ; that is what Christ has obtained for us.[21]

According to P. Althaus, Luther follows two lines of argumentation concerning the foundation of the office: one "from below" and one "from above," without the two forming for Luther a contradiction. On the one hand, Luther grounds this office starting from the general priesthood of all baptized Christians: all Christians, in virtue of their priesthood, are empowered and called to service in word and sacrament. So that no confusion may result, the community entrusts the *public* service to a single person, who carries out this duty in the name of the Church.[22] "Thereby occurs a delegation of the authority which the entire community and each person has, to one person, whom it chooses out of its own ranks."[23] The difference between the one who occupies the office and the other members of the community lies purely on the level of service: *"a laico nihil differat nisi ministerio."*[24] On the other hand the fullness of authority of the office is grounded in its institution by Christ: the power to preach is "called, grounded, and supervised" by God.[25] Althaus summarizes his interpretation in the following way: "The particular office to which one is called out of the community of the general priesthood for Luther has no other substance and also no other authority than the priesthood of all the others."[26]

Other interpretations mention a change in Luther on this point. In the writings from 1519–23 the office seems to be derived more from the universal priesthood, while later Luther emphasizes more strongly its divine institution.

On the question of offices, since the nineteenth century there has been an academic dispute among Lutheran theologians. "For one group spiritual office is a concretizing of the general service to which the Church as a whole is commissioned, with special attention to proclamation and

---

Amt, Ordination, Sukzession (Düsseldorf, 1974) chs. 6–8 (here the positions of several contemporary Protestant dogmatists are presented: ch. 6, Lutheran theology; ch. 7, Reformed theology); W. Stein, *Das kirchliche Amt bei Luther* (Wiesbaden, 1974); J. Rohls, *Theologie reformierter Bekenntnisschriften* (Göttingen, 1987) 282ff.; A. Ganoczy, *Ecclesia ministrans. Dienende Kirche und kirchlicher Dienst bei Calvin* (Freiburg, 1968) 195ff.

21. WA 7:57.

22. "Aliud enim est ius publice exequi, aliud iure in necessitate uti: publice exequi non licet, nisi consensu universitatis seu Ecclesiae. In necessitate utatur quicunque voluerit" (WA 12:189).

23. Althaus, *Die Theologie*, 280.

24. WA 6:657.

25. WA 50:647. See also WA 30 II, 598; 37, 192, and 269 among others.

26. Althaus, *Die Theologie*, 281.

the administration of the sacraments; the others stress the direct foundation of Church offices in the commissioning of the apostles. . . . There
is room for both orientations in the Church of the Augsburg Confession."[27]

At the same time, the opinion has been presented that the office does
not devolve from the universal priesthood. "The authority of the office
should not be understood as delegated from the community";[28] "the
office as a divine institution is not a delegation of the community, even
when this has been entrusted to the Church."[29]

For the meaning of offices and their relation to the community, the
Malta report of 1972 established "that the office, besides standing within
the community, also stands over against the community."[30] This formulation, which was represented in the document by both Roman Catholic
and Lutheran theologians, has been taken over in other ecumenical documents.[31] "Over against the community" means that the office, in virtue
of the call through the Church and thereby in virtue of the commission
by Christ, represents Christ in the proclamation of the Word and in the
administration of the sacraments. The "in" here orients the ecclesiological problem in the direction of an ecclesiology based on *koinonia* and synodality. "[This fullness of authority] is rather an authority with the
commission to service in the community and for the community. For that
reason the exercise of the authority of this office should include the participation of the entire community. . . . The Christian liberty, brotherhood, and responsibility of the entire Church and of all its members must
find its expression in conciliar, collegial, and synodal structures within
the Church."[32]

"This relation between the 'in' and the 'over' characterizing office and
ecclesial community is constitutive of the proper teaching about office and

27. *Kirchengemeinschaft in Wort und Sakrament.* Bilaterale Arbeitsgruppe der Deutschen Bischofskonferenz und der Kirchenleitung der VELKD (Paderborn-Hannover,
1984) no. 61.

28. Gemeinsame römisch-katholische/evangelisch-lutherische Kommission, *Das
geistliche Amt in der Kirche,* no. 23, in DwÜ, 337.

29. *Kirchengemeinschaft in Wort und Sakrament,* nos. 61 and 60; The distinctive
ecclesial authority "is a divine establishment; thus it does not grow out of an ulterior
arrangement or appointment of the Church."

30. *Das Evangelium und die Kirche,* no. 50, in DwÜ, 261.

31. *Das geistliche Amt in der Kirche,* no. 23, in DwÜ, 337; *Kirchengemeinschaft
in Wort und Sakrament,* no. 62; *Evangelium-Sakramente-Amt und die Einheit der
Kirche,* eds. K. Lehrmann and E. Schlink (Freiburg-Göttingen, 1982) 188 (*Gemeinsame Erklärung des Arbeitskreises: Zeichen der Einheit der Kirche,* in connection with
CA 6.2).

32. *Das geistliche Amt in der Kirche,* no. 24, in DwÜ, 337.

its correct exercise according to the gospel. The community is directed to solidarity with the apostolic office; at the same time the office must be received by the ecclesial community."[33]

The contemporary institution of synods, in which not only office-holders but also lay personnel take part, is a development of the nineteenth century under the influence of secular categories.[34] Originally the Lutheran Church recognized only the synod of pastors. The Augsburg Confession states: "*Ecclesiae apud nos docent.*"[35] "The subject of '*docere*' are those who hold Church office. . . . Following that, for the Augsburg Confession there is an institution founded upon a *ius divinum* that decides on what belongs to true gospel proclamation and the correct administration of the sacraments. We would call this institution a 'synod,' which is responsible to the office holders, but at which also *persons who are not ordained may be present.*"[36]

The mutual reciprocity[37] of office and community, whereby "both belong together and need one another,"[38] belongs, in the Lutheran conviction, to the essential principle of the Church: "No single office is constituted by itself as a successor to the apostles, without the communication and cooperation of the entire Church."[39] This theme goes together with the problem of apostolic succession (see below chap. XII, part 5).

3. Theological Reflection

Some of the most important ecclesiological pronouncements of Vatican II are located in the second chapter of the Constitution on the Church. Here we wish to give a foundation for these statements. This reflection, which includes aspects of exegesis as well as the history of dogma, has three moments: first a general clarification, then a reflection on participation in the priestly office of Christ, and finally a reflection on participation in the prophetic office of Christ. These three moments should be understood as a unity, that is, as elements that complement and complete one another.

a. Foundations

For the relation between community and office the New Testament texts that speak of the priesthood of the *entire* community, that is, of the

33. *Gemeinsame Erklärung des Arbeitskreises* 4, 2, 188.
34. See R. Bäumlin, "Synode," in RGG 6:569–71.
35. CA 1, in BSLK 50.
36. Thus P. Brunner, "Remarks on the Conference by W. Kasper," in *Evangelium-Sakramente-Amt,* 131.
37. Kinder, *Der evangelische Glaube,* 160.
38. P. Althaus, *Die christliche Wahrheit* (Gütersloh, 1966) 510.
39. W. Pannenberg, *Thesen zur Theologie der Kirche* (München, 1974) these 111.

priesthood of *each* baptized Christian, are without special significance, for they only emphasize what concerns everyone, without making a distinction between the various members of the community.

The elements that must be kept in mind were already exhaustively presented in chapter V. Here is a summary:

According to the history of the apostles, the relation between the apostles and their communities were such that one could write: "The apostles and the elders made their decisions together with the entire community" (Acts 15:22).

Paul is certainly conscious of his authority over the community. In spite of that, he will not act in isolation from the community.

The structure of charisms in the Pauline community, whose model is Corinth, as well as the community structure in Antioch, which in this respect was similar to the Pauline communities, shows that all the community members had a coresponsibility, each in their own way, in the Church.

Matthew 28:18, a text in which the commissioning of the apostles by Jesus Christ is described and in which a sort of "community structure" is transmitted, shows the basic organic connection between the apostles and the communities.

The Pastoral Letters stress the decisive role of the offices for the preservation of the apostolic tradition. Although these communities were originally Pauline, the charismatic structure of the Church now falls into the background or disappears altogether. Catholic theology has typically—and shall we say one-sidedly—based itself on this understanding of the Pastoral Letters in order to justify its conception of the offices. However, we should not forget that 1 Peter, a text that falls equally within the borders of an originally Pauline community or arose in contact with one, presents a synthesis of the role of the presbyter (5:1-4) and the role of the charisms (4:10-11), so that both elements, the officeholder and the services of all community members, are viewed as completing and complementing one another. In other words, the role of the officeholder includes rather than excludes the operations of the other Christians and their coresponsibility.

Through these elements the significance of the universal priesthood for life in a community that is hierarchically structured can be concretely laid out. It is a matter of a complementary connection between both elements.

The function of office, already emphasized in the New Testament, shows itself clearly in the Church's answer to the Gnostic movement. Specifically, the old Church orthodoxy sees the officeholder as the witness of the authentic apostolic Tradition. The lists of successors to which Irenaeus and Tertullian among others refer are intended to show that a community and its teaching stand in continuity with the apostolic Tradition.

During discussions in the Churches, the officeholders immediately came to the forefront, certainly as witnesses and to that extent as representatives of the community. The synods of bishops (and the later so-called ecumenical councils) should be understood in this perspective. Here the *charisma veritatis certum* of the bishops, of which Irenaeus speaks, is mirrored.[40] The spirit of the old Churches with regard to the relation between office and community is clearly and simply laid out by Cyprian. "Since the beginning of my tenure as bishop I have made it a rule for myself not to decide something according to my personal counsel, without requesting the opinion of you priests and deacons, and without consulting my entire people." "I must make myself familiar with these specific cases and carefully consider the solution, not only with my fellow bishops, but also with my entire people."[41]

Before ordination a candidate had to present his belief to the community.[42] Because the bishop had specific responsibility for this community, he was the first to verify the apostolic foundation for his belief. This element has remained the same down to today. It is in this light that we should understand the fact that Eusebius of Caesarea gave his community an account of why he had endorsed the confession of faith of Nicaea.[43]

For the historical description of the connection between community and office, and therefore of the role of the teaching office, the Arian crisis plays a significant role. John Henry Newman emphasizes that "the dogma of Nicaea was maintained during the greater part of the 4th century: 1. not because of the unchanging steadfastness of the Holy See, the councils, or the bishops, but 2. through the *consensus fidelium.*'"[44] Even when this interpretation requires some nuancing, it still may be said that through the Arian crisis a perspective became clear that casts into sharper

40. *Adv. Haer.* 4.26.2.

41. *Ep.* 14.4 and 34.4. Both texts are quoted from the document "Einheit vor uns" (Paderborn-Frankfurt, 1985; 65 note 160) of the United Roman Catholic/Evangelical Lutheran Commission.

42. *Constitutiones Apostolorum* 3, in F. X. Funk, *Didascalia et Constitutiones Apostolorum 1* (Paderborn, 1905) 77f.

43. PG 20:1536-44.

44. J. H. Newman, "On Consulting the Faithful in Matters of Doctrine," in *The Rambler* (July 1859) 198-230 (here 214) = Newman, *Polemische Schriften,* Ausg. Werke 4 (Mainz, 1959) 255-94 (here 273). E. Schillebeeckx has a similar position: "Das Problem der Amtsunfehlbarkeit," *Conc* 9 (1973) 198-209 (here 205). J. Lebreton has another interpretation in "Le désaccord de la foi populaire et de la théologie savante dans l'Église chrétienne du IIIe siecle," *RHE* 19 (1923) 481-506 and 20 (1924) 5-37. Lebreton does not distinguish between the faithful and the hierarchy, as Newman does, but between the faith of the people and the speculations of the theologians. Congar follows him in *Der Laie,* 465 note 66.

relief than traditional Catholic theology the connection between community and officeholder.

b. Sharing in Christ's Priestly Office

In the New Testament the priestly categories are only used to apply to the people of God as a whole (1 Pet 2:5, 9; Rev 1:6; 5:10; 20:6), and never for an office. The usual term for office is *diakonia,* "service."

The term used in 1 Peter 2:5—*pneumatikas thysias,* or "spiritual offering"—should be understood in light of the general use of cultic terminology in the New Testament.[45]

Latreuein/latreia is the term used for apostolic service (Rom 1:9) or for the lives of Christians for God (Rom 12:1; Phil 3:3; Heb 12:28).

The priestly office of Christ is referred to by *leitourgia/leitourgein* (Heb 8:6). The term is also used for Christians. Philippians 2:17 speaks of the *thysia* and *leitourgia* of the faith; that is, the life in faith of Christians is understood as an offering and a sacrifice. Paul names himself a *hiereus* of the gospel and understands his function of proclaiming the gospel in a priestly way, for through the acceptance of the gospel the heathen becomes an offering (*prosphora*) to God (Rom 15:16).

The term *thysia,* used for the sacrifice of Jesus Christ (Eph 5:2; Heb 9:23, 26), is also used for Christians, who should present their entire lives to God (Rom 12:1; Phil 2:17; and 1 Pet 2:5). In Philippians 4:18 the alms are referred to as a sacrifice.

Thus the terminology of offering is primarily used for the lives of Christians in the faith. Paul exhorts the believers to bring *themselves* forward as a living and holy sacrifice; that should be their spiritual worship (Rom 12:1). At no point is the Eucharistic celebration specifically described with a term indicating sacrifice. However, since the Christian life can never be separated from the Eucharistic celebration, it should not be excluded that such terminology can equally be invoked for the formal Christian cult.[46]

Although office in the New Testament is never described with priestly categories, Paul uses such terminology for his own apostolate, as Romans 15:15-16 shows clearly—2 Corinthians 5:18, 20 and Philippians 2:17 should also be considered here—so that one may speak of "indications of a priestly vocabulary" in the New Testament.[47]

45. Bibliography: S. Lyonnet, "La nature du culte dans le NT," in *La liturgie après Vatican II,* Unam sanctam 66 (Paris, 1967) 357–84 (esp. 368ff.); H. Schlier, *Die Zeit der Kirche,* ch. 7; H. Schürmann, "Neutestamentliche Marginalien zur Frage der 'Entsakralisierung,' " *SEELS* 38 (1968) 38–48, 89–100 (esp. 43ff.).

46. Lyonnet, *La nature,* 378.

47. Rapport de la Commission internationale de Théologie, *Le Ministère sacerdotal* (Paris, 1971) 71. See the Lima Document on authority, no. 17, in DwÜ, 572.

We find a sacrificial terminology for the Eucharist and a priestly terminology for office only in post-New Testament writings. Clement of Rome
describes the activity of the officeholder as *prospherein ta dora,* that is,
as bringing forward the gifts.[48] Ignatius of Antioch strongly emphasizes
the connection between bishop and altar.[49] Justin characterizes the Eucharist without any hesitation as a sacrifice (an offering of praise) and
stresses the role of the presider during the *prospherein.*[50] These witnesses
from the end of the first and the first half of the second centuries suggest
what is to be found fully expressed in the first ordination formulary for
bishops to come down to us from the *Traditio apostolica* of Hippolytus:
the presider prays that the bishop-candidate may receive the *pneuma
hegemonikon* and the *pneuma archieratikon,* that is, the spirit of leadership and the spirit of the high priest's charism. Through ordination a
special spiritual gift is bestowed upon the candidate.[51] In this way a fundamental difference between the bishop, including his presbyters, on the one
hand and the community on the other is described.

The question whether a Eucharistic celebration would be possible
without an ordained minister would not have been understood by this
Church. The Eucharistic celebration was the celebration of the community, in which everyone in their own way concelebrated. The bishop pronounced the high prayer alone, the presbyters were silent, and the entire
community sealed everything with an "Amen." The *ekklesia* itself was
the integral subject of the liturgical-Eucharistic transaction.[52] This is witnessed by numerous passages from the Church Fathers and liturgists.
Throughout the liturgy collective and communitarian expressions were

48. *1 Clem.* 44.4, ed. J. A. Fischer, *Die apostolischen Väter* (München, 1981) 80.
As an introductory bibliography: J. Martin, *Die Genese des Amtspriestertums in der
frühen Kirche,* Der priesterliche Diesnt 3 (Freiburg, 1972); K. S. Frank, "Zum Opfer-
verständnis in der Alten Kirche," in *Das Opfer Jesu Christi und seine Gegenwart in
der Kirche,* eds. K. Lehmann and E. Schlink (Freiburg-Göttingen, 1983) 40-50.

49. For example, *Phil.* 4: "Be therefore mindful to constitute *the one* Eucharist—
for one is the flesh of our Lord Jesus Christ, and one is the cup to be joined with
his blood, one the altar of sacrifice, just as one the bishop together with his presbyters"
(Fischer, 197); *Trall.* 7.2: "Whoever is within the space of the altar is pure; whoever
is outside the altar space is not pure, that is, whoever does something without bishop,
a presbyterate, and deacons, that person is not pure in conscience" (Fischer, 177).

50. *1 Ap.* 67. See also *Dial.* 41.3 and 117. Justin speaks of the thanksgiving over
the bread and cup as of the sacrifice which Jesus Christ commanded the Christian
community to offer up.

51. *Traditio apostolica* 3, ed. B. Botte, *La tradition apostolique de s. Hippolyte*
(Münster, 1963) 8.

52. The title mentioned in the bibliography of the work by Congar, *L'ecclesia,* which
basically I am following.

used: *"nos offerimus," "offerunt," "Ecclesia offert," "celebrant."* In the epicleses of the Eastern Church the plural is also used; this is a sign that the entire community of believers actively celebrated the liturgy.[53] Gregory the Great (d. 604) reports that the priests of the community of Saint Pancratius often did not come to the church on Sunday, so that the disappointed faithful had to return to their homes without a liturgy. The terminology is important: The faithful had come in order to concelebrate the mysteries (*missarum solemnia celebraturi*). According to the handwriting, a later editor altered the text, changing *celebraturi* to *audituri,* that is, "to *hear* a mass."[54] As late as the twelfth century the following text could be found in the Western tradition: "The priest does not all by himself offer [*sacrificat*] and consecrate, but with him the entire community of the faithful who are present consecrates and offers."[55]

The fundamental conviction of the entire patristic tradition is that the minister exercises his office in the celebration of the sacrament in the name of Christ (*in persona Christi*).[56] An expression of this conviction is the fact that the words of institution, which at the time of the canon of Hippolytus were understood as the foundation for the thanksgiving of the Christian community, were later viewed as *consecrating* words, that is, as words which the minister speaks in the name of Christ. Various factors have contributed to the fact that the conception of the patristic Church, with its ecclesiological presuppositions, has been almost entirely forgotten. One of these factors is the emphasis placed on the consecrating power of the priest.

In the West, two texts have taken on a classical status. The deacon Florus of Lyons (d. ca. 860) comments on the *"qui tibi offerunt"* in the Roman canon in the following way. "The priests of the Church offer. Through them and in them [*per ipsos et in ipsis*] the entire Church presents the praise-offering. That which is actualized distinctively [*proprie*] through the service of the priests, occurs in general through the belief and devotion of all [*fide et devotione cunctorum*]."[57] Innocent III (d. 1216) writes: "The priests offer, but yet all the faithful: for what is brought about specifically [*specialiter*] through the ministry of the priest occurs in

53. The Orthodox theologians Afanassieff and Evdokimov (see note 15) both refer to these facts.

54. PL 77:867.

55. Geric d'Igny: PL 185:87.

56. The *Western* Church Fathers: Cyprian, *Ep.* 63.15; Ambrose, De Mysteriis 54; Augustine, *Ep.* 89.5; De baptismo 6. *Eastern* Church Fathers: Theodore of Mopsuestia, *Cat. Homil.* 15.24; John Chrysostom, *Hom. 17 ad Hebr.:* PG 63:131; *In Levit.* 9, 22; PG 93:89; Narsai, *Hom.* 18.

57. PL 119:47f.

general through the assent of the faithful.''[58] If this *proprie et specialiter* is emphasized and the question of what is necessary for the validity of a sacrament is raised, as Scholastic theology did, then the following answer may be expected: the faithful contribute nothing, for strictly speaking the validity depends exclusively on the ministerial authority, which only the priest possesses.[59] This answer clearly indicates that the minister is seen as separate from the community. This would be avoided if it were emphasized that the minister exercises his office *in persona ecclesiae.*[60] Thomas Aquinas sees no difficulty in saying that the minister of the sacrament exercises his office *in persona ecclesiae,* since he is a minister of the Church.[61] The *in persona Christi* should not be seen in isolation from the *in persona ecclesiae.*

The question frequently posed in recent times, whether a Eucharistic celebration would be valid without the presence of any ordained officials, is often answered only in legal categories, without any consideration for the ontological connection between office and community.[62] Should the case arise that a Eucharistic celebration might be possible without an official, one should emphasize that such a celebration can in no way take place against the office; that is, if the possibility exists, it does so only in emergency situations.[63] Since the Eucharistic celebration should be regarded as the center of the life of the community (see chap. VIII), the community has a fundamental right to an official, so that it can properly celebrate the Eucharist.[64] The pastoral principle of the Church (*salus animarum,* "the care of souls") demands fundamentally that no human or Church

58. PL 217:845D. This text is quoted in the encyclical *Mediator Dei:* DS 3851 = NR 722.

59. Thus Congar, *L'ecclesia,* 277.

60. See B. D. Marliangeas, *Clés pour une théologie du ministère. In persona Christi. In persona ecclesiae* (Paris, 1978); Marliangeas, " 'In persona Christi,' 'In persona Ecclesiae,' " in *La liturgie apres Vatican II,* Unam sanctam 66 (Paris, 1967) 283–88; Y. Congar, "Ein Mittler," in Gemeinsame römisch-katholische/evangelische-lutherische Kommission, *Das Geistliche Amt,* (Paderborn-Frankfurt a. M., 1981) 127–34; H. Legrand and J. Vilström, "Die Zulassung der Frau zum Amt," ibid. 102–26 (here 115ff.).

61. *Summa theologiae* 3.64.8. ad 2; 3.64.9. ad 1; 3.82.6. But in 3.82.7. ad 3, Thomas changes the "in persona Christi," in whose name the priest consecrates, to the "in persona Ecclesiae."

62. Representatives of the theologians who have raised this question are the following: H. Küng, *Die Kirche* (Freiburg, 1967) 520ff.; L. Boff, *Die Neuentdeckung der Kirche,* (Mainz, 1983) 100–09 (with an excellent bibliography). See also Y. M. Congar, "Quelques problèmes touchant les ministères," *NRTh* 93 (1971) 794.

63. W. Kasper raises this in *Conc* 5 (1969) 169.

64. See J. Blank, P. Hünermann, and P. M. Zulehner, *Das Recht der Gemeinde auf Eucharistie* (Trier, 1978) especially Hünermann's work.

law, such as that concerning the celibacy of the minister in the Latin rite, form an obstacle to the concrete realization of this right of the community.

In summary we may say: office and community, or, in the words of *Lumen gentium,* the universal priesthood and the ministerial priesthood, that is, the hierarchical priesthood, are allied and coordinate. The participation of the priest and the participation of all the baptized faithful in the priesthood of Christ are two different things. That is what the difference *essentia et non tantum gradu* means. Since both types of priesthood are allied with one another, one should not see office as isolated from the community. It would be an erroneous conception of the office and of priestly spirituality to see the official as a super-Christian.

c. Sharing in Christ's Prophetic Office

Lumen gentium treats the prophetic character of the people of God under two aspects: that of the sense of the faithful and the anointing of all believers, and that of the outpouring of the Spirit of God over the entire people of God and the sharing in the gifts of the Spirit (charisma).

The same Spirit who was poured out on the apostles at Pentecost was and is given to each believer through baptism (Acts 2:38, 39). The fulfillment of God's promise proclaimed by the prophets takes place not only with the apostles, but with the entire people of God.

As it warns us against false prophets, 1 John 2:20-27—the text is quoted by *Lumen gentium*—invokes as a criterion for the confession of Christ the interior norm of faith: every Christian has received an anointing from God and is therefore in a position to withstand error. The anointing is a work of God through his Spirit within the believer, an inner illumination through the Holy Spirit. Paul refers to this working of the Spirit when he speaks of the charisms.

The constitution bases its confidence that the Church remains in the truth on this working of the Spirit in the entire community, the Spirit who leads the Church into the truth (see John 16:13). The truth is experienced by the community as *communio.*

"Sensus fidelium"[65] *and the Teaching Office.* In the patristic literature the term *sensus fidelium* played a special role as an expression of the

---

65. Bibliography: Congar, *Der Laie,* 530ff. (on the Church Fathers); M. Seckler, "Glaubenssinn," in LThK 4:945-48; W. Beinert, "Bedeutung und Begründung des Glaubenssinnes (*sensus fidei*) als ein dogmatisches Erkenntniskriterium," *Conc* 25 (1971) 217-303 (with bibliography); M. Löhrer, "Träger der Vermittlung," in MySal 1 (1965) 547-55; M. D. Koster, "Der Glaubenssinn der Hirten und Gläubigen," in Koster, *Volk Gottes im Werden* (Mainz, 1971) 131-50 (with important references to the history of theology); H. Vorgrimler, "Vom 'sensus fidelium' zum 'consensus fidelium,' " *Conc* 21 (1985) 237-42.

belief of the Church and of the tradition lived by the Church. Y. M. Congar summarizes the fundamental ideas of the Fathers under the following two principal arguments:

"1. If someone declines to believe as the entire Church believes, he implicitly declares the belief of an entire people to be in vain; however, this is impossible.

2. Demonstrations on behalf of a doctrine that devolves from the concrete practice and the belief of the community."[66]

The theme "a belief of the universal community of the Church" is encountered frequently in Catholic theology, especially in authors within the Augustinian tradition. The Council of Trent opposed the new doctrines of the Reformers by referring to the understanding of the entire Church, for example, in the Decree on the Eucharist: "Thus have all our forefathers, who lived in the true Church of Christ, openly believed"; the Reformers' interpretation is "opposed to the universal understanding of the Church" (DS 1637 = NR 569). Pius IX and Pius XII refer to the *sensus ecclesiae* as a justification for the dogmas concerning Mary.[67]

The teaching office is based upon the *sensus ecclesiae,* to the extent that it is an expression of the apostolic tradition living within the Church. For that reason, every member of the Church is dependent upon this *sensus ecclesiae.* The ecclesial teaching office is a *listening* Church with reference both to the normative apostolic proclamation and to the growth of tradition.

The Catholic conception thereby contains a special difficulty: the teaching office authentically teaches something that has been delivered to the entire community of believers. It clarifies something that belongs to the entirety of the community. A portion of the Church, the teaching office, is appointed as the clarifying agent for what the totality lives and passes on. Naturally, Holy Scripture remains throughout the *norma normans,* against which the *sensus ecclesiae* must be constantly tested.

The teaching office is to critically interpret and to test the presented charisms. It must be open to any incursions of the Spirit, wherever they may occur in the Church.

The word *charism* should not remain an abstract word in the Church. We should recall here a passage from *Lumen gentium* that is often for-

66. Congar, *Der Laie,* 530f.

67. Pius IX: The bishops "scripto significarent, quae esset suorum fidelium erga Inmaculatam Conceptionem pietas ac devotio, et quid ipsi praesertim Antistites de hoc ipsa definitione ferenda sentirent": Bull "Ineffabilis Deus" (8 December 1854), in Pii IX, Acta 1/1, p. 97ff. Pius XII: "Haec singularis catholicorum Antistitum et fidelium conspiratio . . . cum concordem Nobis praebeat ordinari Magisterium doctrinam, concordem inquam christiani populi fidem, quam idem Magisterium sustinet ac dirigit": Bull "Munificentissimus Deus," in *AAS* 42 (1950) 768.

gotten: the bishops "can judge more exactly and better with the help of the experiences of the lay community in both spiritual and secular matters" (no. 37, 3). In this text the reciprocity of bishop and laity is concretized. Through this intermingling the essential ecclesiological term *communio* may also be clarified.

Laity and Officials in the Proclamation of the Word. Prophetic participation in the office of Christ has its concrete expression in the proclamation of the Word of God. As to what is specific to the office with reference to the Word, one must distinguish various levels.

To the extent that preaching is a *kerygmatic exhortation,* that person will be the better preacher who lives more in grace and the Spirit. Accordingly, a lay person—a man or a woman—could perhaps preach better than the pope himself.

To the extent that preaching is *proclamation of the belief of the Church,* and to the extent that it requires specific theological knowledge, perhaps a lay theologian could preach better than an official.

If these two principal statements are taken into consideration, then the question arises about the characteristic relation between office and the proclamation of the Word. K. Rahner has answered this question in the following manner: "The priest is one who has been appointed by the entire Church to a specific community as the official proclaimer of the Word of God, in such a way that the highest sacramental degrees of this Word are bestowed upon him. Simply expressed, he is the proclaimer of the gospel in the mission and name of the Church."[68]

According to CIC 1983 (canon 767, 1), the homily is reserved to a priest or deacon, since it is itself part of the liturgy. The laity may be allowed to preach in a church only outside the context of a Eucharistic celebration (canon 766). Noteworthy is the foundation on which this canon rests, specifically the Constitution on the Sacred Liturgy, in which the homily is described as "part of the liturgical matter" (no. 35, 2; see also no. 52).

Lay preaching in the context of the Mass must remain an exception, if one does not wish to underestimate the importance of preaching in comparison with the celebration of the sacrament. The official is ordained with reference both to the proclamation of the Word and to the celebration of the sacrament. Of course, his function must be seen in its ontological connection with the community; therefore, lay preaching in the context of a Mass, even if this is viewed as exceptional, shows symbolically the active role of all members of the community in the matter of the liturgy. For that reason it would have been more appropriate to formulate this canon in a less rigid way.

---

68. K. Rahner, "Der theologische Ansatzpunkt für die Bestimmung des Wesens des Amtspriestertums," *Conc* 5 (1969) 196.

d. Summarizing Thesis:
All Members of the Church Are Responsible

This concluding thesis is founded on the express statement of the Second Vatican Council that the laity—that is why we spoke above of *all* members of the Church—"carry out their part of the mission of the entire Christian people both in the Church and in the world" (*LG* no. 31; see also *AA* no. 2, 2).

The stated thesis excludes the possibility that the Church will be viewed as exclusively the property of clerics, that is, of ordained officials. The Church is a *communio* of all who believe in the Lord, that is, a society of believers. This element is not canceled by the fact that some carry a special responsibility, since the latter does not cancel the general responsibility of all.

L. Bouyer's statement is pertinent: "The role of the pope only has meaning within episcopal collegiality and with reference to this. The role of the bishops, including that of the pope, presupposes and requires the collegiality of clerics. It is, however, decisive that the entire service of the apostles and all their successors only have meaning and even existence within the context of a community of believers. One could call this the third form of collegiality within the Church, and the one that coincides with its catholicity in its deepest sense."[69]

The council distinguishes the formation for spiritual directors or pastors (*consilium pastorale*) that pertains especially to selected clerics, members of religious orders, and lay people (Decree on the Bishops no. 27, 5), from the formation for priests (Decree on the Presbyterate no. 7). The difference is described in the following terms: "Formation for the care of souls pertains as well to the laity, for the tasks of a spiritual director require it" (ibid. n. 41). Since the function of the Church should not be viewed as anything other than the care of souls, and since the function of office is a pastoral function, should we not say that pastoral formation should be a precondition for priestly formation?[70] If the situation is otherwise, then should we not take this as an indication that such a Church is still too clerical? Unfortunately, we can observe this fact all too often, and this means that the text from *Lumen gentium* quoted above (no. 37, 3) has not been sufficiently put into practice.

---

69. L. Bouyer, *Die Kirche* (Einsiedeln, 1977) vol. 2, 253. In the same direction, commentary by J. Ratzinger, *Das neue Volk Gottes* (Düsseldorf, 1969) 210ff. (pastoral implications of collegiality).

70. Thus J. Höffner, "Zur Theologie des Seelsorgerates und Priesterrates, Beitrag zum kirchlichen Amtsblatt des Bistums Münster," in *Unsere Seelsorge* 17 (1967) no. 6, 14. On the other side, P. J. Cordes, "Kommentar zum Dekret über Dienst und Leben der Priester," LThK, E 3, 175.

4. Toward a Theology of the Laity[71]

Around 1950 Catholic publications dedicated special editions to the theology of the laity. It is striking that journals devoted to questions in spirituality, and not primarily theological reviews, occupied themselves with this theme.[72] Much of the credit for this goes to the theologians Y. M. Congar, G. Philips, K. Rahner, and E. Schillebeeckx. The teaching of *Lumen gentium* on the laity should be seen as a synthesis of their theological labor.

The Constitution on the Church first sets out a typological description of the laity:

> Under the term "laity" is here understood all those who believe in Christ, with the exception of those who are members of vowed communities and those orders recognized in the Church: that is, those believers in Christ who, made into the one body of Christ through baptism, have been made into the people of God and participants in their own way in the priestly, prophetic, and royal offices of Christ, and to the extent of their powers carry out the mission of the entire Christian people both in the Church and in the world. (no. 31)

It is interesting to see what the constitution indicates as specific to the laity: its worldly character.[73] "The worldly character [*indolis saecularis*] belongs distinctively to the laity" (no. 31, 2).

The council's reflection is based on a comparison with two other states in the Church, that of the consecrated life and that of being a member of an order recognized by the Church. Those are called "lay" who are not officeholders and who do not belong to any order. The lay status is

---

71. Bibliography: Congar, *The Laity;* Congar "Laie," in *Handbuch theologischer Grundbegriffe,* ed. H. Fries, vol. 2 (München, 1963) 7–25; G. Philips, *Der Laie in der Kirche* (Salzburg, 1955; French original, 1954); K. Rahner, "Über das Laienapostolat," in *Schriften* 339–73 (here 339–51); E. Schillebeeckx, *Theologische Peilingen 4,* "De Zending van de Kerk" (Bilthoven, 1968) ch. 2, nos. 1–6 (a collection of different articles on this topic); Schillebeeckx, "Die typologische Definition des christlichen Laien," in *Barauna* 2:269–88; A. Sustar, "Der Laie in der Kirche," in *Fragen der Theologie Heute* (Einsiedeln, 1958) 520–48; H. Heimerl, *Kirche, Klerus, Laien. Unterscheidungen und Beziehungen* (Vienna, 1961); Heimerl, "Laienbegriffe in der Kirchenkonstitution des Vatikanums II," *Conc* 2 (1966) 219–24; A. Antón, "Principios fundamentales para una teología del Laicado en la Eclesiología del Vaticano II," in Gr. 68 (1987) 103–55. For the history of the term *laity:* I. de la Potterie, "L'origine et le sens primitive du mot laïc," *NRTh* 80 (1958) 840–53; J. B. Bauer, "Die Wortgeschichte von 'Laicus,' " *ZKTh* 81 (1959) 224–28.

72. Evidence in Schillebeeckx, "Die typologische Definition," 283 note 30.

73. *Schema Constitutionis de Ecclesia* (Rome, 1964) 127 = Acta Synod. 3/1, 281: per notam quodammodo specificam "indolis saecularis."

a positive condition, on the basis of its participation through baptism and confirmation in the priestly, prophetic, and royal offices of Christ.

The mission and responsibility of the laity are based on their baptism and confirmation. It is a matter here of a *distinctive* mission and responsibility that is not derivative from the mission and responsibility of the hierarchical priesthood, unlike for example, Catholic Action, which understands itself as a participation in the hierarchical apostolate (Pius XI). Thus the mission and responsibility of the laity can be described as "an office," in the sense that it belongs distinctively to it, although the lay person occupies no Church office on the basis of a consecration. Both officeholders and laity participate in the one apostolate of the Church, if in different ways. As *Apostalican actuositatem* no. 2, 2 says, there is a difference of service, although a unity of mission (*diversitas ministerii sed unitas missionis*). The emphasis on the proper responsibility of the laity within the Church precludes the possibility that the Church could be thought of as the exclusive business of clerics.

The council's statement that it is its secular character that specifically characterizes the lay state must be seen in connection with the distinction between the laity and members of orders. The eschatological perspective belongs to the essence of the Christian life. Christians engage themselves in the world (the incarnation) and in a certain way relativize the world on the basis of their eschatological hope. Christians are in the world and must commit themselves to the world, but they should not live according to the spirit of the world, in the negative New Testament sense of this word.[74]

There are various ways in which the eschatological perspective can be lived by Christians. Some orient their lives radically on the eschaton; through their lives they witness to the eschatological hope. The model of this style of life are the monks: "Omnis de saeculo fugitivus, id est monachus"—a person who withdraws from the world is a monk. In general these belong to orders through the three vows they take, namely poverty, chastity, and obedience.[75]

The larger portion of believers, however, remain before God in the condition in which they were called (see 1 Cor 2:20, 24). These Christians should equally live out of the eschatological hope, but they do this to the extent to which they prepare the conditions for the kingdom of heaven

74. "Laici scilicet in mundo sunt et in eo laborant, sed 'malitiae mundi' adversantes, 'mundum ipsum' ab intra sanctificant. Haec antithesis correspondet duplici significatione vocabuli 'mundi' in textibus biblicis"; *Schema Constitutionis* 128 = Acta Synod. 3/1, 282.

75. For the characterization of both groups, see *GS* no. 38; *LG* no. 31 on the "evangelical counsels": *LG* no. 42; on those ordained: *LG* no. 6.

through their engagement with the world (*materiam regni coelestis parantes*), as *Gaudium et spes* no. 38 puts it.

Through this distinction from those who belong to orders, what is specific to the laity is made more precise: "This positive 'specific qualification' consists in the Christian relation of the laity to the secular."[76] Since a relation to the secularity of the world belongs to what is universally human, one can extract from this no distinctive description that would have ecclesiological relevance for a definition of the laity. This comes if one speaks of the *Christian* relation to the secular. Thereby what is characteristic of the Church's mission is applied to the description of the laity.

The Church's mission is primarily religious. As a consequence she has also a specifically ecclesial mission in the world and for the world, namely, "the ordering of the earthly processes of humanization . . . toward salvation."[77] Since relationship to the world is one essential element of the Church, the *Christian* relation to the world, that is, to secularity, may also count as an essential element of the *ecclesial* term *laity*. From that point of view the laity may be described in its specific character with ecclesiological relevance.

Lumen gentium speaks of a mission of the laity in the Church and in the world. This statement could be understood in the following way: since the Church has a task for the world, every mission in the Church also contains a task in the world. A consequence would be that "the laity are not primarily characterized by their exclusively secular activity, but rather through their active participation in the activity of the Church." This is the way the second schema of the constitution of 1963 formulates this relationship.[78]

Once it is noticed that the constitution emphasizes the secular character of the laity, an important nuance is added when it is said that the laity should be characterized by its Christian relation to the world, in analogy to the Church's mission to the world. The world is an integral element of the Church as well as of the Christian life of its members.

Through the laity—or better, *especially* through the laity, so as not to prejudice the engagement of the officials in and for the world[79]—the Church is present in secular structures. Through the laity, or more ac-

76. Schillebeeckx, "Die typologische Definition," 279.

77. Ibid.

78. *Schema Constitutionis de Ecclesia* (Vatican, 1963) pars 2, 15 = Acta Synod. 2/1. See in Schillebeeckx ("Die typologische Definition," 271–77) the comparison of the three formulations of this text.

79. The limitation of the (political) engagement of officials in and on behalf of the world is postulated from their function as servants of the unity of the community. Naturally this limitation is dependent historically and culturally upon the changing situation of the community.

curately through their attempts to live as Christians in secular structures, the Church experiences both the advantages and the disadvantages of concrete secular structures. There is a particular sort of responsibility within the Church for the laity (and only for them) to appropriate, and that specifically because of their presence in the world, that is, on the basis of what characterizes the laity as a state of life. To this experience the officials and those who belong to religious orders can in principle not contribute, by reason of their different state of life. This means that the hierarchy cannot carry out its own apostolate without the contribution of the experience of the laity. *Lumen gentium* refers to the positive significance of the laity's experiences when it speaks of the necessity for a trusting communication between pastors and laity. "With the help of the laity, the bishops can better and more accurately judge both in spiritual and in secular matters" (no. 37, 4).

Thus, what the laity on the basis of their state of life, that is, on the basis of their attempt to live as Christians within the structures of the world, have to say in the Church can be regarded as a charism. The difference intended by God between man and woman must also be regarded as a source of charisms. Women's experiences must be taken into account within the Church. We should also integrate the positive experiences of the role of the different social groups which the "specialized" Catholic Action has produced. The parish should be understood as a community made up of distinct communities.

It is to be desired and required that the voices of the laity receive the importance at every level—pastor, bishop, and the universal Church—that corresponds to the coresponsibility of the laity within the Church.[80]

BIBLIOGRAPHY

Congar, Y. M. *Der Laie.* Stuttgart, 1957 (orig. French 1952), chs. 4, 5, and 6.
————. "L'Ecclesia ou la communauté chrétienne sujet intégral de l'action liturgique." In *La liturgie apres Vatican II,* Paris, 1967, 241–68.
Garijo-Guembe, M. M. "Der Begriff der Rezeption und sein Ort im Kern der katholischen Ekklesiologie." In P. Lengsfeld and H. G. Stobbe, eds., *Theologischer Consens und Kirchenspaltung,* Stuttgart, 1981, 97–109, 167–72.

80. In my experience one must decide between the fact that the laity's voice is heard in the Church—for which one needs, naturally, official Church channels—and a participation in the various organizational structures. H. Küng argues for the second alternative in "La participation des laïcs aux décisions dans l'Église. Une lacune dans le Décret sur l'apostolat des laïcs," in *L'apostolat des laïcs,* Unam sanctam 75 (Paris, 1970) 285–308.

Hilberath, B. J. "Das Verhältnis von gemeinsamen und amtlichen Priestertum in der Perspektive von Lumen Gentium 10." *TThZ* 94 (1985) 311–26.

Leeuwen, B. van. "Die allgemeine Teilnahme am Prophetenamt Christi." In Baraúna 1:393–419.

Schillebeeckx, E. "Die typologische Definition des christlichen Laien." In Baraúna 2:269–88.

_____. *Christliche Identität und kirchliches Amt.* Düsseldorf, 1985, 140ff., 146f., 160ff.

Schnell, U. *Das Verhältnis von Amt und Gemeinde im neueren Katholizismus.* Berlin, 1977 (especially chap. 4: After the Council).

XII.
The Hierarchical Composition of the Church: The Bishop with His Co-Workers: The Presbyters and Deacons

It is the understanding of the Roman Catholic Church, as well as of the Eastern Orthodox and the non-Chalcedonian Churches, that the office of bishop—as distinct from the office of presbyter—belongs to the essence of the Church. Authority as such is thus viewed as concentrated in the office of bishop. The Reformation for the first time raised the question whether this office in contradistinction to the office of presbyter was truly constitutive of the Church. This marks a perduring problem in the ecumenical field, in that the Reformation Churches reject such a distinction.

1. The Teaching of *Lumen gentium*

a. The Bishops as the Successors to the Apostles

The third chapter of the constitution is dedicated to the hierarchical composition of the Church, in particular to the office of bishop.

Right at the beginning the constitution states clearly the significance of the bishop's office: "The everlasting shepherd Jesus Christ . . . sent his apostles" and "intended that their successors [*successores*], that is, the bishops, be shepherds in his church until the end of time" (no. 18, 2). The mission bestowed upon the apostles "will last until the end of the world. . . . For this reason the apostles took special care to set up within this hierarchically structured community procedures for the choosing of successors (no. 20), in the sense that they "passed on to their immediate co-workers through a kind of testament the task of shaping and completing the work which they had begun" (no. 20, 2). As evidence of this the consitution quotes, besides the New Testament texts Acts 20:25-27; 2 Timothy 4:6f; 1 Timothy 5:22; 2 Timothy 2:2, and Titus 1:5, also statements from Clement of Rome, Tertullian, and Irenaeus.

The constitution bases its reflection on the witness of the Tradition: "The fact that these successors [*successores*] are to be found in the bishops is clear from the witness of the Tradition [*teste Traditione*], which discerns a succession from the very beginning as if established by the apostles."[1]

The Catholic position states: "The office of apostle to pasture the Church continues to this day, and must be continually carried out by the holy order of bishops. For this reason the holy synods teach that the bishops, on the basis of their divine institution [*ex divina institutione*] are set in the place of the apostles as shepherds of the Church" (no. 20, 3). The constitution refers to earlier teaching documents: to the Council of Trent (DS 1768 = NR 710), Vatican I (DS 3804 = NR 406), and to the Codex (CIC 1917 can. 329, 1; see CIC 1983, can. 375, 1). The Council of Trent and Vatican I say that the bishops are set in the place of the apostles in the sense that they have been instituted by the Holy Spirit. According to Vatican I, the *ex institutione divina* is a *ius divinum* (DS 3058 = NR 443). This means that the office of bishop is constitutive and essential for the Church.[2] It is noteworthy that *Lumen gentium* uses the phrase "the holy synods teach," rather than "the holy synods solemnly teach."[3] That is an indication that "this clarification is not intended apparently as a (new) *ex cathedra* statement,"[4] but rather leaves unchanged the earlier theological qualification.

b. The Sacramentality of the Bishop's Office

Besides this traditional formulation that the bishops are *ex institutione divina* successors to the apostles, the constitution establishes the sacramentality of the episcopal ordination. The authority is bestowed and resides

1. *Schema Constitutionis de Ecclesia* (Vatican, 1964) 83 = Acta Synodalia 3/1, 237.

2. K. Rahner, in LThK. E. 1 (1966) 215 writes: the formulation "ex institutione divina" "implies in any case that the episcopacy does not belong to the merely human, changeable Church law, as though the *post*-apostolic Church could give itself a non-episcopal constitution, or that the episcopal arrangement would fall *outside* the events of revelation that occurred during the apostolic age."

3. The commission had asked the council fathers whether it should be called "solemniter docet"; see *Schema Constitutionis* 84 = Acta Synod. 3/1 238: "Non adhibetur tamen formula solemnis de qua iudicabit Congregatio generalis."

4. Rahner, in LThK. E 1 (1966) 215.

simply in the office of bishop. "Through the episcopal consecration the fullness of the sacrament of ordination is conveyed" (no. 21, 2); the bishop is "distinguished by the fullness of the sacrament of ordination" (no. 26). The constitution here takes over the liturgical custom of the Church as well as the teaching of the Church Fathers (no. 21, 2; see note 55 to the text of the constitution).

As for what concerns the theological qualification of this statement, here also we should pay attention to the expression employed, which runs, "the holy synod teaches," and not "the holy synod solemnly teaches," as the commission had suggested to the council fathers as an alternative.[5] For this reason we are dealing here with a teaching of the Catholic Church that is sanctioned by an ecumenical council, but which, nevertheless, does not have the character of a formal definition.

The council's option is different from that of the theology of the Middle Ages.[6] The latter started with the office of presbyter (*sacerdotium*). Since the bishop did not have any greater power over the Lord's Body (the Eucharist) than a priest, the distinction between the bishop and the presbyter was seen to lie only on the plane of their jurisdictions. For example, Thomas Aquinas stresses that the bishop has power over the priest in what concerns the mystical body (the Church).[7] This consists in the authority to administer confirmation and ordination. The Council of Trent refers to the same things to explain that the bishops "have primacy over the presbyters [*presbyteris superiores*]" (DS 1768 = NR 711). Trent sees the essence of the office in the power to preside at the Eucharistic celebration and to forgive sins (DS 1764 = NR 706, 713). Between Trent and Vatican II, however, the theologians who held the sacramentality of the bishop's office to be an open question were a minority.[8] Vatican II integrated ordination within an ecclesiological context; the power of the office and hence also the power of jurisdiction should be seen starting with ordination. The bishop is ordained as the presider of a concrete community (hence, ordination is not absolute!) whose center is the Eucharistic assembly. "The bishop is distinguished by the fullness of the sacrament of ordination, 'the steward of the grace of the highest priesthood,' preeminently in the Eucharist, which he himself either confects or allows to be confected" (no. 26). The entire authority (*sacra potestas*) of the bishop derives from his ordination, which, following the threefold power of Christ, is character-

---

5. *Schema Constitutionis* 85 = Acta Synod. 3/1, 239: "Dicitur simpliciter 'Docet Sancta Synodus.' Ad Congregationem Generalem pertinet addere, si placet: 'solemniter.' "

6. See L. Ott, *Das Weihesakrament,* HDG 4:5 (Freiburg, 1969) 50ff., 80ff.

7. In 4 Sent. d. 24, p. 2, a. 2, q. 3.

8. See L. Ott, *Weihesakrament,* 136; Lennerz, *De sacramento ordinis,* 80ff.

ized as a teaching office (no. 25), a saving office (no. 26), and a governing office. For that reason the so-called jurisdiction is theologically to be seen from the perspective of the *ordo*.[9] That a nominated bishop should exercise jurisdiction in a diocese before he had received ordination, as would have been possible according to CIC 1917, is theologically problematic. According to CIC 1983, episcopal consecration is necessary before the candidate bishop may take possession of his office (canon 379).

c. The Distinction between Bishop and Presbyter

Even after Vatican II many questions remain open as to what constitutes the difference between bishop and presbyter.

The commission did not wish to express itself on the question "whether the bishop by himself could ordain priests. For that reason it opened up neither the '*quaestio iuris*' nor the '*quaestio facti.*' "[10] The text remains upon the purely factual level: "They bestow holy orders" (no. 26, 3). In what concerns confirmation, the bishop is referred to as the first minister, but not as the "ordinary" administrator (ibid.).[11] Nevertheless, the commission refers to canon 7 of the Tridentine Decree on Holy Orders, which says that "bishops have primacy over priests," that is, the authority to confirm and to ordain is not common to themselves and priests (DS 1777 = NR 719).

With attention to the historical development of the office the constitution states: "In this way the divinely instituted ecclesial offices [*ministerium ecclesiasticum divinitus institutum*] were exercised in various ranks by those who already in ancient times [*ab antiquo*] were called bishops, priests, and deacons" (no. 28). While the office as such is traced back to a divine institution, the concrete forms of the office are described only with the phrase "from ancient times" (*ab antiquo*). The accompanying footnote (no. 63) refers to the text of the Council of Trent, whose canon 6 (DS 1776 = NR 718) states that there exists in the Church a divinely structured (*divina ordinatione*) hierarchy, which consists of bishops, priests, and servers (that is, deacons). The Tridentine formula *divina ordinatione* was the result of a compromise.[12] It was the suggestion of

9. On the problem of "ordo" and "iurisdictio," see Y. M. Congar, "Weihe und Jurisdiktion in der Kirche," in Congar, *Heilige Kirche,* 208–46.

10. *Schema Constitutionis* 87 = Acta Synod. 3/1, 241.

11. With a view to the practice in the Eastern Churches, the term *originarius* was chosen instead of *ordinarius* (*Schema Constitutionis* 99 = Acta Synod. 3/1, 254).

12. On the interpretation of the council: A. Duval, "L'Ordre au Concile de Trent," in *Études sur le sacrament de l'order* (Paris, 1957) 305–08; Ott, *Weihesakrament,* 121ff.; K. Bekker, *Wesen und Vollmachten des Priestertums nach dem Lehramt,* Der priesterliche Dienst 2 (Freiburg, 1970) 100ff.; Dupuy, *Besteht ein dogmatischer Unterschied,* here 268ff.

the archbishop of Granada that the episcopacy should be explained as divine law. The curial party saw in this the danger of an encroachment on the papal primacy and countered, through the archbishop of Rossano, G. Castagna, later Pope Urban VII, with the position that the episcopal power of jurisdiction was conferred directly by the pope. The same archbishop raised the question whether by divine law the bishops were placed above priests, and quoted various theologians and canonists who shared Jerome's position that this distinction did not originate from a direction from the Lord, but only from Church tradition. In spite of these controversies the Council of Trent had no difficulty in describing the bishops (with a reference to Acts 20:28) as the successors to the apostles intended by the Holy Spirit (DS 1768 = NR 711), so that the distinction between bishops and presbyters should be viewed as God's deed. For the council it was not enough to describe this difference as of human origin.

In the opinion of various authors, Trent did not decide the question whether the primacy of bishops over presbyters on the basis of their ordination should be viewed as instituted by Jesus Christ, and thus as an *iuris divini*.[13] The fact that Vatican II invoked the Council of Trent when it used the expression "from ancient times" might be evidence for this.

The importance of the formulation of both council texts for the ecumenical relations between the Reformation and Catholicism with reference to the arrangement of offices has been emphasized by various ecumenical documents, with the intention of presenting the differences as being as small as possible.[14] Still from the Catholic side it must be made clear how both principal statements may be concretely explained, namely, that the bishops are successors to the apostles *ex institutione divina* (in connection with the statements on the sacramentality of the episcopal ordination) and that the arrangement of offices results only "from ancient times."

2. The Ecumenical Problem: The Position of the Reformation[15]

"The *Lutheran Confession* wished to retain the episcopal composition of the Church and with it the distinction in offices. . . . The impos-

---

13. Thus H. Lennerz, *De sacramento ordinis*, 96, no. 167. In the same direction Dupuy, ibid.; Fransen, *Weihe, heilige*, 115.

14. "Das geistliche Amt," no. 48, in DwÜ, 346; *Kirchengemeinschaft in Wort und Sakrament* (Paderborn-Hannover, 1984) no. 68; *Lehrverurteilungen-kirchentrennend?*, vol. 1, eds. K. Lehmann and W. Pannenberg (Freiburg-Göttingen, 1986) 163 (it is emphasized that Trent speaks of divine arrangement, and not divine institution).

15. Bibliography: P. Brunner, "Vom Amt des Bischofs," in Brunner, *Pro ecclesia 1* (Berlin-Hamburg, 1962) 235–92; E. Kinder, *Der evangelische Glaube und die*

sibility at that time of obtaining an agreement in doctrine or to win over the contemporary bishops to consecrate Lutheran officials, led necessarily to a rejection of the received structures. In this urgent situation the institution of officials through non-episcopal officials, or even through the communities, appeared legitimate, if it took place 'ritually,' which here means openly and in the name of the entire Church"; thus do the Lutheran authors of the document *Spiritual Authority in the Church* explain their position.[16]

The Augsburg Confession, no. 28, speaks of the power of the bishops. Their duty is "according to divine law to preach the gospel, forgive sins, decide doctrine, and to reject any doctrine that contradicts the gospels, and to exclude the godless from the Christian community."[17] The Confession's apology makes clear that in Church discipline we are dealing with distinctions set up only on human authority: "gradus in ecclesia, factos etiam humana auctoritate."[18] In the *Tractus de potestate papae* it states that "all who lead the Churches, whether they are called pastors or presbyters or bishops," have the *potestas* which was attributed to the bishops in the Augsburg Confession and in its apology.[19] The argument is grounded primarily on Jerome's testimony.[20] Luther also refers to this on various occasions.[21] The Lutheran conception is summarized by P. Brunner in the following way: "The speech patterns of the Confession documents and Luther's texts is here entirely clear. Bishop and clergyman, *episcopus, presbyterus,* and *pastor* may all be used in the same sense. The various expressions indicate equivalently the same office which arises through vocation. The one office that arises from a vocation is the shepherd's office of the bishop, and it has received its structure not from men, but from God himself. The equivalence *pastor = episcopus* is a proper one."[22]

The *ministerium ecclesiae* concretizes itself in the office of the vicar of a parish, because "both basic functions of the *ministerium,* preaching and administration of the sacraments [of which the Augsburg Confession, no. 5, speaks],[23] are made good by the pastor in service to a specific com-

---

Kirche (Berlin, 1960) 186ff. (with biblio.); A. Dulles and G. Lindbeck, "Die Bischöfe und der Dienst des Evangeliums. Ein Kommentar zu CA 5, 14 und 28," in *Confessio Augustana. Bekenntnis des einen Glaubens* (Paderborn-Frankfurt, 1980) 139–67; G. Tröger, "Bischof. III. Das evangelische Bischofsamt," in TRE 6 (1980) 690–94.

16. No. 42, in DwÜ, 344.
17. CA 27.20-21: BSLK 124.
18. Apol. 14: BSLK 296.
19. *Tractus de potestate papae* 61.60: BSLK 489.
20. Ibid., nos. 62–65.
21. See WA 50, 339, 340, and 399ff.
22. Brunner, *AMT,* 253.
23. In BSLK 58.

munity (*ecclesia*)."[24] With reference to these basic functions, according to Luther all officials are equal, and that *de iure divino*.[25]

Basically the proper execution of the office requires a visitation to the local community. Each local community also requires an *ordained* minister, in the sense of the *rite vocatus* of Augsburg Confession, no. 14.[26] For that reason visitation and ordination are two ecclesial functions which are presumed by every local community. "Ordination and visitation as the necessary services for the local minister to the local community are the legitimate basic functions for whose sake Church leadership exists and toward which it must be primarily structured."[27] This is the way the necessity for superintendents—the term is a translation of *episkopos*—is grounded. Since this function should be understood as one of service to the local community and as a development of the function of such a local authority, it follows quite logically that no further ordination for those who occupy a leadership position is necessary.

From the equality between bishop and vicar it follows that pastors can ordain: "Because according to divine law there is no difference between bishops and pastors or clergymen, there is no doubt that, if a clergyman ordains several qualified persons to Church office in his church, such an ordination is efficacious and right according to divine law," as the *Tractatus de potestate papae* puts it.[28] The same *tractatus* bases this option on the case where bishops persecute the gospel and refuse to ordain evangelical (Lutheran) candidates, so that the Churches may have the authority to ordain such persons: where the Church exists, there exists also the command that the gospel be preached.[29]

Because of the negative reaction of the hierarchy to the Reformation, the problem arose for the Reformers of identifying where the apostolicity of the Church formally resides, and whether this apostolicity is dependent on a board, like that of the bishops, or on the pope. In their opinion, the apostolicity of the Church does not depend upon a hierarchically understood apostolic succession, but rather lies primarily in the agreement of the witnesses of a concrete historical Church with the teaching of the apostles. No formal, hierarchically understood succession will guarantee the purity of the Church: the Church is not maintained through the

---

24. D. Wendebourg, *Reformation und Orthodoxie* (Göttingen, 1986) 327. The entire section on authority offers a good systematic presentation of the theological differences between the leadership of the Würtemberger Church and the patriarch of Constantinople, Jeremias II.

25. WA 2, 228–30.

26. In BSLK 69.

27. Kinder, *Der evangelische Glaube*, 188.

28. 65, in BSLK 490.

29. 66f., in BSLK 491.

bishops. Here are representative quotations from Luther, Melanchthon, and Calvin:

Luther: "Successio ad Evangelium est alligata . . . We must notice where the Verbum is . . . Ubi est verbum, ibi est Ecclesia . . . Credendum est episcopo, non quia succedit episcopo huius loci, sed quia docet Evangelium. The Evangelium should determine the successio."[30]

Melanchthon: "Est [ecclesia] coetus non alligatus ad ordinariam successionem, sed ad verbum Dei; ibi renascitur ecclesia, ubi Deus restituit doctrinam et dat Spiritum sanctum."[31]

Calvin: "Sed in quo sita est successio nisi in perpetuitate doctrinae?"[32]

The importance of this problem has been emphasized by the Lutherans in their Malta Declaration: "From the Lutheran side the significance of a particular succession can be cleared up if the 'succession of teaching' is admitted to be the main issue, and when the transmission of office in an unbroken chain is recognized as by itself no *ipso facto* guarantee for a continuity in the correct preaching of the gospel."[33]

3. Theological Reflection

a. The Foundation of the Catholic Thesis: The Bishops as Successors to the Apostles

The Catholic position corresponds to the understanding of the early Church in its answer to Gnosticism (see the Excursus following chapter 5). Irenaeus, Tertullian, and Origen emphasize that the authentic revelation of Jesus Christ, that is, the authentic proclamation by the apostles, is to be located within the Churches, especially within the Churches founded by the apostles. Irenaeus and Tertullian furnish lists of episcopal succession as evidence for the fact that the Churches remain in continuity with the teaching proclaimed by the apostles.

This understanding has its root in the New Testament, to the extent that in the later sections the role of authority for the preservation of the apostolic inheritance and the apostolic transmission is emphasized. The extra-biblical witness of Clement of Rome, who wrote during the period when the late New Testament writings were being set down, is here of particular importance. It renders more explicit what is already indicated in the New Testament writings. According to 1 and 2 Timothy, Timothy received the commission from Paul to exert himself on behalf of the shepherds, that is, the *episkopoi/presbyteroi* and the deacons. Acts 20:28

30. WA 39 I, 191.
31. *De ecclesia et auctoritate verbi Dei,* in CR 23:598.
32. *Vera ecclesiae reformandae ratio* (1549), in CR, Calvini Opera 7:611.
33. No. 57, in DwÜ, 263. See below chapter 12 section 5.

also justifies local authorities by invoking the will of the apostles. This tendency already present in the later passages of the New Testament will be developed by Clement into a theory:

42.4: "And so the apostles preached in the towns and the countryside and, after first testing them in the Spirit, set up their initial converts as bishops and deacons for the future believers."

44.1: "Also our apostles knew through our Lord Jesus Christ that there would develop controversy around the office of bishop. For this reason they set up, as they had received precise instructions ahead of time, the above-named individuals and thereby indicated that when they died, other proven individuals should take over their work. Thus these were set up, either by they themselves or later by other esteemed individuals, with the agreement of the entire community."[34]

That certain New Testament communities experienced difficulties with the institutionalization of authority is clear from the pseudo-epigraphy, which attempts to make indisputable a very contested solution by invoking the incontestable witness of the apostle. The text from Didaché 15: "Select bishops and deacons from among yourselves! . . . Do not hold them in disdain, for they, together with the prophets are to be esteemed among you," indicates the existence of such a situation. This means that the linear chain Christ → apostles → bishops/presbyters cannot be regarded as a historical reality, in the sense that the leader of every local community was established through such a sequence.

The understanding represented by Irenaeus, Tertullian, and Hippolytus assumes a development of authority after the conclusion of the New Testament. The transition to the distinction between bishop and presbyters is not discernible in Holy Scripture. The first witness to this distinction is Ignatius of Antioch (there is no indication of this distinction in Clement of Rome). However, even after Ignatius the terms *bishop* and *presbyter* were used in an interchangeable fashion, for example by Polycarp, whom Ignatius in his letter calls "bishop,"[35] so that "the *'episkope'* is a title for what the presbyters in fact do: supervision, care, and leadership."[36] The *Shepherd of Hermas* speaks in the majority of cases of *episkopoi* only in the sense of presbyters, whom he calls leaders or presiders (*proegoumenoi*).[37] The following text from Irenaeus also shows such an

34. *1 Clem.* 42.4; 44.1. Translation by J. A. Fischer, *Die Apostolischen Väter* (München, 1981) 79 and 81.

35. *Ad Polyc.*, Greeting; Fischer, 216.

36. Schillebeeckx, *Christliche Identität*, 153. *2 Phil.* speaks of "Polycarp and the presbyters with him." One should obey "the presbyters and deacons as God and Christ" (5.3). Chapter 6 prescribes how the presbyters should behave in their duties; Fischer, 249, 255f.

37. *Vis.* 2.2 and 3.9.3, as well as *Sim.* 9.26.2.

understanding: "Quaproper eis qui in ecclesia sunt *presbyteris* obaudire oportet, his qui successionem habent ab apostolis, sicut ostendimus, qui cum *episcopatus successione* charisma veritatis certum secundum placitum Patris acceperunt."[38] By the end of the second century this development had been completed.

A comparison between Ignatius of Antioch and the *Traditio Apostolica* of Hippolytus shows the importance of this development: Ignatius names as authorities in a community the bishop with his presbyters and deacons. He emphasizes the role of the bishop, for "without him one can neither baptize nor celebrate the love meal"; "those Eucharistic celebrations were held valid which took place in the presence of the bishop or of a person delegated by him."[39] The normal presider at the Eucharist is the bishop: he presides over the assembly of the community. At the same time, a bishop without presbyters and deacons is unthinkable. For that reason the presbyters may be seen as a board of advisors. They are those who may be delegated by the bishop to preside at the Eucharistic celebration.

As with Ignatius, the *Traditio Apostolica* presents the presbyters as advisors to the bishop: the ordination prayer for a presbyter asks that he may receive the spirit of counsel (*spiritum gratiae et consilii*).[40] In the ordination prayer the tasks of the bishop are named: to pasture the holy flock of the Lord, to confect the Eucharist (the exercise of the high priesthood: *primatum sacerdotii*), and to forgive sins. The prayer implores the descent of the spirit of leadership (*spiritus principalis,* following the Vulgate translation of Ps 50:14).[41] The formula for the Eucharistic celebration (the Eucharistic canon) is described after the ordination of the bishop, since it is the bishop's first act after his ordination to celebrate the Eucharist with his community.[42] There is nothing in the *Traditio* concerning the function of the presbyter with reference to the Eucharist, so that one may conclude that during the canon the presbyters remained still.[43] All officials, deacons, presbyters, and bishops, take part in the rite of initi-

---

38. Irenaeus, *Adv. Haer.* 4.26.2.

39. *Smyrn.* 8.2 and 1; Fischer, 211. See also *Phil.* 4; Fischer, 197.

40. *Traditio* 7, ed. B. Botte, *La tradition apostolique de S. Hippolyte* (Münster, 1963) 20. See also *Traditio* 8 (Botte, 24) on the deacon: he does not take part in the counsel of the clerics ("non est enim particeps consilii in clero").

41. *Traditio* 3; ibid., 8.

42. *Traditio* 4; ibid., 10ff.

43. This is also the opinion of G. Dix, "The Ministry in the early Church c. A.D. 90–410," in *The Apostolic Ministry. Essays on the History and the Doctrine of Episcopacy,* ed. K. E. Kirch (London, 1946) 183f.; E. Schillebeeckx, *Christliche Identität,* 166; Vorgrimler, *Sakramententheologie,* 275f.

ation. The concluding ceremony is reserved for the bishop.[44] The bishop appears as the presider of the community. He is the leader. The spirit that one asks for him is compared with the spirit that Jesus Christ bestowed upon the apostles.[45] He carries responsibility for the entire life of the community. He is the priest of the community, the one who baptizes, conducts the Eucharistic service, and offers reconciliation with the Church (the forgiveness of sins). The presbyterium participates in these sacramental affairs, but only in connection with the bishop, that is, without their own pastoral autonomy;[46] we are here dealing with a community with one leader, the bishop, who surrounds himself with a college of presbyters.

In summary, we may say that the sources that have come down to us do not allow us to reconstruct in a precise way the exact manner in which the transition from the function of the apostle to that of the bishop took place; we can only discern two distinct phases.

First, according to the later writings of the New Testament, the existence of an authority in the community corresponds to the will of the apostles. In his presentation of the *ministerialis successio,* Clement of Rome renders explicit what is already indicated in the New Testament.

Second, the emphasis on the role of one person within the college of authorities, that is, the function of the bishop, appears first in the post-New Testament sources and establishes itself everywhere during the second century (monarchic episcopacy).

The significance and the value of such a development can be conveyed only with systematic and consequently dogmatic criteria, since the linear chain of descent Christ → apostles → bishops cannot historically clarify the development from a college of presbyters to the bishop with his board

---

44. *Traditio* 21; Botte, 54.

45. *Traditio* 3; ibid., 8.

46. Schillebeeckx, *Christliche Identität,* 165 note 74 comments: "The presbyters are still not priests (= sacerdotes), even when, with the permission of the bishop, they were allowed to lead the Eucharistic celebration (at least, in many Church provinces)." Thus, taken together, the term *sacerdos* until the fifth century means simply *bishop.* At the end of the fourth and the beginning of the fifth century, bishops in the East were called *archiereis,* and priests *hiereis.* See also B. Botte, "Secundi meriti sumus," *QLP* 21 (1936) 84–88; "*Regularkanoniker von Mondaye.* Der Bischof nach den Ordinationsgebeten," in Y. M. Congar, ed., *Das Bischofsamt und die Weltkirche* (Stuttgart, 1964; French original, 1962) 767–810 (with a basic bibliography: p. 800, and with the prayers of ordination: pp. 801–10); P. M. Gy, "La théologie des prières anciennes pour l'ordination des évêques et des prêtres," *RSPhTh* 58 (1974) 599–617; F. E. Brightman, *Liturgies Eastern and Western. I. Eastern Liturgies* (Oxford, 1896) 598 (hiereus); G. W. H. Lampe, *A Patristic Greek Lexicon* (Oxford, 1961) *archiereus* E (239) and *hiereus* B (669).

of presbyteral advisors.[47] In my experience, there is only one method for evaluating this development: the canon of Holy Scripture and the office of bishop are two "developments" that should not be viewed separately from one another. It would make no sense to accept the canon of Holy Writ while simultaneously rejecting the development of the bishop's office. Those Churches which accepted certain books as belonging to the canon and excluded others as noncanonical[48] were convinced that certain elements such as the office of bishop belonged to the essence of the Church."[49] To deal with the facts before us, the methodological principle of *sola scriptura* is not sufficient.[50]

At the same time, Catholic theology should not forget that in this connection the question arises whether a post-New Testament development may be viewed as a binding decision for the Church throughout its entire history. Here the problem of the *ius divinum* and its concrete formulation in the course of history poses itself; it will be discussed below (in chap. XII, part 3b).

THE DESIGNATION "SUCCESSOR OF THE APOSTLES"

First we must remove a possible misunderstanding that, from the viewpoint of Lutheran theology, may arise concerning this title. The role of the apostles is and remains unique. They were witnesses to the resurrection, and they received their mission from Christ to carry forth their witness with authority and thereby to found the Church. They were the builders and planters not only of the earliest Christian communities, but of the Church of all times and all places (see Eph 2:20; Rev 21:14; and Matt 16:18). In a word, the apostles alone are the foundation stones of the Church, and this role cannot be extended or repeated.

47. The traditional school theology sought to justify the linear chain. J. Salaverri, for example, writes: "Inde a tempore Apostolorum singulis Ecclesiis praeerant Episcopi singuli, qui a medio saec. II ubique erant monarchici. Atqui hoc factum non nisi ex successione iure divino in ordinario Apostolorum munere explicari potest. Ergo Apostolis in ordinario eorum munere iure divino succedunt Episcopi et quidem singuli in particularibus Eclesiis singulis" (*Sacrae theologiae summa*, vol. 1 [Madrid, 1952] no. 347, p. 604). L. Ott argues in a similar way in *Grundriss der Dogmatik* (Freiburg, 1970) 338f.

48. This formulation should be understood as independent from that problem often discussed between Catholics and Protestants, whether the building up of the canon should be seen as the active decision of the Church, or as simply the reception of writings that established themselves in the Church.

49. A. Ramsey, *The Gospel and the Catholic Church* (London, 1936) 63; Dupuy, *Besteht ein Dogmatischer Unterschied,* 271: "Seen dogmatically, the division of offices may be compared with the establishment of the canon"; Dupuy, in MySal 4/2, 516.

50. Congar, *Wesenseigenschaften,* 550.

Catholic theology does not speak of the bishops as successors to the apostles in this narrower sense, although the Middle Ages especially did not observe this difference strictly enough. Many theologians and canonists expressed themselves as if the bishops were the same as apostles and succeeded them in all their functions.[51] Catholic theology distinguishes those apostolic functions which may be transferred from others which are nontransferable. The bishops have this in common with the apostles, that they have received the commission from the Lord Jesus Christ through which the active presence of the absent Lord is brought about. The bishops are successors to the extent that they participate in the authority of service which the apostles had with regard to their communities. The words of the Lord "Who hears you, hears me" (Luke 10:16), which originally were addressed to the apostles, also hold true for the bishops. This transmission is also asserted in the Augsburg Confession 28.22.[52]

b. The Later Development and Its Significance for the Distinction between Bishops and Presbyters

Because of the rapid growth of Christianity, a new unit of Church organization made its appearance, the parish. The connection breaks down between the celebration of the Eucharist and the presider over the community, the bishop. The Eucharist is no longer exclusively celebrated under the direction of the bishop; priests take over the leadership functions in the celebration of the Eucharist that until then were reserved to the bishop.[53] To the bishop is now reserved the prerogative of orders, the consecration of new altars (that is, the establishment of new churches), and governance. In the West the administering of confirmation is added to this list.[54] It is forbidden to the members of the "episcopal choir" to ad-

51. See Y. M. Congar, "Composantes et idée de la Succession Apostolique," *Oecumenica* (1960) 61ff.

52. In BSLK 124.

53. See Synod of Arles (314), can. 15: against the practice that the deacons confect the Eucharist (Mansi 2:473); Nicaea (325), can. 18: against the practice that deacons distribute the Eucharist to the presbyters. As a justification it is mentioned that the deacons "do not have the authority to confect the Eucharist," while the presbyters have this (Mansi 2:675).

54. Jerome offers the first witness that the laying on of hands, or confirmation, was administered separately from baptism, in the case where baptism was administered not in the bishop's city, that is, in the cathedral, but "in villulis aut in castellis." This practice was already widespread before 382, when Jerome wrote: PL 23:164f. This practice is equally testified by the Synod of Elvira around 300: DS 121. In the year 416 Innocent I decreed that the "consignatio" belonged only to the bishop. On the eve of Easter the presbyters administered baptism in the suburban churches of Rome at the same time as the bishop of Rome was baptizing (DS 215). Somewhat later Pope

minister holy orders.[55] The Council of Sardes (343) took up the question whether in small towns, which before had no bishop, now a bishop should be set up. The decision was negative in those cases where a priest was sufficient for the pastoral care of souls.[56]

In conjunction with this development, the *Apostolic Constitutions* list the tasks of the three distinct offices. "Instructed by the Lord, we have entrusted to the bishop *'archierosyne,'* to the presbyter the *'hierosyne,'* and to the deacon the *'diakonia.'* The deacon may neither present the offering, nor baptize, nor present the *'eulogia'*; the presbyter may not ordain/consecrate [*cheirotonia*]."[57]

However, in the ordination formula of the Eastern tradition it is clear that authority as such resides in the office of bishop.[58] As for the ordination of priests, the Copts and Nestorians simply say that the candidate is consecrated to be a "presbyter at the holy altar" or for "the work of priestly service." In the Byzantine rite we find a developed presentation of the priestly function of the presbyter: it obliges him to proclaim the gospel, to present the offering, and to renew the people of God through baptism/confirmation.[59] The original ordination formula that is common to all Eastern rites and is used in every consecration reads, "The divine grace that heals whatever is sick and completes whatever is lacking, has selected this person as bishop [substitute 'priest' or 'deacon']. Let us pray for him, so that the grace of the Holy Spirit may come upon him." This formula goes back most probably to the fourth century (Antioch).[60] Today it is used in every consecration ceremony; however, the words are spoken by a deacon.

Representative of the ordination formula for the Western tradition is a quotation from the ordination prayer for the priest from the *Sacramen-*

Gelasius (492–96) decreed that the presbyters could neither bless nor consignate the chrism: PL 59:50.

55. Synod of Antioch (341), can. 10: Mansi 2:1311.

56. Can. 6: Mansi 3:10f.

57. *Constitutiones apostolorum* 8.46.10-11, ed. F. X. Funk, *Didascalia et Constitutiones apostolorum* (Paderborn, 1905) vol. 2, 560. The formulae for ordination: consecration of a bishop: 8.4.2-5, 12 (ibid., 472–77); ordination to the priesthood: 8.16.2-5 (ibid., 521–23); ordination to the deaconate: 8.17.2-3 (ibid., 523–25).

58. See "*Regularkanoniker von Mondaye.* Der Bischuf," 767–810 (the formula: 810ff.).

59. The texts are in E. Lodi, *Enchiridion euchologicum fontium liturgicarum* (Rome, 1979). For the Copts: no. 2975 = Denzinger, *Ritus orientalium in administrandis sacramentis* (Würzburg, 1863; Graz, 1961) vol. 2, 12f.; for the Nestorians: no. 2978 = Denzinger, 235f. (the second prayer is somewhat more concrete).

60. See B. Botte, "La formule d'Ordination 'La grâce divine' dans les rites orientaux," *L'Orient Syrien* 2 (1957) 285–96.

tarium Veronense (from the last quarter of the sixth century, probably older).

> Through your providence, Lord, you have given the apostles of your Son teachers of the faith as companions, with whose preaching the whole earth has become filled. For this reason we beg you, Lord, vouchsafe for our weakness these helps; the weaker we are, the more we need them. We beg you, Father, bestow upon these your servants the dignity of the office of priesthood [*presbyterii dignitatem*]. Renew in them the spirit of holiness [*spiritum sanctitatis*]. May they receive from you the authority of the second rank [*secundi meriti munus*], may they through the example of their conversion carry out a supervision over our actions. May they be dependable co-workers of our office [*cooperatores ordinis nostri*].[61]

The presbyters are referred to as *cooperatores* of the bishop. With reference to the bishop the document speaks of a "summi sacerdotii ministerium,"[62] while to the presbyters it ascribes a "secundi meriti munus." The relation of the bishops to the priests is understood on the analogy of that of the apostles to their co-workers.

It should be noticed that Vatican II's decree on priests, *Presbyterorum ordinis,* refers to both the Eastern and Western traditions to characterize the function of the presbyter as that of co-worker with the bishop (no. 7, with footnotes 33-37).

The bishop is the one who sits on the *cathedra.* He is the teacher and the leader as the primary priest in the community. Everything is understood in connection with the Eucharistic celebration. The bishop's *cathedra,* from which he preached, was located in the sanctuary around the altar. The "autonomy" of the clergy then raised the question of what distinguishes the presbyter from the bishop.

This question results from an exegesis of the Pastoral Letters. For example, John Chrysostom refers to this problem: "There is no great difference between bishop and presbyter, since presbyters have also received the commission to teach and to preside in church. All that I have said about bishops is also valid for the presbyters. Only with regard to the authority of ordination do the bishops stand higher than the presbyters."[63] The authority to ordain others is also used by Epiphanius as an argument that the presbyter is not equal to the bishop.[64] The synod of Alexandria

---

61. *Sacramentarium Veronense,* eds. L. C. Mohlberg and L. Eizenhöfer (Rome, 1956) no. 954 = Lodi, *Enchiridion,* no. 1071.

62. Ibid., no. 947 = Lodi, no. 1064.

63. *In ep. 1 ad Tim. hom.* 11; PG 62:553.

64. *Panarion* 75.4; PG 42:508.

in 324 reduced a certain Isquiras to the status of lay person, since he had been consecrated by a priest.[65]

Basing himself upon the Pastoral Letters, Ambrose maintains that the bishop is the first presbyter.[66] According to Jerome, one of the presbyters was selected and set above the others, so that order might be maintained in the Church and the danger of heresy banished. The Pastoral Letters are also the main argument for Jerome.[67]

These reflections by Ambrose and Jerome appeared in the early Middle Ages in numerous commentaries on Paul's letters and liturgical works (Isidore of Seville, Alcuin).[68] Gratian, in his decree, repeated the two texts from Jerome.[69] Through these authors the opinion of Ambrose and Jerome exercised a powerful influence on Scholastic theology and canon law.

L. Ott summarizes the Scholastic outlook as follows: "In contrast to the theologians, who with few exceptions seek to reduce the extraordinary power of ordination of the priest to the lower consecration, the canon lawyers show a tendency to expand the extraordinary authority of ordination greatly. The latter interpretation was supported by the opinion maintained by many canonists on the original equality of bishop and priest, an opinion which could invoke the authority of Jerome and which was supported by the authority of Gratian's decree."[70] In light of this opinion, the privileges of ordination which several popes conferred during the late Middle Ages are understandable. Three cases have come down to us: from Boniface IX (February 1, 1400), DS 1145—this privilege was later revoked; from Innocent VIII (April 9, 1489), DS 1435, only for the subdiaconate and diaconate—this privilege was in effect until the eighteenth century; from Martin V (November 16, 1427), DS 1290. Vasquez reports other cases, but he does not give the texts.[71] Theologians like Franciscus of Vitoria and Johannes Maier expressed their objections to such privileges; the latter mentions among the first the privilege bestowed by Martin V

65. In Athanasius, *Apol. c. Arianos* 11.7–12, 3; 76.2–5; PG 25:267, 269, 385.

66. *Liber quaestionum,* ch. 97: "Quid enim est episcopus, nisi primus presbyter, hoc est summus sacerdos? Denique non aliter quam compresbyteros hic vocat et consacerdotes suos"; PL 35:2502. Similarly: *In 1 Tim. c. 3;* PL 17:470.

67. *Ep.* 146.1 (Letter to Evangelus); PL 22:1193; *Comment. in ep. ad Titum;* PL 26:562: "Idem et diceretur in populis: *Ego sum Pauli, ego Apollo, ego autem Cephae* (1 Cor 1, 12), communi presbyterorium consilio ecclesiae gubernabantur. Postquam vero unusquisque eos, quos baptizaverat, suos putabat esse, non Christi, in toto orbe decretum est ut unus de presbyteris electus superponeretur ceteris, ad quem omnis ecclesiae cura pertineret, et schismatum semina tollerentur."

68. Evidence in Ott, *Weihesakrament,* 46.

69. *Decretum* c. 5 D. 95; c. 24 D. 93 (Frieberg, 332, 327).

70. Ott, *Weihesakrament,* 106.

71. *Disp. in III S. Thomae,* disp. 243 c. 4.

on the Cistercian abbots. In modern times several theologians have come out in favor of this right of the papacy.

According to Lennerz, it is impossible that three popes could have erred in so important an issue as sacramental ordination.[72]

Congar also will not accept the notion of a papal error; these are rather exceptional cases: "When we recognize that these facts are exceptional on their proper level, then we should feel the obligation to accept that the ordinary faculties bestowed on the simple priest empower him, *positis ponendis,* not only to be the administer of confirmation, but also of ordination to the diaconate and even to the priesthood."[73]

E. Schillebeeckx emphasizes that priests are co-workers with the bishops, which also includes the possibility that they may transmit the priestly consecration, only, however, as an exception, and only on the order of the highest authority of the Church.[74]

Through these privileges the historical problem comes to a head. Early on, Charlemagne commissioned the priests Willehad and Ludger to consecrate other priests for the mission territories of Friesland and Saxony.[75] The case of Alexandria is also brought out, where the bishop was supposedly consecrated by the college of presbyters; however, this interpretation is not historically defensible.[76]

The case of privileges conferred by the pope should be compared to the history of the theology concerning marriage. Various papal decisions concerning marriage were validated by the canonists. The theologians accepted these decisions on the grounds that a papal error in so important a matter was simply impossible. It seems to me questionable that such a principle is applicable also to the power of ordination, which is always limited to a concrete situation.

Of course, ordination should not be understood as a species of magic; rather, it is a transmission of a function within the Church on the part of a hierarchically structured community. The best evidence for this consists in the fact that ordination has the form of an *epiclesis;* that is, the *entire community* prays, *through* its presiders, that God pour out his spirit

---

72. Lennerz, *De Sacramento Ordinis,* no. 242, p. 143: "in re adeo gravi, qualis est ordinatio sacramentalis."

73. Congar, *Tatsachen,* 314.

74. E. Schillebeeckx, "Priesterschap," in *Theologisch woordenboek,* vol. 3 (Roermond, 1958) 3983f., and in *TTh* 8 (1968) 402-34; G. Philips, *L'église et son mystère au IIe Concile du Vatican* (Paris, 1967) ad locum, accepts this interpretation.

75. MGSS 2:380-83, 410ff.

76. Against Fransen, *Weihen,* 110. J. Lécuyer referred to that in his article: "Le Problème des consécrations épiscopales dan l'Église d'Alexandrie," *BLE* 65 (1964) 241-57.

upon the candidate. The essential presupposition for a valid ordination is that the pneumatological element (the epiclesis) should be carried out according to institutional norms. If the epicletal perspective (the prayer through the community) is taken into account, then perhaps one could extract a positive evaluation concerning the Reformation's ordination, although this ordination was bestowed outside the valid norms of the Church. In any case the Orthodox reaction to this situation should be seriously considered[77] (see below, chap. VII, part 5).

Finally, there remains a fundamental question. The transition to the (monarchical) episcopacy is a historical, post-New Testament decision of the Church. Can this decision be regarded as an enduring norm for the later Church? In 1962 K. Rahner answered this question yes.[78] By contrast, J. Newmann[79] and E. Schillebeeckx[80] expressed a negative opinion. Fundamentally the problem revolves around the so-called *ius divinus,* a terminology that was excluded from *Lumen gentium.*[81]

The difference between the bishop and his presbyters lies in the fact that the one on the basis of his ordination receives the full responsibility for a community, whereas the others are selected to help the bishop and thus are his co-workers. Thus the distinction lies at the level of responsibility (*munus*). The presbyters help the bishop with the service of the community and "represent" him, so to speak. The principle of collegiality between bishop and presbyters follows from this quite naturally. The question of where the bishop's primacy over the presbyter lies with reference to the *potestas ordinis* is not crucial theologically. The point of departure for the proper understanding of the bishop's as well as the presbyters' power to serve is the celebration of the Eucharist. The authority of the bishop should be understood as a concretization of his power with regard to the celebration of the Eucharist. In both cases it is a matter of an

---

77. P. Trembelas, *Dogmatique de l'église orthodoxe catholique,* vol. 3 (Chevetogne, 1968) 318 note 1, believes a future recognition of the validity of the ordinations in the Lutheran Church would be paradoxical, since the apostolic succession has not been preserved there.

78. "On the term 'Jus Divinum' in the Catholic Understanding," in *Schriften* 5:249–77.

79. "Erwägungen zur Revision des kirchlichen Gesetzbuches," *ThQ* 145 (1966) 285–304 (here 294ff.; on Rahner: 296 note 16).

80. "The Catholic Understanding of Office in the Church," *TS* 30 (1969) 567–87 (here 569 note 3).

81. On the "ius divinum": J. M. Miller, *The Divine Right of the Papacy in Recent Ecumenical Theology,* Analecta Gregoriana 218 (Rome, 1980) (with an excellent bibliography; important for the development within Catholic theology: 36–169); Y. M. Congar, "Jus Divinum," *RDC* 28 (1978/nos. 2–4) 108–22.

authority for a community and within a community. In this context an "absolute" ordination is impossible.[82]

The fact that, from the third to the seventh centuries, deacons without holy orders were often ordained directly to be the bishop of Rome shows that the episcopal ordination includes the priestly ordination within itself. The difference between the two lies on the plane where *ordo* and *iurisdictio* intersect. This division of responsibility is at least partially a matter of human law, in that divine law always makes its appearance in a human form.

4. The Function of Bishops

Lumen gentium presents the episcopal functions as participations in the threefold authority of Christ; corresponding to these it speaks of a teaching office (*munus docendi:* no. 25), of a sanctifying office (*munus sanctificandi:* no. 26), and of a governing office (*munus regendi:* no. 27). These three aspects constitute a unity and should be understood in connection with the fact that the bishop is the chief presider at the community assembly for the Eucharist. It is there that the bishop has his *cathedra.*

Like every person in authority, the bishop exercises his office with regard to the community "in the name of Christ." He is the one who "holds the place of Christ and has been sent by Christ" (no. 27). The episcopal function must be understood out of the Eucharistic celebration: it is there that the *Word* of the gospel is proclaimed and the *sacrament* of salvation is made present. For that reason the constitution states that "every valid Eucharistic celebration stands under the bishop's direction" (no. 26, 1) and that "the bishop himself confects the Eucharist, or has this done at his direction" (no. 26, 1). The phrase "has this done at his direction," which is reminiscent of the terminology of Ignatius of Antioch, allows the collegial connection of all who hold authority in the diocese to come to the surface.

---

82. Schillebeeckx (*Christliche Identität,* 188f.) correctly invokes canon 6 of the Council of Chalcedon against absolute ordination: "No one would be ordained in an absolute manner, neither to the priesthood nor to the diaconate. . . . If no Church has been referred to him in an unambiguous way, the holy council decrees that his 'cheirotonia' is null and void . . . and that in no situation may he exercise his functions" (*Conciliorum oecumenicorum decreta,* eds. G. Alberigo and others [Freiburg, 1976] 90). We should regard as nonsense the fact that some contemporary bishops carry the title of an ancient diocese that today no longer exists. If we were to take this canon from Chalcedon seriously, then it is not so easy to justify the fact that the nuncios or certain members of the Roman curia have received consecration as bishops. The ancient Church reserved the title *deacon* for such services.

The bishops' power (*potestas*) in their dioceses is characterized as "personal, ordinary, and direct" (*propria, ordinaria et immediata*) (no. 27, 1), that is, the bishops should not be seen "as representatives of the bishop of Rome" (no. 27, 2). From this explanation arises the question of how, then, the place of the bishop of Rome can be characterized, without giving the impression that the other bishops are only his representatives. The First Vatican Council had already come to grips with this problem. The text of DS 3061 (= NR 446) makes every effort to avoid this impression.

History is often the best teacher. Pope Gregory the Great (d. 604) opposed Patriarch John of Constantinople's naming himself "ecumenical patriarch." Gregory's argument, in a letter which he sent to various bishops, ran as follows: If someone calls himself an ecumenical bishop, then one may conclude that you are no bishops.[83] We will come back to this problem in chapter XIII.

a. The Teaching Office of the Bishops[84]

Among the various offices of the bishops, according to *Lumen gentium* no. 25, proclamation of the gospel occupies a preeminent position. The bishops are described as the "authentic teachers," that is, they proclaim to the people of God the faith that the people must know. The bishops should be "respected as teachers possessing Christ's authority and as witnesses to the divine and Catholic truth." For that reason "the faithful must comply with what their bishops say in the name of Christ concerning belief and behavior [*fides et mores*] and attach themselves to them with religiously grounded obedience" (ibid.).

Following traditional theology, the constitution distinguishes between the exercise of the teaching office by the bishops acting alone and the exercise of this office by the college of bishops acting together with their head, the bishop of Rome; the highest expression of the latter is the ecumenical council.

> The individual bishops do not possess the power of infallibility; however, if they, although split up in the world, maintain community with one another and the successor to Peter, teach authentically concerning faith and morals [*res fidei et morum*] and bring forward

83. "Nam si unus, ut putat, universalis sit, restat ut vos episcopi non satis": PL 77:1005; "si enim hoc dici licenter permittitur, honor patriarcharum negatur": PL 77:773. See D. T. Strotmann, "Der Bischof in der Überlieferung der Ostkirche," in Y. M. Congar, ed., *Das Bischofsamt und die Weltkirche* (Stuttgart, 1964; French original, 1962) 335-53 (the work was first published in *Irénikon* 34 [1961] 147-64).

84. Bibliography: M. Löhrer, "Träger der Vermittlung," in MySal 1, 545-87; A. Houtepen, "Lehrautorität in der ökumenischen Diskussion," in *Verbindliches Lehren der Kirche heute* (Frankfurt, 1978) 120-208.

a certain teaching in agreement as universally binding, they then proclaim in an infallible way [*infallibiter*] the teaching of Christ. This is more manifestly the case if they are united in an ecumenical council as teachers and judges over faith and morals. Then one should attach oneself to their definitions with the obedience of faith. (no. 25, 2)

This passage expands a text from Vatican I (DS 3011 = NR 971). The mode of argumentation of Vatican I with reference to the pope's infallibility of definition, as well as the infallibility of the college of bishops together with the pope, is also taken over by the constitution: "the bishop of Rome enjoys" the infallibility promised to the Church, and it is also "given to the body of bishops" (no. 25, 3; see DS 3074 = NR 454). The constitution's text (remark 79) refers to the comments by the *relator fidei* Gasser from Vatican I, who remarked that the pope should not be seen as separated from the Church.[85]

Foundation of the Task of the Teaching Office. The point of departure for a foundational justification of the task of the teaching office is the role that the Pastoral Letters ascribe to this office, specifically the apostolic commission to protect against heresies. In various later documents of the New Testament, the officials are presented as shepherds of the community, especially against the danger of heretical tendencies.

In the post-New Testament period, disputes concerning the faith were resolved through synods of bishops, who participated as "representatives" of their communities. There are indications of such assemblies dating back even to the middle of the second century.[86] In the dispute concerning the validity of baptism administered by heretics, the Eastern bishops reacted to the position of Pope Stephen (d. 257) with episcopal synods. Dionysius could write to the pope that the Churches of the East were united, after the bishops had come together in synods.[87] The later ecumenical synods

85. "Ideo non separamus papam ab ordinatissima coniunctione cum ecclesia" (Mansi 52:1213). The following remark by Gasser is very interesting: one should not so understand the infallibility of the pope as though it rested first with the pope and then was transmitted from him to the bishops and to the Church ("ac si omnis infallibilitas sit sita in solo papa et a papa derivetur in ecclesiam et illi communicetur": ibid., 1216).

86. "In response to Montanism we have councils in Asia Minor from 160–170 (Eusebius, *Church History* 5.16.10). At the end of the second century (Eusebius, *Church History* 5.23.2), the councils take up the question of the proper date for Easter, and in Africa from the time of Cyprian the question of the *lapsi* or heretics" (C. Vogel, "Einheit der Kirche und Vielheit der geschichtlichen Kirchenorganisationsformen vom dritten bis zum fünften Jahrhundert," in Y. M. Congar, ed., *Das Bischofsamt und die Weltkirche* [Stuttgart, 1964; French original, 1962] 609–62, here 627 note 70).

87. Eusebius, *Church History* 7.5.1.

should be understood in the light of these first synods. The fact that the ecumenical synods produced creeds, that is, *horoi* (definitions), which were intended to distinguish the true faith from heresy (*definire* = mark off), shows that these assemblies saw it as their task to present the *binding* doctrine of the Church. Conciliar decisions were described by the contemporary Church as formulated in truth through the Holy Spirit.[88]

Through God's promise, the Church is indefectible (Matt 16:17). This implies that it will remain in the truth (under the guidance of the Holy Spirit: John 16:13), that is, that it will confess the gospel. Should a specific task be brought to the Church authority, it must then be referred to the confession of the Church.[89] For that reason authority and its function should be understood in the light of God's promise to the Church. This is precisely what the First and Second Vatican Councils intend when they present the infallibility of the teaching office in the light of the infallibility of the Church.

The Ecumenical Problem: The Reformation's Position. Although the Reformation maintained that, in virtue of God's promise, the Church could not abide in error, the insistent stress on the Word of God together with the observation that the papacy had, according to the Reformers' view, suppressed the truth of the gospel, led to the notion that every human intermediary—and the teaching office is one such—must be held suspect.

Luther said on several occasions that

> God had maintained his Church even while Christianity had frequently erred, together with the papacy—and specifically by the fact that He has wonderfully preserved the text of the gospel and the sacraments. . . . In spite of everything, [Luther] spies in the actual history of the Church a line of truth in which the promise that the Holy Spirit would guide the Church is fulfilled in continually new ways. . . . However, this continuity of the Spirit's guidance, this preservation of the true Church, is not identical with the official tradition and the supposed apostolic succession in Christianity, and is not guaranteed through it. . . . God allows the official Church to err, in order to break it repeatedly from relying upon proximate human support instead of relying exclusively upon His Word.[90]

Calvin defended the same position: The Holy Spirit guides the Church, but it allows human things to take place in it, so that it may not put its trust in the human. On the other hand, Calvin construes the Catholic

---

88. Evidence in Y. M. Congar, *La tradition et les traditions* (Paris, 1960) 156ff.

89. See E. Schillebeeckx, "Das Problem der Amtsunfehlbarkeit," *Conc* 9 (1973) 198–209 (here 199).

90. P. Althaus, *Die Theologie M. Luthers* (Gütersloh, 1962) 296; with evidence.

position as if it placed the office of the Church outside of God's Word.[91] Moreover, Luther, Calvin, and the Anglican communion maintain that there have been errors in the councils.

These statements by Luther and Calvin can be found, with small differences, in all the various Protestant theologians; an authentic and infallible teaching authority is for the Protestant understanding an attack upon the sovereignty and freedom of the Word of God, which is the only finally valid authority in the Church. For example, J. L. Leuba sees in the Catholic understanding of the teaching office the three following dangers: (1) the very existence of a teaching office constitutes an authority which stands as a rival to God's unique revelation through Jesus Christ; (2) the teaching authority constitutes a second witness next to the one and only revelation; (3) the existence of a teaching office necessarily implies that the Church rules over God's revelation, rather than the reverse.[92]

In opposition to this it must be emphasized that in the Catholic understanding as well "the teaching office does not stand above the Word of God" (*Dei Verbum* no. 10, 2), but rather under it: the teaching office "serves" God's Word "in that it teaches nothing that has not been passed down" (ibid.). In spite of such clarifications, the Catholic position arouses in Protestant theologians the impression that it does not respect the transcendence of the Word of God. Following W. Kasper, one could summarize the positions of both sides in the following way: "While the Protestant tradition connects the Church's freedom from error exclusively to the Word of God, and believes that this achieves a hearing in the Church ever again *'ubi et quando visum est,'* in God's own time and in his own ways, the Catholic Church retains the decision of the ancient Church, which links the canon of scripture and the rule of faith with the apostolic succession and so sees the Church's abiding in truth *through specific witnesses historically transmitted.*"[93]

It seems to me that the difference between the Catholic and the Protestant conceptions hinges upon their link with theological anthropology. An acceptance (Catholicism) or a rejection (the Reformation) of the axiom *gratia supponit naturam* (grace builds on nature) has as a consequence neither a trust in the human transmission (the Catholic institution of a

---

91. *Institutio* 4.8.13: CR 30:855. "Illi Ecclesiae autoritatem extra verbum Dei collocant."

92. J. L. Leuba, "L'infallibilité, nécessité de la foi et problème de la raison," in E. Castelli, ed., *L'infallibilité, son aspect philosophique et théologique* (Paris, 1970) 216.

93. W. Kasper, "Freiheit des Evangeliums und dogmatische Bindung in der katholischen Theologie. Grundlagenüberlegungen zur Unfehlbarkeitsdebatte," in *Die Theologie und das Lehramt,* ed. W. Kern, QD 91 (Freiburg, 1982) 201–33 (here 216).

teaching office) nor a suspicion of it, whose consequence would again be a one-sided emphasis on the transcendence of God's Word.

b. Additional Remarks

The Relation between the Teaching Office and the Community. The renewed emphasis on the active role of the whole community as well as its sense of the faith makes clear the problem that lies in the Catholic notion: the hierarchy has a *special* responsibility for what has been passed on from the *entire* community (see above chap. XI, part 3: on the *sensus fidelium* and the teaching office). Nonetheless, history clearly shows that the Holy Spirit has also clarified the truth contained in the gospels through charismatic personalities who were not part of the institutional structure (either bishop or pope).

Would it be imaginable that a final definition of the teaching authority would be rejected by the people of God? The answer to this question must take seriously the historical data; it must be produced a posteriori, and not a priori. For that reason various theologians take the Arian crisis as an example of this problem. However, *Lumen gentium* responds systematically and dogmatically: "Moreover, the consensus of the Church can never fail to agree with these definitions, due to the effectiveness of the same Holy Spirit, thanks to whom the entire flock of Christ is preserved in the unity of faith and moves forward" (no. 25, 3). The statement of the council presupposes that the definitions of the teaching authority are in agreement with the content of revelation (*definitiones praedictae cum revelatione necessario concordant*). According to the council acts, the validity of the papal definitions as *ex sese* incontestable (Vatican I) should also be applied to the definitions of councils. That is, they do not need ratification by the people[94] to be valid, as various Orthodox theologians following Chomjakov have maintained.[95] Here it should be remarked that these statements do not exclude the possibility that the entire Church might need time before it can identify with the decisions of the teaching authority and recognize them as useful for its life.

More recently various Catholic theologians have spoken of reception,[96] but in another sense; the term is used to describe the whole Church as

94. *Schema Constitutionis de Ecclesia* (Vatican, 1964) = Acta Synod 3/1, 253.
95. See above chapter 11 section 2a.
96. Y. M. Congar, "Die Rezeption als ekklesiologische Realität," *Conc* 8 (1972) 500–14, a shortened version of the original: "La 'Réception' comme réalité ecclésiologique," *RSPhTh* 56 (1972) 369–403. See also my essay: "Der Begriff der 'Rezeption' und sein Ort im Kern der katholischen Ekklesiologie," in P. Lengsfeld and H.-G. Stobbe, eds., *Theologischer Konsens und Kirchenspaltung* (Stuttgart, 1981) 97–109. For that also B. Sesboüé, "Autorité du Magistère et vie de foi ecclésiale," *NRT* 93 (1971) 337–63 (the author contrasts the "dogmatic mentality" that is widespread in

a living organism. Thereby one emphasizes "the organic and living connection which exists through the action of the Holy Spirit between the officials of the Church and its body, between the earliest witnesses to the faith and the essential guardians of the tradition."[97] The encyclical *Humanae vitae* of Paul VI (1968) offers a good example of reception. The nuancing with which the various bishops' conferences clarified and occasionally completed it is an indication of the complementarity that results through the process of reception in the life of the Church. Naturally, the faithful cannot simply dispense with the teaching of the encyclical.[98] In the last analysis one must wonder with Congar: " 'Non-reception,' or 'disobedient,' or what else?"[99] Such a question indicates the fundamental problem that afflicts this situation where the authority stands simultaneously in ontological connection with the community, that is, *in* it, and in a critical capacity over *against* it.

The stress on the sense of the faith of the entire people of God should not mean that the examination of the charisms, which is the job of the hierarchy (*Lumen gentium* no. 12) would now be thrown into question, so that the hierarchy would be forced simply to comply with the articulated consciousness of the people of God, as the modernists maintained (decree *Lamentabili:* DS 3406 = NR 395). The explanation of the Congregation of the Faith *Mysterium Ecclesiae* raises this danger and quotes the corresponding sections of Lamentabili.[100]

Infallibility or Indefectibility?[101] Even before H. Küng's book *Infalli-*

---

our time with the mentality that was dominant in history); Sesboüé, "Église infallible ou intemporelle," in *Recherches et débats* 79 (Paris, 1973) especially 83-85, 87, 90.

97. P. Fransen, "L'autorité des Conciles," in *Problemes de l'autorité* (Paris, 1969) 59-100 (here 86).

98. See K. Rahner, "Zur Enzyklika 'Humanae Vitae,' " in *Schriften* 9:276-301.

99. Congar, *Rezeption,* 506f.

100. *Mysterium ecclesiae,* no. 2, 5 in *AAS* 65 (1972) 396-408. See the outstanding commentary by K. Rahner, " 'Mysterium Ecclesiae': Zur Erklärung der Glaubenskongregation über die Lehre von der Kirche," StZ 191 (1973) 579-94 = *Schriften* 12:482-500 (here 488ff.: "Die Unfehlbarkeit des Lehramtes").

101. Bibliography: O. Rousseau, et al., *L'infaillibilité de l'église* (Chevetogne, 1962) (important for our context: Ch. Moeller, "Conclusion. Infaillibilité et Verité," 223-55; P. De Vooght, "Esquisse d'une enquête sur le mot 'infaillibilité' durant de période scholastique," 99-146; B.-D. Dupuy, "Le magistère de l'Église, service de la parole," 53-97); W. Kasper, *Dogma unter dem Wort Gottes* (Mainz, 1965); Y. M. Congar, "Infaillibilité et indéfectibilité," *RSPhTh* 50 (1970) 601-18; also in Congar, *Ministerès et communion ecclésiale* (Paris, 1971) 140-65 (with outstanding bibliographical references); K. Rahner, "Zum Begriff der Unfehlbarkeit in der katholischen Theologie," in *Schriften* 10:305-37 (this contribution was included in the report on the symposium on infallibility of January 5-10, 1970, which E. Castelli published [note 92]); *Luther-*

bility?—An Inquiry (Zurich, 1970),[102] several Catholic authors were suggesting the notion of "indefectibility." For example, Y. Congar reviewed the terms which could express "the Church's attempt to live in the truth."

> 1. The term "secure in the faith" (*fidei firmitas*). . . .
> 2. The idea of divine assistance and the providential guidance into the entire truth (John 16:13). G. Thils rightly recommends that we make clear the connection with the theme of truth. . . .
> 3. Finally the notion of indefectibility. Indefectibility means the indestructibility of the faith on which and through which the Church is built. It recognizes there have been unsure paths, as history shows. It admits to shortcomings and partial or momentary lapses of memory, to partial and temporary errors.[103]

In his commentary on the Congregation of the Faith's explanation *Mysterium Ecclesiae*, K. Rahner has emphasized that "ancient forms that endure or which must be replaced with equivalent new formulas, are in practice 'amalgamated' with error."[104]

For his part H. Küng has characterized the problem of the way of the Church toward the truth as an *aporeia*.

> On the one hand we must recognize the *promises* given to the Church. . . . On the other hand we must recognize the *errors* in the Church! What is indisputable is the following: so far no one, neither Vatican I nor Vatican II, nor the theology of the schools, has been able to explain the only thing that has to be explained, which is that the Church, either through her leadership or her theology, cannot make certain statements which from the very outset could not be false. . . .

---

ans and Catholics in Dialogue 6. Teaching Authority and Infallibility in the Church (Minnesota, 1978).

102. For a discussion of the book: (a) K. Rahner, ed., *Zum Problem Unfehlbarkeit. Antworten auf die Anfrage von H. Küng* (Freiburg, 1971). There appear three articles by Rahner: 1. "Zum Begriff der Unfehlbarkeit in der katholischen Theologie," 9–26 = *StZ* 186 (1970) 18–31 = *Schriften* 10:305–37; 2. "Kritik an H. Küng. Zur Frage der Unfehlbarkeit theologischer Sätze," 27–48 = *StZ* 186 (1970) 361–77; 3. "Replik. Bemerkungen zu: Hans Küng. Im Interesse der Sache [in: *StZ* 187 (1971) 43–64. 105–22] 49–70 = *StZ* 187 (1971) 105–22; (b) H. Küng, ed., *Fehlbar? Eine Bilanz* (Einsiedeln, 1973); (c) J. J. Kirvan, ed., *The Infallibility Debate* (New York, 1971); (d) *Conc* 9 (1973) Heft 3, *Wahrheit und Gewissheit;* (e) W. Kasper, "Freiheit des Evangeliums und dogmatische Bindung in den katholischen Theologien," in *Die Theologie und das Lehramt,* QD 91 (Freiburg, 1982) 201–33 (the work was completed in April 1981); (f) *Lutherans and Catholics in Dialogue 6* (especially the articles by A. Dulles, "Infallibility: The Terminology and Moderate Infallibilism"; C. J. Peter, "A Rahner-Küng Debate and Ecumenical Possibilities").

103. Congar, *Infallibilité,* 154f.

104. Rahner, "Mysterium Ecclesiae," 496.

A resolution of the *aporeia* . . . A victory over this dilemma is only possible when the alternatives are sublated to a higher plane: *the Church will abide in the truth despite the errors that are permanently possible!*[105]

In the polemic with H. Küng, K. Rahner engaged himself rather energetically; nevertheless he expressed himself here cautiously:

Theology must reflect much more seriously than she has on the fact that there has been, and certainly today still is, considerable error in the Church and in her theology. We should not dismiss this situation as innocent. This error is not always harmless; it does not merely concern details over which theologians continue to dispute, but rather very often in various ways and in an almost inexpungeable manner it burrows deep into the center of the concrete life of Christians. Also, much more than is commonly believed, error is also "amalgamated" with the truths and dogmas of the Church, which are thereby themselves threatened and damaged in their practical consequences.[106]

Although Congar and Rahner speak with other theologians of errors in the life of the Church, they differentiate themselves from Küng's position in that they naturally accept that the teaching authority can and does present the truth in the Church through correct statements; otherwise a guidance of the Church by the hierarchy would be impossible. A denial of the possibility that the teaching authority can present the truth of the Gospels through correct statements leads to a complete denial of the role of the hierarchy in the Church.

The explanation of *Mysterium Ecclesiae* expresses the position of the teaching authority itself in the following way: "It is not proper for the faithful to recognize in the Church only a general conformity with the truth that could, nevertheless, still mix itself with errors that might be located here and there in the binding statements put out by the teaching authority of the Church or else in the assured context of the people of God in matters of faith and morals.[107]

If contemporary theology suggests the notion of indefectibility, it does so as to take seriously the history of the Church including its darker moments. The Church is guided by the Holy Spirit into the truth. It is the task of the teaching office to mark off (*de-finire*) truth from error and thereby to define authoritatively. In this way the teaching office is an agency for the working of the Holy Spirit, and its function can be understood only in dependency upon and under the operation of the Holy

105. Küng, *Unfehlbar?*, 141ff.
106. Rahner, *Zum Problem*, 45f.
107. No. 4.

Spirit. The decisions of the teaching office are binding for the Christian community in that the teaching office receives the charism of freedom from error (infallibility) for such decisions from the Holy Spirit.

The Incontrovertibility of Dogmatic Formulations.[108] The Church's dogmas are "relative with reference to the primitive witness of the Scriptures." For that reason "they must themselves ever and again be expounded from Scripture [the one and only *norma normans*]."[109] Since human discourse can not fully express a mystery through definitions, and since its language is always historically conditioned, every dogmatic formulation, although it is definitive and incontestable, must be regarded as open to new, complementary formulations. Dogmatic formulations are answers to concrete questions in a concrete cultural context; the answer is and remains always true, however only in relation to the concrete context in which and for which it was formulated. A new cultural context will demand new complementary formulations. Expressed more pointedly: one does not remain orthodox, that is, a correct believer, if one simply repeats the old answers in every new cultural context.

5. "Apostolic Succession"

The document entitled *Spiritual Authority in the Church* states that "The most important question in connection with the theology of the bishop's authority, and the question of the reciprocal recognition of offices, is the problem of the apostolic tradition."[110] As a matter of fact, the Reformers turned against episcopal succession with the argument that true succession consists in one's connection with the gospel (see above chap. XII, part 2). The Catholic understanding is often depicted from the Protestant side as the unfolding of a purely mechanical succession; they then contrast this with a stress on the pneumatological character of succession.

As for the terminology, often the same words are used in different senses. E. Schlink summarizes the different meanings attached to the same words.

---

108. Fundamental bibliography: K. Rahner, "Was ist eine dogmatische Aussage?" in *Schriften* 5:54–81; W. Kasper, *Dogma unter dem Wort Gottes* (Mainz, 1965); E. Schillebeeckx, *Offenbarung und Theologie* (Mainz, 1967) 220ff.; Schillebeeckx, *Das Problem,* here 200–04; C. Molari, "Il linguaggio teologico," in V. Fagiolo and G. Concetti, eds., *La collegialità episcopale per il futuro della chiesa* (Florence, 1969) 227–48; Internationale Theologenkommission, *Die Einheit des Glaubens und der Theologische Pluralismus* (Einsiedeln, 1973) (especially the commentary by J. Ratzinger).

109. Kasper, *Freiheit des Evangeliums,* 230.

110. No. 59, in DwÜ, 348.

By the term *apostolic succession* is meant:

a) The requirement of apostolic service through office.

b) The passing on of the apostolic teaching by the call to office.

c) The consequences of the laying on of hands in the ordination.

d) Particularly the consequences of the bishop's laying on of hands.

Discussions in the theological controversy have concentrated primarily on the question of the supposed unbroken chain in the laying on of hands from the apostles.

Also the notion of the *apostolicity* of the Church is used by some:

a) as a recognition of the historical foundation of the Church in the service of the apostles.

b) as a statement concerning the reality of the Church as determined through the apostolic succession of authority.

c) as a statement concerning the factual preservation of the teaching of the apostles in the Church.

d) as an acknowledgment of the Church's obligation to defend the apostolic teaching and to follow the apostles in its service.

The theological controversy concerns more a factual characteristic of the Church than the obligation of the entire Church with all its members to continue the apostolic service.[111]

The Lima document on authority speaks of the "apostolic tradition in the Church" and of the "succession of the apostolic authority."[112] Systematically, our theme may be presented in four stages.

First, in the Creed the Church is called apostolic. She is built on the foundation of the apostles (Eph 2:20). She must remain in continuity with the proclamation of the apostles. This means that "if one wishes to speak of apostolic succession, one must begin with the apostolicity of the Church in the sense of content."[113] For that reason the "apostolic succession resides at the very least in the continuity of the apostolic teaching," as the document *The Presence of Christ* states.[114] Expressed from the other side: "The paramount manifestation of the apostolic succession is to be found in the apostolic tradition of the Church as a whole."[115] The interest of the later New Testament writings—most clearly in the Pastoral Letters—lies in their further transmission and maintenance of the teaching of the apostles. In the struggle against the Gnostics, the lists of bishops were mentioned out of the felt need to prove that the Church must remain in the authentic apostolic tradition.

111. Schlink, *Apostolische Sukzession,* 138.

112. Subtitle to the fourth section: "Sukzession in der apostolischen Tradition," in DwÜ, 579.

113. "Das geistliche Amt in der Kirche," no. 60 in DwÜ, 349.

114. No. 101 in DwÜ, 512.

115. Lima Document, no. 35 in DwÜ, 579.

Second, the Lima document correctly states that "within the Church, the ordained ministry has a special task to preserve and bring forward the faith of the apostles. The ordered passing on of the ordained authority is thus a powerful expression of the continuity of the Church through history."[116]

This special task is already witnessed in the later texts of the New Testament. In the synods of the ancient Church, at which important substantive problems were discussed, the local Churches were represented by their presiders, that is, by their bishops.

Third, since the responsibility of those in authority does not exclude, but rather implies a coresponsibility of all other members of the community, "the notion of apostolic succession cannot remain limited to the Church authority."[117] Such a reduction would lead to a clericalization of the Church (for a more thorough foundation, see chap. XI). Vatican II's Decree on the Apostolate of the Laity, *Apostolicam actuositatem,* presents a clear foundation for this statement: "There exists in the Church a differentiation of service, but a unity of mission. From Christ the commission was passed on to his apostles and their successors to teach, to sanctify, and to lead in his name and with the fullness of his authority. The laity, by contrast, who also have a share in the priestly, prophetic, and royal authority of Christ, realize in the Church and the world their own part in the mission of the entire people" (no. 2, 2).

Spiritual Authority in the Church formulates in the following way the mutually dependent problems: "The witness [for the gospel] is given to the Church as a whole. For that reason the entire Church as *ecclesia apostolica* stands in the apostolic succession. The succession in the sense of succession of authority figures should be seen as taking place within the succession of the entire Church in the apostolic faith."[118]

"The apostolic succession [of authority] is not only an affair of the validity of the sacraments," that is, of the sacrament of ordination, as if it were "a kind of fluid that would be poured from one validly ordained consecrator to the next."[119] The apostolic succession of authority is succession in the role of presiders of a community that stands in *koinonia* with the other "catholic" communities. As a precondition for his ordination the candidate presents a confession of faith, since the task for which he is being ordained requires a connection with the entire Church and its Creed; the candidate is ordained as a successor to a *cathedra* (the bishop's cathedra). This was the ancient Church's understanding, and today this

116. Ibid.
117. Schlink, *Apostolische Sukzession,* 147.
118. No. 62 in DwÜ, 349.
119. Congar, *Wesenseigenschaften,* 555.

is still the understanding of the Catholic Church as well as of the Orthodox Churches and the ancient Eastern Churches.[120]

For that reason "the apostolic succession is a succession in this task; it consists formally in a sameness [in French: *identité*] of function; its first condition is an identity of belief."[121]

Orthodox theologians of various orientations have all emphasized that the apostolic succession in authority should be seen in connection with the apostolicity of teaching. For example, P. Trembelas writes: "To preserve succession, it is not enough to transmit the priesthood through a canonical ordination by the laying on of hands of the successor of the apostles; rather, it is required that an abiding in the apostolic teaching is simultaneously given. . . . Both elements, preservation of the apostolic teaching and a canonical ordination, are interiorly and inseparably connected, and constitute the apostolic succession. The teaching of the apostles is itself the foundation of the succession."[122] The Russian theologians G. Florovsky[123] and P. Evdokimov[124] express similar views.

With particular regard for the patristic sources, Zizioulas emphasizes that "the apostolic succession is essentially a matter of the charismatic identification of the various societies in time," and thereby a succession in teaching, since "the bishop is not a successor to the apostles in himself, that is, as an individual, but rather as head of this community."[125]

---

120. The documents "Das geistliche Amt," no. 62 (in DwÜ, 349) and "Kirchengemeinschaft in Wort und Sakrament," no. 70, both refer to this fact.

121. Congar, *Wesenseigenschaften,* 556.

122. P. Trembelas, *Dogmatique de l'église orthodoxe catholique,* vol. 2 (Chevetogne, 1967) 389f. The same in J. N. Karmiris, "Abriss der dogmatischen Lehre der orthodoxen katholischen Kirche," in P. Bratsiotis, ed., *Die orthodoxe Kirche in griechischer Sicht,* vol. 1 (Stuttgart, 1959) 58; Chr. Androutsos, *Dogmatikí* (Athens, 1907) 281.

123. "The apostolic succession is not primarily a canonical skeleton of the Church. It is not only a tool to guarantee unity in organization or administration; it is rather a charismatic organ that assures the identity and unity of the living body. Apostolic succession means not only a continuity in episcopal ordination, but also a continuity in authority and function; it is no separated and self-sufficient system, but rather is always fused with the living body" ("Le Corps du Christ vivant. Une interprétation orthodoxe de l'Église," in *La sainte église universelle* [Neuchâtel-Paris, 1948] 9–57, here 39 and 37).

124. P. Evdokimov, *L'orthodoxie* (Neuchâtel-Paris, 1965): "What is distinctive to the Orthodox conception [consists in] neither the individual person nor in his personal authority; rather, the *Church* is the principle of succession" (133). "Succession means . . . the unbroken transmission of the tradition down the centuries until the end of history; and 'apostolic' means history in its historicity, transcended through this witness (Church = Apostles)" (161).

125. *Being as Communion* (New York, 1985) 240 and 238. This work was first published in: *Amt und Ordination in ökumenischer Sicht,* ed. H. Vorgrimler, Der priester-

Various sources from the Fathers and the Middle Ages lead Congar to the following conclusion: "There exists a tradition according to which it is not sufficient to establish the episcopal or papal authority on the plane of simple formulas or juridic legitimacy: it rather depends upon a specific content, especially from the agreement with the faith of the apostles. In short, simple material succession is one thing, formal apostolic succession is another; apostolicity in authority requires apostolicity in teaching."[126]

Congar refers to the "unanimous tradition" of the Middle Ages, "at least down to the Counter-Reformation, on the possibility of a heretical or schismatic papacy": "What is interesting for us is that the loss of authentic teaching of the apostles meant the loss of the apostolic authority."[127] Symeon of Thessalonika (beginning of the fifteenth century) expresses himself in the same way: "The bishop of Rome should be the successor only to the orthodoxy of Sylvester, of Agathon, and of Leo. We would then proclaim him apostolic and bearing the primacy over the other high priests (that is, bishops)."[128] Irenaeus had emphasized that the presbyters (also bishops) who became heretics separated themselves from the succession.[129]

Conclusion: The two aspects, apostolicity in teaching and the apostolic succession in authority, should be seen in connection. "The apostolic succession in the bishop's office consists . . . in a succession in the office of presiding over a [local] community that is set in continuity with the faith of the apostles,"[130] to the extent that it stands in *koinonia* with the other catholic local Churches. The exercise of office in the succession of the apostles requires apostolicity in teaching. This is also clearly shown in the traditional solution to the problem of a possible heretical pope.

---

liche Dienst 5 (Freiburg, 1973) 72–113.

126. Congar, *Apostolicité,* 82.

127. Ibid., 79f. This hypothesis was the result of the problem that in no other situation can the pope be judged. The answer runs: if the pope becomes heretical, he is then no longer pope ("A nemine est iudicandus, nisi deprehendatur a fide devius"). This is the answer given by Deusdedit, Gratian, Innocent III (PL 217:670), Torquemada, Cajetan, Cano, Suárez, Bellarmine, the Salmanti censors. . . . See Y. M. Congar, *Die Lehre von der Kirche. Vom Abendländischen Schisma bis zur Gegenwart,* HDG 3/3d (Freiburg, 1971) 10f., 33, 39.

128. PG 155:120.

129. *Adv. Haer.* 4.26.2 "Iis qui in ecclesia sunt presbyteris oboedire oportet, his qui successionem habent ab apostolis, sicut ostendimus. . . . Reliquos vero qui absistunt a principali successione et quocumque loco colligunt, suspectos habere" (PG 7:1053).

130. *Kirchengemeinschaft in Wort und Sakrament,* no. 71; see also: *Das geistliche Amt,* no. 62, in DwÜ, 349.

Fourth, in general agreement with the Orthodox Churches as well as with the old Eastern (non-Chalcedonian) Churches, the Catholic Church sees the succession of authority realized in the succession of the office of bishop. Is ordination by other bishops the condition *sine qua non* for an apostolic succession in authority? On the ecumenical plane, this is the most important question standing in the way of a mutual recognition of officials.[131] With reference to the ordination of the ecclesial communities which stem from the Reformation, the ecumenical decree of Vatican II (no. 22, 3) speaks of a *defectus ordinis,* that is, a failure in the sacrament of ordination. In the case of Anglican orders there is another problem, namely, the *defectus formae et intentionis.*[132] The Anglican communion has preserved the office of bishop.

On the basis of Augustine's decision, which the West accepted, to recognize the validity of ordination by a Donatist even though it meant ordination by a heretic, the Catholic Church has always recognized the ordinations, as well as the other sacraments, of the Orthodox Churches, although they are separated from the Catholic Church on the basis either of a schism (the Orthodox Churches) or a position which, seen formally, is heretical, such as the rejection of the definitions of the ecumenical councils of Ephesus or of Chalcedon (Nestorian or Monophysite Churches).

With reference to the recognition of the officials of the Lutheran Churches, Catholic theologians have made various suggestions.[133] Basi-

131. On authority, see also the Lima Document, no. 53, in DwÜ, 584.

132. On Anglican ordination, see F. Clark, "Anglikanische Weihe," in LThK 1 (1957) 554; Clark, *Anglican Order and Defect of Intention* (London, 1956); J. J. Hughes, *Absolutely Null and Void. The Papal Condemnation of Anglicans Orders 1896* (London and Sidney, 1968); H. Marot, "Les ordinations anglicanes. Coup d'oeil rétrospectif," *Lumière et vie* 64 (1973) 87-116; M. M.[a] Garijo-Guembe, "Las ordenaciones anglicanas: nuevas perspectivas?" *REDC* 43 (1986) 481-90. See also "Amt und Ordination: Erläuterung no. 6 (Salisbury, 1979) der anglikanisch/römisch-katholischen Internationalen Kommission," in DwÜ, 158.

133. Basic bibliography: W. Kasper, "Zur Frage der Anerkennung der Amter in der lutherischen Kirche," *ThO* 151 (1971) 97-109; Y. M. Congar, "Quelques problèmes touchant les ministères," *NRTh* 93 (1971) 785-800 (here 795ff.); M. Willain, "Ist eine apostolische Sukzession ausserhalb der Kette der Handauflegung möglich?" *Conc* 4 (1968) 275-84; J. M. R. Tillard, "Le *votum eucharistiae:* L'Eucharistie dans la rencontre des chrétiennes," in *Miscellanea liturgica in onore de S. Em. il Cardinale G. Lercaro* (Rome, 1967) 143-94; G. H. Tavard, "The Function of the Minister in the Eucharistic Concelebration," *JES* 4 (1967) 629-49; Tavard, "Roman Catholic Theology and 'Recognition of Ministry,' " in *Lutherans and Catholics in Dialogue 4. Eucharist and Ministry* (Washington-New York, 1970) 301-5 (a good presentation of different theological statements); B. Seboüé, *Serviteurs de l'évangile. Les ministères dans l'église* (Paris, 1971) 114ff.; *Reform und Anerkennung kirchlicher Ämter. Ein Memoriandum der Arbeitsgemeinschaft ökumenischer Universitätsinstitute* (Mainz-

cally these attempts move in the direction of a presbyteral succession to which the Reformation was forced to fall back in an emergency situation. As a complementary principle, and as a response to the objection that "full" authority, that is, the episcopal succession, was not maintained in these Churches, one refers to the principle *ecclesia supplet* or to the Orthodox principle of economy. According to these suggestions, one could recognize the ordination in the Lutheran Churches even though the succession of "full" apostolic authority was not preserved.

The Orthodox have addressed this problem, at least during the last two centuries, with the distinction between *akribie* and *economy*. According to the strict principle of *akribie*, those sacraments administered outside the true (Orthodox) Church are not recognized. However, on the basis of the *economy* the Church may recognize these sacraments under certain conditions. The unconditional presupposition for this is that, in the case of an ordination, an authentic liturgical formulary whose content corresponds to the formularies of the ancient Churches must be used by properly ordained bishops. As for the principle of *akribie*, one is referred to the canonical letter of Basilius as well as to canon 68 of the Apostolic Canons.[134] In practice, these principles are applied in different ways by the various autocephalous Orthodox Churches, so that for similar cases one Church will use the principle of *economy*, while another will apply *akribie*. Thus the Uniate bishops of the Russian Church were recognized as bishops when they converted to Orthodoxy, while the Church of Constantinople in a similar case repeated not only the ordination, but even baptism. With reference to Anglican orders, the Patriarch Meletios of Alexandria, presider of the official Orthodox Commission for Dialogue with the Anglicans (Lambeth, 1930) set the limit of the application of the

---

München, 1973) (especially theses 8.10, p. 17f.); K. Rahner and H. Fries, *Einigung der Kirchen—reale Möglichkeit* (Freiburg, 1983) (thesis 7 with commentary by H. Fries; for reactions, see H. Fries in Fries and O. H. Pesch, *Streiten für die eine Kirche* [München, 1987] 45ff.). Against the recognition of orders on the basis of the ecclesiology of the Reformation communities: J. Hamer, "La terminologie ecclésiologique de Vatican II et les ministères protestantes," in *La documentation catholique*, no. 1589, 68 (1971) 625-28.

134. See P. Trembelas, *Dogmatique*, 331-38, whom I am here following. There are further bibliographical references in Th. Spáčil, *Doctrina theologiae orientis separati de sacramento baptismi*, OrChr[R] 6, 4 (Rome, 1926) 211-25; P. Dumont, preface to the book by J. Kotsonis, *Problemes de l'économie ecclésiastique* (Gembloux, 1971; Greek original, 1957); E. Chr. Suttner, "Ökonomie und Akribie als Normen kirchlichen Handels," *OstKSt* 24 (1975) 15-26; M. M.ᵃ Garijo-Guembe, "Bibliographía fundamental sobre el tema de la 'Economía,' " *DiEc* 10 (1975) 639-44. On the official Orthodox position to Anglican orders, see *Orthodox Statements on Anglican Orders*, ed. E. R. Hardy (New York-London, 1946).

principle of *economy:* "Although the Church in truth has the right to reject the priesthood of schismatics and heretics, she does not have the right to recognize ordinations in Churches in which the apostolic succession [that is, the episcopal apostolic succession] has been broken."[135]

The Orthodox theologian Zizioulas writes that the entire idea of *economy* is itself very unclear, and its empirical application in history is so complex that it is most difficult to use it as a principle for the validity of orders. In his opinion the proper solution can only be found when the connection between the community and those who hold office is kept in mind. "If we do not separate those who hold office from the reality of the community consisting of the *koinonia* brought about by the Holy Spirit, then what makes a concrete office valid is not located in some isolated and objective 'norms,' but rather in the *community* to which this official belongs." In what follows he says that "the recognition of officials in practice becomes a *recognition of communities* in an existential sense." In this situation it comes down to "the entire structure of a community."[136]

Zizioulas' reflections take their departure from the connection between an official and his concrete local community that stands in *koinonia* with the other local communities. He emphasizes, I believe correctly, that the recognition of officials implies a fundamental recognition of the structure of an ecclesial community. It is worth noting that this statement leads to a different conception than that of the Decree on Ecumenism: in the latter a valid office is regarded as the criterion according to which an ecclesial community is accorded the title "Church" or not; in the former one could on the basis of the fact that such ecclesial communities live according to the proclaimed gospel, administer baptism, and celebrate the Lord's Supper in the memory of the Lord, recognize the Church status of these communities. In this understanding, the recognition of officials would be a consequence of the recognition of these communities as Churches. Fundamentally it goes back to the problem of apostolic succession and the "catholicity" of the Church. G. H. Tavard summarizes the situation in the following way: "The apostolic succession does not make the Church Catholic; rather it is the case that the catholicity of the Church guarantees the apostolic succession."[137] In a broader perspective one could say that the more we accept a fundamental agreement in teaching between the Lutheran Churches and the Roman Catholic Church—at least in the sense that former criticisms from both sides need not today

---

135. Quoted by Dumont, 17.

136. Zizioulas, *Communion*, 245 and 243f.

137. "The Function of the Minister," 645. Congar, "Problèmes," 797, considers this thought noteworthy.

constitute a fundamental ground for this separation—the more the problem of the relation between the two communities is altered. The problem of authority would become part of a larger complex, and from this larger complex it could be approached and possibly resolved. Authority should not be isolated, but should always be seen in connection with the entirety that is a Church.[138] Here one should not forget that ordination takes place in the liturgical form of an epiclesis: we pray that the Holy Spirit may descend upon the candidate. Although the prayer is pronounced only by the one ordaining, it is an intercession *by the whole community.*

The official must always be seen as commissioned by a local Church. He receives his function directly from Christ, but *because* the Church selects him. Here the ordination formulary of the Roman Pontificale is entirely clear: "All worthy Father, the Church of _____ asks you to consecrate _____ as bishop."[139] It is a matter of the *rite vocatus* of the Augsburg Confession.[140] In line with the tradition of the Church, Melanchthon in his *Tractatus de potestate papae* refers to the obligation of the Church to proclaim the gospel. From this he concludes that the Church "has the power . . . to call forth, select, and ordain ministers for the Church."[141] Naturally ecclesial norms must here be respected, for it is on the basis of these concrete forms that the bishops as successors to the apostles administer ordination.[142]

The recognition of the ordination administered by another Church could take place through a mutual laying on of hands, and should be seen as in the rubric for reconciliation between Churches: the ancient Church used the same liturgical gesture for ordination, namely, the laying on of hands, as for the reconciliation of sinners and those who had separated

138. See: *Das Geistliche Amt in der Kirche,* no. 82, in DwÜ, 355.

139. Translation by F. Schultz in *Das geistliche Amt in der Kirche* (Paderborn-Frankfurt, 1981) 95. In the ordination to the priesthood it is said: "The Holy Church requests . . ." (ibid., 84) Noteworthy is the difference in the formulation: in a bishop's ordination one speaks in the name of the local Church, while in the ordination to the priesthood one speaks in the name of the universal Church. Was it thus originally? Most probably the language in the ordination to the priesthood resembled that of the ordination to the episcopacy.

140. CA 14, in BSLK 69.

141. 67, ibid., 491.

142. In *Lehrverurteilungen—kirchentrennend? 1. Rechtfertigung, Sakramente und Lehre im Zeitalter der Reformation und heute,* eds. K. Lehmann and W. Pannenberg (Freiburg-Göttingen, 1986) 166, refers in the section on authority to the difficulty that afflicts the question of the power to ordain: "Ordinations which do not take place in accord with these ecclesial and canonical regulations are illegitimate (DS 1777)." The term *illegitimate* corresponds neither to the practice of the Catholic Church nor to the content of the quoted canon, nor to the constitution *Lumen gentium,* which speaks of a "defectus ordinis." See above chapter 12, section 1c.

themselves from the Church. This is also the liturgical gesture with which the rite of initiation concludes. In all these cases, if under different aspects, there is an imparting of the gift of the Holy Spirit. Only after this laying on of hands—and only in specified cases—could the officials who had not belonged to the Catholica exercise further their office within the Catholica.

BIBLIOGRAPHY

Congar, Y. M. "Tatsachen, Probleme und Betrachtungen hinsichtlich der Weihevollmacht und der Beziehungen zwischen dem Presbyterat und dem Episkopat." In Y. M. Congar, *Heilige Kirche,* Stuttgart 1966 (French orig. 1963), 285-316. (The article was first published in *La maison Dieu,* 14 [1954] 107-28; in January 1962 pages 311-16 were added.)

_____. "Die Wesenseigenschaften der Kirche." In MySal 4/1, 543ff. (on apostolicity).

Dupuy, B. "Besteht ein dogmatischer Unterschied zwischen der Funktion der Priester und der Funktion der Bishöfe?" *Conc* 4 (1968) 268-74.

Fransen, P. "Weihen, Heilige." In SM 4:1243-93 = HTTL 8:91-128.

Lécuyer, H. *De sacramento ordinis.* Rome, 1953.

Neumann, J. "Bishof. I. Das Katholische Bishofsamt." In TRE 6:653-82.

Schillebeeckx, E. *Christliche Identität und kirchliches Amt.* Düsseldorf, 1985 (third chapter).

Vorgrimler, H. *Sakramententheologie.* Düsseldorf, 1987, second chapter (with the most complete bibliography, 305ff.).

Zizioulas, J. *He Henotas tas Ekklesias én ta theia Eúcharistia kai to Episkópo katá toús treis prótous aionas.* Athens, 1965.

_____. "The Bishop in the Theological Doctrine of the Orthodox Church." *Kanon* 7 (1985) 23-35.

On Apostolic Succession:

a) Ecumenical Documents
Das Evangelium und die Kirche, (Malta Report), nos. 47-64, in DwÜ 260ff.
Das geistliche Amt in der Kirche, nos. 59-66, in DwÜ 348ff.
Glaubensgemeinschaft in Wort und Sakrament, nos. 70-74, Paderborn and Hannover, 1984, 79-84.
Die Gegenwart Christi, nos. 93-108, in DwÜ 510ff.
Lima-Dokument über das Amt, nos. 34-37, in DwÜ 579ff.

b) Lutheran Contributions
Althaus, P. *Die Theologie M. Luthers.* Gütersloh, 1962, 295ff.
Schlink, E. "Die Apostolische Sukzession und die Gemeinschaft der Ämter." In *Reform und Anerkennung kirchlicher Ämter. Ein Memorandum der Arbeitsgemeinschaft ökumenischer Universitätsinstitute,* Mainz and München,

1973, 123-62 (with an excellent bibliography). There is a reworked version of the article "Die Apostolische Sukzession" in *KuD* 7 (1961) 79-114.

_____. *Ökumenische Dogmatik.* Göttingen, 1983, ch. 20, especially 611ff.

Schütte, H. *Amt, Ordination, und Sukzession.* Düsseldorf, 1974 (a presentation of Lutheran exegesis, nos. 1-5, and of dogmatics, nos. 6-7).

Thurian, M. *Sacerdoce et ministère.* Taizé, 1970, 264ff.

c) Catholic Contributions

Beinert, W. "Ökumenische Leitbilder und Alternativen." In *Handbuch der Ökumene,* eds. H. J. Urban and H. Wagner, vol. 3/1, Paderborn, 1987, 126-78 (here 141ff.).

Congar, Y. M. "Apostolicité de ministère et apostolicité de doctrine; Essai d'explication de la réaction protestante et de la tradition catholique." In *Volk Gottes,* eds. R. Bäumer and H. Dolch, Freiburg, 1967, 84-111; also in *Ministères et communion ecclésiale,* Paris, 1971, 51-94 (with a good historical dossier on the Church Fathers and the theologians of the Middle Ages).

_____. "Die Wesenseigenschaften der Kirche." In MySal 4/1, 554ff. (with bibliography).

Küng, H. *Structuren der Kirche.* Freiburg, 1962, 161ff.

_____. *Die Kirche.* Freiburg, 1967, 419ff.

_____. "Thesen zum Wesen der apostolischen Sukzession." *Conc* 4 (1968) 248-51.

Schütte, H. *Amt, Ordination und Sukzession.* Düsseldorf, 1974 (a presentation of Catholic exegesis nos. 9-12, and dogmatics nos. 13-16).

d) Orthodox Contributions

In general this theme is discussed by Orthodox theologians in connection with the apostolicity of the Church. Several contributions on Anglican orders explore thoroughly the question of apostolic succession; see in this chapter notes 122-24; 132.

Garijo-Guembe, M. M. "Notas sobre la 'sucesión apostólica' en la teología ortodoxa." *DiEc* 11 (1976) 131-54 (a presentation of the positions of various Orthodox authors).

XIII.
The Office of the Pope and the Collegiality of Bishops

0. Toward a Statement of the Question

From the Roman Catholic side, primacy is understood as a service for the unity of the Church. By the Orthodox as well as the Protestants it is at least recognized that the question of service for the unity of the Church—one should speak with patristic theology of the unity of the Churches, as the Orthodox in principle hold to be correct—should and must be situated on a universal plane.

At Vatican II one of the most important discussions concentrated on the topic "The Papacy and the Collegiality of Bishops." Although in this formulation the topic shows a definite Western perspective, the difference between the ecclesiology of the Orthodox Churches and that of the Roman Catholic Church here becomes apparent, especially as concerns their conceptions of the unity of Churches. Y. M. Congar sums up the two understandings in the following terms:

The first conception, which is described as the "model of *communio,*" "existed primarily in the early Church, and has remained dominant in the ecclesiology of the Eastern Churches. This is concerned first with the local Churches, and only secondarily with binding elements that may fuse them together into a unity."

The second conception is characterized as "the model of the unifying organization." That is, one "Church, which builds a single people with even a visible structure as a single people, is what very early the papacy strove after, and which Latin Catholic ecclesiology in general down to today has raised to the level of a theory."[1]

1. Congar, *Wesenseigenschaften,* 399.

197

While the first conception takes the local Churches as its point of departure for reflection, the second conception begins with an ecclesiology of the entire Church. Local Churches are seen *only* as parts of the whole Church. N. Afanassieff, together with his students J. Meyendorff and A. Schmemann, has clearly presented, in his so-called Eucharistic ecclesiology, the significance of this distinction, in that it emphasizes the autonomy and completeness of each local Church as the only compelling argument against primacy: once the notion of an "entire Church" is accepted, the notion of primacy in the Catholic sense follows inevitably.[2]

From the Catholic side one may say that the primacy of the pope can play a different role in the two conceptions. The Catholic definition of primacy by Vatican I is doubtless stamped with the Western mentality (centralism, a discussion on the highest authority in the Church [councils or primacy], etc.). "Anyone who stands on the foundation of Catholic theology may not dismiss the teaching on primacy as null and void. . . . But on the other hand it is impossible for him to regard the shape of the primacy during the nineteenth and twentieth centuries as the only one possible or as necessary for all Christians." These words by J. Ratzinger[3] make very clear which problem Catholic theology must wrestle with: as Ratzinger adds, "[Rome] must ask no more from the East in the matter of primacy than was lived and formulated during the first millenium."

As an analysis of the discussions during Vatican I will show, various Church fathers had difficulties with the doctrine on primacy formulated there, for they had the impression that this formulation would reduce the significance and the role of the bishops. Through its emphasis on the collegiality of the bishops, Vatican II has to a certain extent corrected Vatican I. However, one may still ask oneself whether a consistent vision of episcopal collegiality has been developed, and what kind of collegiality is possible, given the specific characterization of the primacy of the bishop of Rome.

In this chapter we shall first present the Catholic teaching of the first and second Vatican councils (part 1). The difficulties which the other Churches see with the Catholic understanding (part 2) should help Catholic theology to distinguish more sharply between the primacy itself and a specific form of the primacy. Alongside the New Testament statements about Peter (above, chap. VI), the ecclesial discussion about primacy and col-

2. N. Afanassieff, N. Koulomzine, J. Meyendorff, and A. Schmemann, *Der Primat des Petrus in der orthodoxen Kirche* (Zürich, 1961; French original, 1960). See Congar, *Wesenseigenschaften*, 400ff. (with an evaluation of this ecclesiology), as well the bibliography given in chapter 8 (note 2).

3. J. Ratzinger, *Theologische Prinzipienlehre. Bausteine zur Fundamentaltheologie* (München, 1982) 209 (first published in Bausteine für die Einheit der Christen 17, 65 [1977] 6–14).

legiality must be taken into account (part 3), for only in this manner may the possible historical contingency of the formulation of Vatican I be clearly demonstrated. As a further step, the relation between primacy and episcopal collegiality (part 4) as well as the significance of local Churches for a Catholic ecclesiology (part 5) must be considered.

1. The Catholic Teaching

a. The Dogmatic Constitution Pastor aeternus *of Vatican I (DS 3050 = NR 436-54)*

The constitution is divided into four chapters, after each of which a canon follows. Their specific titles and contents are as follows:

Chapter 1: "The Emergence of the Pre-eminence of St. Peter among the apostles." Here Matthew 16:16-19 and John 21:15-17 are invoked to ground the primacy of Peter. According to the constitution, this is a clear teaching of Scripture which the Catholic Church has always (*semper*) followed (DS 3054 = NR 439).

Chapter 2: "The On-going Extension of the Primacy of St. Peter through the Roman Pontiff." It is noteworthy that here quotations from the papal legates at the Council of Ephesus (431), Pope Leo I, Irenaeus of Lyons, and Ambrose of Milan are presented. The successors to the primacy of Peter are instituted by Christ, that is, by divine authority ("ex ipsius Christi Domini institutione seu iure divino": DS 3058 = NR 443).

Chapter 3: "Substance and Nature of the Primacy of the Bishop of Rome." The definition of the Council of Florence (DS 1307 = NR 434) is here quoted verbatim. The papal authority of jurisdiction is here characterized as *ordinaria, immediata,* and *episcopalis.* (However, in the corresponding canon [DS 3064], the term *episcopalis* is omitted.) The function of the bishops in their own dioceses is also discussed.

Chapter 4: "On the Infallible Teaching Authority of the Roman Pontiff." The text refers to the teachings of three ecumenical councils, namely, the Fourth Council of Constantinople, the Second Council of Lyons, and the Council of Florence. Here a historical observation is necessary: not only were these three councils not recognized by the Orthodox Churches as ecumenical, but the Fourth Council of Constantinople was also rejected by Rome. This occurred in connection with the reconciliation between Rome and Constantinople after the controversy over Photius.[4]

4. See V. Peri, "Il Concilio dei Constantinopoli dell' 879-80 come problema filologico et storiografico," *AHC* 9 (1977) 29-42; C. Leonardi, "Das achte ökumenische Konzil," *AHC* 10 (1978) 53-60; V. Peri, "Postilla sul concilio ecumenico ottavo," *AHC* 10 (1978) 61-66.

The council's discussions are concentrated primarily in the final two chapters.

The Primacy of Jurisdiction. The text opposes the positions of Febronius, Eyebel, and Tamburini. According to Febronius, for example, the pope has only a power of supervision and leadership (*potestas inspectionis et directionis*), in which it is much more a matter of moral authority than jurisdictional authority; the pope may suggest laws to the Church, but these acquire validity as laws only through the agreement of the Church. The Church can only express itself through an ecumenical council. The pope exercises in the name of the entire Church only a supervisory and leadership power; his role in the name of the entire Church is limited to patent abuses that require his intervention. Against such opinions the adjectives *ordinaria, immediata,* and *episcopalis* were introduced to describe the papal power. The term *episcopalis* was vigorously debated; in these discussions there were two fundamentally different views about the primacy.

In the first place it was objected that the attribution of episcopal power to the pope would throw into question the role of the bishops in their own dioceses, and would give the impression that the bishops are only representatives of the pope. Two Eastern Uniate bishops especially expressed this position, namely, the Melkite patriarch Jussef and the Russian bishop Papp-Szilagy. Both referred to the Eastern tradition and stressed that such a formula would forever exclude the possibility of a reunification of the Orthodox Churches with Rome, since it nullified the stipulations of the Council of Florence. Papp-Szilagy invoked the teaching concerning *Pedalion,* of the Codex of the Eastern Churches (out of Constantinople): the pope's primacy is like a monarchy; according to this position Christ gave power over the entire Church only to Peter and his successors. Against this position is that of the Orthodox Church, that the bishops' power is not limited to their own dioceses, but rather they are teachers and shepherds of the whole Church; that their concern reaches out and embraces the Church in its entirety, if they are gathered in council and teach something for the Church as a whole.[5]

The majority of the council fathers frequently mentioned the signature of Leo I: "Leo ecclesiae catholicae episcopus": however, this was not a complete quotation, for Leo had continued: "urbis Romae." Against this the minority quoted the sentence from Gregory the Great: "Si unus universalis (episcopus) est, restat ut vos episcopi non sitis."[6]

---

5. Mansi 52:310D. *Padálion tes noetes neos, tes mias, agias, katholikes kai apostolikes ton orthodoxon ekklesias* (Leipzig, 1800).

6. *Ep. 68 ad Eusebium thessal.;* PL 77:1005A. Thus Dupanloup (Mansi 52:574), Strossmayer (ibid., 393), Haynald (ibid., 666).

Cardinal Guidi suggested that either a new chapter or at least a section should be dedicated to the bishops.[7] In the end such a section was added (DS 3061 = NR 446).[8] The general explanation of the German bishops (January/February 1875), which was approved by Pope Pius IX, rejects the criticism that the bishops would only be instruments of the pope without their own pastoral responsibility (see DS 3113 = NR 456).

The fact that the papal power can be characterized as *ordinary (ordinaria)* means that the pope receives this power on the basis of his function, and excludes the possibility that he exercises this authority in the name of anyone else.[9] The papal power is described as *immediate (immediata)* in that he does not need permission from the bishop to intervene in a diocese; that is, his authority need not be exercised through the mediation of the bishops.[10] Even though after the discussions most were of the opinion that the term *episcopalis* should be left out because of the misunderstandings that it could occasion, at the last moment it was included. The relator, Msgr. Zinelli, explained: in that the authority of the pope is of the same nature as that of the bishops, there is no obstacle to using this expression to clarify the nature of the papal power and jurisdiction. The bishops have an episcopal power with reference to their dioceses; the pope possesses an episcopal power with reference to the entire Church. The two powers are of the same nature, with this difference, that that of the bishops is limited to their own dioceses, while that of the pope is without limitation.[11]

Very important for the later development is the answer of the same relator to speeches of Bishops Guilbert and Papp-Szilagy. Both had emphasized that the bishops together with the pope carry the concern for the entire Church (Papp-Szilagy), so that they have a share in the authority to lead the entire Church (Guilbert). The authority of leadership belongs to the episcopacy *to the extent that* it is connected with the pope (Papp-Szilagy).[12] The relator's answer runs: in the Church there is not just one

7. Mansi 51:967D–968A.

8. On the problem of the episcopacy in Vatican I, see Torrell, *La théologie de l'épiscopat*. Also G. Colombo, "Il problema dell'episcopato nella Costituzione 'De ecclesia catholica' del concilio Vaticano I," *ScC* 89 (1961) 344–72; J. Hamer, "Le corps épiscopal uni au pape. Son autorité dans l'Église d'après les documents du premier concile du Vatican," *RSPhTh* 45 (1961) 21–31.

9. "Dividitur potestas in ordinarium et delegatam. . . . Ordinariam, quae alicui competit ratione muneris, delegatam nomine alterius exercetur, in quo est ordinaria" (Mons. Zinelli: Mansi 52:1105).

10. "Immediata est ea potestas quae adhiberi potest sine adhibito necessario scilicet medio" (Mons. Zinelli, ibid.).

11. Ibid., 1104.

12. Papp-Szilagy: ibid., 604; Guibert: ibid., 620 and 1092.

subject with power over the entire Church, as both bishops maintain, but two subjects: the pope by himself, and the episcopacy in connection with the pope. The highest authority rests with the pope alone as head ("veluti capite") and with the head together with the members, that is, with the bishops ("veluti caput et etiam cum membris coniuncto"). If the pope exercises his authority as head, that is, independently from the cooperation of the others ("veluti caput et etiam independenter a concursu aliorum"), then the bishops must agree with their head. For if they did not do this, they then would not be recognizing the complete and supreme authority of the pope. Independently from the pope, the bishops cannot exercise their complete and supreme power in the Church.[13]

To avoid the danger of Gallicanism—which maintains that papal decisions must receive the agreement of the bishops—a canon was added that the pope possesses the fullness of the highest authority (DS 3064 = NR 448). This also rejects the position that one could appeal against a papal decision to a council (DS 3063 = NR 447).

One "limitation" to the authority of the primacy was seconded by the relator of the deputation of the faith: the primatial power must be exercized to build up ("ad aedificationem") the Church, and not to destroy her ("non ad destructionem"). For that reason, and under normal circumstances, the pope should not intervene lightly in another bishop's diocese. The "ordinary" power can and should be exercised in another diocese only under extraordinary circumstances.[14]

The Infallible Teaching Office of the Pope. According to the relator, Msgr. Gasser, the gift of infallibility, which the pope possesses for his *ex cathedra* decisions, extends no further, but no less far, than that of the Church.[15] This also becomes clear in the text of the definition: "Through the divine power he possesses that infallibility with which the Savior intended to equip his Church in its final decisions on matters of faith and morals" (DS 3074 = NR 454).

The pope is seen in the exercise of his function as teacher of the entire Church. The important questions in the discussion were: Whence do the *ex cathedra* decisions acquire their validity? Is the pope required to consult with the Church, that is, with the bishops, beforehand? A comparison of the minority opinion with the explanation of the relator of the deputation of the faith is important here.

The minority invoked the conciliarity of the Churches; to that effect the sentence of Vincent of Lerins was quoted: "quod ubique, quod sem-

13. Ibid., 1108–10.
14. Thus Mons. Zinelli, ibid., 1105.
15. Ibid., 1227: "Infallibilitatem Pontificis nec minus nec magis late patere, quam paetat infallibilitas ecclesiae."

per, quod ab omnibus traditum est."[16] As an example of the weaknesses the papacy had displayed in matters of the faith, the case of Honorius I was introduced (the so-called Honorius question), and Bishop Strossmayer of Djakovo recalled the Council of Chalcedon, at which the council fathers carefully scrutinized the orthodoxy of the *tomus* of Leo I, although according to the papal view the council should have simply accepted it.[17] The Dominican Cardinal Guidi wanted to make sure that the impression did not arise that the pope could exercise his office in an *isolated* fashion. He spoke of the necessity for the pope to consult with the bishops.[18] The sharp reactions to Guidi's position, which was grounded with a reference to the traditional opinion among theologians, shows clearly the opposition of the majority at the council to a common position in Catholic theology. Every possibility of a Gallican interpretation was countered from the very outset.

The Assembly of French Clerics in 1682 had maintained that the pope's decisions, although they should receive the chief weight in matters of faith, were not unchangeable, in case the Church did not concur.[19] According to Msgr. Gasser the reason for the unchangeableness of the papal decisions lay in the papal decrees themselves, and not in some external factor such as the concurrence of the bishops or of the Church.[20] The pope—the relator added—is not obligated with an absolute necessity ("stricta et absoluta necessitas") to consult, since he can recognize what the consensus of the Church is through the clear witness of Holy Scripture, through the consensus of the Church Fathers, and through the statements of the doctors (that is, theologians). There may develop a special case—this the relator conceded—in which the pope holds it to be necessary to consult the bishops through the form of ordinary means on what the Churches think.

16. Thus Ginoulhiac, ibid., 217.

17. Ibid., 398–400.

18. "Haec tandem ratio est, cur ad unum omnes theologi . . . hanc inquisitionem apud episcopos et per episcopos neccessariam innuerunt; ut papa tuto et cum certa scientia, atque matura deliberatione et cognitione ultimum in fide suum judicium proferat" (ibid., 743). For that reason he suggested the inclusion of the following addition to the text: "facta uti moris est, inquisitione de traditione in aliis ecclesiis quoad veritatem definiendam, collatoque aliquando consilio cum pluribus vel paucioribus episcopis . . ." (ibid., 746f.).

19. The explanation of the assembly of French clerics of 1682 runs: "IV. In fidei quoque questionibus praecipuas summi pontificis esse partes, ejusque decreta ad omnes et singulas Ecclesias pertinere, nec tamen irreformabile esse judicium, nisi consensus accesserit" (*DThC* 4, 197; see also 193).

20. "Causam irreformabilitatis sitam esse in ipsis decretis R.P. et non esse ponendam aliunde ex conditione quadam externa, ut esset assensus episcoporum, assensus ecclesiae" (Mansi 52:1317).

However, this case should not be viewed as the norm.[21] Gasser distinguished the moral necessity to consult with the bishops from an absolute necessity which might be viewed as a condition *sine qua non* for such papal decisions.[22]

For the opposition Gasser's explanations came as a disappointment. In the voting over the entire schema (July 13, 1869), the number of those who voted either with "non placet" (88) or with "placet iuxta modum" (62) grew. As a consequence an attempt was made in an international committee to add a clarifying statement on the connection between the pope and the Church. The formulas suggested were "testimonio ecclesiarum innixus" (based on the witness of the Churches) or "et mediis quae semper in Ecclesia catholica usurpata fuerunt adhibitis" (and through the application of instruments which have always been customary in the Catholic Church). These suggestions had no success, since the pope referred a let-

---

21. Here is a selection of the most important points from Gasser's "relatio": "Non separamus papam infallibiliter definientem a cooperatione et concursu ecclesiae, saltem id est in eo sensu, quod hanc cooperationem et hunc concursum non excludimus" (ibid., 1213). "Sed ideo non separamus pontificem ab ordinatissima conjunctione cum ecclesia, Papa enim solummodo tunc est infallibilis, quando omnium christianorum doctoris munera fungens, ergo universalem ecclesiam repraesentans, judicat et definit quid ab omnibus credendum vel rejiciendum. Ab ecclesia universali tam separari non potest, quam fundamentum ab aedificio cui portando destinatum est" (1213). "Demum papam non separamus, et vel minime separamus a consensu ecclesiae, dummodo consensus iste non ponatur ut conditio sive sit consensus antecedens sive sit consensus consequens. Non possumus separare Papam a consensu ecclesiae, quia hic consensus nunquam ipsi deesse potest" (1213f.). "Sed denuo instant et dicunt: consensio ecclesiarum est regula fidei, quam etiam Papa sequi debet, et proinde debet ante definitionem consulere rectores ecclesiarum ut certus sit de consensu ecclesiarum. Respondeo . . . Vero est quod Papa in suis definitionibus ex cathedra eosdem habet fontes sicut Ecclesia: Scripturam et Traditionem. Verum est quod consensio praedicationis praesentis totius magisterii ecclesiae unitae cum capite sit regula fidei etiam pro definitionibus Pontificis. At exinde nullo potest deduci stricta et absoluta necessitas illam exquirendi a rectoribus ecclesiarum seu ab episcopis. Nam haec consensio potest saepissime deduci ex claris ex manifestis testimoniis sacrae Scripturae, ex consensione antiquitatis, id est Sanctorum Patrum, ex sententia doctorum vel aliis modis privatis, quae omnia ad plenam informationem sufficiunt. Proinde stricta illa necessitas, qualis requiritur ad constitutionem dogmaticam, nullo modo potest demonstrari. Potest accidere casus aliquis ita difficilis ut Papa necessarium putet pro sua informatione . . . quaerere ex episcopis, tamquam medio ordinario, quid sentiant ecclesiae, sed talis casus not potest statui pro regula" (1216f.).

22. "In hac stricta et absoluta necessitate consistit tota differentia quae inter nos versatur, et non in opportunitate aut aliqua relativa necessitate, quae judicio Romani Pontificis rerum circumstantias ponderatis prorsus remittenda est" (ibid., 1215). See also the text of p. 1216 (in note 21).

ter directed to himself, containing a recommended position, to the deputation of the faith. In this letter the pope had been asked to express himself even more exactly, so as to close off any means of escape for the Gallicans. The formula suggested ran: "The definitions are in themselves unchangeable, unless the universal agreement of the bishops, whether it be prior, simultaneous, or subsequent, is necessary" ("Definitiones esse ex sese irreformabiles, quin sit necessarius consensus episcoporum, sive antecedens, sive concomitans, sive subsequens").[23] As a consequence the deputation on the faith decided to introduce the formula which has since become famous: "non autem ex consensu ecclesiae" as a clarification of "ex sese." According to Msgr. Gasser, this was only intended to be an expansion of what was already contained in the expression "ex sese": "First a positive statement [with 'ex sese'] is given, and then a negative one [with 'non autem ex consensu ecclesiae']."[24]

b. *The Dogmatic Constitution* Lumen gentium *of Vatican II*

Besides the council's text, on which only the council fathers voted, a "Nota explicativa praevia," that is, a "preliminary clarifying remark" was published.[25] This remark was read to the council fathers by the secretary of the council and was printed in connection with the constitution under the title "Ex actis Concilii" and signed by the general secretary of the council. The "Nota" was drawn up by the commission for the constitution *Lumen gentium* and approved by the Pope. According to the statement of the general secretary, the "Nota" came from "higher authorities" (*superiore Auctoritate*). Pope Paul VI referred to the "Nota" in his address on the occasion of the general vote on the constitution.[26]

The constitution itself establishes that the bishops are successors to the apostles. "As the authority should continue which was given by the Shepherd exclusively to Peter, first among the apostles, and was intended to be passed on to his successors, so the office of apostles to pasture the Church also continues and must always be exercised, according to the holy order [*ordine*] of the bishops" (no. 20, 3). The relationship of the other bishops to the bishop of Rome is described in analogy to the relationship between Peter and the other apostles. "Just as according to the decision of the Lord St. Peter and the other apostles constituted a single apostolic

23. See Aubert, *Vaticanum I*, 273.
24. Mansi 52:1317.
25. See *Primauté et collégialité. Le dossier de G. Philips sur la nota explicativa praevia* (Lumen gentium, ch. III). *Présenté avec introduction historique, annotations et annexes par J. Grootaers* (Louvain, 1986). Grootaers describes in detail the course of the proceedings.
26. L'osservatore romano, 22 November 1964, p. 2.

college, so in a corresponding way [*pari ratione*] are the bishop of Rome, the successor to Peter, and the bishops, the successors to the apostles, bound to one another" (no. 22).[27] The expression "in a corresponding way" is explained in the "Nota" (no. 1) as a "similarity of relation."[28]

The term *college* applied here to the apostles is not understood "in the juridical sense of a circle of equals";[29] rather Peter was "placed at its head" (no. 19). Thus it is emphasized that the college is a compact and perduring group according to the will of the Lord.[30] The relationship obtaining between the pope and the other bishops corresponds to the relation between Peter and the other apostles. The pope alone is the successor to one apostle, Peter. The expression "college of bishops" used in the constitution corresponds to the terms *ordo* or *corpus* in the patristic tradition.[31]

The collegiality of all bishops with one another and with the bishop of Rome is presented and justified in no. 22 under three aspects: (1) already in the ancient discipline the bishops constituted a community with bands of unity, love, and peace; (2) the synods and later the ecumenical councils which took place in order to find "a common rule for the more important situations," "indicate the collegial nature and character of the episcopacy"; (3) the "custom introduced early" that "several bishops [according to can. 4 of Nicaea, at least three are necessary] must be present to take part in the elevation of one newly chosen for the high priest's service," is a sign of this collegiality.

The desire to render more precise the collegiality of bishops in its relation to the head of the college is clearly recognizable in the constitution. The bishops act collegially only if they act together with the head of the college: "with their head and never without this head" (no. 22, 2). "The college or the body of bishops only has authority if the college is understood in communion with the bishop of Rome . . . as its head" (ibid.).

---

27. According to the pope's wishes, the biblical commission was asked about this text. Their answer was the following: exegetically it is certain that, on the basis of their foundation by the Lord, Peter and the other apostles constituted a college. The extension to the pope and the bishops has its foundation in Holy Scripture, in the sense that it gives expression to the clear will of the Lord that the college of apostles he has founded should endure until the end of the world. However, from Holy Writ the form of its realization (*modus exsecutionis*) cannot be established. *Schema Constitutionis de Ecclesia* (Vatican, 1964) 871 = Acta Synod. 3/1, 241f. The commission also refers to the teaching and the life of the Church to justify these statements.

28. The "Nota" refers to: *Modi a Patribus conciliaribus propositi, a Commissioni doctrinali examinati III* (Vatican, 1964) p. 19, no. 57 = Acta Synod. 3/8, 66.

29. *Schema Constitutionis* 81 = Acta Synod. 3/1, 234f.

30. Ibid.

31. *Schema Constitutionis* 89 = Acta Synod. 3/1, 243.

The college so understood, that is, in communion with its head, is characterized like the pope as the "bearer of the highest and fullest power over the entire Church" (ibid.). The exercise of this power is most clearly realized in the ecumenical councils.

The constitution maintains that the bishop of Rome "in virtue of his authority as the representative of Christ and shepherd of the entire Church, possesses the fullest, highest, and universal power [*plenam, supremam et universalem potestatem*] over the whole Church" and that he "may always exercise this freely [*libere*]" (no. 22, 2). The concepts here chosen make clear the council's mind. The following explanation can be found in the acts of the council: "The word *highest [suprema]* is introduced so that it may not appear that the power [*potestas*] of the pope is less than that of the college of bishops, which is described below as highest. It thereby becomes clear that *the Roman Pontiff, in the exercise of his authority, is not dependent upon the bishops,* either at the beginning of a matter or for its continuance. He receives his authority directly from Christ. For that reason the bishops cannot bind him."[32]

The "Nota" adds to this: "It is subject to the judgment of the pope, to whom care for the whole flock of Christ is entrusted . . . as to how this care is transformed into deeds, either personally or collegially. The bishop of Rome proceeds with the leadership, requirements, and sanctioning of the collegial practice in pursuit of the well being of the Church according to his own judgment [*intuitu boni Ecclesiae, secundum propriam discretionem*]" (no. 3). "The pope as the supreme shepherd of the Church may exercise his authority at any time as he pleases [*ad placitum*], as is demanded by his office" (no. 4).

If the question concerning jurisdiction is raised, whether the college of bishops may make demands with reference to the concrete exercise of the papal authority, then according to this text one must answer with a clear negative, since the texts say very clearly that the pope alone may judge; the expressions "ad placitum" and "secundum propriam discretionem" in the "Nota" fundamentally say the same thing as the term *libere* used in *Lumen gentium*. Of course, the expression "in pursuit of the well being of the Church" (*intuito boni ecclesiae*) may be seen as a corrective; however, what is concretely required for the well-being of the Church can, in the last analysis, only be decided by the pope. Ratzinger writes to this effect: "The pope may indeed act without the college, but the college may not act without the pope. Here it must be freely admitted that these statements have reference to the purely juridical level and describe only the authority that may be present or lacking for valid decisions. An interest

---

32. *Schema Constitutionis* 90 = Acta Synod. 3/1, 244.

in the moral aspect of the situation, on the other hand, would doubtless lead to entirely different conclusions."[33]

It is not surprising that the Orthodox response runs: "The *collegialitas* of bishops referred to by the Second Vatican Council . . . is not identical with the synodal system of the ancient Church that is recognized by the Orthodox Churches."[34]

2. Problems of the Other Churches

a. *Problems of the Orthodox Churches*[35]

The ecclesiology of the Eastern Churches may be described as a "communio ecclesiology," that is, as a doctrine about the community of Churches. This was also the original ecclesiology of the patristic Churches. If an important problem arose such as a question concerning the faith, the solution was found through synods. The councils recognized as ecumenical by both the Western and the Orthodox Churches are a clear example of this conception.

Within the *communio* or the *koinonia* of the Churches, the Churches founded by the apostles have played from the very beginning an important role. The patriarchates later took over this role. However, the Church of Rome always occupied the first and preeminent position. The problem is that this preeminence is understood differently by Rome itself than it

33. Ratzinger, *Das neue Volk Gottes,* 187.

34. J. Karmiris, "Zur dogmatischen Konstitution über die Kirche," in D. Papandreou, ed., *Stimmen der Orthodoxie. Zu Grundfragen des II. Vatikanums* (Vienna, 1969) 55-119 (here 70).

35. Bibliography: J. Meyendorff, "Der heilige Petrus, sein Primat und seine Sukzession in der byzantinischen Theologie," in Afanassieff, *Der Primat des Petrus,* 95-117; Meyendorff, *Orthodoxie et catholicité* (Paris, 1965) 50-76 (originally: "La primauté romaine dans la tradition canonique jusqu'au concile de Chalcédone," *Istina* 4 (1957) 463-82; P. Evdokimov, "Kann ein Petrusdienst in der Kirche einen Sinn haben? Russisch-orthodoxe Antwort," *Conc* 7 (1971) 287-89; St. Harklanakis, "Griechisch-orthodoxe Antwort," ibid., 284-87; D. Papandreou, "Überlegungen zur Primatsfrage," in H. Stirnimann and L. Vischer, eds., *Papsttum und Petrusdienst* (Frankfurt, 1975) 51-56; Papandreou, "Bleibendes und Veränderliches im Petrusamt," in J. Ratzinger, ed., *Dienst an der Einheit* (Düsseldorf, 1978) 146-64 (with excellent material on the Orthodox conception); *Konziliarität und Kollegialität. Das Petrusamt in ökumenischer Sicht,* Pro oriente 1 (Innsbruck, 1975) 131-54 (contributions by G. Tomofejeff, D. Staniloae, and I. E. Anastasiou); A. Kallis, "Petrus der Fels—des Stein des Anstosses? Das Petrusamt in der Sicht der Orthodoxie," in V. von Aristi et al., *Das Papsttum: Dienst oder Hindernis für die Ökumene?* (Regensburg, 1985) 43-64; D. Papandreou, "Ein Beitrag zur Überwindung der Trennung zwischen der römisch-katholischen und der orthodoxen Kirche," ibid., 161-67; V. von Aristi, "Das Papsttum und die Zukunft der Ökumene. Stellungnahme aus griechisch-orthodoxer Sicht," ibid., 169-71.

is by the Eastern Churches (see below, part 3 d). The theory of the pentarchy developed later in Byzantium, according to which the unanimity of the five patriarchates recognized by Chalcedon (Rome, Constantinople, Alexandria, Antioch, Jerusalem) is taken to indicate the will of the Churches, expresses this synodal understanding of the Church.[36] Following this conception, Rome's role must be understood within the *koinonia* of the Churches.

It is noteworthy that the clearest concessions of the primatial role of Rome by the Easterners occurred at moments when they were politically weak.[37] In the failed union of Florence (July 6, 1439), the Byzantine bishops who signed the union recognized that the bishop of Rome "occupied the preeminent position over the entire earth" (*in universum orbem tenere primatum*) and that "to him in St. Peter is transmitted the full power to pasture, to direct, and to govern the entire Church by our Lord Jesus Christ" (DS 1307 = NR 434). However, one must not forget that the two clauses which follow this formula were understood by the two sides in different fashions. The reference to the ecumenical councils and their canons ("as it was contained in the reports of the discussions of the ecumenical councils and the holy canons") was understood by the Byzantines as a limitation, *to the extent* that the councils had recognized such an authority (*potestas*) of the bishop of Rome, while the Latins understood this clause as a confirmation, that is, that the councils had already fully recognized the authority of the bishop of Rome. There were also differences in the understanding of the clauses concerning the privileges of the patriarchs: for the Byzantines the rights and privileges of the patriarchs that came out of the ecumenical councils were a limitation on the primacy. The Latins on the other hand understood these rights and privileges as conceded to the patriarchs by Rome.[38]

---

36. This theory already appears in Justinian's novels 123 and 131. Y. M. Congar writes: "Nothing about it was anti-Rome. . . . In its own way the Pentarchy brings the collegially and the synodally oriented understanding of the Church in the East to expression: a form of community of the Church in agreement" (*Die Lehre von der Kirche,* HDG 3/3c, 47).

A. Kallis, *Orthodoxie: Was ist das?* (Mainz, 1979) 32, emphasizes that synodality "should not be confined to the *synod,* for the synod is not an unalterable institution of the Church, but rather a *development* of the ecclesial community and of the consensus in belief of the local Church." However, the term is often used by Orthodox theologians in the sense of a "synodally oriented understanding of the Church," as Congar has formulated it.

37. See below chapter 13, section 3d.

38. See J. Gill, *Personalities of the Council of Florence and Other Essays* (Oxford, 1964) 264ff. ("The Definition of the Primacy of the Pope in the Council of Florence").

Rome's role is expressed by the Orthodox as "primatus honoris": the bishop of Rome "as the first in honor, who has precedence in love," as Patriarch Athenagoras expressed it.[39]

b. Problems of the Lutheran Churches

Martin Luther described the pope as the antichrist in the sense of 2 Thessalonians 2:4 because for him the papacy appeared to suppress the gospel.[40] "The doctrinal decisions of Vatican I confirmed the conviction of many," according to members of the Evangelical Lutheran Commission in *Spiritual Authority in the Church.*[41] Subordination to the primacy of the gospel is for the Lutheran understanding a precondition for the acceptance of any institution for the betterment of the Church. Both in the Malta Report and in *Spiritual Authority in the Church,* the Evangelical Lutheran side concedes that "there is no need for Lutherans to reject the Petrine authority of the bishop of Rome as a visible sign of the unity of the entire Church 'as long as through a theological reinterpretation and a practical restructuring it is subordinated to the primacy of the gospel' (Malta)."[42] This condition locates the problem of the primacy in a wider context, namely, the relation between the Word of God and the teaching office. Although the constitution *Dei Verbum* (no. 10, 2) explicitly says that "the teaching authority is not above the Word of God, but rather serves it," there still exists here a particular problem. In the theme of primacy the problem which divides the Lutheran from the Catholic understanding comes to a head: Word of God and teaching office, as well as teaching office and community.

3. The Church's Historical Understanding of Primacy and the Collegiality of Bishops down to the Split between East and West

It is very clear from the sources that from the very beginning Rome occupied a preeminent position among the Churches. Two aspects espe-

---

39. Tomos Agapis, *Vatican-Phanar (1958–1970)* (Rome-Istanbul, 1971) 380.

40. This formula can also be found in the Evangelical Lutheran creedal texts: BSLK 430f., 484f., 488f., 239f., 300, 1060f.

41. No. 73 in DwÜ, 353.

42. Malta Report, no. 50, in DwÜ, 261; *Das geistliche Amt in der Kirche,* no. 23, in DwÜ, 337. Protestant bibliography: J. J. von Allmen, "Ein reformierter Beitrag zur Frage des Papsttums," in Ratzinger, *Dienst,* 133–45; L. Vischer, "Petrus und der Bischof von Rom," in H. Stirnimann and L. Vischer, *Papsttum,* 35–50; H. Meyer, "Das Papstamt in lutherischer Sicht," ibid., 73–90; J. Moltmann, "Ein ökumenisches Papsttum," in *Papsttum als ökumenische Frage,* pub. by the Arbeitsgemeinschaft ökumenischer Universitätsinstitute (Mainz-München, 1979) 251–61.

cially must here be analyzed: (1) How valid is the foundation of Rome's primacy? (2) How was this primacy understood by the *koinonia* of the Churches?

a. The Martyrdoms of Peter and Paul in Rome as the Foundation for the Preeminence of Rome in the Earliest Testimonies

In his letter to the community in Rome, which he esteems very highly,[43] Ignatius says that he cannot speak to the Romans with the authority of Peter or Paul. The text alludes to the sojourns of both apostles in Rome, probably especially to their martyrdoms,[44] which the first letter of Clement of Rome describes.[45] Irenaeus (successor to Pothinus, who died in 177–78), traces the preeminence of Rome over all the other apostolic Churches to the fact that this community was founded by Peter and Paul.[46] Eusebius speaks of the martyrdom of both apostles in Rome[47] and passes on the testimony of Dionysius, bishop of Corinth, that Peter and Paul together founded the Church of Rome,[48] and that Linus, a student of Paul, exercised the *episkope* over the Church of Rome after the martyrdom of both apostles.[49] The same account can be found in the *Decretum Gelasia-*

---

43. "Ignatius . . . to the Church who has found mercy, life, and light in the lordship of the highest Father and of Jesus Christ his only Son . . .; which also occupies the first place [*prokáthetai*] in the space of the prayers of the Romans, worthy of all praise, honor, divinity, treasure, and prosperity, worthy of salvation [or purity (of belief)], and because you occupy the first place in love [*prokatheméne tes agápis*]" (translation J. A. Fischer, *Die apostolischen Väter* [München, 1981] 183). Catholic theologians of a fundamentalist stripe seized upon this priority in love in Ignatius' text to argue that the Roman Church occupies the leading position in the universal Church (*agápi*—Love = the universal Church). See, for example, J. Salaverri in *Sacrae theologiae summa*, vol. 1 (Madrid, 1952) 622f. B. Altaner and A. Stuiber, *Patrologie* (Freiburg, 1978) 49, and J. A. Fischer, *Die apostolischen Väter*, 129f., among contemporary Catholic patristic scholars, consider this interpretation by the "fundamentalist" theologians to be exaggerated.

44. *Rom.* 4.3; Fischer, 187: "I do not command you like Peter and Paul. Those are apostles, I am a judge; those are free [through their martyrdoms], while I am now a slave. But when I have suffered, then I will be set free in Jesus Christ."

45. *1 Clem* 5.4, 5; Fischer, 31f.

46. "Sed quoniam valde longum est in hoc tali volumine omnium ecclesiarum enumerare successiones, maximae et antiquissimae et omnibus cognitam, a gloriosissimis duobus apostolis Petro et Paulo Romae fundatae et constitutae ecclesiae . . ." (*Adv. Haer.* 3.3.2). "The holy apostles founded the Church and handed over to Linus the 'episcopacy' " (*Adv. Haer.* 3.3.3).

47. Eusebius, *Church History* 2.25.5–8; 3.2; and 3.31.1.

48. Ibid., 2.25.8 "the martyrdom took place at the same time."

49. Ibid., 3.2.

num, whose first part, according to the preponderant weight of research, can be traced back to the Roman synod of 381–82: here Matthew 16:18f. is applied to the Church of Rome. Paul is placed at Peter's side. Both supposedly suffered martyrdom on the same day.[50]

Rome is the primordial and archetypal apostolic Church, since Peter and Paul died there as martyrs. That is the basis for the *potentior principalitas* that Irenaeus attributes to Rome.[51] Irenaeus also emphasizes the apostolic character of other Churches, namely, those of Smyrna (Polycarp) and Ephesus, and says of the Church in Ephesus expressly that "she is an authentic witness to the apostolic tradition."[52] This means that "the Roman Church is such in an especially useful way for the establishment of the apostolic transmission, but she is not such exclusively."[53] Tertullian thinks similarly on the meaning of the apostolic Churches: he speaks of Smyrna and Rome.[54]

Irenaeus interprets the intervention of Clement of Rome in the Corinthian controversy (ca. 90) to claim that he brought the Church of Corinth back to the apostolic tradition.[55]

In the controversy over the celebration of Easter, both sides place themselves within the apostolic tradition: Pope Victor I (189–99) grounds Rome's decision on the apostolic tradition of his Church. Polycrates of Ephesus similarly bases his different position on the apostolic tradition. Thus here apostolic tradition stands against apostolic tradition. The problem was resolved through synods.[56] It is not clear whether the calling of the synods to resolve the date of Easter can be traced back to an initiative by Victor.[57] Victor's readiness to excommunicate other Churches who did not concur with Rome's apostolic tradition illustrates Rome's attitude with reference to its own preeminence in the *koinonia* of the Churches.

One remark with reference to the episcopal succession in Rome is important: according to Irenaeus the succession of bishops was Linus, Anacletus, Clement; on the other hand Tertullian names Clement as the first bishop of Rome, who was installed *by Peter alone.*[58] In my opinion

50. DS 350: "Addita est etiam societas beatissimi Pauli Apostoli . . . qui non diverso, sicut haeretici garriunt, sed uno tempore, uno eodemque die gloriosa morte cum Petro . . . coronatus est."

51. The text quoted in note 45 continues: "Ad hanc enim ecclesiam propter potentiorem principalitatem necesse est convenire omnem ecclesiam . . ." (*Adv. Haer.* 3.3.2).

52. *Adv. Haer.* 3.3.4.

53. Baus, *Von der Urgemeinde,* 400.

54. Tertullian, *De Praescr. Haer.* 36; PL 2:44.

55. *Adv. Haer.* 3.3.3.

56. See Eusebius, *Church History* 5.23 and 24.

57. See Vries, *Entwicklung des Primats,* 121.

58. Irenaeus, *Adv. Haer.* 3.3.3; Tertullian, *De Praescr.* 32: "sicut Romanorum

this is a clear indication that, already in the time of Tertullian, the Roman succession incorporated a theologized view of history.

b. The Invocation by the Roman Bishops of the Petrine Texts

According to the testimony of Firmilian/Cyprian, the Roman bishop Stephen appealed around 250 to the sentence "You are Peter" to support his claims: "Qui sic de episcopatus sui loco gloriatur et se successionem Petri tenere contendit . . . Stephanus, qui per successionem cathedram Petri se praedicat."[59] This is the first certain witness to such a use of this sentence. It is debated whether Pope Callistus (217–22) appealed to this text.

The way the "You are Peter" was normally interpreted at this time is shown by Tertullian's polemic during his Montanist period against a bishop (*pontifex maximus*)—it is not clear whether it was Agrippinus of Carthage or Callistus of Rome—who invoked Matthew 16:18 to justify his authority to forgive all sins, even up to and including incest. What is interesting here is not Tertullian's exegesis, according to which it is a matter of an authority which refers only to Peter as a pneumatic Christian, but rather the exegesis of the bishops against whom Tertullian is polemicizing: according to them, Matthew 16:18f. refers to any Church that stands in connection with Peter.[60] This text indicates the catechetical tradition of Africa, which anchored the power of the Church to forgive sins in Matthew 16:18f. and John 20:22.[61]

In his controversy with Pope Stephen concerning the baptism by heretics, Cyprian supported himself with Matthew 16:18f. Because Stephen comes forward as the successor to Peter, it is obligatory to give obedience to Rome's decision. Cyprian opposed this, referring to Paul, from whom Peter, in the controversy over whether circumcision was necessary for Gentile Christians, had demanded no such obedience on the basis of his primatial position.[62] In the same way for Cyprian Rome is the enduring cathedra

---

Clementem a Petro ordinatum edit." According to Eusebius, Linus is the first after the martyrdom of both apostles (*Church History* 3.2), that is, after Peter (ibid., 3.4.8); the successors to Linus were Anacletus and Clement (ibid., 3.15).

59. In Cyprian, *Ep.* 75.17; CSEL 32:821.

60. "Si quia dixerit Petro Dominus: super hanc petram aedificabo ecclesiam meam, tibi dedi claves regni coelorum; vel: quaecumque alligaveris vel solveris in terra, erunt alligata vel soluta in coelis, id circo praesumis et ad te derivasse solvendi et alligandi potestatem, id est ad omnem ecclesiam Petri propinquam?" (*De pudicitia* 21).

61. See Ludwig, *Primatworte,* 14, with reference to H. Bruders.

62. "Nam nec Petrus super quem aedifivit [dominus] ecclesiam suam, cum secum Paulus de circumcisione postmodum disceptaret, vindicabit sibi aliquid insolenter aut adroganter adsumpsit, ut diceret se primatum tenere et obtemperari . . . sibi oportere" (*Ep.* 71.3; CSEL 3/2:773).

of Peter, the *ecclesia principalis,* to which the priestly unity goes back.[63] That the Church is grounded on Peter means for Cyprian that the unity of the Church shows itself in the unity of its origin, since Peter was the first to receive authority from the Lord.[64]

Origen wonders if the words of Matthew's Gospel refer "exclusively to Peter." The occasion for his doubt was apparently Rome's interpretation. Using John 20:22 he argues for the equality of all the apostles. He takes up Matthew 16:19 and interprets "Peter" as "every complete person": "Every follower of Christ is Peter."[65] This interpretation became firmly established in the East: Every person who proclaims the true faith is designated by various ecumenical councils as Peter.

The Roman synod of 381–82 anchored the claims of Rome and its bishops with Matthew 16:18 and emphasized that the preeminence of Rome came from the Lord and not from a Church synod.[66] Leo I used the same argument in rejecting canon 28 from Chalcedon. The Pope was disturbed that the canon did not mention the apostolic and Petrine character of the chair of Rome.[67]

c. The Unity of the Church as a Koinonia of Churches and the Role of Rome within such a Conception[68]

The ecclesiology of the early Church should be characterized as an ecclesiology of *communio* or a *koinonia. "Communio* is the bond of unity

63. "Navigare audent [the heretics] et ad Petri cathedram atque ad ecclesiam principalem, unde unitas sacerdotalis exorta est" (*Ep.* 59.14; CSEL 3/2:683).

64. "Loquitur Dominus ad Petrum: Ego tibi dico, inquit, quia tu es Petrus etc. [Matt 16:18f.]. Et eidem post resurrectionem suam dixit: Pasce oves meas [John 21:27]. Super illum aedificat ecclesiam et illi pascendas oves mandat. Et quamvis apostolis omnibus post resurrectionem parem tribuat potestatem, unam tamen cathedram constituit et unitatis originem adque rationem sua auctoritate disposuit. Hoc erant utique ceteri quod fuit Petrus, sed primatus Petro datur et una ecclesia et cathedra una monstratur. Et pastores sunt omnes, sed grex unus ostenditur, qui ab apostolis omnibus unanimi consensione pascatur" (*De cath. eccl. unit.* 4; CSEL 3/1:212). The meaning of this text becomes clear in the continuation of the text in ch. 5: "Quam unitatem tenere firmiter et vindicare debemus, maxime episcopi qui in ecclesia praesidemus, ut episcopatum quoque ipsum unum atque indivisum probemus. . . . Episcopatus unus est, cuius a singulis in solidum pars tenetur" (ibid., 5; CSEL 3/1:214).
There is a second presentation in ch. 4 that goes back to a later redaction and "most probably does not come from the pen of Cyprian" (Ludwig, *Primatworte,* 26).

65. *In Matth.* 12.10; PG 13:997. See the analysis by Ludwig, *Primatworte,* 41.

66. DS 350: "sancta tamen Romana Ecclesia nullis synodicis constitutis ceteris Ecclesiis praelata sit, sed evangelica voce Domini et Salvatoris primatum obtinuit."

67. See note 76.

68. See L. Hertling, "Communio und Primat," in *Una sancta* 17 (1962) 91–125 (originally in *Miscellanea pontific,* [Rome, 1943]); Y. M. Congar, "Von der Gemein-

between bishops and the faithful, the bishops with one another, the faithful with one another, which is effective and simultaneously manifest through the Eucharistic *communio.*"[69] For the ancient Church there were two mutually complementary axioms: (1) each belongs to that Church where he receives communion, and (2) if anyone establishes another *communio,* he establishes another Church.

The unity of the Church shows itself in the fact that the various local Churches live in *communio,* so that the faithful of one local community or their bishop may communicate with another community.

The opposite of living in *communio* is ex-communication, that is, a break in this communion. According to this conception, any bishop could excommunicate any other. If it turned out that the other bishops and Churches did not stand behind him, then the excommunication fell back on himself. Firmilian of Caesarea referred to this when he wrote to Pope Stephen (d. 257): "You have yourself committed a great sin in separating yourself from so many communities. For you have thereby cut yourself off; do not deceive yourself: the real schismatic is the one who makes himself into a rebel against the *communio* of Church unity."[70]

Life in the *koinonia* was regulated by synods. This is the way the problem of baptism by heretics was solved.[71] The case of Paul of Samosata, the bishop of Antioch, who in 268 was excommunicated by a synod and removed from office shows that life in the *koinonia* was ordered by a definite structure of the chairs of the bishops: the participants in the synod wrote a letter to the bishops of Rome and Alexandria "so that they might write to him [Domnus, the new bishop of Antioch] and receive communion letters in reply from him."[72] We have here the three bishops' chairs which fifty years later the Council of Nicaea would name the bearers of a "primacy" with *exousia/potestas,*[73] and the preparatory stages to a patriarchate understanding of the Church, which the ecumenical councils would later dismantle.

---

schaft der Kirchen zur Ekklesiologie der Weltkirche," in Congar, ed., *Das Bischofsamt und die Weltkirche* (Stuttgart, 1964; French original, 1962) 245ff. (especially 249ff.).

69. Hertling, "Communio," 92.

70. In Cyprian, *Ep.* 75.24; CSEL 3/2:825: "Peccatum vero quam magnum tibi exaggerasti, quando te a tot gregibus scidisti! Excidisti enim te ipsum, noli te fallere, si quidem ille est vere schismaticus qui se a communione ecclesiasticae unitatis apostatam fecerit."

71. Eusebius, *Church History* 7.4 and 5.

72. Ibid., 7.30.17.

73. Nicaea, can. 6, in *Conciliorum oecumenicorum decreta,* ed. G. Alberigo et al. (Barcelona, 1962) 8.

At Nicaea the primacy of Alexandria was understood in analogy to the primacy of Rome, because there was a similar "custom"[74] with reference to the bishop of Alexandria as with the bishop of Rome. In the third canon of the First Council of Constantinople and especially in canon 28 of Chalcedon, Constantinople is given the place immediately after Rome (*ta presbeia*) because Constantinople was the new Rome.[75] Thus, Constantinople was raised at the expense of Alexandria. The problem lay in the fact that Rome stressed the principle of apostolic origin,[76] while the council fathers at Chalcedon worked with the principle of accommodation to the civil structure.

The later theory of the pentarchy, according to which an agreement of the five patriarchates is an indication of the true faith of the Church, brings the conciliarity of the ancient Church to expression.

The invocations of the Roman Church should be understood in the light of this life in *koinonia;* this is especially clear through the fact that in the same cases invocations were also made to the other important bishoprics.

d. Rome's Role in the Understanding of the Eastern Churches

The Example of the Council of Chalcedon (451). The Council of Chalcedon is a particular example of the Roman outlook, as well as that of the Eastern participants in the council (it should here be remembered that the minority at the First Vatican Council raised this topic).

For Pope Leo I (as well as for the Roman legates at the council), the question of faith was settled by his "Tomus" (a dogmatic document) to Flavius (449) and by his judgment of the Robber Synod of Ephesus. "The Pope grounded his teaching authority through the assistance of the Holy Spirit, which he claimed for himself, but also from his status as the suc-

---

74. Ibid.

75. The texts: ibid., 28 and 75. It is important to notice that canons 9 and 17 of Chalcedon (ibid., 67 and 71) in practice establish the second place of Constantinople, since one can appeal against the metropolitan either to the exarch of the diocese or to the archbishop of Constantinople. On canon 28 see, besides the interpretation of Catholic authors like E. Herrmann ("Chalkedon und die Ausgestaltung des Konstantinopolitanischen Primats," in A. Grillmeier and H. Bacht, eds., *Das Konzil von Chalkedon*, vol. 2 [Würzburg, 1962] 459–90) and A. Wuyts (in *OChPer* 17 [1951] 265–82) also Meyendorff, *Orthodoxie et catholicité.*

76. Synod of 380–82: DS 350 (the text in note 66): the Roman legates at Chalcedon quoted can. 6 of Nicaea according to the Latin translation, which had as its introduction: "Romana Ecclesia semper habuit primatum." These words do not appear in the Greek text. Leo I, *Ep.* 14.11 *ad Anastasium;* PL 54:675; *Ep.* 104 *ad Marcianum;* PL 54:993f. Leo's argument runs: "non dedignetur regiam civitatem, quam apostolicam non potest facere sedem."

cessor to Peter, from whom he had received the commission to safeguard the truth."[77] Leo believed he was the authorized witness to the faith of the Church. He identified the faith of all Catholics with his own position and presumed that the synod *must* accept his tome.[78]

However, Leo's "Tomus," against the wishes of the Roman delegates, was thoroughly discussed. The imperial commissioners asked the bishops to venture an opinion on whether Leo's letter was in agreement with the creed of the Church, that is, those produced by Nicaea and Constantinople.

> On the basis of its own authority the council deliberated whether there was agreement between the old recognized teaching authorities and Leo's letter. Thus, for the council, Leo's statements are not necessarily by themselves the unconditionally valid and incontestable truth, simply on the basis of the teaching authority of the pope, as would have to be the case if Leo had spoken in the name and with the authority of Peter. . . . In the position of the council, authority only came to Leo's letter to the extent that it was accepted by the synod.[79]

The council participants acclaimed the tome: "Peter has spoken through Leo. This is the teaching of the apostles. . . ." Against the background of this experience, this acclamation means that the council fathers recognize the agreement of the Bishop Leo with the authentic teaching of the apostles: Leo's point of view is in line with Peter's position. In the background stands the understanding that whoever proclaims the truth in the Church is Peter.

The document of the council fathers to the Pope in which they ask him to confirm the twenty-eight canons recognizes Leo's primacy. Leo is described as the "interpreter of St. Peter's voice"; he "has allotted the glorification of his [Peter's] faith to all."[80]

Why did even the emperor as well as Anatolios, the archbishop of Constantinople, and the entire synod so exert themselves to secure the Pope's recognition of the canons? Two factors here played a role: first, without the concurrence of the West, the council would not have been ecumenical, so that its decisions would not have had validity;[81] second, the agreement of all the patriarchs was necessary, since the question was a new order of precedence among the patriarchs.[82]

---

77. W. De Vries, "Die Struktur der Kirche gemäss dem Konzil von Chalkedon (451)," *OrChrP* 35 (1969) 63–122 (here 9).

78. Evidence ibid., 90ff.

79. Ibid., 103f.

80. In Leo, *Ep.* 98; PL 54:952, 954.

81. Thus E. Caspar, *Geschichte des Papsttums von den Anfängen bis zur Höhe der Weltherrschaft*, vol. 1 (Tübingen, 1930) 534.

82. Thus Vries, *Struktur*, 110.

Although canon 28 was not at first added to the collection of canons, as one would have expected—which is itself a clear indication that those in the East were very attentive to the authority of the bishop of Rome—the specifications of the canon were immediately valid law in the East. Anatolios says explicitly that confirmation of the proceedings is reserved to the authority of the bishop of Rome.[83]

W. de Vries writes correctly: "The primacy is indeed recognized more clearly in Chalcedon than in other councils. However, even here Rome could not fully establish its claim to absolute leadership in the Church. The awareness of collegial authority of the bishops at the council was too strong for that."[84] This point of view was later spelled out explicitly at the Second Council of Nicaea (787) in a Horos: "The tradition of the Catholic Church receives its confirmation through a common decision."[85] The criticism of the Synod of Aquileia called by Ambrose against the Synod of Constantinople (381) was that the problems in the Church can only be resolved through the participation of all.

Express Recognition of the Role of Rome on the Part of the Eastern Bishops. In the time between the sixth and tenth centuries there are various Roman documents on the papal primacy with reference to the universal Church, especially for the East: for example, the creed of Pope Hormisdas (DS 363–65), through the acceptance of which by about 250 Eastern bishops the Akazian schism (484–519) was ended; the *Libellus satisfactionis*[86]—the *Libellus* is very similar to the *Formula Hormisdae*—which everyone who wished to take part in the Council of Constantinople of 869–79 had to sign. At this synod Photius was removed and Ignatius was again installed as patriarch. It is worth mentioning what Photius himself wrote to the Pope: "One could well ask: who is the teacher who taught you to behave in such a fashion? It is most certainly and before all others the ranking member of the apostles, Peter, whom the Lord placed at the head of all the Churches, when he said to him: pasture my sheep (John 21:17). And yet he is not this all by himself; he includes also the holy synods and constitutions. It is also the holy and orthodox decrees that have come down from the Fathers, as your own god-like and pious letters testify."[87]

The clearest recognitions from Easterners of Rome's primacy occurred in crisis situations, and came from those who were either in a minority

---

83. "Cum et sic gestorum vis omnis et confirmatio auctoritate vestrae beatitudinis fuisset reservata" (Leo, *Ep.* 132; PL 54:1084).

84. Vries, *Struktur*, 11.

85. *Concilorum oecumenicorum decreta*, 110.

86. Mansi 16:27E–28D. German translation in D. Stiernon, *Konstantinopel 4* (Mainz, 1975) 311–13.

87. Mansi 17:396D. On Photius see Dvornik, *Byzanz*, 115ff.

or were being persecuted. In the dispute over monotheletism (middle of the seventh century), we have testimonies from Sophronius of Jerusalem, Maximus the Confessor, and John the Patriarch of Constantinople.[88] The defenders of the devotion to icons in the East could find support only with the papacy. It is thus not surprising that, like Nicephorus, the Patriarch of Constantinople, they emphasized the apostolic and Petrine character of the seat of Rome.[89]

It is still very worth noticing how the letter from the pope to the empress, which was read to the participants at the seventh ecumenical council, on the devotion to icons, was translated: in the Greek version the quotation of the Lord's promises to Peter, on which the papal claims to primacy were grounded, are repeatedly missing. Only a brief allusion to these words of the Lord remains in the text. Further, at every point where the pope mentions Peter as the founder of the seat of Rome, the Greek version adds Paul as well.[90]

An ongoing source of conflict lay in the fact that, especially following the pseudo-Isidorian decretals, the popes sought to intervene in ecclesial problems in the East, just as they did in their own metropole or in their patriarchate. The East had recognized the preeminence of Rome and the primacy of her bishop, but this recognition was always understood within the framework of the autonomy of the local Churches, that is, of the patriarchates, and in connection with the decisions of the councils. In this understanding Rome is the *prima sedes,* but she can never be understood as the *caput, fons, origo,* and *cardo,* as the popes expressed it.[91]

4. Theological Reflection

In this section I would like to set out a theological legitimation of primacy. Doubtless such an attempt has become more difficult, as various Catholic authors have indicated. What is crucial is to make clear at the outset what sort of primacy I am attempting to legitimate. Catholic

---

88. Sophronius: "Go to the apostolic seat, where lie the foundations of the true teaching" (Mansi 10:893). Maximus: "This seat [Rome] is the foundation of all the Christian Churches of the world. She is received and exercises leadership, authority, and the power to bind and to loose over all the holy Churches of the world in all things and for all things" (ibid., 692). Patriarch Johannes adopts the usual Roman description and names the pope the head of the Church (Mansi 12:196).

89. "Without them [the Romans], no piece of dogma discussed in the Church, even if before it was approved by canonical laws and church practice, can be regarded as authorized or overthrown, for they truly possess the first place in the priesthood and owe this position to the leader of the apostles" (PG 100:597).

90. Mansi 12:1082.

91. See Congar, *L'ecclésiologie,* 365.

theology is very aware that the formulation of primacy in the First Vatican Council occurred against the background of the unfolding of the second millenium, and is stamped with this specific historical context.[92]

a. A Theological Legitimation of Primacy

Traditional Catholic theology sought to legitimate primacy on the basis of a twin foundation.[93] First and above all else mention is made of the preeminence which Peter received within the circle of apostles from Jesus Christ himself: the band of apostles was formed by Jesus Christ into a college with Peter as its head or "ranking leader." Here Matthew 16:18f. plays the most important role. On the other hand it is conceded that "Jesus specified successors neither for Peter nor for the other apostles." However, "a succession follows *from the nature of the thing itself,* namely, from the missioning of Peter (Matt 28:18ff.), who moves out toward the four corners of the earth and toward the end of history."[94]

The second basis for legitimation is the earlier history of the Church. Qualifying that, however, it must be noticed that "for its first thousand years there are numerous testimonials to the ecclesial consciousness of the preeminence of the bishop of Rome (the primacy); however, these testimonials are general and nascent."[95] Here especially the witnesses of Clement of Rome, whose letter "testifies to a deep sense of response to the entire Church," of Ignatius of Antioch, and of Irenaeus ("propter potentiorem principalitatem") are emphasized. In this context the actual practice is carefully studied: "The bishop of Rome in the second century was consulted for his decision in matters of controversy, for example, in that over the celebration of Easter. . . . From the fourth century on we come upon the fact that the bishops sought protection in Rome against threats

---

92. See H. J. Pottmeyer, "Kontinuität und Innovation in der Ekklesiologie des II. Vatikanums. Der Einfluss des I. Vatikanums auf die Ekklesiologie des II. Vaticanums im Lichte des II. Vatikanums," in *Kirche im Wandel,* ed. G. Alberigo, Y. M. Congar, and H. J. Pottmeyer (Düsseldorf, 1982) 89–110.

93. As an example, the article "Papst" by M. Schmaus in SM 3:970–91, or in HthTL 5:317–34 is selected.

94. Schmaus, 973/320. There are similar reflections in Congar, *Wesenseigenschaften,* 585: "It is true that the successor to Peter is not expressly created in his position as first in initiative and representation. We reach this conclusion through rational reflection: the texts that ground Peter's primacy look forward to the future and fall under the law of the economy of salvation according to the rhythm of promise and fulfillment. What is at stake in all this is the continuation *of the Church,* as one can extract from John 21:15 and more expressly from Matt 16:18 ('the gates of hell shall not prevail against thee')."

95. Schmaus, 974/321.

to their rights, that in questions of law one appealed to Rome, over whose decision an appeal was considered useless."[96]

With reference to this argument the following fundamental remarks must be made: it is striking how cautiously respected Catholic exegetes today express themselves on the topic of the successors to the apostles (see above, chap. V, part 4b). Naturally, this has consequences for this subject. Moreover, the Petrine text does not speak expressly about the successors to Peter. However, the text does open up to the future: "the gates of Hell shall not prevail against it" (Matt 16:18). The fact that the theme of Peter is discussed in different New Testament texts and in a wide geographical dispersion testifies to the continuation of the function of Peter within the Church.

From the exegetical point of view, one should, with the Anglican-Roman Catholic Commission, at least say, "It is indeed possible that a primacy for the bishop of Rome does not contradict the New Testament and is a part of God's plan for the unity and catholicity of the Church— even when one also recognizes that the New Testament texts do not offer a conclusive foundation for this."[97]

As for what concerns the historical texts (see the remarks made above in chap. XIII, part 3), it is important above all to notice how in the patristic sources the preeminence of Rome is grounded: always mentioned first are the martyrdoms of both Peter and Paul in this city; only later is Peter alone referred to in the founding. It was only possible for the Roman bishops to appeal to the Petrine texts for this second aspect. The statements of the texts, that both apostles suffered martyrdom "at the same time," "on the same day," is extremely noteworthy. Through these statements the problem of the origin of the Roman community, and the tension between the two poles of evangelization (Peter and Paul), was resolved.

On the basis of the martyrdoms of Peter and Paul, Rome was the *"sedes apostolica* in a preeminent sense."[98] A second important element for the emergence of Rome's preeminence is the fact that Rome was seen as the successor to Jerusalem: "The transference to Rome meant in the eyes of the nascent Church the final transition from the Church of the Jews to the Church of the Gentiles."[99]

The different formulations and specifications in Irenaeus, Tertullian, and Eusebius of the chain of successors in Rome clearly shows that the

96. Schmaus, 976/322.
97. *Autorität in der Kirche 2*, no. 7, in DwÜ, 179.
98. Thus also Ratzinger, *Das neue Volk Gottes*, 127.
99. Ibid., 128. W. Kasper is of the same opinion in "Dienst an der Einheit und Freiheit in der Kirche," in J. Ratzinger, ed., *Dienst an der Einheit* (Düsseldorf, 1978) 81–104 (here 84).

statement "the bishop of Rome is the successor to Peter" rests upon a theological appreciation of history. Speaking strictly historically, the only chain we can establish is: Christ → Peter/Paul → the bishops of Rome. On this basis I believe we may say correctly that

> these words (Matt 16:17-19) serve fundamentally *to legitimate after the fact* a leadership role and a claim to leadership that had evolved gradually out of extremely various historical motives and conditions. . . . At the beginning there was no theological theory about the Petrine authority and succession invoking an explicit word of Jesus, from which one could then deduce the preeminence of the Roman Church, of the episcopal chair of Rome, and finally of the bishop of Rome. At the outset there were only historical experiences. These experiences of the faith *led to a re-reading of the Scriptures.*[100]

These statements take seriously what may be concluded from the historical sources. Methodologically, this means that one cannot operate with the principle of *sola scriptura*. The same categories are relevant here as with the question of the bishop's authority. To justify the monarchical office of bishop, the development that led to it was compared with the development of the canon of Holy Scripture: both belong together (see above, chap. XII, part 3a). The topic of "papal authority" should also be integrated within this perspective. That is, *the canon of Holy Scripture, the office of bishop, and the primacy are realities which must be regarded together.*

In accord with this reflection, one should regard the primacy as "God's plan" and "God's intention," or as having arisen "on the basis of divine providence." This is the vocabulary used by the Anglican-Roman Catholic Commission's *Authority in the Church II.*[101] Is this the meaning of the word *institution* in the formulation of Vatican I (DS 3058 = NR 443): "on the basis of the institution by Christ the Lord himself, that is, on the basis of divine law"? The position of the congregation of the faith on May 6, 1982 was no.[102] It is my belief that they were then operating with an understanding of *ius divinum* that was very narrowly defined.

---

100. Ibid., 84. Similarly in this direction, Döring, *Papsttum,* 318, and W. Klausnitzer, *Das Papsttum im Disput zwischen Lutheranern und Katholiken* (Innsbruck, 1987) 501; "A later re-reading may even discover a basis in scripture that was not even perceived earlier."

101. Nos. 11 and 13: DwÜ, 180f. According to the commission the expression "ius divinum" should be understood as at least saying that "this primacy brings to expression God's intention for his Church," but it "does not need to be understood unconditionally in the sense that the universal primacy was established directly by Jesus during his earthly life as an enduring institution" (no. 11).

102. 3.2, in HerKorr 291.

However, in what concerns the structures of the Church, one should "with reference to divine law . . . work with a wide, unconstricted understanding."[103] Fundamentally it is the same problem as when one wishes to justify the "divine" institution of specific sacramental matters. In case the question can not be any further clarified exegetically, there is no other way than the one presented above to justify the primacy.

b. Primacy within the Framework of Collegiality

The starting point for modern reflection on the primacy in Catholic theology is the evident difference between the formulation of Vatican I (the highpoint of the practice of the second millenium) and life in unity as a *koinonia* of the Churches at the time of the early Church (first millenium). The life in unity before the split between East and West shows that the Eastern Churches had accepted a primacy *within* a collegiality and co-responsibility of all the bishops. Even before the break, however, they had the impression that Rome was shifting the notion of primacy outside that of collegiality.

The East sees the bishop of Rome as first among the bishops. "In the public community understanding its role consisted in safeguarding, from its higher vantage point, the unity of the Church and, corresponding to the tradition and canons which regulated the life of the Church, to adjudicate any cases that threatened this unity." Rome understood itself as "caput, fons et origo, fundamentum et basis, cardo." This terminology is simply unknown in the East, which sees in it the danger that the autonomy of the local Churches will not be respected. It is not by accident that the greatest crises between East and West (Photius, Kerullarios) "occurred during times in which Rome and the West defended in the strongest terms a doctrine of the Church in which the latter was presented as a single realm under the pope's authority."[104] Later this perspective became stronger, especially because of the Western controversy over conciliarism and Gallicanism. In practice "the one [either collegiality or primacy] was emphasized at the expense of the other."[105]

The relevance of a patristic idea of collegiality should be distinguished from the modern, speculative collegiality: while the patristic understanding is oriented toward the reestablishment of the organism of the individual Churches within the unity of the entire Church, the modern conception is concerned with the *plena et suprema potestas* of the college over the entire Church and its competition with the *plena et suprema potestas* of

---

103. Congar, *Wesenseigenschaften*, 537.
104. Congar, *Von der Gemeinschaft der Kirchen*, 256.
105. *Autorität in der Kirche 1*, no. 22, in DwÜ, 168.

the pope.[106] At Vatican II, because of the formulation of Vatican I and the entire Western tradition of the second millenium, the problem was discussed at the juridical level. As a consequence, not only was it strongly emphasized that, without the pope, the episcopal college is no real college, but also that the pope may decide all by himself whether he will discuss a topic alone and independently, that is, with the counsel of persons selected by himself, or collegially, that is, with the counsel of the college of bishops or with selected representatives therefrom. To this the comment was correctly made: "If attention had been directed more to the moral aspect of the business, entirely different conclusions would have been reached. . . . While it is true that the purpose of collegiality cannot be to set up something like a parliament in place of a monarchy, it is rather to bring back into effectiveness and validity the reality of *ecclesiae* within the *ecclesia*,"[107] that is, to make the collegiality of the Churches a living reality.

The primatial office exists to serve the unity of the Church and to safeguard the apostolic message: the pope has a particular responsibility to safeguard the apostolic message. *Pastoral authority* describes the meaning of this office much better than *primacy of jurisdiction*. This type of understanding better articulates the integration of the pope within the Church: in terms of the local Churches, and therefore within the circle of the other pastors. A primatial office does not diminish the function of the bishops nor the autonomy of the local Churches, but rather strengthens them. Catholic theology must recognize the fears of the other Churches. For example, the Anglicans express themselves on this issue in the following way: "The claim that the pope possesses an immediate jurisdiction, whose borders are not clearly delimited, is for Anglicans a source of anxiety; it seems to them that in this way no barrier is placed in the way of an illegitimate and uncontrolled use of this authority."[108]

It was conceded by the relator of the *deputatio fidei* at Vatican I that primacy has limits to its exercise: primacy must always be used in such a way as to build up (*in aedificationem*) and never to tear down (*in destructionem*) the Church.

In the specification of these statements, different factors play an important role. It must be said as a foundation that the exercise of the primatial office today demands a special sensitivity to the religious, theological, cultural, and ecumenical climate which reigns in particular Churches. Here arises the entire problem of a legitimate pluralism within life in unity. Each local Church must be able to live in autonomy. However, one must also

---

106. Thus Ratzinger, *Das neue Volk Gottes,* 102.
107. Ibid., 103 and 105.
108. *Authorität in der Kirche 1,* no. 24, in DwÜ, 169.

not forget that each local Church is related to the other local Churches, to the extent that they must live in the *koinonia* of the Churches. The fact that different bishops' conferences can decide, and decide differently, with regard to the specification of universal norms should be accepted as a natural consequence of the autonomy of the local Churches. A clear example of this is the various concrete forms chosen by the various conferences of bishops with reference to the possible application of the third formula for confession.

From the perspective of the autonomy of the Churches the function of primacy may be described as a supervision of life in *koinonia,* that is, within the truth of the gospel.[109] The more the autonomy of the local Churches is emphasized in the life of the Church, the clearer and sharper will appear what is specific to the primacy. The contemporary heavily centralized notion that reigns in the Catholic Church is often justified as a consequence of the primacy. However, in reality this is a practice that should be fundamentally distinguished from the notion of primacy. In what concerns the function of the bishop of Rome, the role of metropolitan and patriarch of the West should be separated from his primatial function. This means concretely: if one begins from primacy as the fundamental reality in the Church, there results the point of view of the 1983 codex, which is still in effect. However, if one were to start from the reality of the local Churches who live in *koinonia* under the leadership of the bishop of Rome, then the codex could have turned out entirely differently.[110]

A comparison of the various theological statements of Vatican II with the content of the encyclicals of Pope Pius XII (especially *Mystici corporis* and *Humani generis*) shows clearly that certain concepts, which in the light of the statements of these encyclicals would have been considered at least partially suspect, nonetheless established themselves at the council. This example of life in the Church shows clearly the different types of consequences the exercise of the primacy can have within or outside the context of collegiality.

An understanding of the primacy and its practice within the framework of collegiality leads to the necessity of synodal structures for the life of the Church. At such regularly scheduled synods the various local Churches should present their own reflections. This was the purpose that

---

109. The corresponding canon of Vatican I rejects the opinion that "the bishop of Rome possesses only the power of supervision or manager, and not the highest power of jurisdiction over the entire Church" ("tantummodo officium inspectionis vel directionis, non autem plenam et supremam potestatem iurisdictionis in universam Ecclesiam"; DS 3064 = NR 448). The expression is used here in another perspective.

110. This remark appears to me important for the question of what role the primacy should play in case the still separated Orthodox Churches should be reunited.

brought about the reestablishment of the synod of bishops (cf. canon 342, CIC 1983).[111] This modern institution has for a precedent the Roman synods, with whose help the popes of the early Church reached their decisions (for example, the "Tomus" of Pope Leo I for the Council of Chalcedon). One has a difficult time imagining that the pope could object to such synodal reflections. That such should be the normal situation results from the *collegial* structure of authority, which the Catholic understanding of the primacy does not exclude.

Now arises, in sharpened form, the issue of the infallible teaching authority of the pope. The choice of the formula "ex sese et non ex consensu ecclesiae" has been described as "unfortunate."[112] It has been often misinterpreted. If the pope speaks *ex cathedra,* he presents the truth of the Gospels according to the tradition of the Church. This means he is speaking *ex consensu ecclesiae.* In my opinion Orthodox theologians have correctly turned around the formula of Vatican I to describe the function of authority.[113] On the ontological level the pope is dependent upon the *sensus ecclesiae:* the pope is only empowered to define a truth to the extent that the Church is already, if obscurely, testifying to it.[114] For that reason the *relatores fidei* at Vatican I maintained firmly that they were not separating, and could not separate, the pope from the Church.

That there could be a juridical condition, in the sense of a condition *sine qua non,* for the papal decisions was rejected by the *deputatio fidei* at Vatican I. *Lumen gentium* expressed itself in the same direction. In practice, both Pius IX and Pius XII consulted the local Churches and especially the bishops for their definitions concerning Mary.

---

111. With regard to the question of what a synod is, the reflection of the extraordinary synod of bishops of 11–28 October 1969 is still relevant. See Idoc International no. 8 (15 September 1969) with the preparatory schema and no. 14 (15 December 1969) with the reports by Seper, Marty, and McGrath; *DC* 66 (1969) 957–72; G. Caprile, *II Sinodo dei Vescovi. Prima assemblea straordinaria* (Rome, 1970); J. Grootaers, "Die Bischofssynoden von 1969 und 1974: Mangelhaftes Funktionieren und signifikative Ergebnisse," in *Kirche im Wandel,* 275–97. See also J. Ratzinger, *Kirche, Ökumene und Politik,* 49ff. According to the codex—as specified in the summoning of the first extraordinary synod of bishops—a bishops' synod has only a consultative character, "unless in certain circumstances the pope has transferred to it the power to pass a decision" (can. 343).

112. Thus, among many others, Kasper, *Dienst,* 99.

113. See above chapter 11, section 2a.

114. See G. Dejaifve, "Ex sese, non autem ex consensu ecclesiae," *Sal* 24 (1962) 283–95 (here 294f.) = in *De Doctrina Concilii Vaticani Primi* (Vatican, 1971) 506–20 (here 519). It is noteworthy that this article was included in the memorial volume on Vatican I published by the Vatican. Various other theologians, such as H. Fries, G. Thils, Y. M. Congar, and I myself have expressed the same opinion.

In this context it is worth noticing that various Catholic theologians have recently returned to the question posed during the Middle Ages of the case of a heretical pope, a situation which also remained in the theological consciousness after the Reformation. This doctrine states: In case the pope should become a heretic, he is no longer pope of the Church.[115] According to Congar this hypothesis is "necessary and helpful as a hypothesis and limit situation, in order to set the pope *in,* and not *over,* the Church, as if he were no longer *within* the Church."[116] For his part, W. Kasper holds this "canonical doctrine" to be "fully in conformity with the system . . . indeed urgently necessary."[117]

Two aspects must always be kept in mind. On the one hand, the bishop of Rome has a special commission within the *koinonia* of bishops and of Churches. On the other hand, this special commission of the bishop of Rome does not mitigate the commissions of the other bishops (*ius divinum* of bishops) nor the meaning of the *koinonia* of the Churches. The second aspect means: "The pope is not chief of the college of bishops (*supra*) without at the same time belonging (*in*) to this college, and thus without obeying the ontological law of this college. For that the juridical perspective must be given up, and an ontology of communion and fraternity, which is that of the Church, must be embraced."[118]

The pope has a special commission for the unity of the Church to the extent that he is bishop of the local Church of Rome,[119] where Peter and

---

115. An overview is given by H. Küng in *Strukturen der Kirche* (Freiburg, 1962) 228–44.

116. Y. M. Congar, *Ministères et communion ecclésiale* (Paris, 1971) 198. The entire article "Synode épiscopal, Primauté et Collégialité" (187–227) is recommended.

117. Kasper, *Dienst,* 98.

118. Congar, *Ministères,* 198.

119. Orthodox theologians raise the following objection against the primacy: "Like every commission within the Church, office is a gift of grace, a grace that is bestowed with the sacrament of orders. . . . In its hierarchy, the Church recognizes three stages, and there simply is no gift of grace that is higher than that of the bishop. The Orthodox Church recognizes no charisma or sacrament of the primacy" (thus A. Schmemann, "Der Begriff des Primates in der orthodoxen Ekklesiologie," in N. Afanassieff et al., *Der Primat des Petrus,* 122). This argument was also used by Russian theologians before the Revolution. See Th. Spáçil, "Conceptus et doctrina de Ecclesia juxta Theologiam orientis separati," OrChr[R] 2, 2 (Rome, 1924) nos. 45 and 135, pp. 60 and 98ff. Catholic theology agrees with the Orthodox in the point of departure for reflection. Nevertheless, it believes that the presider over a specific bishop's see possesses a special responsibility for the *koinonia* of the Church, that is, for the Church as a totality, on the basis of his function as presider over this local Church, that is, on the basis of orders. One should not apply here, however, the distinction developed later in the West between *ordo* and *iurisdictio.*

Paul died as martyrs. It is essential that the two apostles, as well as their tension-filled *koinonia,* not be forgotten. Therein lies a programmatic principle for the *Catholica.* It is also necessary that the local Churches live in autonomy. The opposite would be the attempt to create a uniform episcopacy, the result being that any bishop who was not known to be true to Rome (in the sense of the Curia) would be suspect. With J. A. Möhler, we may describe the pope as the reflex or response of the entire Church, precipitated into a person.[120] Against the danger of a narrow ecclesial regionalism,[121] primacy brings the perspective of the universal Church to bear.

5. Toward a Theology of the Local Churches[122]

There are few elements in Vatican II which have relevance to a theology of the local Churches.

In *Lumen gentium* (no. 23, 4), this theme is discussed in the context of the collegiality of bishops. The model for the local Churches is that of the old patriarchal Churches. The bishops' conferences are presented in analogy with these Churches, although the autonomy granted them in the current Codex is very small. The constitution speaks of possible differences with reference to discipline (canon law), to liturgical practice, as well as to theological and spiritual tradition. However, the unity of the faith and the divine appreciation of the entire Church must remain undamaged. "Local Churches" means not only individual dioceses (see the Decree on the Bishops, no. 11), but also, following the model of the patriarchal Churches, federations of dioceses.

120. J. A. Möhler, *Die Einheit in der Kirche oder das Prinzip des Katholizismus,* ed. J. R. Geiselmann (Darmstadt, 1957) 230.

121. See J. Meyendorff, "Kirchlicher Regionalismus: Strukturen des Gemeinschaft oder Vorwand des Separatismus," in *Kirche im Wandel,* 303–18.

122. Bibliography: (a) Catholic authors: B. Neunheuser, "Gesamtkirche und Einzelkirche," in *Barauna* 1:547–73; W. Beinert, "Die *'Una Catholica'* und die Partikularkirchen," in *ThPh* 42 (1987) 1–25; Beinert, "Das Petrusamt und die Ortskirchen," in *Petrus und Papst,* vol. 1, 95–116 (esp. 112ff.); Antón, *Primado y colegialidad,* esp. 79ff. (with bibliography); H. M. Legrand, "Nature de l'Église particulière et rôle de l'évêque dans l'Église," in *La charge pastorale des évêques,* Unam sanctam 74 (Paris, 1969) 103–21; H. de Lubac, *Les églises particulieres dans l'église universelle* (Paris, 1971). (b) Non-Catholic authors: J. D. Zizioulas (Orthodox), *L'etre ecclésial* (Geneva, 1981) = Being as Communion (New York, 1985) (esp. chs. 3, 5, 6); R. Sienczka (Lutheran), " *'Ecclesia particularis.'* Erwägungen zum Begriff und zum Problem," in *KuD* 12 (1966) 319–33; J. J. von Allmen (Reformed), "L'Église locale parmi les autres Églises locales," *Irénikon* 43 (1970) 512–37.

Such introductory reflections still contain a programmatic significance. The Catholic Church has here a new path stretching out before it. The way in which it proceeds down this path will be decisive for giving the function of the bishop of Rome a new form within the *koinonia* of Churches.

Fundamentally a theology of the local Churches must take the differences in the theological, liturgical, and canonical realms, as these existed for the first thousand years both in the East and in the West, as a model. Unity in no way implies uniformity. The principles that the decree on ecumenism emphasized for dialogue with the other Churches must also be applied within the Roman Catholic Church.

BIBLIOGRAPHY

General:

Antón, A. *Primado y Colegialidad*. Madrid, 1970 (with an outstanding international bibliography).

Bermejo, L. M. *Towards Christian Reunion. Vatican I; Obstacles and Opportunities*. Auand-Gujarat, 1984.

Brandenburg, A. and H. J. Urban, eds. *Peter and Paul*. Vol. 1: Münster, 1977; vol. 2: Münster, 1978 (collection of articles by various authors). Important contributions in this work:

Beinert, W. "Die Exzentrizität des Papstes. Über die Unfehlbarkeit des römischen Bishofs in der Kirche": 2:56–86.

_____. "Das Petrusamt und die Ortskirche": 1:95–116.

Döring, H. "Das 'Ius Divinum' des Petrus-Amtes. Ansätze zu einem gemeinsamen Verständnis": 2:87–118.

Kasper, W. "Dienst an der Einheit und Freiheit der Kirche. Zur gegenwärtigen Diskussion um das Petrusamt in der Kirche": 2:119–41.

Congar, Y. M. "Die Wesenseigenschaften der Kirche." In MySal 4/1, 395ff., 570ff. (Primacy and Episcopacy).

_____. "Die Lehre von der Kirche. Von Augustinus bis zum Abendländischen Schisma" (HDG 3:3c); Vom Abendländischen Schisma bis zur Gegenwart (HDG 3:3d), Freiburg, 1971.

Dejaifve, G. *L'église de Vatican I à Vatican II*. Rome, 1976 (collection of various essays).

Döring, H. "Papstum." In NHThG 3:313–28.

_____. *Grundriss der Ekklesiologie*. Darmstadt, 1986, 273ff.

Legrand, H. "La Réalisation de l'Église en un lieu." In *Initiation à la Pratique de la théologie*, vol. 3, Paris, 1983, 257ff. (Communion between the Churches).

Ratzinger, J. *Das neue Volk Gottes. Entwurfe zur Ekklesiologie*. Düsseldorf, 1969, 121ff. (Primacy and Episcopacy), 171ff. (Episcopal collegiality according to the teaching of the Second Vatican Council).

_____. *Kirche Ökumene und Politik.* Einsiedeln, 1987, 35–48 ("The Primacy of the Pope and the Unity of the People of God," originally in J. Ratzinger, ed., *Dienst an der Einheit,* Düsseldorf, 1978, 165–79), 49–63 (Questions concerning the structure and jobs of the synod of bishops).

Schulz, H. G. "Ortskirche und Gesamtkirche. Primat, Kollegialität und Synodalität." In D. Papandreou, ed., *Église locale et Église Universelle,* Chambesy, 1981, 177–97.

Tillard, J. M. R. *L'évêque de Rome.* Paris, 1982.

On Vatican I:

Aubert, R. *Vaticanum I.* Mainz, 1965 (especially chs. 7, 10, and 11).

Betti, U. *La costituzione dommatica 'Pastor aeternus' Del concilio Vaticano I.* Rome, 1961.

Dewan, W. F. "Potestas episcopalis auf dem Ersten Vatikanischen Konzil." In Y. M. Congar, ed., *Das Bischofsamt und die Weltkirche,* Stuttgart, 1964 (French original, 1962), 689–718.

Kasper, W. "Primat und Episkopat nach dem Vaticanum I." *ThQ* 142 (1962) 47–83.

Minnerath, R. *Le Pape, évêque universel ou premier des évêques?* Paris, 1978.

Pottmeyer, H. J. *Unfehlbarkeit und Souveränität. Die päpstliche Unfehlbarkeit im System der ultramontanen Ekklesiologie des 19. Jahrhunderts.* Mainz, 1975.

Schatz, Kl. "Päpstliche Unfehlbarkeit und Geschichte in den Diskussionen des 1. Vaticanums." In *Dogmengeschichte und katholische Theologie,* eds. W. von Löser, K. Lehmann, and M. Lutz-Bachmann, Würzburg, 1985, 187–250.

Thils, G. "Potestas ordinaria." In Y. M. Congar, *Das Bischofsamt und die Weltkirche,* Stuttgart, 1964, 719–38.

_____. *L'infaillibilité pontificale. Source-conditions-limites.* Gembloux, 1969.

_____. *La primauté pontificale. La Doctrine du Vatican I. Les voies d'une revision.* Gembloux, 1972.

Torrell, J. P. *La théologie de l'episcopat au premier concile du Vatican.* Paris, 1961.

Ecumenical Documents:

Anglican-Roman Catholic International Commission, The Final Report, London, 1982: Authority in the Church 1 (Venice, 1976); Authority in the Church: Elucidation (Windsor, 1981); Authority in the Church 2 (Windsor, 1981); German translation in DwÜ 159–90.

Bibliography on the Reaction to the Document, in J. F. Puglisi and S. J. Voicu, *A Bibliography of Interchurch and Interconfessional Theological Dialogues,* Rome, 1984, 69ff., 75ff.

Groupe de Dombes, *Le ministère de communion dans L'église universelle.* Paris, 1986, and in *DC* 68 (1986) 1122–42.

Papal Primacy and the Universal Church, eds. P. C. Empie and T. A. Murphy, (Lutherans and Catholics in Dialogue 5), Minneapolis, 1974.

The Positions of the Congregation of the Faith, in *L'osservatore romano,* May 6, 1982, 3f.

Ratzinger, J. *Kirche, Ökumene und Politik.* Einsiedeln, 1987, 67–87 ("Probleme und Hoffnungen des anglikanisch-katholischen Dialogs," originally in: International Catholic Journal *Communio* 12 [1983] 244–59), 87–96 (Afterword 1986).

On the Historical Problematic:

Baus, K. "Von der Urgemeinde zur frühchristlichen Grosskirche." In KG (J) vol. 1, Freiburg, 1962, 180f., 399ff.

Congar, Y. M. "Zerrissene Christenheit. Wo trennten sich Ost und West? Wien and München, 1959 (especially chs. 3–5) (French original "Neuf cents ans après," in 1054–1954. *L'Église et les églises,* vol. 1, Chevetogne, 1954, 3–95).

_____. *L'ecclésiologie du haut moyen age.* Paris, 1968, 340ff.

Dvornik, F. *Byzance und der römische Primat.* Stuttgart, 1966 (French original, 1964).

Horn, S. O. *Petrou Kathedra. Der Bishof von Rom und die Synoden von Ephesus (449) und Chalkedon.* Paderborn, 1982.

Ludwig, J. *Die Primatworte Mt 16, 18, 19 in der altkirchlichen Exegese.* Münster, 1952.

McCue, J. "Der römische Primat in den drei ersten Jahrhunderten." *Conc* 7 (1971) 245–49.

_____. "The Roman Primacy in the Patristic Era. The Beginning Through Nicaea." In *Papal Primacy and the Universal Church,* eds. P. C. von Empie and T. A. Murphy (Lutherans and Catholics in Dialogue 4), Minneapolis, 1974, 44–72.

Stockmeier, P. "Das Petrusamt in der frühen Kirche." In G. Denzler and others, *Zum Thema Petrusamt und Papsttum,* Stuttgart, 1970, 61–79.

Twomey, V. *Apostolikos thronos. The Primacy of Rome as Reflected in the Church History of Eusebius and the Historico-Apologetic Writings of S. Athanasius the Great.* Münster, 1982.

Vogel, C. "Einheit der Kirche und Vielheit der geschichtlichen Kirchenorganisationsformen vom dritten bis zum fünften Jahrhundert." In Y. M. Congar, ed., *Das Bischofsamt und die Weltkirche,* Stuttgart, 1964, 609–62.

Vries, W. de. "Die Kollegialität auf Synoden des ersten Jahrtausends." In G. Denzler and others, *Zum Thema Petrusamt und Papsttum,* Stuttgart, 1970, 80–91 (a summary of his work on the eight ecumenical councils = *Orient et occident. Les structures ecclésiales vues dans l'histoire des septs premiers conciles oecuméniques,* Paris, 1974).

_____. "Die Entwicklung des Primats in den ersten drei Jahrhunderten." In *Papsttum als ökumenische Frage,* pub. by the Arbeitsgemeinschaft ökumenischer Universitätsinstitute, Mainz and München, 1979, 114–33 (with an outstanding bibliography and a presentation of the different interpretations of the texts. A discussion of reviews of the book, 134ff.).

Fourth Part:

The Mission and Task of the Church

The Church must always be understood in terms of her mission, which she has received and continues to receive from her Lord. In the words of *Ad gentes:* "The pilgrim Church is essentially a 'missionary' Church (that is, one sent, and continually on the way), since she traces her origin back to the sending of the Son and the sending of the Holy Spirit, according to the plan of God the Father" (*AG* 2; see also *Lumen gentium* no. 17).

Since all share in the office of Christ (*Lumen gentium* no. 12; *Apostolicum actuositatem* no. 2), the Church, that is, the community of all believers, not just those who hold office, must appropriate, as *Lumen gentium* no. 17 says explicitly, the apostle's words, "Woe unto me, if I do not proclaim the gospel!" (1 Cor 9:16).

However the mission of the Church and its implications have been understood, she has always, in the course of her history, proclaimed the gospel; she has always held this to be her essential task. The history of the Church is the history of her missionary expansion.

The fact that the Church realizes herself in the Eucharistic celebration (chap. VIII) highlights her missionary character in the sense that the word she proclaims must be seen in connection with the Word that Jesus Christ himself is, and that becomes sacramentally present in the Eucharistic celebration; the Church has no other word to proclaim than Jesus Christ with his gift of salvation for all of humanity (the world). The Lord proclaimed by the Church becomes present in the community's worship. Any separation between the Church's worship and her missionary character would have to be seen as an unfortunate error. Unfortunately, in certain celebrations of the Eucharist this missionary character does not come to expression sufficiently, and the impression is given that the community is celebrating itself. In such cases the perspective under which the Church is described as the sacrament of salvation is lost sight of: *Lumen gentium* presents the Church as the sacrament in Christ, in the sense that she is "sign and instrument for the closest union with God as well as for the unity of mankind" (no. 1). The same statement is made by *Gaudium et spes* (no. 42, 3) when it speaks of the help which the Church seeks to extend to human society.

Through its missionary task, the Church understands itself as the sacrament of the world. Through the accomplishment of its function, which "belongs to the religious order" (*GS* 42, 2), the Church is convinced that it contributes to the construction and the solidification of the society of humankind according to God's plan (ibid.).

In this final part of our book, the formal task of the Church, that of evangelization, will be presented with its consequences and implications (chap. XIV). Thereby may the relation of the Church to the world, and of the world to the Church (chap. XV), finally be described in a new light.

XIV.
Evangelization and Its Implications

1. Toward a Statement of the Question

The tension between the "horizontal" and "vertical" dimensions of the faith is the most obvious issue which divides contemporary Christians. This division transcends traditional separations along confessional lines. At the Fifth United Assembly of the Ecumenical Council of Churches in Nairobi in 1975, this division between representatives of "verticalism," that is, those who are concerned primarily with a direct relation to God, the spiritual dimension of the gospel, and a conversion of heart, and representatives of "horizontalism," that is, those who stress a social liberation that is to be achieved through political engagement in the name of the gospel, became quite manifest.[1] This tension may also be detected within the Roman Catholic Church, even at official meetings such as the synods of bishops on evangelization (1974) and on catechesis (1977).

It seems to me symptomatic that movements such as the theology of revolution, political theology, or liberation theology have developed within Western theology. In what could be a general description of such theologies, J. B. Metz characterizes the presentation of political theology as "a *critical corrective* to a certain tendency toward privatization in contemporary theology (in its transcendental, existential, and personalistic varie-

1. See the report from Nairobi: *Ergebnisse—Erlebnisse—Ereignisse,* eds. H. Krüger and W. Müller-Römheld (Frankfurt, 1978). In the index consult the entry "Evangelisation." As to the thrust of the Orthodox criticism, see the positions of the Russian-Orthodox Church against the danger of "Horizontalism" in *Irénikon* 49 (1976) 186–204. See also the reflections of Orthodox theologians in *Orthodox Contributions to Nairobi* (Geneva, 1975).

ties).'' ''As such a critical corrective, political theology is motivated by the intention to deprivatize the world of theological concepts, the language of proclamation, and spirituality.''[2]

Without surveying the errors and ambiguities to which such theologies can give rise, we may still say that their theological expression was necessary to make clear that Christian belief requires engagement in the world. The statement in *Gaudium et spes* no. 43 that Christians may not ignore their earthly duties is a clear indication that the connection between Christian belief and social engagement was not clear, or not clear enough, to many Christians. In this sense, the movements mentioned have helped to remind Christian faith of its social implications.

The task of the Church is to be understood in continuity with the mission of Jesus. For that reason it is not surprising that theological reflections on the implications of the mission of the Church have consequences in the presentation of Christology.[3] In the following we shall first describe the mission of the Church according to recent official documents; subsequently we shall present a theological reflection on the entire problematic.

2. The Mission of the Church according to the Official Documents

a. Vatican II

Lumen gentium: In no. 17 the constitution describes the missionary character of the Church, which is grounded in the missionary commission of the apostles by Jesus Christ—here Matthew 28:18-20 is quoted—just as the latter was sent by the Father. The actual goal of the mission consists in the expansion of the Christian faith together with the means of salvation, especially love: for the Church ''is specifically animated by the Holy Spirit to cooperate so that God's plan, which placed Christ as the source of salvation for the entire world, will in fact be carried out. In proclaiming the good news, the Church seeks to bring its hearers to belief and the confession of faith, she prepares them for baptism, frees them from slavery to error, and makes them members of Christ'' (*LG* no. 17).

---

2. J. B. Metz, ''Politische Theologie,'' in HTTL 6:51-58 (here 52f.).

3. In my opinion the book by L. Boff, *Jesus Christus der Befreier* (Freiburg, 1986), is a clear example of this; see 24ff. (''Two Levels of Social Awareness and Two Corresponding Theologies''), as well as his depiction of the kingdom of God in Jesus' preaching (52ff.). See also J. Sobrino, *Christology at the Crossroads* (London, 1978) 346ff. (''Theses towards an Historical Christology''; especially 4.5; 6; 8.15; 9.6; 11.4, and 11.9).

Ad gentes: The basic statement of *LG* no. 17 is developed in the decree *Ad gentes.* According to the decree the mission of the Church "is therefore accomplished through that activity by which, in obedience to Christ's command and led by the grace and love of the Holy Spirit, it becomes present to all individuals and peoples in its full actuality, so as to lead them through the testimony of its life, its preaching, the sacraments, and the other ways of sharing faith and grace, to freedom and to the peace of Christ; in this way should the free and certain way to full participation in the mystery of Christ be opened to them" (*AG* no. 5, 1).

The decree formulates the principle that "today and always the missionary activity retains its meaning and necessity undiminished" (*AG* no. 7, 1), a necessity which is based on the character of the Church as the sacrament of salvation (equally with a reference to *LG* no. 14). This principle does not exclude the possibility that there are people who reach salvation who, through no fault of their own, neither have heard the gospel nor have come to an explicit recognition of God (*LG* no. 16; *AG* no. 7, 1). Even though the divine will intends the salvation of all people in their concrete situations (and thus we may speak of "anonymous Christians"), still this cannot be viewed as a criterion for the understanding of the formal task of the Church.[4]

The formula for the mission of the Church is the proclamation of the gospel; however, the gospel has consequences for the development of humanity: "As a matter of fact, the gospel was in history, even profane history, a catalyst for human freedom and progress, and offers itself still as a catalyst for fraternity, unity, and peace. There are indeed reasons why Christ is celebrated by the faithful as the 'Hope and Savior of the peoples' " (*AG* no. 8).

Gaudium et spes: The last statement leads to one of the most important aspects of the reflections of the Second Vatican Council, developed in the constitution *Gaudium et spes.* The decree on the mission and the constitution on the Church in the modern world were published by the council on the same day. The fourth chapter of the first part of *Gaudium et spes* is concerned with "the task of the Church in the modern world" (the chapter title). In the preparatory stage of the document, whose decisive text is no. 41, it was first emphasized that "the plan of salvation includes the plan of creation" (no. 50). As a consequence, the text spoke of the universal mission of the Church ("de missione universali Ecclesiae"): "In that the order of salvation encompasses the order of creation, the

---

4. On this theme K. Rahner writes: "It would thus be foolish to believe that talk of an 'implicit Christology' would have to diminish the significance of mission, the proclamation of the Word of God, of baptism, etc." (K. Rahner, "Mission und 'implizite Christlichkeit,' " in HTTL 5:88–91, here 90.

Church's service extends itself necessarily from its own point of view over all objects and over all human problems . . ."[5]

Before we take up the final version of the text, we must review the notion of the constitution. *Gaudium et spes* formulates the fundamental principles of a Christian anthropology: "It is a matter of the rescue of the human person, it is a matter of the proper construction of a human society. Thus the human being, one and entire, with body and soul, heart and conscience, reason and will, stands at the center of our discussion" (*GS* no. 3, 1). The four chapters present first the human problem on the individual and social level, and then the human person in the light of Christ. The matter is organized according to the following plan:

Chapter 1: The worth of the human person (the person in the image of God; sin, the value of reason, truth and wisdom . . . atheism) → Christ, the new man (no. 22).

Chapter 2: Human community (. . . the essential equality of all men and social justice . . .) → the incarnate Word and human solidarity (no. 39).

Chapter 3: Human activity in the world (the value of human activity, . . . human activity corrupted by sin) → Human activity brought to its fulfillment in the mystery of Easter (no. 38); the new earth and the new heaven (no. 39).

Chapter 4: The task of the Church in the contemporary world → Christ, alpha and omega (no. 45).

The structure of the four chapters shows clearly that the constitution confronts humankind and its problems with the perspective that arises from the gospel, that is, from the significance of Christ as Savior. The council finds in Christ the authentic solution for the fundamental problem of humankind: "The Church [believes] it has much to contribute to a more human shaping of the family of men and to their history" (no. 40, 3); "since it has been entrusted to the Church to make known the mystery of Christ, the final goal of humankind, she discloses to humanity simultaneously the understanding of its own existence, that is, the final truth concerning humankind" (no. 41, 1).

In the light of her formal religious task, the Church recognizes that she can offer support to the human community: "The Church's distinctive mission, which Christ has passed on to her, does not directly have to do with the political, economic, or social order; the goal which Christ has given her belongs instead to the religious sphere. However, there flows even out of this religious mission a commission, light, and power that allows her to contribute to the building up and solidification of the human

---

5. Reference by M. D. Chenu, "Die Aufgabe der Kirche in der Welt von heute," in G. Baraúna, ed., *Die Kirche in der Welt von heute* (Salzburg, 1967) 226–47, here 230.

community according to divine laws" (no. 42, 2). Otherwise expressed: Because of its mission, because of the Christian identity of its members, the Church can help humankind toward the full realization of their personhood.

It is noteworthy that the constitution refers to Christian identity when it speaks of the help which the Church can transmit to humanity: "The power . . . that the Church has to share with the human community is that faith and that love which works itself out in the actions and truth of life [*in illa fide et caritate, ad effectum vitae adductis, consistit*]" (no. 42, 3). The constitution emphasizes the obligation of Christians to commit themselves to the building up of the world and to the betterment of their fellow human beings (nos. 34, 3; 39, 3; 42, 2; 43, 1; 57, 1), however, it sees this engagement as a consequence of their Christian identity, that is, of a life that is stamped with the supernatural virtues (faith, hope, and charity). For that reason it warns against the danger of separating faith from daily life: "Such a split . . . belongs to worst errors of our time" (no. 43, 1).

The constitution opposes the dualism that such a division implies. M. D. Chenu remarks that the constitution's text "avoids the usual expressions that indicate a difference between natural and supernatural," and prefers instead "more synthetic terms that are more in keeping with the gospel."[6] This statement is all the more interesting in that G. Gutiérrez also bases himself upon it to develop his theology of liberation.[7]

For his part, Y. M. Congar regrets that the constitution does not distinguish more clearly between two ways in which the Church may operate, specifically, its own formal mission "to lead the world to the gospel," and "the operations of the Church in the world, that is, those activities which she carries out in the world and for the world *according to its own structures and activities,* and which remain in their own order": "Almost nothing is said about the relation which must be established between these two activities of the Church, which together constitute its mission as a whole. It is all the more important to emphasize that this relationship is extremely close."[8]

Is this just a difference between various theologies? As a matter of fact, the decree on the lay apostolate, which was published by the council

6. Chenu, *Die Aufgabe der Kirche,* 237.

7. G. Gutiérrez, *Theologie der Befreiung,* 59ff.: "The Schema for the Distinction of Levels in the Crisis." This schema was used by the Catholic Action in France. Gutiérrez supports the understanding of *Gaudium et spes* against that of *Apostolicam actuositatem* (58 and note 26). In his theological reflection he refers to "the single call to salvation" (66ff.). See also the section "The Unity of History" (140ff.).

8. Y. M. Congar in LThK. E 3, 398.

a few days before *Gaudium et spes,* expresses itself more in the style of Congar.

Apostolicam actuositatem: The decree speaks of a twofold task of the Church:

The Church "should spread the lordship of Christ over the entire earth to the glory of God the Father, and thereby allow all humankind to share in life-bringing salvation, and through these men, the entire world should be ordered to Christ in truth" (no. 2, 1).

"Christ's work of salvation has for its goal the salvation of humankind, but it also includes the building up of the entire temporal order. For that reason the mission of the Church does not consist only in communicating the message and grace of Christ to humanity, but also in penetrating and completing the temporal order with the spirit of the gospel" (no. 5).

The two tasks are spelled out even more concretely in nos. 6 and 7. With reference to the first task, no. 6, 1 says: "The apostolate of the Church and all of its members is directed in the first place to making known Christ's message to the world through word and deed, and to communicating his grace to it. This takes place in a special way through the ministry of the Word and the sacraments." In this way the proclamation of the gospel, which is oriented toward the kindling of belief (no. 6, 3), and the administration of the sacraments are presented as tasks of the Church, since "the Church has no other task than to save humankind."[9]

No. 7 speaks of the second task of the Church, which the council commission described with the words "toward a Christian formation of the temporal order [*de ordine rerum temporalium christiane instaurando*]." This terminology appears with slight variations several times in the decree.[10]

The distinctive significance and legitimate autonomy of the temporal order are stressed in the same article (no. 7, 2; see also *GS* no. 36). To it is added the description of the role of sin in human history: "In the course of history temporal things were disfigured through serious misuse. Burdened with original sin, humankind frequently produced various errors concerning the true nature of God, human nature, and the fundamental obligation of society's norms" (no. 7, 3; see also *GS* no. 37). In the light of this statement it appears understandable that it is presented as the task of the entire Church "to labor so that humankind will become capable of properly constructing the entire temporal order, and through Christ to orient it toward God" (no. 7, 4).

A comparison of the statements of the decree with those of *Gaudium et spes* shows that the two documents occupy two different perspectives which, however, do not contradict one another. They are addressed to

9. Acta Synod. 4/6, 50 (Modi ad no. 6, "12").
10. F. Klostermann has gathered the different texts in LThK. E 2, 621f.

two different audiences: while *Apostolicam actuositatem* has in mind an inner-Church readership, *Gaudium et spes* is addressed to all people of good will. These different audiences require two different orientations: the constitution may take as its point of departure only the fact that the Church may, because of the content of its mission, also deliver a word on human dignity. That is the reason it emphasizes that its religious mission also has consequences for the development of the temporal order. Thus the constitution assumes a difference between the two tasks of the Church which is explicitly formulated in the decree.

It was emphasized by theologians already before and during the council that the two tasks of the Church must be seen as tightly bound together. Congar—who should be regarded as one of the representative theologians on this topic—wrote in 1963:

> This single mission of the Church to the world unfolds itself as regards its content in a twofold way. First and *foremost* it includes the task to lead humanity toward the gospel (conversion), so that they may be transformed into members of the people of God. *Further and as a consequence of this* she receives the task to exert herself as an influence on the secular society, to order it according to God's will and to orient it towards God's kingdom as its goal, as far as this is possible short of its eschatological completion.[11]

These sentences present the fundamental concepts which are established in *Apostolicam actuositatem*.

b. Post-Conciliar Documents

The contemporary problematic of evangelization was the object of discussion at the Third Synod of Bishops in 1974. There reference was made to the document produced by the Second Synod of Bishops in 1971, *Justice in the World*.

The conclusion of the 1971 document states: "It thus appears to us that an active engagement on behalf of justice and a cooperation in the transformation of the world is indeed a constitutive dimension [*tanquam ratio constitutiva*] of the proclamation of the gospel, specifically of the mission of the Church for the salvation and liberation of humanity from whatever situations of suppression."[12]

The manner in which this thesis statement from the synod was understood becomes clear from the content of the entire document. It first em-

11. Y. M. Congar, "Laie," in HThG 2 (1963) 7–25 (here 15).
12. Introduction. The document in *AAS* 63 (1971) 923–41, a German translation in *HerKorr* 26 (1972) 36–42 (here 37). Page numbers in what follows refer to the German translation.

phasizes the connection between our attitude toward our fellow human beings and our attitude toward God: "According to the Christian message, the relation of man to his fellow men is a constitutive part of his relationship to God."[13] Then the inseparability between love of neighbor and justice is asserted. From that it is concluded that the mission of the Church contains not only the call to humanity to turn away from sin and towards the love of God, but also a concern with the brotherhood of all people and hence the demand for justice in the world. The argument consists in rendering explicit the implications of the gospel proclaimed by the Church: the Church "has a unique and specific responsibility that is identical with her mission: to lay down before the world a witness to the requirement of love and justice, as these are contained in the gospel." For that reason "the mission to proclaim the gospel demands . . . that we engage ourselves entirely for the universal liberation of humanity even in its current existence in this world."[14]

A new perspective appears in the statement that otherwise the credibility of the gospel proclamation is thrown into question: "For if the Christian message of love and righteousness does not demonstrate its effectiveness through engagement for justice in the world, it will be all the more difficult for the peoples of our time to believe in it."

At the synod of 1974, Msgr. R. Terrella, the secretary for the theme "Justice in the World," explained that at the synod of 1971 the expression "constitutive dimension" (*ratio constitutiva*) should be interpreted in the sense of an integrating part (*parte integrante*), and not in the sense of an essential part (*parte esencial*).[15]

An in-depth analysis of the problematic was mounted by the synod of 1974.[16] On the work of the synod we have a synthesis of the statements of the participants that was edited by one of the secretaries of the synod and then read officially to the participants. However, we have no genuine concluding document that had been discussed and formally published at the end of the synod.[17] A list of the themes taken up was presented to the pope, to serve as a possible foundation for the publication of an apostolic exhortation. This is how *Evangelii nuntiandi* (1975) was written.

From the declaration of the synod, no. 12 touches our topic:

13. 2, 1, p. 39.

14. 2, 2, p. 39.

15. 2, 1, p. 39.

16. See G. Caprile, *Il sinodo del Vescovi 1974* (Rome, 1975) 602; B. Kloppenburg, "Evangelization y Liberacion," in *Medelin. Teología y pastoral para América Latina I* (1975) 6–35, here 22.

17. See D. Grasso, "Zum Lernprozess synodaler Arbeit—erläutert an der Entstehung von 'Evangelii nuntiandi,' " in ". . . *denn Ich bin bei Euch*" (FS J. Glazik and B. Willeke) (Cologne, 1978) 101–8, here 108. See also Caprile, *Sinodo*, 990 and 1011.

Among the many questions which we on the synod took up, we were most especially concerned with the type of relations that exist between evangelization and the total healing or full liberation of individuals and peoples. On this unusually important question we have been struck by the profound unity that must ever anew be established in a close connection between evangelization and liberation. The stimulus for this was not only our deep solidarity with our own faithful and all people, in whose lives and common fate we ourselves share, but primarily the gospel that God has entrusted to us out of his mercy, which is a fresh message of healing for all peoples and for all of human society. This salvation begins and announces itself already in this world, even it can reach its complete fulfillment only beyond the present life.

Impelled by the love of Christ and instructed by the gospel, we put our trust in the fact that the Church, when she most authentically carries through the work of evangelization, announces, and even already begins to bring about, a total healing of humankind and their complete liberation. As a society that is completely dedicated to evangelization, the Church is obligated to conform herself to the pattern of Christ, who expressed his own mission in the following words: "The Spirit of the Lord is upon me; the Lord has anointed me. He has sent me to bring good news to the poor, to announce freedom to those in chains, and sight to those who cannot see" (Luke 4:18).

True to its gospel commission, the Church as a truly poor, begging, and fraternal community has much to contribute to the total healing and complete liberation of people. Out of the gospel she will craft deeper arguments and discover ever new impulses to call for a generous insertion in service to all humankind, especially the poor, the weak, and the oppressed, and she will help to overcome the social consequences of sin which lock people in unjust social and political structures. Supported by the gospel and strengthened by its grace, the Church will be able to preserve this striving toward liberation from errors, so that the latter does not become concentrated upon purely political, social, or economic matters which the Church naturally must attend to, but rather leads finally toward a complete freedom from sin, from personal or collective egoism, and toward a full, transcendent communion with God, and with human beings as brothers. In this way the Church will advance, in the gospel way that is proper to her, the true and complete liberation of all individuals, groups, and peoples.[18]

In the contributions of various participants to the synod, often in the name of the bishops' conferences which they represented, attention was

---

18. *HerKorr* 28 (1974) 622–24, here 623.

drawn to the danger that in practice, the faith could become politicized. Opposition was raised against "a tendency toward secularity" (*de tipo temporalista*). An exaggeration of such a tendency would be the suggestion that the Church must first liberate the poor, and only then begin to evangelize. Several participants at the synod expressed themselves against such an opinion.[19]

The fact that there were numerous statements along this line makes clear the importance of the exhortation *Evangelii nuntiandi,* a papal document which should be seen in connection with the reflection of the synod.

Evangelii nuntiandi[20] (in its fundamental thrust): The substance of evangelization is discussed in the third part of the document: "Evangelization will always be—as the foundation, center, and simultaneous high point of its dynamic—a clear proclamation that in Jesus Christ, the Son of God who became man, died, and rose again, salvation is offered to every person as a gift of the grace and mercy of God himself" (no. 27). To ground this statement, which touches the kernel of the Christian message, reference is made to Ephesians 2:8 and Romans 1:16. This salvation is of a type—the text continues—which exceeds every boundary, one that comes to completion in a communion with the one Absolute, with God: thus, a transcendent, eschatological salvation, which has its beginning indeed already in this life, but reaches its fulfillment only in eternity. The exhortation formulates the goal of evangelization in the following terms: "Beyond the proclamation of a message, evangelization in its entirety consists in having the Church take root, which, however, cannot happen without its sacramental life, which in turn has its high point in the Eucharist" (no. 28).

For evangelization to be complete, the connection between evangelization and the concrete personal and social life of people must be attended to (no. 29). For that reason the message concerning justice in the world as well as concerning liberation must be seen in connection with the Church's mission of evangelization: "The Church has . . . the duty to proclaim the liberation of all people; the duty to aid this liberation to become a reality, to give witness to it and to support it until it reaches its full completion. This is thoroughly in harmony with evangelization" (*omnia haec non sunt aliena ab evangelizatione:* no. 30). According to the exhortation, there is in practice a close connection between evangelization and human advancement, development, and liberation. This connection is illustrated on three levels: anthropologically, to the extent that the person who is to be evangelized cannot be seen in separation from

19. There is an interesting presentation in Kloppenburg, *Evangelización,* 14ff.

20. The text is in *AAS* 68 (1976) 1–76. See also the work listed in the bibliography by J. Sobrino.

his or her social and economic problems; theologically, to the extent that one cannot separate God's plan of creation from his plan of salvation; and "evangelically," on the basis of love (no. 31).

In its conclusion, the exhortation emphasizes that, concerning the Church's task, the "preeminence of her spiritual mission must be strengthened." This entails a refusal "to replace the proclamation of the kingdom of God with the proclamation of human liberation": "The contribution of the Church to liberation would be incomplete if she neglected to preach salvation in Jesus Christ" (no. 34). However, the exhortation also rejects the notion that "the Church's mission is reduced to the merely religious sphere" (ibid.).

The bishops' synod of 1977, whose theme was catechesis, stressed with reference to an authentic catechesis human advancement as a gospel demand ("ad humanam promotionem sumptam tanquam contentum et nuntium evangelicum").[21] The same synod drew attention to the situation that arises in the elaboration of the catechetical thematic: one orientation emphasizes more the spiritual aspect, another emphasizes the struggle with political problems and tries to strengthen political engagement. The synod's solution was that one should not represent the radical positions, which stress one or the other aspect, in a one-sided manner, since the gospel message is thereby damaged. The dichotomy must be overcome, specifically through a dialectical tension between the orientations, so that they mutually enrich one another ("sed inveniat quandam tensionem dialecticam inter duos polos, ita ut hi mutuo faecundentur").

The last document to be mentioned is the *Instruction of the Congregation of the Faith concerning Christian Freedom and Liberation* (March 22, 1986).[22] Referring to *Gaudium et spes* no. 42, 2, this document maintains that "society's political and economic affairs do not directly belong to the Church's mission" (no. 61). On the connection between evangelization and the advancement of justice, the following is said:

> Thus if the Church declares itself for the advancement of justice in human society or encourages the lay faithful to exert themselves there according to their vocation, she is not abandoning her mission. However, she is mindful of the fact that this mission is not primarily directed by and cannot be reduced to concern for the temporal order. For that reason she maintains very clearly and with great care the unity as well as the difference between evangelization and human progress:

21. See Caprile, *Il sinodo*. On page 573 the author offers a summary of the doctrine (*propositiones*), since the text was not officially published. I use here the Latin text which I received through private channels, from Spanish bishops.

22. A German edition in: *Verlautbarungen des apostolischen Stuhls*, no. 70 (Bonn, 1986).

the unity, because she seeks the good of all humanity; the difference, because these two tasks are part of her mission for different reasons. (no. 64)

Contemporary theology emphasizes the term *liberation*. On that point the instruction remarks that "the soteriological dimension of liberation . . . may not be reduced to the social dimension" (no. 71).

3. Theological Reflection

A reflection on the task of the Church must take its point of departure from the explicit content of evangelization, that is, from the preaching of the apostles after Easter/Pentecost. The apostles proclaimed Jesus as the Christ, as the one raised up by God the Father: for example, Acts 2:22-24 and 36 (Peter's address); 1 Corinthians 15:3-7 (the earliest *kerygma* of the Church); Acts 17:31f. (Paul's speech in Athens). The missionary task of the apostles and therefore of the Church at that time consisted, in the words of the Risen One to the apostles, in making all peoples into disciples of Jesus Christ (Matt 28:19), to proclaim the gospel (Mark 16:15), thus to preach conversion in the name of Jesus for the forgiveness of sins (Luke 24:47). The recovery offered to human beings by God in Jesus Christ is a liberation from the slavery to sin, or the sins under which they suffer (salvation). The liberation proclaimed by Jesus (the announcement of the kingdom of God) refers primarily to the eschaton.

In the different epochs of its history the Church has naturally carried out its mission in different ways, depending on the cultural and historical situation. This does not imply that the Church has always sufficiently or consistently achieved this mission in all of its implications.

In a reflection on evangelization one must distinguish between the religious mission of the Church and the implications of this mission, which may be different in distinct historical situations. This is the thrust of the various official documents. *Gaudium et spes* quite clearly states: "From this religious mission [flow] a task, a light, and a power which can contribute to the building up and solidification of the human community according to divine law" (no. 42, 2). An emphasis on this difference seems necessary in order to preserve Christian identity. What specifically the community of Christians (the Church) has to contribute to society comes out of its faith in Jesus as the Christ, and out of the hope which the community of believers carries not only for itself and for all individuals, but also for society as a whole (see 1 Pet 3:15): "Be at all times ready to take responsibility for one another, for an account will be demanded of you of the hope that is in you." The preservation of the identity of the Christian faith presumes that the missionary task of the Church to make all people into disciples, and thereby to plant the Church everywhere throughout the world, is being taken seriously.[23]

Contemporary theological reflection correctly tries to overcome the dualism which results from talk about the Church's two tasks. For that reason it emphasizes that they are tightly bound together, as one can see in various official documents.

If we raise the question of the relation between the experience of grace and social structures for the primitive community of the New Testament, we must point out first of all that Jesus was not a social revolutionary.[24] Still, Acts 4:32 shows clearly that conversion implies a certain social obligation: "No one called what he had his own, but rather they had all things in common."

If we ask ourselves whether there are any signs in the New Testament of a connection between personal conversion and the improvement of social structures, there appears at first only the short letter of Paul to Philemon. Y. M. Congar refers to this letter to justify the distinction between the Church's tasks. "Paul is not proclaiming the dismantling of the institution of slavery, but rather as he sent the runaway slave Onesimus back to his master Philemon, he suggested to the latter that he regard Onesimus as a companion in the service of the gospel; he thereby shows that Christ has knit new relationships between people."[25] Another Dominican and a spokesman for a progressive orientation, E. Schillebeeckx, writes: "Thus I regard Paul's letter to Philemon as a 'social ex-

---

23. See the discussion of the book by L. Rütti, *Zur Theologie des Mission. Kritische Analysen und neue Orientierung* (München-Mainz, 1972) by Y. M. Congar in *ThRv* 69 (1975) 353–60. Rütti ends his work with the following words: "On the basis of the universal promise to the world, the Christian mission aims not primarily at the maintenance and spread of the Church, but rather at fashioning an energetic responsibility of hope in the world; it seeks therein and on that basis to win over humans to this hope and to this work" (348). Congar, *Peuple messianique,* 179f., comments in the following way: "The authentic decree on mission, that is, about the tasks of the Church, would for Rütti be not *Ad gentes divinitus,* since it bears the error of ecclesial-centrism, but rather *Gaudium et spes,* even though this pastoral constitution is stamped with a Church-World dualism, which is the authentic 'original sin' of this entire theology." Bibliography for a theology of mission: P. Rossano, "Theologie der Mission," in MySal 4/1, 593–34 (with bibliography); Y. M. Congar, "Theologische Grundlegung (nos. 2–9) [des Dekretes über die Missionstätigkeit der Kirche]," in J. Schütte, ed., *Mission nach dem Konzil* (Mainz, 1967) 134–72.

24. See, for example, O. Cullmann, *Jésus et les révolutionnaires de son temps* (Neuchâtel-Paris, 1970); J. Guillet, "Jésus et la politique," *RSR* 59 (1971) 531–44; Congar, *Peuple messianique,* 110–44 (with bibliography).

25. Congar in LThK. E 3, 399.

change' between two Christians, and not as question of Christian principles (unfortunately!)."[26]

The case offered Paul, at least from today's viewpoint, a good opportunity to provide an answer to a fundamental question. This the apostle did not do. Very likely 1 Corinthians 7:21-24 and 29-31 supply the reason for this.

Before we take up the Pauline text, a preliminary remark must be made. The early Christian community could not allow itself to appear as a socially revolutionary movement; that would have hindered the spread of Christianity. They could have decided not to accept slave holders as members of the community. However, they did not take such a step. We may discover the reason for this in the passage mentioned.

Paul sets out as a basic principle that "each should remain in the state in which he first heard God's call" (v. 20; see also v. 24). Most probably the apostle is here taking up a problem set before him by the community. It is important for him to open up a new perspective: through baptism we are all free in the Lord *and* slaves of Christ. This perspective should lead to new relationships between individuals. The problem of social structures is not here being addressed by Paul. Why? His reflections in verses 29-30 provide an answer: "The time is short. For that reason anyone who has a wife should in the future so act as if he had none . . .; whoever buys, as if he did not buy. . . . For the form of this world is passing away."

Similar counsels can be found in other Pauline texts, for example in Romans 12:2: Do not conform to this world. For Christians this world is dangerous, to the extent that "in her present form she can lead us astray from the goal of becoming Christians."[27] In the face of his contemporary world Paul presents an eschatological reservation. The ultimate ground for Paul's statements lies in human sinfulness itself.[28] Expressed in contemporary terms, "Our concrete worldview as believers still remains 'concupiscent,' that is, it perdures in our inability to master the worldliness of the world in an expression of free, disinterested disposition through faith."[29] Such thoughts, and also probably the expectation of the imminent coming of the Lord, influenced Paul's ethical position and counsel.

New contemporary experiences have thrown up new problems for the Christian community. Remarkably, the eschatology which in the course

---

26. Schillebeeckx, *Christus*, 547. For the problem in general, see R. Schnackenburg, *Die Sittliche Botschaft des Neuen Testamentes*, vol. 1 (Freiburg, 1980) 250–53 (with bibliography).

27. Schnackenburg, *Sittliche Botschaft*, 253.

28. Here attention should be paid to Romans 8:18-30.

29. J. B. Metz, *Zur Theologie der Welt* (Mainz, 1973) 40 note 44.

of the Church's tradition has led only too often to a *fuga mundi,* a flight from the world, is now understood in a new way as a fundamental element for the engagement of Christians and for the ecclesial community in the world. J. B. Metz has formulated this new perspective very clearly:

> Eschatology in a Christian theology must be understood not only regionally, but also radically: as the form of *all* theological statements. . . . The relation between faith and world may be expressed theologically in terms of a "creative-critical eschatology." . . . The eschatological promises of the biblical tradition—freedom, peace, justice, and reconciliation—must not be privatized. They make ever new claims upon the society's responsibility. . . . This "eschatological reservation" leads us into, not a negative, but rather a critical-dialectical relationship to our society's condition.[30]

The implications of the content of evangelization show themselves most clearly in statements on the love of neighbor. According to the Christian tradition, love of neighbor cannot be separated from the love of God (see Matt 22:34-40; Matt 25:31-46 [the final judgment]; 1 John 4:20). Even more, love of neighbor is a verification of our love of God.[31] Christians may not rest so long as unjust structures govern society, even if they engage themselves in charitable work. This means that a serious proclamation of the gospel will come up against various social problems with which the Christian and the community of Christians (the Church) must come to grips precisely on the basis of their faith. Insertion and engagement in the social problematic is an implication of what the Church proclaims and must proclaim: love of neighbor.[32]

30. Ibid., 83f., 105f. This theological perspective can also be found in other theologians. For example, J. Moltmann, *Theologie der Hoffnung* (München, 1964); W. Pannenberg, "Der Gott der Hoffnung," in Pannenberg, *Grundfragen systematischer Theologie* (Göttingen, 1967) 387–98; K. Rahner, "Zur Theologie der Hoffnung," in *Schriften* 7:213–17; E. Schillebeeckx, *Gott, die Zukunft des Menschen* (Mainz, 1969) 142ff.

31. See K. Rahner, *Schriften* 6:277–98 ("On the unity between love of God and love of neighbor"); Rahner, *Grundkurs des Glaubens* (Freiburg, 1982) 301f.; W. Thüsing, "Strukturen des Christlichen beim Jesus der Geschichte. Zur Frage eines neutestamentlich-christologischen Ansatzpunktes der These vom anonymen Christen," in E. Klinger, ed., *Christentum innerhalb und ausserhalb der Kirche* (Freiburg, 1975) 100–12.

32. L. Boff defends the notion of an "articulation growing out of social analysis" in place of a merely "sacramental articulation." The point of departure for both is the love of neighbor. An articulation based on social analysis would be characteristic of liberation theology, in the sense that only this type employs the method necessary to uncover clearly the causal mechanisms for the scandalous misery of humanity (*Jesus Christus,* 24ff.); L. and Cl. Boff, *Wie treibt man Theologie der Befreiung?* (Düssel-

A complementary element here is the teaching of Vatican I on the fact that God may be naturally known. This must be understood as a logical presupposition for the acceptance of a divine revelation. In connection with this teaching one can say: God appears as the transcendent "Third" in all our human experiences, in our inter-human relationships, so that "the recognition of God cannot be separated from the human commission to establish justice and love in our inter-human relationships."[33] E. Schillebeeckx writes correctly: "It makes me wonder anew each time I hear Christians ask *to what extent* being a Christian requires exerting oneself for the improvement of the world, a strenuous opposition to war, racial discrimination, and all forms of injustice. For an analysis shows that the acknowledgment of God merely formulates in other words what is at stake and going on in the actualization of good and opposition to evil in the world."[34] On the problem contained therein of the distinctiveness of being a Christian, K. Rahner says pertinently:

> Christianity does not thereby simply add a vertical dimension to the horizontal as something new and extra, nor does it, dividing this, impose it as a *double obligation* on man; rather, it merely unveils what, in a very inexact and misunderstood picture can be called the vertical dimension, or verticality, which is in fact the ultimate radicality, the final worth, and the deepest reality hidden in the relation of man to his fellow men, to be a "Thou" [the personal, intimate form], which God uses when He speaks to us.[35]

What the Christian community says and can say with regard to humanity and its problems, and thus with regard to society and its problems, can be derived from the nature of its message; that is, it must be understood as a consequence of the Christian identity: only on the basis of God's yes to humanity in Jesus Christ proclaimed by the Church does the Church have anything to say to the world. Its word is a consequence of its task of evangelization. Out of the religious content of the Church's proclamation arise new perspectives for the relation between people and for society as a whole.

This means that the Church may not renounce its missionary religious commission if it does not wish to give up its very identity. For that reason one must distinguish between evangelization and its implications. Only

---

dorf, 1988) 34ff. In that man retains a *concupiscent* connection to the world, one must pay attention that the method of our faith does not dry out. Christian faith must always contain, and be able to maintain, a critical dimension.

33. E. Schillebeeckx, *Personal Begegnung mit Gott* (Mainz, 1964) 47.
34. E. Schillebeeckx, *Gott, die Zukunft des Menschen* (Mainz, 1969) 69.
35. Rahner, *Heilsauftrag*, 560.

in this way can what is distinctive about being a Christian be preserved from other forms of ideology.

4. Concluding Theses

1. The differentiation between the two tasks of the Church, between evangelization and its implications, is necessary to illustrate and preserve the distinctive identity of the Christian and the Church. On the basis of its distinctive mission—and only on this basis—does the Church have anything to say concerning society (and about the world).

2. Evangelization is the essential task of the Church, and it alone grounds the Church's missionary character. It would be a great error to attempt to reduce this mission to the struggle for justice.

3. The distinction between the tasks of the Church should not be understood in the sense of a separation; rather, there is an irreducible connection between the two. The Church has articulated this connection in different ways at different moments of its history. The interpretation that seems to be demanded today presupposes several factors, most especially the societal, political, and cultural developments in the world. Any proclamation of the gospel today must not forget this close connection, since the credibility of the Church's message depends upon it.

4. Two elements belong to the Christian way of being and acting in the world: engagement and eschatological reservation.[36] Through engagement we experience indications of the transcendental dimension to human existence, that is, the "wither" of our immanent or inner-worldly reality, which we were already aware of through faith.

Engagement demands a methodology for the analysis of reality. This methodology must be taken seriously, and yet faith must maintain a critical function with regard to its implementation.

BIBLIOGRAPHY

Alfaro, J. *Speranza cristiana e liberazione dell'uomo.* Brescia, 1972, ch. 12 (Christian hope in its effort for human liberation).

Congar, Y. M. *Un peuple messianique. L'église sacrement du salut.* Salut et Libération, Paris, 1975 (2nd part).

Gutiérrez, G. *Liberation Theology* (orig. Spanish, Salamanca, 1972).

Kühn, U. *Kirche.* Gütersloh, 1980, 153–59 (the mission of the Church in the world, a presentation from the Lutheran perspective).

36. See *Gaudium et spes* no. 38, and below, chapter 15.

Rahner, K. "Grundprinzipien zur heutigen Mission der Kirche." In HPTh 2/2, 547–67.

_____. "Heilsauftrag der Kirche und Humanisierung der Welt." In *Schriften* 10:547–67.

Schillebeeckx, E. *Christus und die Christen.* Freiburg, 1977, 543ff. (the New Testament experience of grace and social structures), 744ff. (salvation from God, experienced through people and the world).

Sobrino, J. *Resurreccion de la verdadera Iglesia. Los pobres lugar teologico de la eclesiologia,* Santander, 1984, 267–314 (evangelization as mission/task of the Church).

XV.
Church and World

1. Presentation of the Problematic

Schema 13 of the Second Vatican Council was dedicated to the topic
"Church and World," and indeed finally became known as the Pastoral
Constitution on the Church in the Modern World. Its first part presented
the Church's teaching on people, on the world, and on the relation of
the Church to both. Two chapters are here of special importance: chapter 3, on "Human Activity in the World," and chapter 4, entitled "The
Task of the Church in the Modern World." In this latter chapter the
reciprocal relationship of Church and world is presented; the discussion
is not only of the help which the Church can offer to individual people
and to society as a whole (nos. 41–43), but also of the contribution which
the modern world can make to the Church (no. 44).[1]

Throughout, the constitution views the world in its legitimate autonomy (no. 36, 2) with optimism. Nevertheless, it reminds us that human
activity is corrupted by sin (no. 37). Already at the council the optimism
of the constitution was criticized by a minority on the basis of the biblical
use of the term *world*.

Even before the council the topics of the constitution had become the
subject of theological reflection. In French circles Y. M. Congar in 1952
suggested the importance of "Kingdom, Church, and World" for a theology of the laity: "This question today occupies many people. Recently
it has been discussed sometimes under the title 'theology of history,' some-

---

1. On the structure of the first part of the constitution, see above chapter 14, section 2a.

times under the title 'theology of secular reality.' "[2] The question which concerns those theologians who have special interest in developing a theology of the laity is, does what people do in the world have any significance with regard to the eschaton? If the answer is yes, then what significance? Will what people do be integrated within the eschaton, or does the eschaton refer to such a completely different reality that one may not speak of integration? In Catholic theology there were two opinions. Some were of the opinion that there exists a certain continuity and connection between activity in this world, even between the cosmic process as a whole, and the final kingdom. Others emphasized the discontinuity: "1. God alone will usher in the kingdom from above. 2. The entire duration of this world and of the gospel leaven in it is marked by a sign of contradiction and the struggle of opponents against the kingdom of God."[3]

The defenders of continuity attempted nothing less than to bring both elements of the life of a Christian, that is, the secular and the religious, together into a unity. The work of Teilhard de Chardin is here especially striking.[4] For him it was evident that only continuity may lead to an integration of the person.

While the council was in progress, E. Schillebeeckx formulated the crucial question in the following terms: "Can and must the faithful, as members of a Church with eschatological expectations, accept this *dualism* between Church and world? Are those great secular expectations which are in ferment among humanity really foreign to the essence of the theological life of humanity in union with the living God?"[5]

Fundamentally a question is here posed which, at least on the surface, stands in opposition to the traditionally dominant conviction in the Church that to be a Christian requires a flight from the world, a *fuga mundi*. Without doubt such a *fuga mundi*, in combination with a specific conception of eschatology (as a freeing of the soul into another world) has stamped Christian existence for hundreds of years. It is no wonder that Christians as such, that is, on the basis of their faith, showed no particular interest in the historical development of humanity.

Gaudium et spes is convinced that not only does the Church offer help to humanity, but that also it may derive help from the modern world toward the fulfillment of its task (nos. 41–44). This means that the dialogue is reciprocal. It is proper to ask, on the basis of what theological prin-

2. Congar, *Laie,* 136. In note 76 he lists some of the most important works so far produced.

3. This is the way Congar (ibid., 141) summarizes the thought of an energetic representative of discontinuity, L. Bouyer.

4. See especially his work, *Le milieu divin* (Paris, 1957).

5. Schillebeeckx, *Wereld en Kerk,* 128.

ciple may one speak of a reciprocal dialogue? What is the relation between the help which the Church may receive from the contemporary world to that which the Church already experiences from revelation?

Here the main task must be to present the theological principles on the basis of which the statements of Vatican II can become comprehensible. A necessary presupposition for systematic reflection is the New Testament's understanding of the world and of the Church in its relationship to the world.

2. Biblical Perspectives

a. Sense and Significance of the World[6]

Without doubt the term *world* has a negative meaning in the New Testament. This is seen very clearly in the following text from the Johannine corpus: "Love not the world, nor what is in the world! Whoever loves the world does not love the Father. For all that is in the world—the desire of the flesh, the craving of the eyes, and boasting of possessions—is not from the Father, but from the world. The world and its desires pass away; however, whoever does the will of God remains to eternity" (1 Jn 2:15-17). Paul also says something similar: "Do not conform to this world [literally: to this age]" (Rom 12:2). Paul's understanding will here be taken as typical.

For Paul the world is subject to the judgment of God. However, God has reconciled the world to himself in Christ (Rom 11:15; 2 Cor 5:19; see also Col 1:20). Here world means, though perhaps not exclusively, fallen humanity. The world's wisdom (1 Cor 1:20) is identical with the wisdom *kata sarka* (1 Cor 1:26). The Christian must no longer live according to the wisdom of this world, that is, "according to the desires of the flesh" (Gal 5:16f.; see also Rom 7:14ff.), but rather according to the Spirit. Paul's theological statements concerning the world are related to his anthropology. He speaks negatively of the world in a relative sense, that is, in relation to the human situation, for human beings are "interiorly" divided

6. Bibliography: H. Balz, "kósmos" in EWNT 2:765-73 (with an important bibliography); R. Schnackenburg, *Die Johannesbriefe* (Freiburg, 1974) Exkurs 6; Schnackenburg, "Der neue Mensch—Mitte christlichen Weltverständnisses," in Metz, *Weltverständnis*, 184-202; K. H. Schelkle, *Theologie des Neuen Testaments 1* (Düsseldorf, 1968) 27-64 (with bibliography); F. Mussner, "Welt I." in LThK 10, 1021-23. H. Sasse distinguishes three meanings to the term *kósmos* in the New Testament: (1) as the entire universe, all of creation; (2) as the context for humankind, the stage of history, the earth; (3) as humankind, or fallen creation, the arena for salvation history; in TWNT 3:883-96.

(Rom 7:14ff.); according to a later expression, human beings are "concupiscent."

Romans 8:18-22 presents paradigmatically the connection between humankind and the world as creation: the entire creation today lies in slavery, in a situation which must be understood in connection with human sin or with the sin that reigns in humankind, if we leave the grace of God out of the picture. "Through man's fall from God, creation itself is equally torn out of its proper relation to the creator and has thereby lost its deeper significance."[7] The contemporary situation of creation is described by Paul in parallel fashion to the human situation: men and women are waiting for the salvation of their bodies in the eschaton (v. 23)—the first gift of the Spirit, which Christians have already received, indicates this eschatological liberation. The situation of creation is similar: it is waiting for the eschatological salvation from slavery, into which human sin has brought it (vv. 22-23).

The term *world* also has the sense of creation: the world is described as the creation of God (and only of God, against any suggestion of dualism). On the basis of his salvation the early Christian community recognized in a liturgical hymn Christ as the transmitter of creation: "Everything is made by him and through him" (Col 1:16). If from its very beginning creation testifies to God's intention in Christ, then one must speak of a connection, according to the eternal plan of God, between creation and salvation. Salvation discloses this inner tendency of creation. Creation must be understood "soteriologically."[8]

b. The Church according to God's Eternal Plan

The letters to the Colossians and the Ephesians emphasize the connection of the Savior to creation. In such a context it was possible to depict the Church according to the eternal plan of God. This happens in the Letter to the Ephesians.[9]

God's plan of salvation is described in Ephesians 1:3-14. Through Jesus Christ God has made manifest to us the mystery of his will (v. 9); in him Christians have heard the Word of Truth (v. 13). The goal of God's plan of salvation consists in gathering together and uniting all things in Christ (*anakephalaiosasthai:* v. 10). This idea also appears in Ephesians 1:20ff. where Psalm 8:7 is invoked: "He has laid all things at his feet" (v. 22).

7. Schnackenburg, "Der neue Mensch," 190.

8. L. Scheffczk, *Schöpfung und Vorsehung,* HDG 2, 2a (Freiburg, 1963) 13ff. (the Christian stamp of the belief in creation in the New Testament).

9. See H. Schlier, *Der Brief an die Epheser* (Düsseldorf, 1963); Schlier, *Die Zeit Der Kirche* (Freiburg, 1962) 159-86 (The Church according to the Letter to the Ephesians) 299-307 (The Church as the Mystery of Christ—according to the Letter to the Ephesians).

The author returns to the mystery that Christ is and which was hidden in God from eternity in 3:8f. The Church is the instrument through which knowledge of this mystery is received (v. 10). Here the author speaks of the "powers and dominations of the heavenly realm," a terminology probably of Gnostic origin. The Church is "the manifestation of God's wisdom. With her and in her God's wisdom appears anew. With her and in her it appears among the worldly powers. . . . In and by and through herself, she, the Church, makes the mighty and powerful experience the wisdom of God, whose 'heavenly' creation she herself is. She is thus a public manifestation of the mystery of the cosmos."[10]

In Ephesians 1:20-23 the author speaks of a double superiority of Christ to every power and domination (v. 21) and to the Church (v. 22). The first is not of the same type as the second: in the second it is a matter of a superiority in salvation and rescue; in the first, on the other hand, it is a matter of victory over the powers of evil, whose might will first be broken in the eschaton.

The Church, the place of rescue and salvation, is described as the *pleroma* of Christ: "He has placed all things at his feet, and placed him, who towers as head over all things, over the Church. She is his body and is fulfilled by him, who governs all things completely" (vv. 22-23).

When we overlook various nuances, the exegetes[11] agree that a function is here passed on to the Church, in the sense that it is the instrument of Christ's activity (that is, of the fullness of Christ), "who fills all things everywhere" (a literal translation of verse 23).

In summary: the Church is the reality realized by Christ. Its function can only be understood in dependence upon Christ. As Christ's instrument, and only as Christ's instrument, does it have a function for the whole, that is, for the world. God's salvific plan for the world is made manifest through the Church (Eph 3:16): "So now the powers and dominations of the heavenly realm should receive through the Church knowledge of the multifaceted wisdom of God."

3. Systematic Reflection

a. The Dialectical Tension between Church and World as a Fundamental Theological Perspective

The exegetical references given above (see Col 1:15-20; Eph 1:3ff.) show that according to God's plan, there is a "unity between the reality of sal-

---

10. Schlier, *Der Brief an die Epheser,* 157.
11. See ibid., 99; L. Cerfaux, *La théologie de l'église suivant S. Paul* (Paris, 1965) 270ff. (ch. 14). On the term *pleroma* see G. Delling, "plároma" in TWNT 6:297-304, H. Hübner, "plároma" in EWNT 3:262-64 (with bibliography).

vation and the reality of creation."[12] The Savior is the mediator of creation; even more, from its very beginning creation was oriented toward Christ.

The fact of the incarnation itself, that is, that the Son of God became man, raises the perspective under which the community of believers can and must view the "world": as the reality made by God and in which salvation in Jesus Christ has entered. For that reason, with J. B. Metz one can speak of "the truth of the incarnation as the horizon which determines the Christian understanding of the world."[13] The world's profanity, its "enduringly secular" character,[14] appears to the Christian in the light of belief. The Church in the narrow sense is the public presentation as well as the conscious concretization of what Christ has already achieved for all of humanity, even if humanity as a whole is largely unaware of this. As God's grace has made itself visible in Jesus, however, this grace tends toward a visible form, toward becoming a "church."

Between Jesus' resurrection and his coming again there is "a dualism between Church and world."[15] There will remain "a certain differentiation and a dialectical tension between *Church* and humanity."[16] Even if with E. Schillebeeckx[17] one can speak of a softening of the borders between Church and humanity on the basis of the union between creation and salvation, still at no time are these borders nor the dialectical tension between them ever collapsed.

b. The Church as Sacrament for the World

If the difference mentioned above is taken seriously, then a question poses itself: how may we characterize more precisely the nature of the relation of the Church to the world?

Since the Christian community speaks about the world on the basis of its faith, or, since the Christian community experiences in salvation the positive meaning of the world according to God's eternal plan for salvation, which has been concretized and revealed in Jesus, it can do nothing else but proclaim this. In its proclamation of the grace-filled

12. An expression of K. Rahner, *Sendung und Gnade* (Innsbruck, 1959) 51. See also Rahner, "Grundsätzliches zur Einheit von Schöpfungs- und Erlösungswirklichkeit," in HPTh 2/2, 208–28; Schillebeeckx, *Wereld en kerk,* 153; G. Gutiérrez, *Theologie der Befreiung* (Mainz-München, 1972) 141ff.; G. Muschalek, "Schöpfung und Bund als Natur-Gnade-Problem," in MySal 2, 546–58.

13. Metz, *Theologie,* 29. The same opinion can be found in other Catholic theologians, such as K. Rahner and E. Schillebeeckx.

14. Metz, *Theologie,* 29.

15. Congar, *Laie,* 128.

16. Schillebeeckx, *Wereld en Kerk,* 146.

17. Ibid., 149.

announcement of God in Jesus, the Church presents itself as the God-intended mediator between Christ and the world. Hence its function as the instrument chosen by God for the spread of the lordship of Christ in the world may be characterized as *sacramental*.

_ *Gaudium et spes* (no. 45, 1) describes the Church as the " 'all-embracing sacrament of salvation' (*LG* no. 48) that simultaneously reveals and realizes the mystery of God's love for mankind." This is the foundation for the "good things that the Church has to share with the human family" (ibid.). On the basis of its announcement the Church is *sacramentum mundi*. It is a sign of God's love for humanity; it is the visible offer of God's salvation which is present in it; if not only in it, but rather also in the whole world, that is, outside the Church, then not without connection to the Church, since God's grace always possesses an ecclesial character: the activity of Christ everywhere in the world can only be experienced in the light of the Church's announcement.

The Church is distinguished from the world to the extent that it is that part of humanity which has a knowledge of the concrete love of God for humanity in Jesus Christ. It is part of the world to the extent that "the pilgrim Church [carries] the form of this world, which is passing away, and counts herself among the creation that until now still sighs and lies in groaning as it awaits the revelation of the children of God (see Rom 8:19-22)" (*Lumen gentium* no. 48, 3).

The sacramental character of the Church should enable it to meet the danger of absolutizing itself, since a sacrament is precisely a sign from God for something *else,* that is, for the proclamation of salvation. To understand itself as the sacrament for the world means that the Church must recognize its own *provisional* character:[18] it is *not* the kingdom of God, and it must always live oriented toward the kingdom of God (see above, chap. X, part 2).

To the extent that "the restoration . . . promised us and which we are awaiting has already begun in Christ, receives its continuation in the sending of the Holy Spirit, and through the Spirit perdures in the Church" (*Lumen gentium* no. 48, 2), the Church may be characterized from a certain perspective by an expression that we find frequently among the Church Fathers,[19] as the "transfigured world."[20]

---

18. See K. Rahner, *Schriften* 6:350f. (the Church and Christ's Parousia).

19. Origen calls the Church "the world coming into order." For Augustine also the Church is "the world that is holy, reconciled, rescued, with goodness coming out of its evil." See Auer, *Kirche und Welt,* 492f.

20. The Orthodox theologian N. A. Nissiotis uses this title for his work on the Church and the world: "L'Église, monde transfiguré," in Nissiotis, *L'église dans le monde,* Églises en dialogue 2 (Tours, 1966) 11-80 (especially 37ff.).

The function of being the sacrament for the world imposes concrete demands upon the Church: it cannot properly carry out its function as sacrament for the world if individuals in the Church are not treated with respect, and if there are not adequate lines of communication by which the theological principle that should govern relationships within the community, notably between officials and the community, can be put into practice.

We cannot forget that, until the eschaton, the Church is also "world" in the negative sense, in the sense that it remains "ecclesia semper reformanda" (see chap. X, part 1).

The Church's function for the world is of a prophetic character (in the sense of being both *critical* and *utopian* for society). The Church must continually recommit itself to presenting images and approximations of the eschatological kingdom on earth.[21]

c. The "World" in Its Twofold Meaning

Next to this negative sense of the term *world* there is also a positive sense to emphasize: the world is God's creation that is given to us to cultivate and develop according to our nature. A theology of the incarnation underlies this interpretation.

As God's creation the world has its own autonomy: "Precisely through their status as creatures do all particular realities have their secure individuality, their own truth, their own goodness, as well as their own structure and order" (*Gaudium et spes* no. 36, 2; see also *AA* no. 7, 2). The "autonomy of temporal things" cannot, however, mean that "created things would be somehow independent from God" (*GS* no. 36, 3).

"To Christianize the world"—that is the expression that has been repeatedly used to characterize the Church's task. The Decree on the Apostolate of the Laity, for example, speaks of the "Christian transformation of the temporal order" (no. 19) or of the "penetration and perfection of the temporal order by the spirit of the gospel" (no. 2, 2) among other expressions.[22] "What its Christianization of the world means," writes J. B. Metz, "in a basic sense is that the world becomes more itself—it means to bring it into its own distinctive and proper form, to safeguard the scarcely discerned, hardly hoped for heights or depths of its 'being a world,' features that are made possible by grace, but which, however, are currently buried or hidden by sin."[23] It is worth noting that Metz here

---

21. See K. Barth, *Christengemeinde und Bürgergemeinde* (Zollikon-Zurich, 1946). On the terminology "sacrament of the kingdom," see Commissio theologica internationalis, *Themata selecta de Ecclesiologia* (Vatican, 1985) 10.2 and 10.3 = International Theologenkommission, *Mysterium des Gottesvolkes* (Einsiedeln, 1987) 84ff.

22. F. Klostermann has gathered the various expressions in LThK. E 2, 621.

23. Metz, *Theologie der Welt*, 44.

invokes the terms *grace* and *sin*. A few pages before this he has spoken of the "unconquered reality," since "our concrete . . . relation to the world is still 'concupiscent,' that is, it remains in its inability to master the worldly character of the world in a free (disinterested) disposition through faith."[24]

If the world is viewed as a thing made by God and thus as a good reality, then one may interpret the formula "to Christianize the world" as "to bring the world more into itself." However, if the world is seen in its relation to humankind, then it is not sufficient to speak of "bringing the world more into itself," since our relation to the world remains "concupiscent": because of our inner tension (original sin, concupiscence), we relate to the world not with our authentic inner freedom; rather, because of the lack of this inner freedom we are often slaves to the world. For that reason the freedom of which the Church speaks must be understood not only as a liberation from societal structures which oppress humankind, but also as a freeing of us at our deepest center. The two perspectives are inseparable.

Gaudium et spes (no. 37: "Human Activity Corrupted by Sin") points this out when it speaks of human activity in the world (chap. 3).

In what concerns the relation of worldly progress to the growth of the kingdom of God, the constitution emphasizes the difference between the two, but not without pointing out that worldly progress "has great significance for the kingdom of God, to the extent that it may contribute to a better ordering of human society" (no. 39, 2). Human progress is appreciated as "the presupposition for the preparation for the heavenly kingdom" ("materiam regni caelestis parantes": no. 38), a formula that should be understood in light of the axiom *gratia supponit naturam*. Theologically one may say: "The fruit of human endeavor and the positive shape of human plans [will be] taken up in the final bestowal of grace and thereby restored to humankind."[25]

d. The Help which the Church Receives from the Modern World

So runs the title of no. 44 of the pastoral constitution. Although the Church understands itself as the catalyst of history, the constitution recognizes "how much she owes to history and to the development of humankind" (no. 44).

The New Testament itself shows that the reception of Greek categories aided the primitive community to develop and to deepen new perspectives for its central announcement concerning Jesus the Christ. This

24. Ibid., 40 and note 44.
25. Congar, *Laie*, 164.

is also shown by the law of all evangelization, of which the constitution (no. 44, 2) speaks.

In that the Spirit of God is active in all human history, the constitution recognizes the necessity and the duty "to look to the signs of the times, and to interpret them in the light of the gospel" (no. 4) or "to attend to the various voices of our time, to distinguish, interpret, and to evaluate them in line with the Word of God" (no. 44, 2). The goal of this is to more deeply experience, to better understand, and to more ably proclaim the revealed truth (ibid.).

Through God's revelation the Church carries within itself the ultimate Word of hope, not only for itself, but also for the world. It can recognize the ultimate truth of the world in the light of the plan of salvation which has been revealed to it.

On the other hand, an analysis of the history of the Church discloses clearly that this Church has experienced a special help from the development of humanity in appreciating the depth of God's saving Word. The hopes and plans of humankind reveal themselves thus to the Church to be a type of foreign prophecy, through which it may deepen its own proclamation. In this way help for the other becomes help from the other. Along this provocative path moves *Gaudium et spes,* for it is convinced that salvation and creation constitute a unity according to God's plan of salvation.

In the eschaton the world and the Church will be identical. Until that time they will remain, despite their reciprocal relationships, distinct.

BIBLIOGRAPHY

Here we can give only a small selection from the rich bibliography available on this topic.

Auer, A. "Kirche und Welt." In F. Holböck and Th. Sartory, eds., *Mysterium Kirche,* vol. 2, Salzburg, 1962, 479–570 (with a bibliography).

Chenu, M. D. "Die Aufgabe der Kirche in der Welt von heute." In G. Baraúna, ed., *Die Kirche in der Welt von heute,* Salzburg, 1967, 226.

Congar, Y. M. *Der Laie.* Stuttgart, 1957 (French original, Paris, 1952), 98–184 (Kingdom, Church, and World).

Metz, J. B., ed. *Weltverständnis im Glauben.* Mainz, 1965. Especially important in this volume are the following systematic contributions:

Congar, Y. M., "Kirche und Welt," 102–12.

Schillebeeckx, E., "Kirche und Welt. Zur Bedeutung von 'Schema 13' des Vaticanum II," 127–42.

Ratzinger, J., "Der Christ und die Welt von heute," 143–60.

_____. *Zur Theologie der Welt.* Mainz, 1968.

Rahner, K. *Schriften zur Theologie* 8:580-92 (on the theological problematic of the "New Earth"), 593-609 (immanent and transcendent perfection of the world), 637-66 (theological reflection on secularization).

Schillebeeckx, E. *Wereld en Kerk* (Theologische Peilingen Deel 3). Bilthoven, 1966 (ch. 2, no. 2: "Kirche und Welt," also published in Metz, *Verständnis*).

_____. *De sending van de Kerk* (Theologische Peilingen Deel 4). Bilthoven, 1968 (ch. 1, no. 3: "The Church as 'Sacrament of the World' ").

_____. *Gott die Zukunft des Menschen*. Mainz, 1969, 100-18 (The Church as the sacrament of dialogue).

Smulders, P. "Das menschliche Schaffen in der Welt." In G. Baraúna, ed., *Die Kirche in der Welt von Heute*, Salzburg, 1967, 201-25 (with bibliography).

List of Abbreviations

AAS	*Acta Apostolicae Sedis*
Baraúna	G. Baraúna, ed., *De ecclesia. Beiträge zur Konstitution "Über die Kirche" des Zweiten Vatikanischen Konzils,* 1 and 2. Freiburg, 1966.
BSLK	*Bekenntnisschriften der evangelisch-lutherischen Kirche.* Ed. German Lutheran Church Committee. Göttingen, 1967.
CIC	Code of Canon Law (Codex Iuris Canonici).
DS	H. Denzinger and A. Schönmetzer. *Enchiridion symbolorum, definitionum et declarationum de rebus fidei et morum.* Barcelona, 1965.
DwÜ	*Documente wachsender Übereinstimmung. Sämtliche Berichte und Konsenstexte interkonfessioneller Gespräche auf Weltebene 1931-1982.* Eds. H. Meyer, H. J. Urban, and L. Vischer. Paderborn-Frankfurt, 1983.
EWNT	*Exegetisches Wörterbuch zum Neuen Testament.* Eds. H. Balz and G. Schneider. Stuttgart-Berlin-Köln-Mainz, 1980-83.
HDG	*Handbuch der Dogmengeschichte.* Freiburg, 1956ff.
HFu	*Handbuch der Fundamentaltheologie.* Eds. W. Kern, H. J. Pottmeyer, and M. Seckler. Freiburg, 1985-86.
HPTh	*Handbuch der Pastoraltheologie. Praktische Theologie der Kirche in der Gegenwart.* Eds. F. X. Arnold, V. Schurr, L. M. Weber, and K. Rahner. Freiburg, 1964-69.
HTTL	*Herders theologisches Taschenlexikon.* Ed. K. Rahner. Freiburg, 1972-73.
LThK	*Lexikon für Theologie und Kirche,* 2nd. ed. Eds. J. Höfer and K. Rahner. Freiburg, 1957-65.

LThK.E.	*Ergänzungsband: Das Zweite Vatikanische Konzil, Dokumente und Dokumentation.* 3 vol. 1966–68.
MySal	*Mysterium salutis. Grundriss heilsgeschichtlicher Dogmatik.* Eds. J. Feiner and M. Löhrer. Einsiedeln-Zurich-Köln, 1965–81.
NHThG	*Neues Handbuch theologischer Grundbegriffe.* Ed. P. Eicher. München, 1984f.
NR	J. Neuner and H. Roos. *Der Glaube der Kirche in den Urkunden der Lehrverkündigung.* New edition by K. Rahner and K. H. Weger. Regensburg, 1983.
Rahner, SCHRIFTEN	K. Rahner. *Schriften zur Theologie.* Einsiedeln-Zurich-Köln, 1954–84.
SM	*Sacramentum mundi. Theologisches Lexikon für die Praxis.* Eds. K. Rahner and A. Darlap. Freiburg, 1967–69.
ThWNT	*Theologisches Wörterbuch zum Neuen Testament.* Eds. G. Kittel and G. Friedrich. Stuttgart, 1933–73.
TRE	*Theologische Realenzyklopädie.* Eds. G. Krause and G. Müller. Berlin-New York, 1976ff.

DOCUMENTS OF THE SECOND VATICAN COUNCIL

LG	*Lumen gentium*
AA	*Apostolicam actuositatem*
AG	*Ad gentes*
CD	*Christus Dominus*
DV	*Dei Verbum*
GS	*Gaudium et spes*
PO	*Presbyterorum ordinis*
UR	*Unitatis redintegratio*

All other abbreviations are used according to the list in TRE, compiled by S. Schwertner, 1976.